"UNLESS YOU BELIEVE,

YOU SHALL NOT UNDERSTAND"

"Unless You Believe,

You Shall Not Understand"

LOGIC, UNIVERSITY, AND SOCIETY

IN LATE MEDIEVAL VIENNA

MICHAEL H. SHANK

PRINCETON UNIVERSITY PRESS

PRINCETON, NEW JERSEY

PUBLICATION OF THIS BOOK WAS MADE POSSIBLE
BY A GRANT FROM THE PUBLICATIONS PROGRAM OF THE
NATIONAL ENDOWMENT FOR THE HUMANITIES,
AN INDEPENDENT FEDERAL AGENCY

THIS BOOK HAS BEEN COMPOSED IN LINOTRON BEMBO

CLOTHBOUND EDITIONS OF
PRINCETON UNIVERSITY PRESS BOOKS
ARE PRINTED ON ACID-FREE PAPER, AND BINDING
MATERIALS ARE CHOSEN FOR STRENGTH AND DURABILITY.
PAPERBACKS, ALTHOUGH SATISFACTORY FOR
PERSONAL COLLECTIONS, ARE NOT
USUALLY SUITABLE FOR
LIBRARY REBINDING

PRINTED IN THE UNITED STATES OF AMERICA
BY PRINCETON UNIVERSITY PRESS, PRINCETON, NEW JERSEY

LIBRARY OF CONGRESS CATALOGING-IN-PUBLICATION DATA

SHANK, MICHAEL H.
UNLESS YOU BELIEVE, YOU SHALL NOT UNDERSTAND : LOGIC, UNIVERSITY,
AND SOCIETY IN LATE MEDIEVAL VIENNA / MICHAEL H. SHANK.
P.   CM.
BIBLIOGRAPHY: P.
INCLUDES INDEX.
ISBN 0-691-05523-8 (ALK. PAPER)
1. APOLOGETICS—MIDDLE AGES, 600–1500. 2. LOGIC, MEDIEVAL.
3. TRINITY—HISTORY OF DOCTRINES—MIDDLE AGES, 600–1500.
4. UNIVERSITÄT WIEN—HISTORY. 5. HEINRICH, VON LANGENSTEIN,
CA. 1325–1397—CONTRIBUTIONS IN APOLOGETICS OF THE TRINITY.
6. VIENNA (AUSTRIA)—CHURCH HISTORY. 7. CHRISTIANITY AND OTHER
RELIGIONS—JUDAISM—HISTORY. 8. JUDAISM—RELATIONS—CHRISTIANITY—
HISTORY. I. TITLE.
BT1117.S53 1988
239'.09436'13—DC19   87-36889

TO

WILMA AND DAVID SHANK

CAROL TROYER-SHANK

sine quibus non

CONTENTS

Preface   ix

Bibliographic Abbreviations   xv

Critical Symbols   xvii

CHAPTER ONE   Vienna and the Rise of Its University   3

CHAPTER TWO   Intellectual Life in the Revived University   26

CHAPTER THREE   On Paralogisms in Trinitarian Doctrine (I):
The Early Fourteenth Century   57

CHAPTER FOUR   Trinitarian Paralogisms Come to Vienna:
Henry of Oyta and Henry of Langenstein   87

CHAPTER FIVE   On Paralogisms in Trinitarian Doctrine (II):
The Viennese Students   111

CHAPTER SIX   Langenstein and the Viennese Jews   139

CHAPTER SEVEN   "Unless You Believe, You Shall Not
Understand"   170

CONCLUSION   201

APPENDIX   The Notebook of Johannes Bremis   205

Bibliography   221

Index   249

PREFACE

When the twilight years of the Habsburg Empire inundated Europe with a flood of creative activity—in music, psychology, painting, philosophy, architecture, literature—no one doubted that Vienna was an important cultural center.[1] Five hundred years earlier, the French and the Italians would have laughed at such a thought. Indeed the Holy Roman Empire chafed under its image as the realm of the uncivilized, and Vienna was no exception. By the late fourteenth century, the Habsburgs already controlled the city. Though only dukes, they were ambitious and forward-looking, intent on improving both their lot and the standing of their capital. Within a matter of decades, they would take the helm of the Holy Roman Empire, and keep the imperial title in the family until this century. They founded a university under inauspicious circumstances in 1365, not long after the Great Plague ravaged Europe. The corporeal plague was soon followed by a spiritual one, as two popes claimed the undivided allegiance of the faithful and their rulers.

Ironically, the Great Schism of the Western Church proved a great boon to the cultural development of the Empire. By forcing many German academics to leave Paris, it unwittingly encouraged the transfer of learning eastward. In the late fourteenth century, new universities sprang up in the Holy Roman Empire. Unlike Paris and Oxford during this period, these fresh institutions were not burdened by their former glory or by unflattering comparisons with their past vigor. The University of Vienna, which had been ailing, was revived for good in 1384, thanks to prominent theologians recently displaced from Paris.

As a result of the Schism, then, Vienna stood in direct continuity with the intellectual heritage of the French university, which was not only the leading theological school of Europe but also one of the high places of medieval natural philosophy. Thus the University of Vienna provides an unusual opportunity to study the fate of the Parisian tradition in the later fourteenth century. In addition, throughout the fifteenth century, Vienna housed a succession of competent astronomers,

[1] See especially Schorske, *Fin-de-siècle Vienna*; Janik and Toulmin, *Wittgenstein's Vienna*; and, for the essential pictorial dimension, Waissenberger, *Vienna, 1890–1920*.

whose works radiated their influence throughout Central Europe, most notably into the Cracow of Copernicus's youth.[2] In other words, the University of Vienna is an ideal circumscribed context in which to explore the transition from medieval to early modern science. A better understanding of this institution in the century following its revival would not only illuminate the reception of Parisian natural philosophy in the generation after its heyday and the state of astronomy in the generation before Copernicus; it would also shed light on a neglected period in university history.

These broad considerations about the importance of Vienna provided the motivation for the present study, which covers a small subset of these questions. The first part of this book is a contribution to the intellectual history of the early University of Vienna. It focuses on a question at the interface between the faculty of arts and the faculty of theology: to what extent was Aristotle's syllogistic logic a suitable tool in theology, and trinitarian theology in particular? Between Duns Scotus and Gregory of Rimini, a number of theologians had examined the problems that emerged when the premises of standard syllogisms contained Trinitarian terms. Typically they accounted for apparent contradictions by providing an analysis of fallacies or by suggesting minor modifications of Aristotle's syllogistic. This debate came to Vienna with Henry of Langenstein and Henry of Oyta, the two leading theologians who emigrated from Paris. Initially, both men agreed that Aristotle's rules of syllogizing were universal, and valid in theology; to hold otherwise would incur the ridicule of the infidels. Yet, near the end of his life, Langenstein rejected the consensus of the age and his own earlier position. He denied that Aristotle's rules of reasoning retained their formality and universality when dealing with terms that signified the divine being. Aristotle's syllogistic was no longer ontologically neutral, for it was unsuited to treating the fundamental propositions of the faith. Langenstein's change of mind drove a wedge between the methods of the faculties of arts and theology, and eliminated a point of contact between Christians and infidels.

Langenstein's about-face demands an explanation, particularly because he adopted such an unusual position in the last years of his life. The second part of this book examines his change of mind and its influence in light of its environment—an instance of an intellectual historian compelled by his sources to pay attention to urban politics, ecclesiastical history, the suppression of heresy, and Jewish-Christian

---

[2] See Grössing, *Humanistische Naturwissenschaft*; Markowski, "Beziehungen," passim.

relations. I argue that a key factor in Langenstein's reversal was the presence in Vienna of a vigorous Jewish community, which he had tried to convert by argumentation. Within two months of the lecture in which he rejected the validity of Aristotle in theology, Langenstein admitted that the Jews had failed to convert. In his apologetic program, he had required that the infidels give up their demand for demonstrative arguments, which the Jews were apparently unwilling to do, particularly in the matter of the Trinity, the traditional point of contention in any such effort.

Langenstein's reversal made a notable impression on his students, who mentioned it in their formal theological works. If they had any ambiguity about his position, the Council of Constance, which convened to restore the unity of the Church, helped some of them make up their minds. In responding to the Hussite heresy, the council leaders accused John Hus and his disciple Jerome of Prague of confusing logic (suited to natural philosophy) with rhetoric (suited to the moral sciences and the interpretation of scripture). For the council, such confusion lay at the root of some of the erroneous interpretations that Hus claimed to have derived from scripture. At Constance, where several of Langenstein's students participated in the proceedings, the debate ended with the burning of Hus and Jerome at the stake. Several years later in Vienna, in the tense atmosphere of the Hussite wars, a new attempt was made to convert the Viennese Jews. Constance had emphasized the inappropriateness of logic in matters of faith, and traditional apologetic means had disappeared. Belief therefore had to precede understanding. In 1421, those who refused to accept this proposition were burned at the stake. In highly charged contexts, even abstract ideas can have concrete consequences.

In the subtitle, mere commas separate areas of study that historiography has divided along well-defined disciplinary boundaries. Only a strong sense that the material at hand demanded an interdisciplinary approach succeeded in overcoming my hesitation to trespass on the territories of such distinct specialties, each with its own methodologies, approaches, and languages.

The methodological pluralism that presently characterizes the history of science as a discipline—specifically in the Department of the History of Science at Harvard, where this work began and matured—has no doubt contributed to my conviction that our understanding of most historical problems will gain in depth and texture by examining them from several points of view. Although a single vantage point may be admirably suited to the representation of a simple object, whose unseen features can be extrapolated from the seen, it leaves something to be desired when the matter at hand is complex in several dimensions.

One word about terminology. The term "nominalism" figures prominently in almost every work that touches on the intellectual history of the late Middle Ages. In the following pages, by contrast, it will play a very limited role, for the most part in historiographical discussions. This calls for a brief explanation. The term appears to have grown out of a twelfth-century debate over the ontological status of universal terms. Roscellinus, whose views are preserved only in the writings of his opponents, allegedly claimed that universal terms had no more substance than the "breath of the voice" (*flatus vocis*) that uttered them. A second view, defended by Abelard, held that universal terms referred to concepts, mental abstractions from individual entities. A third position asserted that universal terms signified entities that existed apart from the perceiving or abstracting mind. Although Roscellinus appears to have been the only genuine "nominalist" in this debate, the term has been widely used to describe Abelard's position.

In the secondary literature on the fourteenth century, however, the term "nominalism" has acquired a number of connotations associated with the differences between the thirteenth and fourteenth centuries. William Courtenay has identified these connotations as particularism, skepticism, fideism, voluntarism, and an undue emphasis on the absolute power of God.[3] In addition, "nominalism" has come to be identified with the outlook and concerns of an entire century and more. This is hazardous for several reasons. First, much remains unknown about the later fourteenth century. At this stage in the research, it is premature to assume that the central questions raised in this period were identical to those of the early to mid-fourteenth century. Second, because exploratory work requires finer tools than synthetic evaluations, the many connotations of the term are ill-suited to the requirements of a project at its beginning. Finally, current research suggests that it is perilous to generalize from a thinker's position in one area to his position in another. Recent work on the natural philosopher John Buridan, for example, has shown that his views in ethics share none of the features traditionally associated with nominalism, although he is routinely considered a nominalist in natural philosophy. Similar prob-

---

[3] Courtenay, "Nominalism and Late Medieval Religion," 27ff; idem, "Nominalism and Late Medieval Thought: A Bibliographical Essay," 616–734; and idem. "Late Medieval Nominalism Revisited: 1972–1982," 159–164.

lems emerge in the assessment of Nicole Oresme's work. The terminological difficulties are illustrated by the fact that such a thinker as
Ockham, on whose positions scholars are in agreement, is labeled in a
variety of ways.[4]

It is, of course, possible to construct definitions of nominalism that
have a determinate content. In his study of Ockham's logic, for example, E. A. Moody defines a nominalist *in logic* as someone who
holds that logic deals not with being or beings (metaphysics), but with
modes of signification; not with things signified, but with relations
between signifiers.[5] Unlike many of the widely used connotations of
the term, this specific understanding is unambiguous, and therefore
useful as an analytical tool. Even Courtenay, who has all but called for
a moratorium on the use of the word "nominalism," agrees that
Moody's definition is worth retaining. This is, however, not the kind
of definition that lends itself to generalizations. The expression *via
moderna*, which is often equated with "nominalism," was first used in
the fifteenth century (ca. 1425). It therefore falls outside the chronological boundaries of this discussion.[6] The term "Ockhamist," on the
other hand, is most properly reserved for thinkers whose work bears
the imprint of Ockham in specific positions. Given the inevitable ambiguities of these terms in current historiography, it has seemed preferable to describe the positions of individual thinkers rather than to
give them labels that only spread confusion.

This book would not have been possible without several comple-
mentary support networks. I owe my heaviest intellectual debt to John
Murdoch. The stimulus of his seminars and writings, and his conta-
gious enthusiasm for the medieval university, provided the initial inspiration for my research. I am thankful for all of his help and advice
along the way. The late Jan Pinborg introduced me to the rigors and
rewards of paleography, and made the hands of late medieval logical
texts less forbidding. I am indebted to Steven Marrone, Katherine
Park, and Edward Tenner for helping me think seriously about pub-
lishing. For their constructive criticisms at various stages of the project, I thank Melissa Chase, Harold Cook, William Courtenay, Thomas
Emmert, Talya Fishman, Hester Gelber, William Jordan, Paul Oskar
Kristeller, Alfonso Maierù, Steven Marrone, Charles Purrenhage,

---

[4] Wieland, "The Reception and Interpretation of Aristotle's *Ethics*," 667–668; Hansen, *Nicole Oresme and the Marvels of Nature*, 104ff; Courtenay, "Late Medieval Nominalism Revisited: 1972–1982," 162.

[5] Moody, *The Logic of William of Ockham*, 52–53, 306ff.

[6] Gilbert, "Ockham, Wyclif, and the 'Via Moderna,' " 85ff.

Katharine Tachau, Paul Uiblein, Linwood Urban, David Vampola, Mark Verman, and Herwig Wolfram.

The Fulbright-Hays Program and the Bundesministerium für Unterricht und Kunst of the Austrian government supported me during two years of research in Vienna. The Social Science Reseach Council and the American Council of Learned Societies generously supplemented these funds for the first year, and supported the first six months of writing. To Harvard University, I am indebted in three tangible ways: the Lehman Fund made possible a crucial research trip to St. John's University; the Department of the History of Science freed me to teach less and write more during my final year of graduate study; and the "Presidential Leave" for assistant professors in their fourth year supported me during a semester of revisions. The contributors to, and administrators of, these funds have my gratitude.

For the privilege of working in their libraries, I thank especially Dr. Eva Irblich and the staff of the Handschriftenabteilung of the Österreichische Nationalbibliothek (Vienna) for two years of gracious hospitality, as well as the staffs of the following: the Institut für österreichische Geschichtsforschung, the Katholisches Theologisches Institut, and the Universitätsarchiv of the Universität Wien; the monastic libraries of the Schottenstift (Vienna), Klosterneuburg, and Melk; the manuscript collections of the Universitätsbibliothek Graz, the Bayerische Staatsbibliothek (Munich), the Staatsbibliothek Preussischer Kulturbesitz (Berlin), and the Alcuin and Hill Monastic Manuscript Libraries of St. John's University (Collegeville, Minnesota); the Widener and Houghton Libraries at Harvard. The Institute for Ecumenical and Cultural Research (St. John's University) provided a superb environment in which to bring the whole project to conclusion. I thank Nicholas Steneck for his extended loan of several microfilms.

The most consistent and unstinting support during a decade of "work in progress" has come from Carol Troyer-Shank. Insofar as it is expressible, my deepest gratitude goes to her. As for the rest, "What we cannot speak about, we must pass over in silence."

Collegeville, Minnesota
March 1987

BIBLIOGRAPHIC ABBREVIATIONS

AFA, I *Acta Facultatis Artium Universitatis Vindobonensis*, 1385–1416. Ed. P. Uiblein (Vienna, Graz, and Cologne, 1968)

AFA, II *Acta Facultatis Artium, liber secondus*, ms. (Vienna, Archiv der Universität)

AHDLMA *Archives d'Histoire Doctrinale et Littéraire du Moyen Âge*

AR *Acta rectoratus*, ms. (Vienna, Archiv der Universität)

ATF *Akten der theologischen Fakultät der Universität Wien (1396–1508)*. Ed. P. Uiblein (Vienna, 1978)

Auctarium *Auctarium Chartularii Universitatis Parisiensis*. Vol. 1: *Liber procuratorum nationis Anglicanae (Alemanniae) in Universitati Parisiensi*. Ed. H. Denifle and E. Chatelain (Paris, 1894)

Beiträge . . . *Beiträge zur Geschichte der Philosophie und Theologie des Mittelalters* (Münster i. W.)

Chartularium *Chartularium Universitatis Parisiensis*, 4 vols. Ed. H. Denifle and E. Chatelain (Paris, 1889–1897)

CHLMP *The Cambridge History of Later Medieval Philosophy*. Ed. N. Kretzmann, A. Kenny and J. Pinborg (Cambridge, Eng., 1982)

GStW *Geschichte der Stadt Wien*. Ed. under the auspices of the Alterthumsvereine zu Wien (Vienna, 1897–1918)

MGH *Monumenta Germaniae Historica*

MIÖG *Mitteilungen des Instituts für österreichische Geschichtsforschung*

MUW, I *Die Matrikel der Universität Wien*. Vol. 1: *1377–1450* (Graz and Cologne, 1954)

NF Neue Folge

NS New Series

ÖNB Österreichische Nationalbibliothek (Vienna)

OP *Opera philosophica*

OT *Opera theologica*

· xv ·

PIMS   Pontifical Institute of Mediaeval Studies (Toronto)

PL   *Patrologiae cursus completus . . . ser. lat.* Ed. J. P. Migne (Paris, 1841–1891)

RHE   *Revue d'Histoire Ecclésiastique*

RS   *Repertorium Commentatorium in Sententias Petri Lombardi.* 2 vols. Ed. F. Stegmüller (Würzburg, 1947)

RTAM   *Recherches de Théologie Ancienne et Médiévale*

SMRT   *Studies in Medieval and Reformation Thought.* Ed. H. Oberman (Leiden)

CRITICAL SYMBOLS

(!)	sic
(?)	uncertain reading
[ ]	physical damage to the manuscript
⟨ ⟩	editorial addition
{ }	editorial deletion
[[ ]]	scribal deletion
/	page break
add	*addit, addunt*
hom	*homoioteleuton*
interl	*interlineatura*
inv	*invertit, invertunt*
mg	*marginalium*
om	*omittit, omittunt*
transp	*transponit, transponunt*

"UNLESS YOU BELIEVE,

YOU SHALL NOT UNDERSTAND"

CHAPTER ONE

Vienna and the Rise of Its University

Est vero in hac nostra marchia civitas
Wienna . . . nulli autem omnium urbium,
quas vel in Germania vel Gallia vel
Ytalia viderim, inferior.

GUTOLF OF HEILIGENKREUZ
(late thirteenth century)

T HE REPUBLIC of the Christian faith is composed of three parts,
wrote the Cologne canon Alexander of Roes in the late thirteenth century. "The priesthood (*sacerdotium*) in Italy keeps the
faith, kingship (*regnum*) in Germany rules so that the faith can be kept,
and learning (*studium*) in France teaches the faith that ought to be
kept."[1] The separation of powers that Alexander advocated in this ele-
gant scheme served above all a political purpose, specifically the attempt to limit the encroachments of the French crown on the traditional prerogatives of Italy and the Holy Roman Empire. Almost in
passing, it confirmed another notable development within European
society: the growing perception that the university was a power in its
own right. Nowhere was this power more obvious than in the far-
reaching influence of the University of Paris, which Alexander and his
contemporaries considered to be the exemplar of preeminence in
learning. In the late thirteenth century, former Parisian masters not
only administered the possessions of the Church and decided the limits
of the faith; they even sat on the papal throne.

Throughout the fourteenth century, however, Alexander's model of
Christendom became ever more implausible as a description, and fanciful as a prescription. The most extended and virulent conflict over
regnum during this period would involve not Germany, but the
Hundred Years' War between France and England. Alexander's apprehensions about France, which grew out of its domineering role in the

---

[1] Grundmann, "Sacerdotium—Regnum—Studium," 6.

election of Pope Martin IV in 1281, proved to be fully justified. During the following decades, matters continued to deteriorate until 1303, when agents for Philip the Fair of France held the elderly Boniface VIII prisoner for three days. The pope died a month later. His successor, the Italian Benedict XI, was pope less than a year. The Frenchman who was elected to succeed him remained for a while in Avignon, a French city surrounded by papal territories, where he awaited the outcome of the posthumous trial of Boniface VIII. This temporary sojourn would eventually last three quarters of a century—the "Babylonian Captivity" of the papacy in Avignon. While Italy was losing its grip on *sacerdotium*, France was losing some of its preeminence in *studium*. Already in the thirteenth century, France could claim no monopoly on higher education.[2] During the following century, however, particularly in the years between the beginning of the Avignon papacy and the end of the Great Schism, new universities mushroomed at an unprecedented rate throughout the Holy Roman Empire. When Alexander wrote, there were no universities east of Padua. By the outbreak of the Hussite wars, two dozen new ones had been founded throughout Europe, at least seven of which endured in and around the Holy Roman Empire.[3]

Contrasting sharply with this efflorescence of university foundations is a more common picture of the fourteenth century, in which images of decline and disaster predominate.[4] This general interpretation of a period punctuated by real as well as metaphorical plagues has much to recommend it. Although more research into the social and economic history of the fourteenth century still remains a desideratum, broad trends have emerged. The arrival of the fourteenth century signaled the conclusion of an era of economic growth, and the beginning of a series of large-scale disasters. The Great Famine of 1315–1317, the collapse of the most important banking houses between 1327

[2] There were by 1348 fifteen Italian universities, eight French, six Iberian, and two British. See Grundmann, "Vom Ursprung der Universität im Mittelalter," 10.

[3] They included Prague (1347/1348), Cracow (1364/1397), Vienna (1365/1384), Heidelberg (1385), Cologne (1388), Erfurt (1379/1392) and Leipzig (1409); see Rashdall, *The Universities of Europe in the Middle Ages*, 211ff. By 1400, some fifty-five universities had been founded in Europe, a number of them ephemeral, however. See Denifle, *Die Entstehung der Universitäten*, 219ff.

[4] See for example Huizinga, *The Waning of the Middle Ages*, whose English title is more pessimistic than the "herbstij" (harvest-tide) of the Dutch original; Perroy, "A l'origine d'une économie contractée," 167–182; Graus, "The Crisis of the Middle Ages and the Hussites," 76–103; Tuchman, *A Distant Mirror*; and Fliche and Martin, eds., *Histoire de l'Eglise*, XIV, 1: *L'Eglise au temps du Grand Schisme et la crise conciliaire (1378–1449)*.

and 1343, the onset of the Hundred Years' War, and the Great Plague at mid-century followed each other in short succession.[5] The "Black Death" cut the population of Europe by one-third to one-half. This demographic collapse had unprecedented consequences. Unlike the victims of war and famine, the survivors of the Great Plague found themselves with a surplus of goods and food. Full storehouses and bleak prospects for the future encouraged a decline in productivity often combined with unbridled consumption, which eventually generated ripples of rising prices until the end of the century.[6]

In matters spiritual, the Church was widely thought to be in decline. This perception was of course not new: reformers had decried abuses throughout the Church's history. In the fourteenth century, however, the voices of the critics grew more numerous and insistent. From the "Babylonian Captivity" of the papacy in Avignon to the end of the Great Schism, observers as different as William of Ockham, William Langland, and Saint Catherine of Siena all agreed that the Church was not what it ought to have been, and they often said so stridently.[7]

To those historians of philosophy who see Thomas Aquinas as the pinnacle of medieval thought, the critical spirit associated with nominalism has signified decline as well.[8] In a similar vein, but with much less argumentation, a recent history of medieval technology dates the onset of technological decline at the Bishop of Paris's condemnation of 219 Aristotelian and Averroist propositions in "1277, when mysticism gained ascendancy over reason."[9]

For all of these reasons, the language of decline has seemed eminently appropriate to characterize the fourteenth century as a whole. More recently, the more dramatic concept of "crisis" has overtaken the

[5] Pirenne, *Economic and Social History of Medieval Europe*, chap. 7; Miskimin, *The Economy of Early Renaissance Europe, 1300–1460*, chap. 1.

[6] Lütge, "The Fourteenth and Fifteenth Centuries in Social and Economic History," 325, 338–339.

[7] See the prologue to Langland's *Piers the Plowman*; Ockham's "Dialogus de imperio et pontificia potestate," in *Opera omnia*, 1. On St. Catherine, see Ullmann, *The Origins of the Great Schism*, 60–61.

[8] At their most eloquent, these views are typified by Etienne Gilson, for whom Ockham "marks the end of the golden age of scholasticism." He "unleashed and encouraged forces which he himself could not possibly control after setting them free" (*History of Christian Philosophy in the Middle Ages*, 498). For a sound critique of this point of view, see Moody, "Empiricism and Metaphysics in Medieval Philosophy," 145–163. For an excellent summary of the historiography of nominalism, see Courtenay, "Nominalism and Late Medieval Religion," esp. 26–31; idem, "Late Medieval Nominalism Revisited: 1972–1982," 159–164; and Ozment, *The Age of Reform*, chaps. 1–2.

[9] Gimpel, *The Medieval Machine*, 242.

imagery of decline.[10] But the era was not one of unmitigated doom, even for contemporaries. In addition to such cultural contributions as the harpsichord, polyphony, the dissemination of paper, eyeglasses, and the mechanical clock, historians of science have long considered the fourteenth century to be one of the high points of medieval thought. Nor have the only optimists been historians. Indeed there were grounds for optimism, which the leader of the recently founded University of Vienna exuded. In the eyes of Henry of Langenstein, the decline of the University of Paris was obvious, but it merely represented another passing phase in the *translatio studii*—the transfer of learning from the ancient wisdom of Moses and the Egyptians to Athens, then to Rome, and finally to Paris. But Paris had now had its day; it was waning. In the Empire, however, learning was waxing. Around 1386, Langenstein wrote with exuberance:

> Behold the universities of France are breaking up, the sun of wisdom is eclipsed there. Wisdom withdraws to light another people. Are not three lamps of wisdom now lit among the Germans, that is three universities (*studia generalia*) shining with rays of glorious truth? Let now that Italian Boethius be silent, let him no longer say "We have seen a few marked by German fury," for blindness has now fallen in part on Israel so that the multitude of the Gentiles might be enlightened.[11]

In Vienna, where Langenstein had recently moved from Paris, the mood was buoyant. At long last the Empire was beginning to overcome its sense of inferiority in European culture.[12]

---

[10] See the works by Fliche–Martin and Graus (n. 4 above). Heiko Oberman concurs, but suggests that the term "birthpangs" may be more appropriate yet. See his "The Shape of Late Medieval Thought," 3–25, esp. 11.

[11] Sommerfeldt, "Zwei Schismatraktate Heinrichs von Langenstein," 469. The translation is adapted from Thorndike, *University Records and Life in the Middle Ages*, 257. Contrary to Sommerfeldt, the three universities are Prague, Vienna, and Heidelberg, and the date is ca. 1386. See Ritter, "Studien zur Spätscholastik I," 31, n. 2, for the corrections. For similar evaluation of Paris, by Richard of Bury in 1344, see John Murdoch, "*Subtilitates Anglicanae* in Fourteenth-Century Paris," 51.

[12] This sense of inferiority was not quick to disappear. Throughout the fifteenth and sixteenth centuries, German intellectuals remained very sensitive about their image in the eyes of Europe. Although the astronomer Regiomontanus (d. 1476) occasionally identified himself as "Joannes Germanus" in letters to his Italian colleague Bianchini, the preface to his *Disputationes contra deliramenta cremonensia*, shows that he was keenly aware of the association between "German" and "barbarian." See Schmeidler, ed., *Joannis Regiomontani Opera collectanea*, 515. The letters to Bianchini have been edited by Curtze,

As an aspiring center of learning, Vienna was promising enough. From the modest outpost that had once sheltered Marcus Aurelius's garrison on the northeast border of the Roman Empire, Vienna by the late Middle Ages had grown into a sizable city. This development undoubtedly had much to do with its location at the intersection between the east-west Danube traffic and the north-south Semmering road that linked the Danube to Venice. When the Babenberg dukes first ruled the surrounding area in the late tenth century, Vienna was a city without walls. In the wake of increasing economic activity in the late twelfth century, however, Leopold v of Babenberg erected extensive fortifications around the entire settlement, which now included his own residence. The walls extended as far as the present-day Ringstrasse, ambitiously enclosing a large area that was not yet inhabited, but that presumably would soon be.[13]

In Lower Austria, the Habsburgs came to power in the thirteenth century. They used a brief stint at the helm of the Holy Roman Empire, together with holy matrimony, as steppingstones to expansion. With their acquisition of Carinthia, Krain, and Tyrol during the fourteenth century, Austria became a strategic territory from the commercial point of view. The Habsburgs now controlled several important trade routes between Germany and Italy, including the road to Venice by way of the Semmering range and Villach.[14]

Although the geography and the demand for goods were propitious enough, these advantages were tempered by the heavy restrictions that taxation placed on trade in the late Middle Ages. One scholar has counted as many as seventy-seven tolls on the relatively short Lower Austrian course of the Danube.[15] These limitations notwithstanding, Vienna benefited to some extent from the transit of eastbound English, Rhenish, and Flemish cloth, and of cattle moving westward from

---

"Der Briefwechsel Regiomontans," I, e.g. 195, 242. For examples from the late fifteenth and early sixteenth centuries, see Strauss, ed., *Manifestations of Discontent*, 64ff.

[13] The cost of this large undertaking was covered in part by the enormous ransom exacted from the English to free Richard the Lionhearted, who on his return from the Crusades was taken prisoner near Vienna by Duke Leopold v. See Hantsch, *Die Geschichte Österreichs*, I, 72–73; and Hummelberger and Peball, *Die Befestigungen Wiens*, 14.

[14] See Luschin von Ebengreuth, "Die Handelspolitik der österreichischen Herrscher im Mittelalter," 311–327, esp. 324; Vancsa, *Geschichte Nieder- und Oberösterreichs*, II, iii.

[15] Kulisher, *Allgemeine Wirtschaftsgeschichte des Mittelalters*, I, 301.

Hungary.[16] Luxury goods and consumer products destined to the court accounted for a substantial portion of the local manufacturing.[17] The city also profited from the trade between the Lower Austrian and Styrian iron mines and their clients in Northern and Eastern Europe. Last but not least, viticulture, controlled for the most part by the burgesses, constituted the backbone of the Viennese economy, which depended on exports of local wine to Bavaria and the Sudetenland.

The importance of viticulture for the city's livelihood might seem to imply that the bourgeoisie played a leading role in city politics, but this was only partially the case. Vienna had a three-tiered social system that distinguished it from many of its Flemish or North German counterparts. The guilds and the patricians were not entirely powerless, of course, but the decisive element in fourteenth-century Viennese politics was the presence of the Habsburg court. After 1275, when the construction of the ducal stronghold, the Hofburg, began within the city walls, the town faced a concrete reminder of the proximity of ducal power: there could be no doubt that what was good for the Habsburgs was good for Vienna. Only rarely—and in the end unsuccessfully—did the city display the streaks of independence so characteristic of the cities of the Low Countries during these years.[18]

One scholar has gone so far as to claim that during the fourteenth century the city of Vienna had no political history. In the first third of the fourteenth century, the patrician families that had played an important role in earlier city history were either in decline or had completely disappeared. Throughout that century, the Habsburgs steadily consolidated their power. The city council took care of perfunctory administrative duties, but played no discernible political role. The few conflicts crystallized around problems of Habsburg succession.[19]

---

[16] Brunner, *Die Finanzen der Stadt Wien*, 8–9.

[17] Brunner, "Die Politik der Stadt Wien," 8.

[18] The winter uprising of 1287–1288 forced Albert I to leave Vienna for his stronghold atop the Kahlenberg (now the Leopoldsberg), which dominates the city. But the rebellion was soon quelled. In February 1288, the city of Vienna swore obedience to the duke, who exacted a high price for contrition—the renunciation of the privileges that Rudolph I had conceded to the city. See Vancsa, *Geschichte Nieder- und Oberösterreichs*, II, 61–62. The formal renunciation of the privileges is printed in Tomaschek, ed., *Die Rechte und Freiheiten der Stadt Wien*, I, No. xx, 66–67. In 1309, following the murder of Albert I in 1308, there erupted another uprising, which involved the Viennese artisans. Vancsa links it to an antidynastic conspiracy initiated by the Duke of Bavaria, and not to internal stirrings of independence.

[19] Brunner, "Die Politik der Stadt Wien," 7–9; Vancsa, "Politische Geschichte von 1283 bis 1522," in *GStW*, II, pt. 2, 507–508.

Thus, when in their privileges the Habsburgs referred to the city as *unsere Stadt*, they were expressing not merely fondness for their place of residence, but also an uncontested political fact.

The fine texture of Viennese social fabric is not well known. Based on the 1405 census, recent estimates suggest that two thousand burgesses constituted the core of the citizenry. These figures include males above the age of eighteen who had received from the city council "the citizen's rights" in exchange for the obligation of living in Vienna in their own households. According to one scholar, the population comprised the following categories: approximately 100 patricians, 300 merchants, and 1,600 artisans (1,130 technical artisans, 300 small shopkeepers, and 170 members of various auxiliary services—physicians, gardeners, winetasters, etc.). On the assumption of five persons per hearth in the early fifteenth century, the total population of the city has been estimated at fifteen to twenty thousand, including 1,000 persons associated with the university, 500 Jews, 1,500 courtiers and related occupations, 1,500 religious, and 2,000 journeymen, beggars, prostitutes, etc.[20] Since the second half of the fourteenth century witnessed demographic upheavals, it is very difficult to know precisely the size of the population at any given date.

Whatever the exact figures, the broad outlines of the various social groups are discernible, and the dukes seem to have been particularly skilled at playing off various factions against each other. Rudolph IV (d. 1365), for example, consciously favored the burgesses against the old patrician families. Otto Brunner has argued that the peculiar social and political constraints on Vienna, combined with its idiosyncratic economic activities, account for the relatively stable social and political history of the city, especially by comparison with towns like Bruges, Liège, or Florence. With heavy investments in viticulture and the wine trade, a large portion of Viennese society placed a high premium on compromise to avert violent solutions that would ruin the city's economic base for years to come.[21] The citizenry, not the Habsburg court, was almost always the compromising party, however, and this for good economic reasons: unlike the Viennese townsfolk, the Habsburgs disposed of considerable sources of income beyond the city.

[20] Perger, "Beiträge zur Wiener Verfassungs- und Sozialgeschichte im Spätmittelalter," 14. These figures (particularly the number of persons per hearth) may be high. The carefully documented data for Pistoia in 1427 averages 3.6 persons per household; see Herlihy, *Medieval and Renaissance Pistoia*, 110.

[21] Brunner, "Die Politik der Stadt Wien," 8.

Like many other medieval towns, Vienna boasted a long, if decen-
tralized, tradition of learning well before the foundation of the university. Various religious orders had established houses in and around the
city. In the mid-twelfth century, the Babenberg ruler Heinrich Jaso-
mirgott had invited Irish Benedictines from St. Jacob's in Regensburg
to found a sister monastery in Vienna.[22] The newcomers settled within
the city walls, on the location of the present-day Schottenstift. Along
with their reputation for holiness, they also brought a library. Traces
of a school that taught the *trivium* have survived, but its influence is
difficult to evaluate.

By the fourteenth century, however, the Benedictines themselves
were on the decline.[23] The torch of reform passed on to the Augustinian Eremites, established in the vicinity of Vienna since the mid-thirteenth century. They eventually came to occupy a prominent position
within the educational hierarchy of the order. By 1327, when they re-
located inside the city walls, the Viennese House had been the *studium*
of the Augustinian order's Bavarian province for some twenty years.
According to received wisdom, their teachings reflected the views of
Giles of Rome, at least until the mid-fourteenth century when the influential theologians Thomas of Strasbourg and Gregory of Rimini
succeeded each other at the head of the order.[24]

Beyond the scattered libraries and schools of its religious orders,
Vienna in the thirteenth century also supported a school associated
with the parish of St. Stephen.[25] In 1296 Duke Albert I, who had been
the patron of the school, transferred its jurisdiction to the burgomaster
and city council. In the same ordinance, he gave the rector of St. Stephen's oversight responsibilities not only for the Bürgerschule, but for
the other schools in the city.[26] Although the names of several other

[22] Rapf, *Das Schottenstift*, 9ff; Hauswirth, *Abriss einer Geschichte der Benedictiner-Abtei
U.L.F. zu den Schotten in Wien*, 2ff.

[23] Lhotsky, *Die Wiener Artistenfakultät*, 31.

[24] Rennhofer, *Die Augustiner-Eremiten in Wien*, 41–46. The recent discovery of their
joint epitaph in the Augustinerkirche confirms the fact that Gregory of Rimini and
Thomas of Strasbourg had both spent some time in Vienna; see Chapter 4 below.

[25] Mayer, *Die Bürgerschule*, 6f. The existence of the school can be inferred from Emperor Frederick II's privilege of 1237 for the city of Vienna; see Tomaschek, ed., *Rechte
und Freiheiten* I, no. VI, 16.

[26] Tomaschek, ed., *Rechte und Freiheiten*, I, no. XXIII, 70. See also Albert Hübl, "Die
Schulen," in *GStW*, V, 351ff. Another school *im Spital* is first mentioned in 1376; see
A. Mayer in *GStW*, II, pt. 2, 956–957.

rectors have survived,[27] Conrad of Megenberg's tenure as headmaster of the Bürgerschule (1342–1348) stands out as one of the high points of learning in Vienna before the foundation of the university. The details of his activities as a teacher remain obscure. He presumably brought to his vocation the same interest in the dissemination of knowledge that led him to produce both a German version of Sacrobosco's *On the Sphere* as well as *Das Buch der Natur*, allegedly the first natural history in German—even if it was heavily indebted to Albertus Magnus.[28] Interestingly, these scientific interests went hand in hand with a vociferous antipathy for Ockhamism.[29] Little else is known about the school curriculum during these early years.[30]

Although the Bürgerschule and religious orders provided an educational tradition around which a university could be built, these antecedents played a lesser role in the formal emergence of the *studium generale* than did Habsburg and ecclesiastical politics. Vienna was, as Paul Uiblein has pointed out, the first university founded at the initiative of a man who was neither a king, nor an emperor, nor a pope.[31] The

[27] A Magister Ulrich in the early fourteenth century, for example, impressed one of his students, who remembered his master in his poetry; Büdinger, "Über einige Reste der Vagantenpoesie in Österreich," 333–336.

[28] Pfeiffer, ed., *Das Buch der Natur von Konrad von Megenberg*, introduction, esp. xi. He also composed Latin questions on Sacrobosco, preserved in Munich, Bayerische Staatsbibliothek, Clm 14687, fols. 71–95; see Thorndike, *The Sphere of Sacrobosco and Its Commentators*, 37. For a brief biography, see Krüger, "Krise der Zeit als Ursache der Pest?" 842.

[29] See his *De commendatione clerici*, first printed anonymously by Thorndike (*University Records and Life*, 409), but subsequently identified as a fragment from Conrad's *Oeconomica*; see Pelzer and Kaeppeli, "L'*Oeconomica* de Conrad de Megenberg retrouvée," 559–616. Conrad appears to have played a leading role in attempts to limit the influence of Ockhamism in Paris ca. 1340; see Courtenay and Tachau, "Ockham, Ockhamists, and the English-German Nation at Paris, 1339–1341," 74–75.

[30] The school continued to prosper long after the foundation of the university. The flyleaves of ÖNB 213 contain a list of books lent ca. 1350, presumably by the headmaster of the Bürgerschule, Leutold. The volumes include Priscian, Donatus, Prudentius, the *ars vetera*, a "volume of philosophy," a treatise on the *modi significandi*, and Boethius's *Consolation of Philosophy*. It is not known whether the books belonged to Leutold or to the school library; see Gottlieb, *Mittelalterliche Bibliothekskataloge Österreichs*, 428–430. Albert III's university privilege of 1384 mentions the teaching of the *artes liberales* at the school, as one might expect (Kink, *Geschichte*, II, 62). A detailed ordinance pertaining to the curriculum survives for 1446; and a mid-sixteenth-century map still indicates the location of the school. See Mayer, *Die Bürgerschule*, 16ff.

[31] Uiblein, "Die österreichischen Landesfürsten und die Wiener Universität im Mittelalter," 383. For the background, legal as well as traditional, of the notion of *studium generale*, see Cobban, *The Medieval Universities*, chap. 2.

institution grew out of the long-standing rivalry between Austria and
Bohemia, specifically from the keen competition between Charles IV
of Luxemburg and his ambitious son-in-law, Duke Rudolph IV of
Habsburg. In 1346, even before his election as Holy Roman Emperor,
Charles had petitioned the papacy for the privilege of establishing a
university in Prague. In 1347, Clement VI, who had met Charles during the latter's years at the French court and later supported his election
to the imperial throne, issued the bull that authorized the first *studium
generale* of the Empire.[32]

Not to be outdone by his father-in-law, Duke Rudolph IV took steps
to obtain papal permission for a *studium generale* in Vienna. He envi-
sioned a full-fledged university, with not only a faculty of arts but also
the three higher faculties of medicine, law, and (especially) theology.
As his envoy to Avignon, Rudolph enlisted Albert of Saxony, the
Paris-trained natural philosopher.[33] But Urban V's bull authorized only
an incomplete university: he explicitly denied Rudolph's petition for a
faculty of theology.[34] Was the pope so conscious of the advantages of
doctrinal centralization that he did not wish to multiply theologizing
entities beyond necessity? Or did Emperor Charles sense a threat to
the viability of the nearby Prague *studium*, and lobby successfully
against the efforts of his son-in-law?[35] Whatever the reason, it obviously caught Rudolph by surprise: his own privilege, which explicitly placed Vienna in the tradition of the "transfer of learning" (*translatio studii*) from Paris, listed theology as the first discipline to be taught
at the new university.[36]

Although Rudolph signed the privilege on his deathbed, it illustrates

[32] On Charles's impression of Petrus Rogerii (later Clement VI), see his autobiography
Vita Caroli Quarti, trans. Hillenbrand, 84ff, 172ff; and Seibt, *Karl IV. Ein Kaiser in Europa, 1346–1378*, 119, 149f, 179ff. Similar rivalries lurk behind a number of other German university foundations, notably Heidelberg and Greifswald. See Grundmann, "Ursprung," 12; and Ritter, *Die Heidelberger Universität*, 36. On the foundation of Prague,
see Rashdall, *Universities*, II, 215; and Denifle, *Die Entstehung der Universitäten*, 586.

[33] See Heidingsfelder, *Albert von Sachsen*, 29–30.

[34] The bull (dated 18 June 1365) is published in Kink, *Geschichte*, II, 26–28, esp. 27.

[35] At the university level, the Avignon popes authorized the teaching of theology in
only nine of the eighteen institutions for which they issued privileges. For an overview
of the situation and the historiographical options in the case of Vienna, see Denifle, *Die
Entstehung der Universitäten*, 607, 703–706. Theology presumably remained at the heart
of the Augustinian *studium* in Vienna; for analogous cases, see Verger, "*Studia* et universités," 175–203, esp. 192ff. I thank Katherine Tachau for this reference.

[36] Lhotsky, *Die Wiener Artistenfakultät*, 208. The best, but rare, edition of the privilege
in its German and Latin versions is in [Uiblein], ed., *600 Jahre Universität Wien*, 6–25. I
thank Paul Uiblein for bringing this edition to my attention.

both his undying ambition and the unilateral character of relations between the city and the duke. By granting immunities to scholars, the privilege effectively removed a portion of the urban population from city control. It therefore drastically affected the rights, privileges, and finances of the townspeople. Yet the charter that granted so many freedoms to students and masters was enacted—typically enough—without consulting the city. As it had done before, Vienna obediently accepted this new infringement upon its jurisdiction: no evidence of objections or protests seems to have survived.[37]

Rudolph's death unwittingly granted the city several years of reprieve. The first rector, Albert of Saxony, left Vienna within the year, following his preferment to a bishopric in Halberstadt.[38] The Habsburg territories were soon divided between Rudolph's two adolescent brothers, Leopold III and Albert III, who promptly fell into an intense and devastating rivalry. For the university as well as the city, these tensions proved disastrous. There was talk of dividing the city of Vienna—and even the ducal quarters in the Hofburg—into two parts, each to be ruled by one of the brothers.[39]

Little is known about the life of the university during these years. But a climate of political factionalism combined with sweeping economic problems can scarcely have contributed to the well-being of the fledgling institution.[40] No official university records have survived for these years. In the Vienna matriculation registers, which open with the names of 9 masters of arts and 282 students, the first entry is undated and is perhaps a summary of all earlier matriculation records. The next entry, dated 24 June 1377, contains 139 names.[41] These figures suggest

[37] In the "privilege" of 1296, for example, the city lost its right to make binding judicial decisions. See Voltelini, "Zur Wiener Stadtverfassung im 15. Jahrhundert," 296; and Brunner, *Die Finanzen der Stadt Wien*, 14.

[38] Heidingsfelder, *Albert von Sachsen*, 33.

[39] Vancsa, "Politische Geschichte von 1283 bis 1522," 515; and Zeissberg, "Der österreichische Erbfolgestreit," 12.

[40] For these years, see Denifle, *Die Entstehung der Universitäten*, 608–614. Anna Campbell has cited the difficulties of several new universities founded between 1348 and 1370 as indirect evidence for a general decline linked with the Black Death, later followed by a recovery in the last quarter of the fourteenth century. The suggestion is plausible, but short on evidence; see her *The Black Death and Men of Learning*, 163.

[41] *MUW*, I, I, 1–4. Following Kink, Mayer has suggested that the faculty of arts survived during these years as a dependency of the Bürgerschule at St. Stephen's until Johann von Randegg started the matriculation records for the *studium* in 1377; see Mayer, *Die Bürgerschule*, 11. During these lean years, the faculty of law seems to have been successful in attracting students; see Uiblein, "Beiträge zur Frühgeschichte der Universität Wien," 308.

a *studium* of very modest size, for the number of late medieval students who completed their studies in the faculty of arts typically represented only a small fraction of matriculants.[42] Quality made up for quantity. One of the first graduates of the faculty of arts was Berthold of Wehingen, later Albert III's chancellor, who would play a decisive role in the history of the Viennese *studium*. His influence on Albert, and his acumen in following up an unexpected consequence of the Great Schism, were, as we shall see, instrumental in giving the university a new lease on life.

·

The road that led to the revival of the university was a tortuous one. After the papal court's lengthy residence in Avignon, Gregory XI had valiantly attempted to return it to Rome in 1377.[43] But he died very soon after his election. If his reign was too short to reestablish the papal residence in Rome, it proved long enough to revive in the Romans the hope of tasting once again the fruits of such a return. For Rome, the arguments from tradition and propriety were complemented, if not overshadowed, by a powerful economic incentive. The pope's move to Avignon in the early fourteenth century had deprived Rome of the lucrative pilgrimage trade, and the Eternal City had been languishing ever since.

With such high stakes riding on the outcome, the papal election of 1378 took place in a tense atmosphere. By all accounts the Roman populace did in fact riot outside the conclave. How much pressure they thereby exerted on the cardinals to select at least an Italian, if not a Roman, is difficult to determine. In any event, the Archbishop of Bari became the next pope, taking the name Urban VI. There is no good reason to doubt that, pressure or not, the electoral college considered the election fully valid. But the sickly Urban VI proved to be both an irascible character and a tactless politician: within a few months, he had alienated many of the cardinals who had elected him. By midsummer, a movement was afoot to declare the April election invalid.

---

[42] Jacques Paquet reports that the attrition rates between matriculation and reception of the master's degree range from a low of 83.8 percent (Tübingen) to a high of 96.5 percent (Erfurt) during the late Middle Ages; see Paquet and IJsewijn, eds., *The Universities in the Late Middle Ages*, 13, n. 20.

[43] This section is based upon the following works: Fliche and Martin, *Histoire de l'Eglise*, XIV, 1: *L'Eglise au temps du Grand Schisme et de la crise conciliaire (1378–1449)*; and Ullmann, *The Origins of the Great Schism*. For an interesting contemporary perspective on the events, see Jean Froissart, *Chroniques*, Book III.

Although political motives surely influenced these considerations, Urban's heavy-handed manner contributed significantly to his own deposition. The stormy circumstances of his election offered an ideal excuse to the disgruntled cardinals. By August, a group of them gathered at Anagni to annul Urban's election. In September 1378, they deposed Urban and chose a new pope, the pro-French Robert of Geneva, who took the auspicious name of Clement VII. But Urban refused to step down. Fortified by Roman fears of another return to Avignon and by German apprehensions about another papacy under French control, he did not find himself without support.[44]

The Schism soon deepened the many political rifts within European politics. The ecclesiastical and legal issues involved in the double election and the deposition were not easy to resolve. Meanwhile the various temporal powers found plenty of reasons for favoring one pope over the other. Accordingly, they did not wait to see what the Church would do: within a year, much of Europe had taken a position on the legitimacy of one of the two popes.[45]

The impact of the Schism was felt far and wide, not least at the University of Paris, where all of these political, economic, and legal issues came to a head. The French king had definite political reasons for supporting Clement VII: the papacy of Urban signified a loss of access to, if not control over, one of the wealthiest and most powerful forces in Europe. As the acme of European learning and theology, Paris found itself in a particularly difficult position. The university had much to say about an eventual resolution of the Schism: the weight of its opinion might be decisive. Although at first unwilling to prejudge the issue, the university soon came under heavy royal pressure. King Charles V declared that he expected full-fledged commitment to Clement from the local *studium generale*. Before the end of 1379, the Norman and French nations of the faculty of arts had joined the three higher faculties of theology, medicine, and law in pledging their support to the Avignon pope.

The French crown, however, would stand for nothing less than unanimous support for Clement VII. Faced with constant royal badgering, the recalcitrant Picard and English-German nations confronted an awkward dilemma. The "English" nation, which was by the 1360s the smallest of the four and predominantly German, had already pro-

---

[44] On this episode, see Swanson, *Universities, Academics, and the Great Schism*. The German opposition to French interference with the papacy is discussed in Grundmann, "Sacerdotium—Regnum—Studium," 7ff.

[45] Ritter, "Studien zur Spätscholastik I," 28.

tested on several occasions the unfair treatment of its members at the hands of university officials.[46] The Germans were, in addition, keenly aware of their reputation for cultural backwardness. The Schism only exacerbated their insecurities. Most of the secular rulers in their home territories favored Urban, and were prepared to enforce sanctions against supporters of the "antipope." Clerics from the Empire who had been preferred to benefices in their homelands faced the very tangible threat of losing their means of support.[47] When the Duke of Anjou, acting as regent for Charles VI, violently rejected the conciliatory route proposed by the university in 1383, most of the Germans saw no solution but to leave Paris for their homelands.[48]

It was at this point that Berthold of Wehingen, the chancellor of the Habsburg dukes, realized that this exodus offered the University of Vienna an unusual opportunity. According to a contemporary chronicle, he persuaded Albert III to call several of the prominent exiles from Paris to the aid of his university.[49] Although the earlier papal charter of 1365 had explicitly denied Vienna a faculty of theology, the Schism made it possible to overcome this obstacle. In the early 1380s, when both popes were attempting to consolidate their political support, Habsburg territories were a disputed region. True to their sibling rivalry, Leopold had sided with Clement while Albert favored Urban.[50] Albert's envoys to Rome evidently pleaded their case with flair. In 1384 Urban issued a new bull, which at last authorized the university of Rudolph IV's dream—a full-fledged *studium generale*, complete with a faculty of theology.

Berthold's strategy proved successful. The call to Vienna struck a responsive chord in Langenstein, who not only was available, but also clearly felt a sense of mission in coming to the hinterlands. Several years earlier, in the *Epistola concilii pacis*, he had complained that the Church was neglecting the provinces: "Why is it that today all make for the hub of Christendom, which abounds with rich benefices and which is, so to speak, a center of quiet, while the parts of the church

[46] For the relations between the English-German nation and the chancellor, see *Chartularium*, III, 203–205, 269, 307; *Auctarium*, I, cols. 488–490; and Boyce, *The English-German Nation*, 29f.

[47] Ritter, "Studien zur Spätscholastik I," 30, 32.

[48] Swanson, *Universities, Academics and the Great Schism*, 41.

[49] "Wiener Annalen (1349–1404)," in *MGH, Deutsche Chroniken*, VI, 233.

[50] Sauerland, "Rede der Gesandtschaft des Herzogs Albrecht III. von Österreich an Papst Urban VI," 449ff.

on the circumference, where the ungodly walk, have been neglected and unvisited?"[51]

After securing the services of Henry of Langenstein, Henry of Oyta, and Gerard of Kalkar, Vienna could boast that its faculty of theology included some of the most prominent German doctors of theology trained in Paris.[52] The university thus acquired almost overnight an attractiveness that the nearby *studium* in Prague must have found difficult to match. Beyond these academic factors, nationalist considerations further accentuated the appeal of Vienna for many German students in Prague. For some years already, clashes between Germans and Czechs had disrupted academic life in Prague. The tensions reached a peak late in 1384 over the problem of filling vacancies in the residential colleges. The Archbishop of Prague, who was also chancellor of the university and supported the Czech minority, clashed with the German rector Conrad of Soltau on this issue. In one of the scuffles, the rector himself was assaulted.[53] Whether drawn or driven, a significant number of students from Prague did in fact defect to Vienna during the first years that followed the revival of the university.[54]

.

In 1384, the Vienna that all these newcomers encountered was by all appearances a growing city. The church towers that rose above the city walls testified to the importance and prosperity of the religious orders. The Spiritual Franciscans had recently expanded the Minoritenkirche. The Carmelites had been in the city for two decades. To the older towers of the Benedictine Schottenstift and of St. Michael's parish had recently been added the new ascetic steeple of the Augustinerkirche.

[51] Henry of Langenstein, "Epistola concilii pacis," trans. James Cameron, in Spinka, ed., *Advocates of Reform*, 135–136.

[52] One exception was Conrad of Soltau, who taught in Prague until Marsilius of Inghen convinced him to come to Heidelberg soon after that university opened in October 1386. Marsilius himself did not complete his commentary on the *Sentences*—and therefore become a full-fledged theologian—until the very end of his life; see Ritter, *Die Heidelberger Universität*, I, 60.

[53] "Chronicon Universitatis Pragensis," in *Geschichtschreiber der Husitischen Bewegung in Böhmen* [Fontes Rerum Austriacarum, Scriptores, II (1856)], 13–14; Kibre, *Nations*, 170–171. See also Vaclav Chaloupecký, *L'Université Charles à Prague*, 113ff.

[54] Of the sixty-five masters who made up the core of the teaching staff in the early years, at least thirty-six had earlier ties to Prague (see the list in the Acts of the Faculty of Arts, 13 September 1385; *AFA*, I, 4–5 and the index). Henry of Oyta, who had returned to Prague soon after the Schism broke out, also came to Vienna about this time; see A. Lang, *Heinrich Totting von Oyta*, 34–36.

When the Augustinian Eremites settled inside the city walls, they chose a strategic location adjoining the Hofburg, in the midst of the former Hochstrasse, which recently had been renamed Herrengasse, the "Street of the Lords."[55] Then as now, street names were changed to honor the past, and ironically the Herrengasse was no exception. Rudolph IV's legislation had dealt a severe blow to the old landowning patriciate, which had already suffered major setbacks before the Great Plague. The rising class that stepped into its place was composed of members of the luxury- and consumer-related guilds, such as goldsmiths, butchers, and furriers.[56] This group of parvenus, whose fate was closely tied to the fortunes of the Habsburg court, came to play an increasingly important role on the city council and in civic life generally.

Rudolph IV's legacy had touched other aspects of city life as well. In the center of town, construction was slowly underway on his other dream, a monumental cathedral to replace the older Romanesque church of St. Stephen. The Habsburgs hoped to free Vienna from its episcopal subordination to the diocese of Passau, and worked to elevate the city to the rank of bishopric in its own right. The recent establishment of a chapter of canons associated with St. Stephen's took a first step in this direction. An impressive new edifice commensurate with Habsburg ambitions would be another. Indeed a cathedral would have the additional attraction of matching Emperor Charles IV's parallel efforts in Prague.[57] By the early 1380s, construction had presumably begun on the expansion of the older church. The foundations for the southern tower of the edifice—today one of Vienna's landmarks—had been laid in 1365, but construction above ground was far from complete. One recent explanation blames the slow progress on technical problems, adducing the need to let the foundations dry before erecting the massive tower.[58] But economic and political considerations surely played a decisive role in the construction delays. At the time, Austria

[55] Perger and Brauneis, *Die mittelalterlichen Kirchen und Klöster Wiens*, 126, 138, 155ff; Zykan, *Der Stephansdom*, 15 (map).

[56] Brunner, "Die Politik der Stadt Wien," 9, no. 15.

[57] Perger and Brauneis, *Die mittelalterlichen Kirchen*, 11; Zykan, *Stephansdom*, 70. Ernst Kelter has drawn attention to a spate of splendid ecclesiastical building projects in Germany in the years that followed the Black Death. The renovations in Vienna and Prague were therefore not merely isolated efforts, but were parts of a larger trend; Kelter, "Das deutsche Wirtschaftsleben," 202.

[58] Zykan, *Stephansdom*, 90. The detailed records of construction expenditures by the *Kirchenmeister* begin only in 1404; see Uhlirz, ed., *Die Rechnungen des Kirchmeisteramtes von St. Stephan zu Wien*.

was still embroiled in the vicious fraternal feud that disrupted life throughout the Habsburg territories. To make matters worse, Habsburg finances remained in shambles throughout the late fourteenth century.[59] According to the *Wiener Annalen*, the Great Plague had decimated two-thirds of the world's population. Whatever its accuracy, the figure hints not only at the psychological impact of the epidemic, but also at the extent of its social and economic disruption.[60] During Rudolph IV's reign, large expenditures for military purposes had drained Habsburg coffers. At Rudolph's death in 1365, his debts came to 60,000 florins.[61] Twenty years of feuding between his brothers Albert and Leopold did little to alleviate these financial problems.

Given these constraints, it is surprising that the revival of the Vienna *studium* occurred at all, for it too involved a large financial commitment on the part of the duke. The initial expenses were not trivial: 680 *Pfund*, 230 of which paid the yearly pensions of Langenstein and Oyta. In addition, Albert had endowed a new Collegium ducale, consisting of a building with lecture halls and living quarters for a dozen masters of arts and one or two members of the theology faculty, who each received a pension of 20 *Pfund*.[62].

Under normal circumstances, the duke might have borne such a financial commitment with relative ease. But these were not the best of times. Like Habsburg territories in general, the city of Vienna was still beset with severe problems. According to the *Wiener Annalen*, another epidemic in 1381 killed so many people (the chronicler gives the unbelievable figure of 15,000) that the price of wine soared for lack of laborers. Many houses were deserted and much land lay fallow. In 1383, the wine—the city's main cash crop—was generally bad. An exceptionally cold winter in 1384 affected the vineyards adversely. In 1385, very little wine was produced. The following year, the high price of wine again proved worthy of mention. And in 1390, wine produc-

---

[59] In 1364, Rudolph IV had exacted from his brothers a pledge to complete the construction of St. Stephen's. But neither Albert III's will (August 1395) nor the Hollenberg Treaty (November 1395) mentions any funds for St. Stephen's—a sure sign that more pressing financial worries had eclipsed the promise. See Perger, "Ein neues Geschichtswerk über den Wiener Stephansdom," 80; and Lhotsky, "Wien im Spätmittelalter," 21. Zykan (*Stephansdom*, 89) conjectures that Albert withheld the funds for St. Stephen's to spite the city.

[60] "Wiener Annalen," 231.

[61] Vancsa, *Geschichte Nieder- und Oberösterreichs*, II, 168.

[62] For the duke's expenses, see Karl Schrauf, "Die Universität," in *GStW*, II, pt. 2, 980.

tion was abnormally low.[63] This sequence of disastrous vintages worsened an already ailing economy. The shortage of funds brought about
by these cumulative causes made monetary shortcuts hard to resist.
Between 1373 and 1389, the *Wiener Pfund* registered a 20 percent de-
crease in silver content by comparison with the Hungarian gulden.[64]
The need for revenue was so great that in his new university foundation charter of 1384, Albert had to defend himself from the charge that
he had revived the Viennese *studium* for financial gain.[65] He subjected
the town to unusual taxes in an attempt to replenish the Habsburg
treasury, and this at a time when city debts were running very high—
more than half the total city budget.[66] These hard times contributed
little to the city's social stability. By the late fourteenth century, relations between the Viennese Jews and the local population were tense.
By the late 1370s, already one-third of the houses in Vienna were
mortgaged to Jewish moneylenders.[67] Repeated crop failures and epi-
demics further drained the resources of the populace, which resorted
to loans for temporary relief.

Following Leopold's death in 1386, Albert became the sole ruler,
and the internal political strife came to an end for a decade, even if the
economic situation remained very precarious. By 1387–1388, the future of the university was still far from secure. Several leaders—among
them Langenstein and Gerard of Kalkar—worried about the viability
of the institution. These doubts almost certainly contributed to Kalkar's departure for Cologne in 1388, where he worked on the foundation of a university there.[68] They also prompted a letter from Langenstein to Duke Albert, pleading for more extensive financial support,
for much-needed repairs, and for funds to purchase books. Without
these additional monies, he argued, the university might not survive.[69]

But Albert III was in no position to be generous. The depth of his

---

    [63] "Wiener Annalen," 231–235. The scarcity for 1390 is confirmed in Henry of Lan-
genstein's *Treatise on Contracts*, which was written during that year: "videmus in illo
tempore quo vina deficiunt quia magis indigemus eis fiunt cariora." See Gerson, *Opera
omnia*, 187ᵛa.

    [64] Brunner, *Die Finanzen der Stadt Wien*, 24.

    [65] Kink, *Geschichte*, II, 54; and Uiblein, "Die österreichischen Landesfürsten und die
Wiener Universität im Mittelalter," 390.

    [66] Brunner, *Die Finanzen der Stadt Wien*, 418–419.

    [67] The city administration was likewise indebted to members of the Jewish commu-
nity, but it also had borrowed heavily from members of the nobility; see Brunner, *Die
Finanzen der Stadt Wien*, 412ff, and Chapter 6 below.

    [68] See Shank, "Academic Benefices and German Universities," 37ff.

    [69] Sommerfeldt, "Aus der Zeit der Begründung der Universität Wien," 306.

financial predicament may be gauged by his desperate attempt in 1389–1390 to collect revenue by taxing not only the townsfolk and the Jews—his habitual sources of income—but also the clergy.[70] The papacy responded swiftly by imposing the interdict on Habsburg lands. But the Schism did not permit such high-handed treatment of badly needed political allies, and Boniface IX rescinded his decree the following year.[71]

When Langenstein was not asking for money, however, he remained sanguine. In 1391, he reused his panegyric of 1386 about the flowering of learning throughout the Empire in a letter to Rupert of the Palatinate, the patron of the new University of Heidelberg. In the intervening five years, though, his figures had already become obsolete: the foundation of the University of Cologne in 1388–1389 forced him to revise the number of new *studia* to four.[72]

For good financial reasons, the university continued to cultivate close connections with the Habsburg court throughout Albert's reign. When the financial needs of the university increased, Henry of Langenstein did not hesitate to appeal to the duke's vanity to obtain more money. The university was reborn under Albert's tutelage, and he took much pride in this accomplishment. He not only mentioned the university first in his will, but he also showed a keen interest in its affairs. The duke sought to encourage good relations between the city and the university, if only for the sake of keeping the peace in his capital. Such a goal was not always easy to attain. When the city population forgot the income it derived from the students, it resented this group of intruders who escaped almost completely from its control. Among other privileges, students and masters paid no taxes, were covered by ducal immunities, and were tried by their own courts in cases involving Viennese citizens.[73] Thus Albert occasionally had to mollify the city by intervening with threats and other injunctions aimed at controlling what Rashdall has called "the wilder side of University life."[74] In turn, the university cultivated Albert's solicitude with attentions of its own. It tactfully remembered the anniversaries of its "founders and

[70] See Tomaschek, ed., *Rechte und Freiheiten*, I, no. c, 201; and "Wiener Annalen," 235.

[71] Vancsa, *Geschichte Nieder- und Oberösterreichs*, II, 179–180. The text of the reinstatement is printed in Kurz, *Österreich unter Herzog Albrecht III*, 228.

[72] Sommerfeldt, "Die Stellung Ruprechts III. von der Pfalz zur deutschen Publizistik bis sum Jahre 1400," 311. Sommerfeldt mistakenly dates the letter to 1394; for the correction (1391), see Ritter, "Studien zur Spätscholastik I," 197–199.

[73] See Rudolph's privilege of 1365 in Lhotsky, *Artistenfakultät*, 212ff.

[74] Uiblein, "Landesfürsten," 390–391; Rashdall, *Universities*, III, 427.

their progenitors," initiated a procession and Mass in supplication for the peace and tranquillity of the realm (May 1389), and organized a procession to welcome Johanna, Albert III's wife.[75]

These official connections were complemented by personal ties that further strengthened the relationship between the Habsburgs and the university. The duke took a genuine interest in learning, and commissioned a number of translations for his own use.[76] His chancellor, Berthold of Wehingen, was also intimately involved with the university, not only as the instigator of its revival, but also as the duke's attorney in university affairs.[77] Albert's personal physician was a member of the faculty of medicine.[78] His chaplain Frederick of Gars, who doubled as the preceptor to young Albert IV, was also a member of the university.[79] According to the chronicler Leopold Stainreuter, who later served as Albert's chaplain and knew the court well, Henry of Langenstein and Henry of Oyta were the duke's spiritual advisers.[80] Henry of Langenstein also filled an important ambassadorial role. After Leopold's death made possible the reunification of Habsburg lands under Albert III's rule, it was Langenstein who composed the speech that Albert's envoys delivered before Pope Urban VI to mark the return of all Austrian lands to Roman obedience.[81]

The city also took advantage of the expertise in its midst. The sentence of excommunication that Boniface IX had imposed on Habsburg lands lasted long enough to crystallize opposition to fiscal edicts that Rudolph IV had imposed upon the city several decades earlier. The Viennese leaders turned to the university for an opinion about their claims. This request resulted in three works on contractual relations by Henry of Langenstein, Henry of Oyta, and Johann Reuter.[82]

---

[75] See *AR*, I, 14ᵛ, 15ᵛ, 23ʳ, passim; and Uiblein, "Landesfürsten," 390f.

[76] Hohmann, *Heinrichs von Langenstein 'Unterscheidung der Geister' Lateinisch und Deutsch*, esp. 258ff; and Heilig, "Leopold Stainreuter von Wien," esp. 262.

[77] Uiblein, "Landesfürsten," 391.

[78] See the reference to the university official "magistrum Chunradum medicum ducis" in *AR*, I, 6ʳ.

[79] *MUW*, I 12.

[80] [Stainreuter], "Die österreichische Chronik von den 95 Herrschaften," 210. Konrad Heilig identified Stainreuter as the author of this anonymous treatise in his "Leopold Stainreuter von Wien," 225–289. Langenstein's German penitential treatise *Von Erchantnuss der Sund* was written for young Albert IV at the request of his father. See Rupprich, *Das Wiener Schrifttum des ausgehenden Mittelalters*, 154.

[81] Sauerland, "Rede der Gesandtschaft," 448–458.

[82] Trusen, *Spätmittelalterliche Jurisprudenz und Wirtschaftsethik*, 20. Langenstein's *Tractatus de contractibus* is discussed in Chapter 6 below.

If the university was a source of prestige, income, and advice for the duke and the city, it also presented opportunities for its own members. In the late Middle Ages, learning was for a few students an end in itself, witness the decision of some masters of arts (such as John Buridan) not to pursue the career-oriented higher degrees and remain teachers in the faculty of arts, or the Polish woman who "for the love of learning" dressed as a man to attend lectures at the University of Cracow.[83] For many others, the university was one of the few channels that made upward social mobility possible.[84] Education had always offered a few poor bright boys a chance to rise. The Church had actively encouraged such opportunities in very concrete fashion—with financial support. The Third and Fourth Lateran Councils had decreed that a benefice in each cathedral chapter should support one master assigned to the education of the poor.[85] For some members of the medieval university who matriculated as impoverished fourteen-year-olds, a successful academic career was a first and crucial step to positions of power, not only within the university, but also in the Church and at court. The Dominican theologian Robert Holcot went so far as to correlate academic success with humble origins.[86]

The opportunities of the university in this regard are strikingly illustrated by the order in which the members of the University of Vienna mingled with members of the nobility in the Corpus Christi Day procession. According to the *Acta rectoratus* (13 June 1389), the students and bachelors of the arts faculty marched first, followed by the teachers of medicine and their bachelors, the teachers of law and their bachelors, and the teachers of theology and their masters. Next came the deans of the faculty of arts with its teachers, the dean of the faculty of medicine with its masters along with the "less illustrious nobles"; then the dean of the faculty of laws with its professors, along with the "simple illustrious" nobles, followed in turn by the dean of the faculty of theology with its *licenciati*, along with "illustrious nobles" such as dukes and counts. At the very end of the procession, in the place of

---

[83] Moody, "Buridan, Jean," 603; and Shank, "A Female University Student."

[84] Jacques LeGoff implies as much, even though he contends that the university had developed a caste mentality by the late Middle Ages; see his "How Did the Medieval University Conceive of Itself?" in *Time, Work, and Culture in the Middle Ages*, 133. See also Overfield, "Nobles and Paupers," 175–210.

[85] Murray, *Reason and Society*, chap. 9, esp. 218.

[86] "We commonly see that the sons of the rich and powerful do not learn, and that the sons of the simple poor men are raised to the highest ecclesiastical dignities by reason of their character and science." Smalley, *English Friars and Antiquity*, 199, quoting from Oxford, Bodl., 722 (2648), 19ᵛ.

honor, walked the rector of the University.[87] Although members of
the nobility marched in positions of distinction for no reason other
than their birth, the rector, who walked in the place of honor, was
elected from among the members of the university; he was a scholar
who frequently had no special social rank and who sometimes even
had enrolled as a pauper.[88] The large proportion of paupers who matriculated at Vienna during the first half-century of its existence suggests that, whatever the deeper causes of these trends might have been,
at least on the surface the intentions of the Lateran Councils were being
realized with a modicum of success.[89]

The reemergence of the University of Vienna was made possible by
a number of extra-academic factors. Chief among these was the
Schism, which dealt a severe blow to the morale of Christendom but
which proved a distinct boon to higher education in the Holy Roman
Empire, and to Vienna in particular. By making academic life in Paris
impossible for German students and masters, the Schism forced the
latter back to their homelands, where the ambitions of local princes
came into play. In Vienna, Albert III took advantage of these circumstances to improve an institution that his brother had founded largely
on paper, by bringing prominent theologians to the young university.
Nationalist stirrings in Prague further contributed to boosting the en-
rollment at Vienna, making it attractive for advanced masters to transfer. The diversity of these factors suggests something of the complex-
ities that entered into the life and growth of the university.

The expectations that the new university embodied were at least as
diverse. The Church had always viewed its universities as training centers for the clergy, but Urban VI also used his privilege for Vienna as a
means of currying support from an important potential ally. To the
Habsburgs, their support of the university not only enhanced their
prestige, but also counted as a charitable and pious act with possible
economic benefits. Teachers such as Langenstein saw the revived insti-

---

[87] *AR*, I, 16ʳ.

[88] Birth conferred advantages on students from the nobility not only with respect to
seating in lectures, but also in academic evaluation and prospective career opportunities.
See Fletcher's discussion of Freiburg and Tübingen in his "Wealth and Poverty in the
Medieval German Universities," 411–412. See also the remarks of Petit, quoted in F. M.
Powicke, "The Medieval University in Church and Society," in his *Ways of Medieval Life
and Thought*, 203.

[89] Between 1377 and 1425, almost 28 percent of the students matriculated as paupers
(2,861 out of 10,197); see Overfield, "Nobles and Paupers," 184, 200. At Cologne, between 1395 and 1465, one student in six was a pauper; see Eulenberg, *Die Frequenz der
deutschen Universitäten*, 71.

tution as a personal opportunity and as a mission, but also as the symptom of an important shift in the locus of education: France no longer stood at the pinnacle of learning, while the Holy Roman Empire at last was on the road to cultural maturity. To the students, the *studium* represented the road to learning and, beyond that, the prospect of social, economic, and ecclesiastic advancement. The factors that gave the University of Vienna a second life, and the hopes that it embodied, placed the institution in the crossfire of conflicting demands and expectations from its various constituencies. It was against the background of these expectations, and in the context of Vienna's very concrete urban environment, that the university turned to more abstract concerns associated with academic life.

CHAPTER TWO

Intellectual Life in the Revived University

Urbanus quintus te glorificavit ab intus,
inclita Wienna. Plus quam volatile penna,
doctrine meritis per climata fama volabis.
Ecce per Albertum codicem tibi pandit apertum,
qui nichil incertum dereliquit in arca repertum,
quem fecit expertum studium, quem lingua
    desertum.

JOHN OF HILDESHEIM,
O. Carm. (1365)

NOT EVERYONE in the late fourteenth century would have agreed with Henry of Langenstein that the "sun of wisdom was eclipsed" in France. Since eclipses are notoriously dependent on the observer's coordinates, it is doubtful that the French in particular saw this one. From the vantage point of the self-exiled Germans, however, the Schism had transformed the cosmopolitan University of Paris into a dim provincial shadow of its former self. And yet, critical of their alma mater though they were, even Langenstein and his colleagues could not avoid the afterimage of Paris, from which they freely drew inspiration. The very documents of Habsburg officialdom reflected the lingering glory of the French *studium*. Rudolph IV's original university privilege of 1365 and Albert III's new privilege of 1384 proudly stressed the continuities between Vienna and Paris.[1] When Langenstein wrote Duke Albert to request more funds, he measured the inadequacies of the Viennese facilities against the standards of Paris, which he had known so well. His short letter alluded to the archetype no fewer than five times.[2] The customs of Paris also played a normative role in the statutes of the faculty of theology, which were approved in 1389. The French university was mentioned with

[1] Kink, *Geschichte*, II, 4, 50.
[2] See Langenstein's "Informacio serenissimi principis ducis Alberti de stabiliendo studio Wiennensi," edited in Sommerfeldt, "Zur Zeit der Begründung," 305–306.

pride, albeit with the recognition that it had suffered a decline.[3] As these official documents suggest, Paris remained the exemplar that Vienna tried to emulate at the institutional level. Taken in isolation, however, the legal and administrative records of a university present at best a warped picture of its academic life. Even when official pronouncements discuss curricular matters, they give few details, and they almost never treat events in the lecture room or the disputation hall. In the case of Vienna, it is legitimate to wonder whether the Parisian institutional model had a counterpart at the intellectual level. After all, professors such as Henry of Langenstein, Henry of Oyta, and Gerard of Kalkar not only had studied at Paris, they had also spent the flower of their teaching careers there. Were Parisian intellectual concerns dominant in Viennese thought? Or did the *studia* in other cities also play a role—e.g. Prague, which contributed many students to Vienna; or Bologna, where several other early Viennese theologians were trained?

Detailed answers to such questions would add much to our understanding of late medieval university history, and specifically to issues surrounding the transmission of Parisian natural philosophy to Central Europe. Recent work on Paris suggests that the analytical tools and key concepts of natural philosophy developed in the faculty of arts exercised a strong influence on theology, not only in such standard theological works as commentaries on Peter Lombard's *Sentences*, but also in student notebooks, and in the reaction of theologians who resented the intrusion.[4] For Vienna, the materials pertinent to these issues are very numerous and, for the most part, unexplored. For this reason alone, a reliable overview of the intellectual landscape of Vienna is not likely to emerge in the near future. It is nevertheless important to continue the task that a few scholars have begun. Following a rapid survey of the historiography on the philosophical outlook of Vienna, which illustrates a few of the problems that confront the researcher in this field, this chapter examines an unusual student notebook that sheds light on the academic life of the young university, and on its intellectual relations with Paris.

·

Like the intellectual history of the late Middle Ages generally, the philosophical orientation of the University of Vienna has long been a

---

[3] Kink, *Geschichte*, II, esp. 93–94.
[4] See Murdoch, "From Social into Intellectual Factors," esp. 271–289.

murky topic. In the fifteenth and sixteenth centuries, the genetic connection between Paris and the revival of the Viennese *studium* provided
sufficient grounds to link the latter with nominalism. This association
was based on the mistaken assumption, perpetuated in student hand-
books and in the early scholarly literature, that the Parisian natural
philosopher John Buridan had founded the University of Vienna.[5]
During the nineteenth century, histories of the university generally
took either institutional or bio-bibliographic approaches to their subject, and found correspondingly little to say about intellectual life.
When they did, they usually confined themselves to extrapolations
from the presumed positions of the early Viennese leaders, who were
overwhelmingly categorized as "nominalists," Ockhamists, followers
of the *via moderna*.[6]

Historians such as Rashdall and Ehrle argued from curricular prescriptions that Vienna bore the marks of Ockhamist influence. Their
case rested on the statutory requirements, which included texts on logical topics (*suppositiones, ampliationes, appellationes, insolubilia, consequentiae,* Peter of Spain's *Summulae,* and so on), as well as lectures that
drew on works by Marsilius of Inghen, Albert of Saxony, and William
Heytesbury, who are traditionally seen as nominalists.[7] The early literature generally characterized Viennese philosophical inclinations in
monolithic fashion. A few scholars attempted finer distinctions between the faculties, or between members of various orders.[8] During
the 1920s, Gerhard Ritter was one of the few scholars who hesitated to
identify the philosophical orientation of the Viennese *studium* for lack
of adequate studies of its leading figures.[9]

[5] See the *Manuale scholarium* (trans. R. F. Seybolt), a dialogue between two students in
the late fifteenth century. The tradition of Buridan's role in the foundation of Vienna
goes back at least to Stephen Hoest's speech to the members of the *via moderna* in the
faculty of arts at Heidelberg in 1469; see Ritter, "Studien zur Spätscholastik II," 153. The
legend was then widely publicized by Aventinus in the sixteenth century. See Aventinus,
Sämtliche Werke, III, 200, 474; Duhem, *Le Système du monde,* X, 142–143; and Trapp,
"Augustinian Theology in the Fourteenth Century," 183–184, n. 43.

[6] Kink, *Geschichte,* I, pt. 1, 79–82; Hartwig, *Henricus de Langenstein,* I, 55; Aschbach,
Geschichte, I, 78–82, 363. Denifle (*Die Entstehung der Universitäten,* 604ff) omitted the
philosophical issue altogether.

[7] Rashdall, *The Universities of Europe in the Middle Ages,* II, pt. 1, 242–243 (on this point
the revised edition does not differ from the edition of 1899); Ehrle, *Der Sentenzenkommentar Peters von Candia,* 162–167.

[8] Wappler, *Geschichte der theologischen Fakultät,* 26, portrayed the institution as predominantly nominalist, but with some realists drawn mainly from the Dominican order.
Along the same lines, Häfele (*Franz von Retz,* 283) depicted his Dominican hero as a
staunch defender of realism in a nominalist environment.

[9] Ritter, "Studien zur Spätscholastik II," 44.

The 1930s mark a turning point both in the interpretations of Vienna's philosophical position and in the approaches used to ascertain it, even though the historiography that saw the *via moderna* as dominant did not die during those years.[10] Increasingly, scholars expressed doubts about the wholesale association of Vienna with nominalism, and began to base their evaluations on the writings of figures whom they took to be representative.[11] Albert Lang's earliest account of the first Viennese leaders had also placed Langenstein and Oyta in the camp of the "moderate nominalists."[12] Later, however, in his monograph on Henry of Oyta, he published the first serious study of an early Viennese theologian, concluding that Oyta's views were eclectic but showed a marked sympathy for Thomas Aquinas. If, as Lang argued, Henry of Oyta had influenced decisively the intellectual stance not only of his colleague Langenstein, but of the early university as a whole, the institution could scarcely be termed nominalist without qualification.[13]

Since the 1960s, the labels have proliferated, with no sign of consensus in sight. Isnard Frank has claimed that the dominant orientation among the professors at the early university was "not only realist, but even Thomist."[14] Alphons Lhotsky has suggested that the Augustinian influence on the early university should not be overlooked. He played

[10] In 1948, George Sarton could still draw on this early literature to claim that Albert of Saxony, Henry of Langenstein, Henry of Oyta, and Nicholas of Dinkelsbühl were all "moderate Occamists" who "created in Prague and Vienna the philosophical preparation for the purely scientific work to be accomplished later"; see Sarton, *Introduction to the History of Science*, III, pt. 2, 1091.

[11] Heilig, "Mittelalterliche Bibliotheksgeschichte," 20. Heilig's doubts were based on the number of columns required to list the works of Aquinas (5), Scotus (⅓), Ockham (¼), and Gerson (9) in an index of medieval library holdings in Lower Austria. His approach did not distinguish the genres represented (e.g. sermons vs. formal theological works). Rough though it was, Heilig's conclusion had the merit of stimulating a reexamination of the received wisdom.

[12] A. Lang, *Wege der Glaubensbegründung*, 211ff. His evaluation of Langenstein, however, rested on Munich, Bayerische Staatsbibliothek, Clm 11591, the so-called *Lectura Eberbacensis*, which is unfortunately the commentary on the *Sentences* by James of Eltville. The same flaw mars J. Lang, *Christologie*, 335, 368–369. For the correct identification, see Trapp, "Augustinian Theology," 252, n. 93; and Appendix below. Parts of J. Lang's analysis can be salvaged as a much-needed contribution to our knowledge of James of Eltville.

[13] A. Lang, *Heinrich Totting von Oyta*, 241. (Häfele's earlier work on Franz von Retz [n. 8 above] was primarily bio-bibliographic.) Maurice de Wulf offers an interesting (though unsubstantiated) institutional solution to the problem of eclecticism: Henry of Langenstein and Henry of Oyta had been nominalists in Paris, but became Thomists in Vienna; *Histoire de la philosophie médiévale*, III, 183–188, esp. 185–186.

[14] Frank, *Hausstudium*, esp. 146, 153.

down the importance of an early "rationalistic-critical" influence of
Paris on Vienna in general, and on Langenstein in particular, by pointing to the latter's brief stay at the Cistercian monastery of Eberbach
(ca. 1382–1383), with its mystical atmosphere inspired by St. Bernard
of Clairvaux. But, Lhotsky argued, Langenstein's arrival in Vienna coincided with yet another revision of his views on universals, this time
under the influence of St. Thomas mediated by the Viennese Dominicans.[15] Finally, two recent works have pointed in yet another direction.
Based on an examination of Langenstein's genuine commentary on the
Sentences, Rudolf Damerau has called the latter's Eucharistic teaching
"Ockhamist-Scotist,"[16] while Karl Binder has associated Scotism with
the founders of the University of Vienna. For Langenstein, Binder's
evidence is tenuous. He relies on Justin Lang's analysis of the so-called
Lectura Eberbacensis, ascribed to Langenstein but actually by Jacobus de
Altavilla,[17] and on three citations of Scotus by name. For Henry of
Oyta, Binder draws on Albert Lang's monograph and on very general
similarities between the positions of Oyta and Scotus.[18] Scotism may
well have played a role in Vienna, but more evidence is necessary to
make the claim plausible.

The lack of consensus about the philosophical orientation of Vienna
and its early leaders is in part a consequence of the superficial criteria
used to establish it. Citations of authorities and lists of surviving manuscripts are useful pieces of information. But they do not constitute
decisive evidence for a philosophical position, nor can they substitute
for careful study of indigenous Viennese works, beginning preferably
with those of established authorship or authenticity. Critical editions
and intellectual biographies based on genuine writings, then, will remain important desiderata for some time to come.

But the disarray in the historiography reflects more than simply an
absence of adequate editions and monographs. Many of the works ex-

---

[15] Lhotsky, *Die Wiener Artistenfakultät*, 57–58. Vanderjagt takes a similar position in
his article "Henry of Langenstein," *Dictionary of the Middle Ages*, VI, 167.

[16] Damerau, *Die Abendmalslehre*, 32–54, esp. 33. Damerau's transcriptions and arguments must be used with caution. To his credit, however, Damerau recognized the doctrinal differences between Clm 11591 (the so-called *Lectura Eberbacensis*) and Langenstein's so-called *Lectura Parisiensis* (Alençon, Bibliothèque de la ville, codex 144); see
below and Appendix.

[17] See n. 12 above and Appendix below.

[18] To make his case for Scotist influences, Binder points to Oyta's discussion of future
contingent propositions, and to his omission of a proof for God's existence from motion—positions that belong to the common heritage of fourteenth-century thought; see
Binder, "Zum Einfluss des Duns Scotus," 750–754.

amined above have associated the nominalist-realist distinction, which was at home in the twelfth century, with the *via antiqua–via moderna* dichotomy of the fifteenth century. They usually bridge the gap between these periods with Ockham, who is considered both a nominalist and a *modernus*. Heiko Oberman's typology of mid-fourteenth-century nominalism has given a new meaning to the old category. According to Oberman, nominalism represents less a specific philosophical position about the ontological status of universals than a methodological approach that uses the absolute power of God as an analytical tool, primarily in theological discussions.[19] This suggestion has proved helpful in sharpening the focus of the debate, but not in settling it. For when a single category encompasses "a common attitude" in figures as different as Bradwardine, Holcot, and John of Ripa, it has outlived its usefulness as a precise analytical tool. It tells us more about an entire historical period than about the fine shades of philosophical or theological discussion within that period. For the late Middle Ages, however, it is crucial to make more headway on both leading and secondary figures as a prerequisite to characterizing in detail the period as a whole. In an excellent survey of the historiography of nominalism, William Courtenay has illustrated the various connotations that the term "nominalism" has acquired, and his example should make students of the late fourteenth century very wary of using it.[20] More recently yet, Neal Gilbert has argued that the term "modernus," although long used in its ordinary language meaning, became the proper name of a philosophical position only after the Council of Constance (1414–1418). Since the earliest explicit reference to a struggle between the *via antiqua* and the *via moderna* goes back to Cologne in 1425, the meanings of "nominalism" in the fourteenth century and of "modernus" in the fifteenth remain open questions.[21] With this recognition of the necessity and inadequacy of taxonomy, let us turn now to the specimens themselves.

When Rashdall compared the curricula of Vienna and Paris, he cautiously suggested that Vienna was "less conservative" and stressed mathematics to a greater extent.[22] It is tempting to infer from the statutes of these two institutions alone that the curricular differences between them were genuine. One must remember, however, that when

---

[19] Oberman, "Some Notes on the Theology of Nominalism," 47–76.

[20] Courtenay, "Nominalism and Late Medieval Religion," 26–59.

[21] Gilbert, "Ockham, Wyclif, and the 'Via Moderna,'" 85–125, esp. 106; Trapp, "Clm 27034," 320–321; Ritter, "Studien zur Spätscholastik II," 39.

[22] Rashdall, *Universities*, II, 242–243.

Langenstein and his colleagues came to Vienna, they brought with them twenty years of intimate acquaintance with the *practice* of teaching in the faculty of arts, and recent experience with the customs of the faculty of theology as well. Since Langenstein and Oyta seem to have played a leading role in formulating the Viennese curricular requirements, it is likely, that the Viennese statutes reflect the actual practices of Paris more closely than the older Parisian statutes themselves.

Among the topics of the ordinary disputation, Albert III's statutes explicitly mention *sophismata*, those logical puzzles so telling of the fascination with logic during the fourteenth century. Likewise, the section on private instruction lists the fees for such works as Buridan's questions on Aristotle's *Physics* and Albert of Saxony's commentary on *On the Heavens*.[23] Although university statutes are not always a trustworthy guide to academic practice, the Acts of the Faculty of Arts prove that in the early years some of these prescriptions were indeed carried out. Not surprisingly, they report a steady diet of lectures on Aristotle's logical and philosophical works. In addition, a few scattered references betray an interest in the logical and natural-philosophical outlook of mid-fourteenth-century Paris. The commentaries of William of Ockham on the *Physics*, and of John Buridan on the *Physics*, *On the Soul*, and the *Metaphysics* also appear in the lecture assignments,[24] alongside courses on such standard fourteenth-century logical fare as *consequentiae* and *insolubilia* (sometimes with the names of specific expositors such as John of Holland or Marsilius of Inghen). One reference to the "logic of Heytesbury" (*loyca Hesbri*) is especially noteworthy, for this work represents a high level of logical sophistication.[25] Marsilius of Inghen's works on a variety of topics were also used at Vienna, including his commentaries on logic and on the *On Generation and Corruption*, among others.[26] These commentaries were among the latest products of Paris. Their use in Vienna was probably not a coincidence. Marsilius had long been a colleague of Langenstein at Paris, both in the faculty of arts, and in the gatherings of the small English-German nation. Indeed the two men appear to have been on good terms. After the Schism drove them from Paris, they remained in con-

---

[23] Lhotsky, *Artistenfakultät*, 254–255. On *sophismata*, see Kretzmann, "Syncategoremata, Sophismata, Exponibilia," 217ff.

[24] *AFA*, I, 81, 142, 289, 303.

[25] *AFA*, I, 54. See also Wilson, *William Heytesbury*; and Heytesbury, *On "Insoluble" Sentences*.

[26] *AFA*, I, 79, 137, 169, 171, 185, 265, passim.

tact with each other from their positions of leadership in Vienna and Heidelberg.[27]

In addition, manuscript evidence confirms the fact that some of these statutory prescriptions were indeed carried out.[28] Various logical questions by Ludolf Mestermann (or Meistermann), who taught in the faculty of arts from 1385, have survived in one manuscript from the early 1390s.[29] A manuscript of Buridan's questions on Aristotle's *Physics* was copied at the university in 1390.[30] For all of their interest, however, these details reveal little about the way these works were used, or the extent of their influence on the assumptions and positions of the Viennese masters.

Not until 1390 did the faculty of arts begin to keep records of the courses assigned to its masters. Before that time, almost nothing is known about day-to-day academic life in Vienna. For the faculty of theology, which was the most prestigious of the higher faculties, even less information has survived. Since its records begin only in 1396, even the official angle on theological activity during these early years is poorly documented. These lacunae have left few sources beyond the works of the early teachers. Whatever its philosophical orientation, the influence of Gerard of Kalkar lasted only a few years, from 1384 to the autumn of 1387.[31] Soon after his own arrival, Langenstein began lecturing on Genesis: the first date in the autograph of his lectures is 1385.[32] These lectures on the first six days of Creation combine biblical exegesis with a wealth of information about late medieval science in a theological context. Steneck's analysis of their scientific and natural-

---

[27] See Ritter, "Studien zür Spätscholastik 1," 12ff, 34ff, 196f.

[28] This is not always the case. A number of discrepancies can be found between the assigned courses in the faculty of arts and some of the courses that were actually being taught. The list of lectures compiled by a Viennese student (ca. 1405) in Vienna, Dominikanerkonvent, codex 187/153 (Frank, *Hausstudium*, 153, n. 103) bears little resemblance to the official lectures for the specified year in *AFA* 1.

[29] Lhotsky, *Artistenfakultät*, 91. ÖNB 5252, which contains these lectures, is dated "Vienna 1392"; see Unterkircher, ed., *Katalog der datierten Handschriften in Österreich*, 1, 77, figs. 235–236.

[30] ". . . finite Anno domini M° 1390 in die Sancti stephani prothomartiris per cristiannum vrouwyn de zusato In venerabili studio wyennensi" (ÖNB 5424, fol. 163ʳ); Unterkircher, ed., *Katalog*, 1, 80, fig. 222.

[31] Shank, "Academic Benefices and German Universities," 37, 45 n. 41. Kalkar had been a disputation partner of Peter of Candia at Paris in the late 1370s. Ehrle groups Kalkar with the theologians who were strongly influenced by nominalism in Paris, but claims that the disputation in which Gerard participated at Cologne in 1389 was oriented toward realism; see Ehrle, *Der Sentenzenkommentar Peters von Candia*, 147–148.

[32] Shank, "Academic Benefices and German Universities," 42, n. 2.

philosophical content is especially interesting, for it suggests that the boundary line between the arts and theology was very fluid. The younger theology students who sat through these biblical lectures were introduced in passing to a wide spectrum of late medieval science.[33] In a more traditional vein, Henry of Oyta's *Quaestiones super Sententias*, which he presumably had first presented in Paris, were reread at Vienna ca. 1389. According to Albert Lang, they represent an "eclecticism of nominalist hue," a shift from Oyta's position during his years in Prague.[34] But the dates in the autographs of Langenstein's lectures on Genesis, and the colophons in copies of Henry of Oyta's questions on the *Sentences*, shed only a dim light on the activities of the faculty of theology during its early years.

Fortunately, one unusual manuscript (Vienna, ÖNB 4371) has survived to bear witness to those early years. It goes beyond the professorial lectures to capture vividly the interests of the first bachelors of theology at Vienna. The poor physical condition of the manuscript and a cataloguing mistake have conspired to keep it out of the scholarly limelight all these years.[35] Precariously preserved on mildewed paper and in faded ink, the volume is a miscellany notebook once owned by a Johannes Bremis (d. 1390). It contains extensive transcriptions and rough drafts of *principia* disputations that Bremis and three other theology students held before the faculty of theology in Vienna, most probably during the academic year 1388–1389.[36] These disputations include not only Bremis's own arguments, but transcripts of the arguments defended by his opponents. Bound with those rough drafts are fragments from Bremis's personal library. A detailed analysis of the notebook and its contents will require a separate monograph.[37] Meanwhile, the following pages serve to illustrate both the interest

[33] Steneck, *Science and Creation*, 141ff. Steneck wisely avoids circumscribing Langenstein's position with the standard fourteenth-century philosophical categories. He concludes that Langenstein approaches Aristotelian science from an Augustinian point of view. Instead of establishing the basis for a rational ascent to God, science inspires the soul to love the Creator.

[34] According to the colophon of Munich, Bayerische Staatsbibliothek, Clm 8867, these questions were "read anew" in 1389. A. Lang has argued that they originated in Paris between 1378 and 1380 (*Oyta*, 63, 66–68, 139ff). See Chapter 4 below.

[35] The *Tabulae codicum manu scriptorum praeter Graecos* (III, 253) of the National Library in Vienna inexplicably identifies codex 4371 as a commentary on book I of the *Sentences* by Nicholas of Dinkelsbühl.

[36] For a more detailed description of the manuscript, a discussion of its date, and the circumstances that led to its survival, see Appendix below.

[37] An edition is currently in preparation.

that the codex presents for the intellectual life of the early University of Vienna and the hazards of prematurely reducing the outlook of its members to ready-made categories.

.

After completing his lectures on the Bible, every theology student was expected to lecture on the four books of Peter Lombard's *Sentences*. Before being authorized to start on a given book, however, the candidate was required to "principiate" (*principiare*). In their *principia*, several students of theology debated issues suggested by the book on which they were about to lecture, took each other's theses to task, and criticized each other's arguments before the entire faculty of theology. Although the Viennese statutes do not specify precisely when the *principia* were to be held, the prescriptions in Bologna, which are very detailed and familiar to three of the early Viennese professors, spread the four disputations over the academic year, at intervals of several months.[38] Among other recommendations, the students were urged to treat their debate partners (*socii*) with respect, and to avoid frivolous discussions. They were also permitted to use a few notes during the debate.[39] Beyond this, their task was to prove their mastery of the subject matter and their competence to deal with the subtleties of theological argumentation.

The *principia* in ÖNB 4371 stand out for several reasons. They are the earliest documents of this kind for the University of Vienna, contemporary with the formulation of the statutes of the faculty of theology.[40] Their content therefore constitutes a precious source of information for a period that is still poorly understood. The eighty-odd folios of the disputation spell out in detail a host of interesting theses. The arguments and counterarguments bring assumptions to the fore; they also show dialectical tools and invectives at work, and theological positions in the making. Not least, they prove conclusively that the

---

[38] Ehrle, *Der Sentenzenkommentar Peters von Candia*, 39ff; idem, *I più antichi statuti*, 20ff; Marcolino, "Augustinertheologe," 174ff. The three theologians trained in Bologna were Conrad of Ebrach, O. Cist., Leonard of Carinthia (or of Villach), O.E.S.A., and Frederick of Nürnberg, O. Carm.; see Uiblein, "Lebensgeschichte," 97, and idem. "Die ersten Österreicher," 85. The importance of these statutes for Vienna is discussed briefly by Uiblein in his "Zu den Beziehungen der Wiener Universität," 178.

[39] See the statutes of the faculty of theology in Kink, *Geschichte*, II, 93–127, esp. 102ff.

[40] Work on the statutes proceeded between 10 April 1386 (*AR*, I, 5ʳ) and 1 April 1389, when they were approved by the faculty (Kink, *Geschichte*, II, 93).

first generation of Viennese theology students was not only aware of, but also in dialogue with, recent developments in Parisian theology.

But the interest of the notebook goes beyond content. Unlike the carefully edited *principia* that typically preface the published version of a commentary on the *Sentences*, these rough drafts offer insights into the way the debates were composed and delivered. They also provide an opportunity to check the practice of the *principium* debate against the recommendations of the statutes. As we shall see, the *principia* themselves show that students of theology were occasionally nonchalant about the university guidelines on propriety and orthodoxy.

The debates preserved in this codex involve four protagonists—Johannes Bremis, Hermann Lurtz of Nürnberg, Johann of Meigen, and Lambert of Gelderen—whose biographical sketches reflect the diversity of the student body and teaching staff of the early university. Since very little has been written about Johannes Bremis, the following details about his life will help place this manuscript in context. Although his name usually occurs without the "de" of origin, the last reference to him in the Acts of the Faculty of Arts proves that he had come from Bremen: *Johannes quondam de Bremis*, "formerly from Bremen."[41] In the 1370s, he attended the University of Prague, where he obtained his degrees of bachelor of arts and master of arts in 1377 and 1380, respectively.[42] Between 1380 and 1384, he supervised the determinations of six students, and on one occasion was selected to examine candidates for the bachelor's degree.[43] He is perhaps identical to the Johannes Nicolai de Bremis who obtained a law degree at Prague in 1381.[44]

It is not known precisely when Bremis left Prague for Vienna. His name does not appear in the Viennese matriculation lists, which are not all extant for the early 1380s. The first official record of his presence at the recently revived university is his election as proctor (*procurator*) of the Saxon nation on 14 April 1385.[45] The Acts of the Faculty

[41] *AFA*, I, 51. Bremis's name appears in Aschbach, *Geschichte,* I, passim; and Uiblein, "Johann Stadel von Russbach," 10, 13, passim. He should not be confused with the Franciscan Johannes Bremer (fl. 1420–1455), about whom Ludger Meier has written in some detail; see "Der Sentenzenkommentar des Johannes Bremer," 161–169, and later articles.

[42] *Monumenta historica universitatis Carolo-Ferdinandeae Pragensis*, II, pt. I, 177, 192.

[43] Ibid., 201, 207–208, 212, 214, 218.

[44] Ibid., 127. If this surname is indeed correct, he may have been a prebendary of the parish church in "Brygenes, Ripen. dioc. vac. per obitum Johannes Nicolai" (13 September 1396); under "Ebbo, Johannis" in [Tellenbach, ed.], *Repertorium Germanicum*, II (1933), col. 232.

[45] *AR*, I, 3ʳ.

of Arts mention his name for the first time on 22 April.[46] The statutes of Albert's III's new Collegium ducale, dated 26 April of the same year, include him among the ten original members.[47] After this date, Bremis's name appears relatively frequently in the Acts of the Faculty of Arts, in a variety of positions of responsibility. His colleagues elected him examiner in December 1386 and May 1387.[48] Between January 1387 and July 1389, he sat on no fewer than six committees, with tasks that ranged from mediating disputes to finalizing the statutes of the faculty of arts.[49] Following the death of the Roman pope Urban VI in October 1389, Bremis played an active role in the university's preparations for its first *rotulus*, or "roll of petitions" for benefices.[50] In particular, he served the Saxon nation of the university as "enroller" (*inrotulator*), the officer appointed to collect the fees from the hopeful supplicants for ecclesiastical benefices.[51] The last known detail about Bremis's life is also associated with these preparations. According to a list of expenses presented to the university in May 1390, he helped the vice-rector Hermann of Treysa and a former colleague from Prague, Paul of Gelderen, drink 4 pfennigs worth of wine when the three men met to correct the *rotulus* shortly before it was sent to Rome in early February 1390.[52] Finally, on 1 July 1390, the Acts of the Faculty of Arts suddenly record Bremis's death, unfortunately without providing any further details.[53] In addition to his notebook, a brief sample of Brem-

[46] *AFA*, I, 2.

[47] See Franz Scherer's rough transcription of the statutes in ÖNB 13763, 404. Franz Ehrle found the unique medieval version of the statutes in codex VII of the Archives of the University of Vienna, the same manuscript that contains a copy of the statutes governing the teaching of theology in Bologna (*I più antichi statuti*, vii–viii). But this manuscript has since disappeared; see Uiblein, "Zu den Beziehungen der Wiener Universität," 179, n. 41.

[48] *AFA*, I, 10, 16.

[49] *AFA*, I, 11, 19, 25, 26, 34, 37.

[50] The universities sent rolls of petitions for benefices to the papal court whenever a new pope was about to be elected, or even upon hearing that the current pope was sick and likely to die; see Watt, "University Clerks," 213–229.

[51] *AFA*, I, 42; *AR*, I, 18ʳ.

[52] "Item 4 denarii pro vino quando magister Paulus cum magistro Johanne de Bremis et mecum correxit rotulum" (*AR*, I, 23ʳ). The expenditure was reported on 11 May 1390, but must have taken place before 13 February, when Hermann of Treysa first assumed Lambert of Gelderen's duties as rector, thereby implying that the latter had left for Rome (*AR*, I, 22ʳ). Since the price of wine fluctuated by a factor of ten between 1386 and 1392, it is difficult to know how much wine 4 pfennigs could buy in 1390. See Sailer, "Geschichte der Preisbewegung," esp. 44.

[53] *AFA*, I, 51.

is's activity in the faculty of arts seems to have survived as a flyleaf in one of Henry of Langenstein's autographs.[54]

Bremis's three debate partners are slightly better known than he in the secondary literature. Hermannus Lurtz de Nuremberga (d. 1399?) earned a master of arts degree from the short-lived *studium* at Fünf-kirchen (Pécs) in Hungary, and was in addition a doctor of medicine. He too taught at Prague for several years. After coming to Vienna in 1386, he served as rector in the summer semester of 1387, and again in the winter semester of 1390. At the time of the debate, he was dean of the faculty of medicine.[55] Lambert Sluter de Gelria (d. 1419), the third *socius*, had spent several years in Paris. His name appears in the records of the English-German nation there between 1375 and 1378. At that time, he was already an advanced student, for the first mention of his name informs us that he had not "determined" in Paris.[56] At Vienna, he served as rector in the summer semester of 1390, at which time he was elected to carry the *rotulus* of university petitions to Rome.[57] Fi-nally, Ioannis de Meigen (d. 1402?) probably received his early training in Vienna, for he is in all likelihood the Mag. Johannes canonicus Wyennensis who matriculated at the University of Vienna before 1377.[58] In 1385, when he served as rector, he was one of the oldest masters teaching at Vienna: in the Acts of the Faculty of Arts, his name follows that of the chancellor Berthold of Wehingen on the "list of masters in order of seniority." Like Bremis, Meigen was one of the first members of the Collegium ducale.[59] Thus far, one work is associated with his name, a *Tractatus distinctionum* that survives in two fifteenth-century manuscripts and in a very rare incunabulum notorious for being the earliest work printed in Vienna (1482).[60]

[54] See Appendix below.

[55] On Lurtz, see Kleineidam, *Universitas Studii Erffordensis*, pt. 1, 265–266; *AFA*, I, xix, 521; Gabriel, *Universities of Pécs and Pozsony*, 26–27; and the statutes of the faculty of medicine (dated 1 April 1389), in Kink, *Geschichte*, II, 157.

[56] *Auctarium*, I, col. 467. The last date on which he is mentioned is the celebration of his admission to the English-German nation (col. 555). See Aschbach, *Geschichte*, I, 419–421, for a brief summary of his activities in Vienna, which include commentaries on the minor prophets (ÖNB 4421, 4423, 4575, 4632, 4635, 4636).

[57] See n. 52 above.

[58] *MUW*, I (1377–1450), I.

[59] *AFA*, I, xix, 4, 533–534; Aschbach, *Geschichte*, I, 410–411. See also Franz Scherer's early nineteenth-century "Chronik der Wiener Hochschule" (ms.), in ÖNB 13763, 404.

[60] See Chapter 4 below. The manuscripts are ÖNB 4951, 154ʳ–163ʳ (copied from the incunabulum); and ÖNB 4963, 119ʳ–127ʳ (copied in 1481). On the incunabulum, which exists in only two exemplars, see Denis, *Wiens Buchdruckergeschicht* (!), 1–2; and Mayer, "Buchdruck und Buchhandel," in *GStW*, III, 610–612.

As masters of arts, the four men taught in the faculty of arts while concurrently studying in the faculty of theology. Their varied backgrounds are typical of the eclectic university membership soon after the institution revived. The *principia* debates in ÖNB 4371 suggest that this academic diversity fostered a lively intellectual climate at the university. The schools of thought and differing assumptions about theological method as well as content sometimes clashed, producing sparks. All in all, the atmosphere of the early years must have been very stimulating indeed. The faculty of theology embodied enough variety to provoke genuine confrontations on matters of substance, yet was probably small enough to avoid large factions.

.

When the debate got underway, it was apparently Johannes Bremis himself who opened it. He therefore had the privilege of setting out its direction,[61] and organized the disputation around the question "Whether eternal salvation for mortals lies only in the faith or law of Christ, which contains matters of utmost profundity?" As was customary, he subdivided this general question into four others, one for each book of the *Sentences*: (1) "Whether the faith of the undivided Trinity surpasses [all other] profundities of theological truth?" (2) "Whether the profundities of Christian truth surpass the limit of the whole created capacity?" (3) "Whether the profundity of the incarnation of the law of Christ can be elucidated fully in this life?" and (4) "Whether there is only eternal salvation in the Christian law?"[62] These questions were to be the foci of the four forthcoming *principia*. After enunciating them, Bremis returned to the first question, the topic of the day, which he in turn divided into four parts: "on theological truth," "on the excellence of the faith," "on the quality and number of the profundities that the faith contains," and "on the most excellent of

---

[61] See Appendix below.

[62] "Utrum in fide ⟨*interl* vel in lege⟩ Christi continente profundissima sit tantum mortalibus salus e[tern]a. . . . Ad huius ergo declarationem formo iiii^or questionum articulos illam tangentes, quorum primus est: Utrum inter profunda theologice veritatis excellat articulus ⟨*interl* fides⟩ individue Trinitatis, et hoc quantum ad primum librum Sententiarum. Secundus articulus: Utrum profunda veritatis Christiane excedant limitem ⟨*interl* totius⟩ capacitatis create, et hoc quo ad secundum Sententiarum. Tertius articulus, quantum ad tertium Sententiarum erit: Utrum profundum Incarnationis legis Christi possit in via ad plenum enodari. Articulus vero 4to libro Sententiarum correspondens est quesitum, videlicet: Utrum sit tantum salus eterna in lege Christiana" (ÖNB 4371, 13^r). From a logical point of view, the position of "tantum" in the last sentence requires the cacophonous translation provided.

these [profundities], namely the mystery of the undivided Trinity."[63] The first and last of these in particular deserve a closer look.

Bremis's discussion of theological truth suggests that he understood truth to be not so much a property of propositions as the property of corresponding to truth itself. This emphasis permeates a number of the conclusions and corollaries in his first *principium*. Truth is something that a creature possesses to the extent that it conforms to the first exemplar. From the point of view of its essential being, every created nature is therefore infinitely true; in other words, its essence conforms perfectly to the first exemplar of that nature. The expression "infinitely true" implies that truth is in some sense susceptible to quantitative variation. And indeed in the following sections, Bremis makes this implication explicit. Thus, although anything may be "truth," it is not the case that any several things are several truths: "Although the essential truth of a thing can be neither increased nor decreased, its accidental truth can be terminated, although not increased."[64] Bremis's views here contrast sharply with those of Ockham and Holcot, for example. For Ockham, truth and falsity were not distinct from the true or the false propositions. Holcot implied as much when he wrote that "properly speaking, no proposition can be truer than another," and claimed that there are no degrees of truth.[65] In contrast, Bremis's outlook recalls earlier views, such as those of Anselm and Henry of Ghent.[66] Indeed, although Bremis cited only Augustine as an authority in this discussion, his shrewd opponent Lurtz immediately saw the similarities with Anselm and Henry of Ghent.[67]

---

[63] ". . . pertractabo in isto principio per ordinem iiii⁰ʳ puncta quorum primum erit de ⟨*interl* veritate⟩ theologica [[vel katholica veritate]], secundum de excellentia fidei; tertium erit de qualitate et numero profundorum que continet fides, 4ᵐ vero erit de excellentissimis illorum, scilicet de misterio individue trinitatis" (ÖNB 4371, 13ʳ).

[64] "Licet res quelibet sit veritas, tamen non quelibet res plures sunt plures veritates" (ÖNB 4371, 14ʳ). "2ᵃ conclusio: tantum quelibet creatura habet de veritate quantum habet respectu primi exemplaris de conformitate . . . ⟨*mg:* Corollarium⟩ Omnis creata natura quantum ad esse suum essentiale est infinite vera. . . . ⟨*mg* 3ᵐ corollarium⟩ Quamvis veritas rei essentialis sit inaugibilis et diminuabilis, accidentalis tamen [[desini]] omnis desinibilis est, licet non augibilis" (ÖNB 4371, 14ᵛ).

[65] Ockham, *Summa logicae*, in *OP* I, 131 (trans. Loux, in [Ockham], *Ockham's Theory of Terms*, 141). See also Boehner, "Ockham's Theory of Truth" and "Ockham's Theory of Supposition and the Notion of Truth," in his *Collected Articles on Ockham*, 174ff and 232ff; Holcot, *In quatuor libros Sententiarum quaestiones*, bk. I, qu. 1 (b1ᵛb).

[66] See Henry of Ghent, *Summa questionum Ordinariarum*, 5ᵛ: "veritas rei non potest cognosci nisi ex cognitione conformitatis rei cognitae ad suum exemplar," with Augustine, Anselm, and Plato cited as authorities. See also Copleston, *A History of Philosophy*, II, 466; Marrone, *Henry of Ghent*, 20–21.

[67] ÖNB 4371, 71ʳ.

Having discussed truth in general, Bremis turned to the varieties of truth. "Although theology and human knowledge communicate[68] in the same truth or truths, yet truth is said to be theological for one reason, philosophical for another." The difference between theological truth and any other truth lies in "the means of asserting it, the manner of considering it, and its end," where theological truths are defined as "only the truths to be believed according to the religion of Christ, and those that follow from them."[69] Yet theology and the religion of Christ are not identical, for "while all [statements] of which the religion of Christ says that they ought to be believed are theological truths, yet not every theological truth must be believed according to the catholic [faith]."[70] For example, it is necessarily the case that one of the following propositions is true: "The Blessed Virgin was conceived in original sin"; "the Blessed Virgin was not conceived in original sin." Since the Immaculate Conception had not yet been settled by a dogmatic pronouncement and was a hotly debated issue in the late fourteenth century, some theologians were clearly defending a false proposition. For Bremis it followed, therefore, that "not every theological falsehood is a heretical depravity" and, hence, that it is possible in some instances to defend a theological falsehood "as a matter of opinion" without sinning. Indeed, "in many theological matters, it is permissible to hold each part of the contradiction as a matter of opinion."[71]

When Bremis decided to use the Immaculate Conception as an illustration, he did not choose haphazardly. In 1387, a dispute had erupted at the University of Paris between the Dominican Juan de Monzón (Joannis de Montesono) and other members of the university

[68] Alluntis and Wolter note that "whatever can be given to more than one subject (individual or person) is said to be communicable" (Duns Scotus, *God and Creatures*, 500). This term seems to be used here in the technical theological sense, to signify an alternation of predicates or properties; see Borchert, *Der Einfluss des Nominalismus*, esp. 8, line 21ff.

[69] "Quamvis in eadem vel eisdem veritatibus communicent scientie humane et theologia, tamen alia ratione veritas dicitur theologica et alia philosophica. Patet quia veritas theologica a veritate qualibet cuiuscumque alterius scientie differt in tribus, scilicet in medio asserendi, et modo considerandi et in fine propter quem. . . . Veritates secundum religionem Christi credende, et que ex hiis sequuntur, theologice sunt, et solum tales" (ÖNB 4371, 16ʳ).

[70] "Licet omnia que religio Christi dicit ⟨*interl* tradit⟩ credenda sint veritates theologice, tamen non omne theologicum verum est credendum katholice" (ÖNB 4371, 16ʳ).

[71] "Sequitur ex ista conclusione quod non omnis theologica falsitas est heretica pravitas. Sequitur secundo quod non omne theologice verum convinci(?) potest katholice credendum. Sequitur tertio quod non semper peccat qui theologicam falsitatem opinative defendit seu affirmat; patet quia in pluribus materiis theologicis licitum est utramque partem contradictionis opinari" (ÖNB 4371, 16ʳ).

over several theses he had defended in his vesper disputation. The proposition that attracted the most attention—"[to hold] that the Blessed Virgin Mary and the Mother of God did not contract original sin, is against the faith"[72]—was a frontal attack on the Immaculate Conception, championed by the Franciscans. In 1389, the year of the Bremis *principia*, the University of Vienna received from Paris two letters on the subject, announcing that the Dominicans had withdrawn from the university after being censured for their denial of the Immaculate Conception.[73] Similar tensions existed in Vienna. In 1388 or 1389, the Dominican professor of theology Franz von Retz preached a Christmas sermon that defended the official position of his order.[74] It is not clear whether there were any vociferous proponents of the Franciscan position in Vienna. But judging from the fact that Langenstein and Oyta both pleaded for moderation in the matter, in writing as well as in sermons, local discussions of the issue evidently had become more heated than the two professors had wished.[75]

Theology deals with the divine, but it is clearly a human activity: not all its claims are necessarily true, and, moreover, they have a limited scope. "In many matters" theology cannot say which of two contradictory propositions is true.

For Bremis, then, under some circumstances theology evidently faces the same predicament as natural philosophy: some propositions are undecidable on the basis of reason alone—such as the eternity of the world for Aquinas or the rotation of the earth for Oresme.[76] This is not to say that theology is on the same plane as natural philosophy, however. What, then, is the relation between these various disciplines? First Bremis establishes the preeminence of the Catholic tradition: "although theology may find itself in contradiction with the conclusions of human tradition, no truth is to be found anywhere which contradicts the Catholic tradition." Theology, like other human enterprises, is subject to error and may generate contradictions when compared

---

[72] *Chartularium*, III, 495.

[73] Ibid., 513–514.

[74] Häfele, *Franz von Retz*, 355ff.

[75] Langenstein and Oyta preached their sermons on 8 December 1389 and 1390, respectively; see Lang, *Oyta*, 231ff, esp. n. 252. See also Binder, *Die Lehre des Nikolaus von Dinkelsbühl*, 80ff.

[76] See Aquinas et al., *On the Eternity of the World*, 19ff; and Oresme's discussion of the rotation of the earth in *Le Livre du ciel et du monde*, 519–539, esp. 539. Interestingly, Oresme notes here that the plausibility of arguments for the rotation of the earth (which seems at first glance to fly in the face of natural reason) can be used to refute those who would undermine the faith by rational argument.

with the results of other endeavors. Whatever may happen, the "Catholic tradition" remains true. Interestingly, Bremis gives one other area a privileged status. The accepted rules of reasoning should not be altered simply because they clash with the results of theology: "one ought not deny any correct rule of logic or philosophy on account of some theological truth." Specifically, Bremis is clear that "in no sect should the expository syllogism or the syllogism *in barbara* be denied." His rationale for this position is simple. The validity of these syllogisms can be demonstrated from things known in themselves. Should anyone propose to deny them, he would meet with ridicule.[77] Having thus preserved the independence of logic, Bremis holds that not everything that is true and correct follows from the theological tradition; yet nothing received which is repugnant to the faith can be correct or true. Other disciplines may have independent ways of asserting truths, but the faith provides the ultimate criterion for separating the true from the false—an interesting maxim, but considerably more difficult to apply than to state, as the vexing problem of the Immaculate Conception might have suggested.

Not surprisingly, then, Bremis holds that theological study can never succeed in attaining demonstrative knowledge (*scientia*) of all the truths it believes. Many of these truths (e.g. "the Trinity, the Incarnation, and the like") are simply unknowable in our present state as "wayfarers" (*viatores*), for they are not deducible from things known in themselves. Yet, "just as every Catholic truth can be founded, stated, and defended on the basis of the proper elements of theological consideration, so [this] truth is sufficient to lead heretics and infidels to the Catholic truth." Indeed according to Bremis, assiduous theological study can find ways "to convert heretics, schismatics, and infidels, if they do what is in them." The association of these three categories of unorthodoxy emphasizes the depth of the tensions between the two papal parties one decade into the Great Schism. But it also shows Bremis's confidence in theological apologetics as the appropriate tool

---

[77] "Quamvis plurime humane traditionis conclusiones repugnent theologice veritati, nulla tamen veritas ubicumque reperta contradicit katholice traditioni. . . . Nullam logice aut philosophie rectam(?) regulam negari oportet propter aliquam veritatem theologicam. . . . In nulla secta aut doctrina negandum est syllogismus expositorius aut in barbara. Patet quia ex per se notis demonstrabile est quod valeat, igitur derisio esset negantis eiusmodum" (ÖNB 4371, 16ʳ). The syllogism *in barbara* is the familiar universal affirmative syllogism of the first figure ('all A are B, all B are C, therefore all A are C'). In an expository syllogism, the middle term is the subject in both premises, and also is singular ('A is B, A is C, therefore C is B'). Incidentally, Bremis stands in complete agreement with Ockham on these issues. See Chapter 3 below.

to use on all deviants. Although he saw a close parallelism between the
foundations upon which theological truth rested and their use in apologetics, he evidently assumed that heretics and infidels could be convinced by arguments with something less than demonstrative force.
For Bremis, the efficacy of theology in such instances was analogous
to that of "the study of medicine, [which] suffices to cure all ill persons
who want to obey."[78] Here Bremis's position has a certain Scotist ring,
with its confidence in reason as a tool of apologetics.[79]

In another intriguing thesis, Bremis proposed that "no world could
be made, or could have been made, whose natural philosophy and
metaphysics would be our theology, even if such a world were to include the entire latitude of creatable things simultaneously, and even if
the wayfarers and philosophers of this world were intellectual creatures
of any higher and more perfect species than are the men and philosophers of this world."[80] This unusual proposition attracts attention for
several reasons. First, the technical term "latitude," which is used here
without explanation, is borrowed from natural philosophy. According
to Nicole Oresme, "a quality is to be imagined to have two dimensions: longitude according to the extension of the subject, and latitude
according to its intensity in degree."[81] For Oresme, a latitude was a
divisible continuum. In the context of Bremis's thesis, however, the
latitude is composed of discrete things ordered in a scale of perfection
containing every possible kind of creature, limited only by the princi-

---

[78] "Quantumcumque studium theologie crescat aut invalescat, attingere non poterit
proprie ad scientiam veritatum omnium quas credit. Probatur quia multe tales in via
sunt proprie inscibiles, [[quod]] quia ex principiis per se notis indeducibiles, sicud veritas
de trinitate, de incarnatione et similes. Cum ista conclusione stat quod sicud ex theologice considerationis propriis omnis katholica veritas potest fundari, declarari et defensari,
ita sufficit hereticos et infideles katholice veritati adducere. Prima pars est satis clara;
secunda pars patet quia per assiduationem theologici studii inveniri possunt vie et ingenia suffi[cientes?] ad convertendum hereticos, scismaticos et infideles, illis facientibus
quod in se est. Et hiis qui in theologico stu[dio?] exercitati sunt laborantibus pro viribus
sicud studium medicine sufficit ad curandum omnes egros qui obedire volunt" (ÖNB
4371, 16ᵛ). On "doing what is in oneself," see Oberman, "Facientibus quod in se est,"
esp. 317–325.

[79] Gilson, *Jean Duns Scot*, 216–217.

[80] "Quod nullus mundus potuit vel posset fieri, cuius naturalis philosophya et methaphysica esset nostra theologia vel [[consimiles?]] ⟨*mg* fides katholica⟩ etiam si comprehenderet talis mundus totam latitudinem creabilium simul et etiam si viatores et philosophi illius mundi essent intellectuales creature quantumlibet altioris et perfectioris
speciei quam sint homines et philosophi istius nostri mundi" (ÖNB 4371, 62ᵛ).

[81] Clagett, *Nicole Oresme*, 63; see also idem, *Science of Mechanics*, chap. 6.

ple of contradiction.[82] This proposition expresses Bremis's conviction that an unbridgeable chasm separated Christian theology from natural knowledge. The two domains were not, and could not be, identical. Although Bremis earlier had seemed to stress the differences between theology and the truths of the faith, here the human side of theology has all but disappeared: in no conceivable world can Catholic theology coalesce with metaphysics and natural philosophy—even granting humans extraordinary, though nondivine, intellectual powers.

Bremis proposed his "possible worlds" thesis in his first *principium*, and Hermann Lurtz immediately took exception to it in his response. Lurtz formulated his objection as a counterthesis: "this conditional [proposition] is necessary: 'If some world were to include the entire latitude of creatable things simultaneously, its natural philosophy and metaphysics would be our theology'." Lurtz evidently thought that Bremis had walked into a trap by adding the conditional clause to his thesis. For Lurtz, there was a necessary connection between the inclusion in the world of the entire latitude of creatable things and the coincidence of natural philosophy with theology. He apparently agreed with Bremis that such a coincidence was impossible, for he went on to prove that the antecedent of his conditional clause was impossible. The reference to the *entire* latitude placed a limit on the absolute power of God, for it implied that God could not make another kind of creature.[83]

The tools used in these arguments are especially noteworthy. When Bremis formulated his thesis in terms of the "entire latitude of creatable things," he was drawing on a well-developed body of concepts within natural philosophy. And Lurtz's response delved further into the details of these fourteenth-century "languages of measurement," as John Murdoch has called them.[84] Thus a debate about the boundaries between theology and metaphysics soon shifted to arguments over the

---

[82] See Murdoch and Sylla, "The Science of Motion," 232, n. 93, who link this language with John of Ripa's *Quaestio de gradu supremo*.

[83] "Hec conditionalis est necessaria: si aliquis mundus comprehenderet totam latitudinem creabilium simul, eius naturalis philosophya et methaphysica esset nostra theologia; contra predictum magistrum Johannem . . . probo propositionem meam sic: istius conditionalis date antecedens est impossibile, igitur ipsa conditionalis est necessaria. Argumentum probo quia si sit possibilis tota latitudo creabilium simul, sit A gratia exempli, tunc sequitur quod potentia dei esset exhausta, quod est impossibile. Consequentia probatur quia deus nichil posset addere isti multitudini" (ÖNB 4371, 75^v).

[84] See Murdoch, "Philosophy and the Enterprise of Science," 51–74; and idem, "From Social into Intellectual Factors," 280ff.

proper application of mathematical rules to the matter at hand. If there is a complete latitude of creatable things, Lurtz argued, then there is a multitude to which God can add nothing. The perfection of this latitude will then be either equal to or less than the perfection of God. Clearly it cannot be equal. But if the perfection of this latitude is less than that of God, then (a) it is exclusively terminated at God's perfection or (b) it stands at some distance from God's perfection. But (a) cannot be the case, for then God would exceed a creature by an infinitely small amount (in which case the perfection of the most perfect creature would be infinitesimally close to the perfection of God). On the other hand, if (b) were the case, then God could create intermediate creatures in the interval of perfection. Hence the multitude of creatable things posited earlier was not the multitude of all creatable things.[85]

In his second *principium*, which survives in two drafts, Bremis attempted to answer the thrust of Lurtz's contention by showing that his opponent's proof did not affect the validity of the original argument. But Bremis failed to point out that the counterargument did require him to drop the "even if" clause from his original thesis. The debate thus immediately shifted to the limit: what does it mean to say that the world can contain the entire latitude of creatable things? For the purposes of discussion, Bremis quickly noted that Lurtz's conditional proposition did not contradict Bremis's own thesis if, as Lurtz had claimed, the antecedent happened to be false. Indeed anything could be inferred from an impossible premise. To cover himself, as well as to justify his original use of the conditional, Bremis noted that Scotus and others had declared that it was possible for the entire latitude of creatable things to be produced. But Bremis cautiously refused to identify wholeheartedly with this position, remarking in the margin of his second draft: "although I shall not assert here how this can be said by those who hold that it is possible."[86] Bremis also refused to

---

[85] "Confirmatur quia vel perfectio A est equalis deo vel minor. Non primum, ut patet de se. Si secundum, vel ergo est exclusive terminata ad perfectionem dei, vel distat ab ea; non primum, quia tunc deus in infinitum modice excederet creaturam ⟨*Bremis in mg*: per excessum irreplebilem distat⟩. Si dicatur quod distat a perfectione dei, tunc deus in ista distantia potest creare creaturas intermedias, et per consequens A non fuit multitudo omnium creabilium, quod est contra ypothesim. Confirmatur quia vel distat iam(?) a perfectione dei finite vel infinite; non finite, quia tunc deus solum finite excederet creaturam. Si infinite distat, tunc deus infinitas alias species potest producere in tali distantia, igitur etc." (ÖNB 4371, 75ᵛ).

[86] "Preterea, contra hoc quod dixi in primo corollario 2ⁱ articuli mei de prerogativa fidei Christi ratione originis et obiectalis dignitatis, quod nullus mundus fieri posset cuius naturalis philosophia esset nostra theologia vel fides katholica etiam si comprehen-

concede that his proposition placed a limit on the power of God.[87] In responding to Lurtz's discussion of the intervals between levels of perfection, he referred to the "distance" that separates two geometrical entities of differing dimensions, such as a line and a plane surface. "Some have argued that a surface is infinitely distant from a line, and yet there is no species intermediate between them," thereby undermining Lurtz's assumption that a distance between the perfection of God and the entire latitude of creatable things is a continuum filled with beings of intermediate perfection.[88]

This brief interchange illustrates how rapidly the original theological issues could fade into the background, as mathematics, logic, and propositional analysis moved into the center of the arena. In this case, Bremis and Lurtz apparently agreed on the relation between theology and natural philosophy. Their disagreement turned on the most effective, consistent, and defensible way of establishing their claims, and here logic played a crucial role.

The portion of Bremis's third *principium* directed against Lurtz does not appear to have survived. But the geometrical issues that had arisen

---

deret totam latitudinem creabilium simul, ponit magister meus reverendus ⟨mg mgr H Lurtz⟩ hanc 7ᵃᵐ suam propositionem 'Hec conditionalis est necessaria: "si aliquis mundus comprehenderet totam latitudinem creabilium simul, eius naturalis philosophia esset nostra theologia," ' quam probat per hoc quod illius conditionalis antecedens [[. . . ad hoc]] dicit esse impossibile.

"⟨mg Sed ad hoc respondeo cum reverentia quod⟩ si antecedens sicut ipse dicit [[est]] esset impossibile [[tunc inferam ita bene oppositum conclusionum suarum sicut ipse infert oppositum mearum. Respondeo cum reverentia quod si hec esset vera]], tunc illa ⟨interl sua⟩ propositio nullo modo esset dictis meis contraria, cum ad idem antecedens impossibile sequatur bene utrumque oppositorum.

"Tamen quia Doctor subtilis ⟨J. Duns Scotus⟩ et plures alii dicunt hoc argumentum non esse impossibile, videlicet quod possit esse tota latitudo creabilium producta ⟨mg quamvis hoc non asseram quomodo dici posset per opinantes hoc esse possibile⟩, dicam ad argumenta per ordinem, quibus oppositum magister meus nititur probare" (ÖNB 4371, 7ᵛ).

[87] "Arguit enim primo quod tunc potentia Dei posset esse exhausta. [[Negatur]] negaretur consequentiam(!) cum reverentia. / Ad probationem: quia deus nichil posset addere isti multitudini, placet michi, tamen quia hanc eandem multitudinem posset infinities destruere et reproducere, clarum est quod sua potentia non esset exhausta. Ad confirmationem: quia sit A multitudo talis omnium creabilium producta, tunc querit magister meus, vel perfectio A est equalis deo, vel minor; et si minor, vel est exclusive terminata ad perfectionem dei vel distat ab ea; et si sic, tunc deus in illa distantia posset creare creaturas intermedias, et per consequens A non fuit multitudo omnium creabilium" (ÖNB 4371, 7ᵛ–8ʳ).

[88] "Etiam multi concesserunt quod superficies infinite distet a linea et quod tamen non posset esse inter superficiem et lineam aliqua species media" (ÖNB 4371, 8ʳ).

in the second *principium* reappear in Lurtz's third *principium*, this time divorced altogether from the theological problem they originally were meant to illuminate. Such a narrowing of the focus is perhaps to be expected in any protracted debate among specialists. Yet it is significant that the direction taken by this sharper focus is mathematical and natural-philosophical in character. The "languages of measurement" had become so integrated into theology itself that debates turned upon their correct application, rather than upon the advisability of using them, for example.

Nor was this trend limited to the question about possible worlds. An examination of Lurtz's third *principium*, for example, shows that here, too, issues originally raised in theological terms during the first *principium* give way to fine points of mathematics and logic. Theological issues are raised, but they rarely stand at the center of Lurtz's argumentation. Even when they are broached, the terms in which they are phrased presuppose a solid background in natural philosophy, as the list of the theses Lurtz defended against Bremis amply illustrates:

—not all individuals of the same species are equally perfect;
—the specific latitude of perfection is to be reached by retreating from the nondegree rather than by approaching the highest degree;[89]
—there is in fact no infinite line, nor any body infinite longitudinally;
—just as it was not possible for the humanity of Christ united to the Word to be made imperfect in many ways, so it was not proper that the Divine Spirit be said to be in some sense imperfect through the power of the *communicatio idiomatum*;[90]
—just as an angel cannot be created immediately after this [instant], so neither can it be altered imperfectly;
—just as an angel in the first instant of its being could not be meritorious, so neither could it in the same instant lose merit by sinning;
—not every created thing that does not possess its accidental perfection is simply an incomplex falsehood;
—a contradiction is involved in claiming that the distinction between the divine persons is the least of all distinctions, and yet that the distinction between the personal property and the divine essence is smaller yet;[91]
—the Holy Spirit could not have been the father of Christ in the case

---

[89] For parallels, see Murdoch, "*Mathesis*," 234ff.

[90] The *communicatio idiomatum* (literally, the "communication of properties") refers to the problem of using the same predicates of the divine and human natures of Christ; see Oberman, *Harvest of Medieval Theology*, 261ff.

[91] This question seems to take off from Scotus's discussions of minimal distinctions; see Gelber, "Logic and the Trinity," 98.

Joseph had been the carnal father of Christ and the Holy Spirit assumed Joseph afterward.[92]

The language and presuppositions of these theses suggest a broad acquaintance with, and delight in, the full range of what John Murdoch has called "the new conceptual languages" or "analytical languages" of the fourteenth century.[93] Intrinsically and extrinsically bounded intervals, instants, and infinity are all brought to bear on the formulation and solution of problems. Thus Lurtz used the language of "intension and remission of forms" (in which changes in the intensity of qualities are assigned degrees with changing quantitative values) to substantiate his first thesis, in which degrees of whiteness, of perfection, and substantial forms are intended and remitted. He also discussed the divisibility of perfection, and the distance between a given species and the one immediately below it.[94] In the same debate, Lurtz referred to the speed with which finite and infinite natural powers corrupt qualities of equal resistance. He suggested, for example, that the entire latitude of specific perfection should not be imagined "according to numbers"; otherwise there could be an irrational proportion between no two species.[95] He argued the case by positing two species A

[92] This example also made its way into Arnold of Sehusen's (Seehusen's, Seehausen's) early fifteenth-century Viennese commentary on the *Sentences* in Munich, Bayerische Staatsbibliothek, Clm 3546, 152^{r}b; see Borchert, *Der Einfluss des Nominalismus*, 146, n. 175. In the original, Lurtz's theses read: ". . . quod non omnia individua eiusdem speciei sunt essentialiter eque perfecta . . . quod latitudo perfectionis specifica magis est attendenda penes recessum a non gradu quam penes accessum ad gradum summum . . ." (81^r); ". . . quod nec est linea de facto infinita nec corpus longitudinaliter infinitum . . . quod sicud non fuit possibile humanitatem Christi unitam verbo multipliciter imperfici, sic fuit inconveniens divinum spiritum vi communicationis ydiomatum aliquomodo imperfectum dici . . . quod sicud angelus non potest creari immediate post hoc, sic nec posset imperfective alterari immediate post hoc . . ." (82^r); ". . . quod sicud angelus in primo instanti sui esse non potuit mereri, sic nec potuit in eodem instanti peccando demereri . . . quod non omnis res creata que non habet perfectionemn suam accidentalem est simpliciter falsum incomplexum . . . quod contradictionem includit quod distinctio personarum divinarum sit inter omnes distinctiones minima distinctiones minima distinctio, et quod tamen distinctio inter proprietatem personalem et essentiam divinam est distinctio minor . . . quod Spiritus Sanctus non fuisset pater Christi in casu quod Joseph fuisset pater carnalis Christi et postea Spiritus Sanctus Joseph assumpsisset . . ." (83^r).

[93] See Murdoch, "Philosophy and the Enterprise of Science," 58f; idem, "The Development of a Critical Temper," 53.

[94] ÖNB 4371, 81^r. On the intension and remission of forms, see Sylla, "Medieval Concepts of the Latitude of Forms," 223–283.

[95] "Tota latitudo perfectionis specifica non est ymaginanda per numeros. Et patet hoc quia aliter sequeretur quod inter nullas duas species esset vel esse posset proportio irra-

and B, such that the perfection of A is twice the perfection of B. If God should change an individual C of species B into an individual of species A, would C ever stand to B as the ratio of the diameter of a square to its side?[96] In his second conclusion, Lurtz made further use of proportions. He also discussed the comparison of various infinite lines, their condensation and rarefaction according to given proportions, the local motion of their parts, the intension of a hot body to the greatest degree of heat.[97] His authorities include Augustine and Anselm, to be sure, but also the mathematician and astronomer Campanus of Novara and the natural philosopher and theologian Nicole Oresme. Yet all these authorities are outnumbered by references to Euclid, and to Aristotle's *Physics* and *On the Heavens*. Elsewhere Lurtz did not hesitate to bring his medical training to bear on theological issues, appealing to arguments by physicians and to the *Canon* of Avicenna.[98]

The debate between Lurtz and Bremis reflects the differences in their interests and education. As a master of arts and doctor of medicine, Lurtz was an experienced dialectician and natural philosopher, and he took advantage of his more extensive training. As one of Lurtz's ironic remarks suggests, Bremis felt less secure on this terrain, and unsuccessfully tried to use evasive techniques:

> the esteemed master [Bremis] did not want to answer these arguments now [about the maximum degree of heat and its relation to infinite intensity], since he considers them rather logical and scarcely relevant to the

---

tionalis" (ÖNB 4371, 81ʳ). This thesis may reflect a concession to Bremis's argument about possible worlds, in which Lurtz had assumed a continuum of perfection.

⁹⁶ "Capio duas species quedam A et B, puta hominis et musce, et pono gratia argumenti quod A sit duple perfectionis ad B, et volo quod deus C individuum quod sit de B specie mutet de specie in speciem quousque veniat in speciem A. Tunc vel C aliquando erit in aliqua specie que se habet ad B sicut dyameter quadrati ad suam costam, vel non. Si sic, ergo inter aliquas species est proportio irrationalis. Consequentia tenet, quia proportio dyametri quadrati ad costam est medietas duple proportionis, ut demonstratum est 10° Euclidis in commento propositionis 7ᶜ, sed medietas duple proportionis est proportio irrationalis igitur, etc. Si ergo dicatur quod C numquam erit in aliqua tali specie, sequitur quod transibit de extremo in extremum et numquam pertinget medium; falsitas patet libro physicorum" (ÖNB 4371, 81ʳ). The "doubling" and "halving" of proportions correspond to squaring and taking square roots; see Murdoch and Sylla, "The Science of Motion," 225ff, and Mahoney, "Mathematics," 164f.

⁹⁷ ÖNB 4371, 81ᵛ.

⁹⁸ "Quod nulla complexio humana esset vera complexio humana nisi forte complexio humana Christi minus(?) est erroneum in medicina, quia medici arguunt scilicet Avicenna primo Canonis et alii cum complexio [compareret(?)] ad formam nullus purus homo haberet veram formam substantialem hominis et per consequens nullus talis esset verus homo sed esset in alia specie animalis; . . . ista est naturaliter impossibilis tam per philosophos quam per medicos" (ÖNB 4371, 73ʳ).

argument. But since I consider them to be very efficacious and to shed some light on the argument, I will save them for him for his next *principium*, and at that time—God willing—he will tell us about their solution.[99]

Bremis's characterization of the arguments as "rather logical" may have been a tactical maneuver to slide out of a tight corner by making his opponent back down. Indeed the statutes of the faculty of theology warned against the use of "philosophical or logical material irrelevant to theology."[100] Bremis's sincerity may perhaps be gauged by the fact that he seems to have held mathematics in high regard (witness a crossed-out thesis to the effect that the study of mathematics could be worthy of eternal life).[101] But his nervousness before Lurtz was not unreasonable. In his third *principium*, Lurtz revealed himself to be a feisty character who peppered the debates with ad hominem attacks on his opponent: "no peasant however thickheaded could concede that the day of judgment will be immediately after this, where [the demonstrative] 'this' points to the present instant, as my esteemed opponent [Johannes Bremis] concedes."[102] In another context he also pointed out that Bremis had set down "many distinctions concerning the noncomplexly true and the noncomplexly false, which—with all due respect—I consider to be nothing but windy words with no foundation whatever, either in philosophy or in theology."[103] To a certain extent, remarks of this sort reflect differences in personality. But they also go beyond these smaller issues to touch on matters of conviction and method. Lurtz evidently was a more eager logician, and he did not hesitate to criticize his opponent whenever he sensed that Bremis was

[99] "Ad istas rationes magister reverendus noluit pro nunc respondere, quia reputat eas aliquantulum loycales et non multum ad propositum. Sed quia ego reputo eas multum efficaces et facere aliquam evidentiam in proposito, ideo reservabo sibi eas ad proximum suum principium et ibi informabit nos Deo dante de earum solutione" (ÖNB 4371, 81ᵛ).

[100] Kink, *Geschichte*, II, 116.

[101] ". . . quamvis in mathematicis non sit finis nec bonum, tamen earum studium esse potest vite eterne meritorium" (ÖNB 4371, 30ᵛ). The thesis occurs twice on this folio, and in each case is struck out.

[102] "Nullus tamen rusticus quantumcumque grossus concederet quod dies iudicii erit immediate post hoc, demonstrando per ly hoc presens instans sicud magister reverendus concedit" (ÖNB 4371, 83ʳ). The seriousness of the insult may be gauged by the first lines of an anti-peasant and anti-Jewish satire in catechetical form composed by a Viennese student in the fifteenth century: "Rusticus que pars est? Nomen. Quale nomen? Judaicum. Quare? Quia ineptus et turpis est ut Judaeus." See Lehmann, *Parodistische Texte*, appended to his *Die Parodie im Mittelalter*, 21. On the use of the insult *rusticus*, see Murray, *Reason and Society*, 237ff.

[103] ". . . ipse ponit multas distinctiones de incomplexe vero et incomplexe falso quas, salva reverentia sui, non estimo nisi verba ventosa non habentia fundamentum aliquod nec ex phylosophia nec ex theologia" (ÖNB 4371, 83ʳ).

indulging in excessive distinctions. In any event, the disputation bears little resemblance to the "empty rhetorical displays" that Ritter has characterized as typical of university life in the fifteenth century.[104]

The surviving records of Bremis's interaction with Lambert of Gelderen are a shade more mild-mannered. In his fourth *principium*, Bremis charged Lambert with impertinence for attributing to him corollaries that were neither his own nor deducible from propositions he held. In the same passage, Bremis implied that Lambert knew neither his logic nor his metaphysics.[105] As in the preceding cases, these barbs were not gratuitous; they reflected basic disagreements in outlook. Thus Bremis argued against Lambert: "That a substantial form should unite informatively with matter and no composite result therefrom, is simply impossible." One could concede, according to Bremis, that a form informs matter before a composite results from it. But it is a mistake, he argued, to assume that our understanding of this process corresponds to an order of ontological priority, "an issue on which the disciples of Ripa (*Ripiste*), whom my master [Lambert] seems to follow, have been deceived."[106]

This reference to *Ripiste* is most interesting. John of Ripa, O.F.M., had commented on the *Sentences* in Paris in 1357. His philosophical theology came under attack in 1362, when the faculty of theology there condemned fourteen theses advanced by Ripa's disciple Louis of Padua. Little else is known about the fate of Ripa's views, save that by 1400, Jean Gerson still worried about their influence.[107] Combes has characterized Ripa's disciples in the last third of the fourteenth century as proponents of "a Platonic realism that went very markedly beyond

---

[104] Ritter, "Romantic and Revolutionary Elements," 23.

[105] "Ex quo patet quam impertinenter, salva gratia sua, contra magister meus intulit duo corollaria quorum opposita nec dixi nec ex dictis meis sunt inferibilia . . . nec sequitur ex dicto meo 'homo est accidentaliter homo aut suppositum est accidentaliter suppositum seu per se subsistens est accidentaliter per se subsistens, ergo per accidens superadditum est homo suppositum vel per se subsistens,' patet scienti loycam et metaphysicam veram" (ÖNB 4371, 46ʳ).

[106] "Conclusio: Formam substantialem uniri informative materie et nullum ex inde compositum resultare est simpliciter impossibile. . . . quamvis forte quoad modum intelligendi nostrum resolutorie(?) prius occurreret [[habitudo]] formam [[informam]] informare materiam quam ex hoc compositum resultare secundum propriam (*interl* formalem) rationem intelligendi hoc et illud; ex hoc tamen non potest argui ordo prioritatis in essendo, sicud sepius decepti sunt [[Ripa et m]] Ripiste quos magister meus videtur sequi . . ." (ÖNB 4371, 43ʳ).

[107] See André Combes's remarks in the preface to his edition of Ripa's *Determinationes*, 9–12; and his "Présentation de Jean de Ripa," 145–242.

that of Duns Scotus."[108] During his student days in Paris in the late 1370s, Lambert had evidently absorbed enough of these ideas to be identified as a follower of Ripa.[109] Equally interesting, Bremis was sufficiently familiar with the views of Ripa not only to recognize them and to connect them with Lambert's outlook, but also to offer a general criticism of their assumptions. Bremis knew whereof he spoke: the thesis that Lambert defended was drawn almost verbatim from Ripa.[110] Lambert enjoyed a long teaching career at Vienna, until his death in 1419. The fact that he once was, and perhaps had remained, a *Ripista*, deserves to be taken into account in assessing the various intellectual currents at the university.[111]

Bremis's interaction with Johann of Meigen, on the other hand, is as proper as the framers of the statutes might have wished. Meigen had been Bremis's teacher, as the latter repeatedly noted throughout the debate, and he treated his master with all due reverence.[112] Although Bremis did take his former teacher to task, he always handled the points of contention with civility. The issues about which they argued were more metaphysical and less natural-philosphical: *necessitas antecedens*, the relative perfection of will and intellect, the relative precedence of the *ratio* of will over the *ratio* of intellect, and so on.[113]

This particular interaction was far from normative, however. The mild-mannered and unimpeachably orthodox recommendations of the statutes of the theological faculty—drafted and approved at the time of the debate—are misleading if construed as faithful descriptions of academic practice. Indeed some of the theses under discussion in the *principia* come close to the heretical conclusions decried in the statutes. Bremis's clash with Lurtz is striking in this regard, especially the last

---

[108] John of Ripa, *Determinationes*, 11.

[109] Lambert should perhaps be counted on the fringes of the "school of *formalizantes*" that Combes has uncovered among the Franciscans in late fifteenth-century Paris; see Combes, *Jean Gerson, commentateur dionysien*, 589ff.

[110] Compare ÖNB 4371, 43ʳ (in n. 106 above) with John of Ripa, *Determinationes*, qu. 1, art. 2, difficultas, 3ᵃ conclusio: "Quamlibet formam substantialem possibile est uniri informative materie et nullum ex ipsa compositum resultare" (74).

[111] André Combes has found traces of Ripa's influence on Nicholas of Dinkelsbühl, who spent his entire academic career at Vienna (1385–1433); see Combes, *La Théologie mystique de Gerson*, II, 367–368, esp. nn. 5–6.

[112] "Reverendus pater et preceptor meus Joannes vicecancellarius" (ÖNB 4371, 77ʳ; see also 70ᵛ and 84ᵛ).

[113] The theses that Meigen defended against Bremis in his third *principium* included the following: "respectu esse vel fore in creatura esse potest in deo aliqua necessitas antecedens" (60ʳ); "voluntas est perfectior quam intellectus" (60ᵛ).

thesis debated in their third and fourth *principia*. Bremis's suggestion
that Joseph might have been the carnal father of Jesus—whether or not
the Holy Spirit assumed Joseph's paternity—cast doubts on fundamental orthodox tenets, including traditional understandings of the
Incarnation, the Trinity, and the sinlessness of Christ. This controversial proposition was carefully phrased in conditional terms, to be sure.
It nevertheless embodied assumptions that courted the charge of blasphemy, and hinted sotto voce at a radical solution to the current debate
about the Immaculate Conception, a solution that was undoubtedly
distasteful to Henry of Langenstein.[114] That some listeners were scan-
dalized is probable. That the debate was not censured is certain.
Bremis had raised the point in his third *principium* (ÖNB 4371, 79^v);
Lurtz responded in his third (83^{r-v}), and Bremis answered again in his
fourth (51^r)—before the entire faculty of theology and at intervals of
several months. Both the extant records of the discussion and its contested content prove that the debate proceeded without restrictions.
Such an intellectual climate can be characterized only as open. The new
theologians were pushing their logical skills, their philosophical arguments, and their theological assumptions to their very limits.

·

   In addition to the debates, the Bremis notebook contains several
other texts that show a keen interest in the recent developments of
contemporary Parisian theology. All are fragmentary; presumably
they constituted a portion of Bremis's personal library.[115] A brief fragment from Henry of Oyta's *Abbreviatio* of Adam Wodeham's commentary on the *Sentences* is bound in the manuscript with portions of
the debate. Only four leaves survive, but all carry traces of Bremis's
annotations and underlinings. Given Oyta's presence on the Viennese
faculty of theology, Bremis's interest in the work is perhaps not surprising, but it should not be minimized either. Indeed, no other copies
of the work appear to have survived in Vienna.[116] Bremis's annotations
also prove that in the early years of the University of Vienna at least,
Wodeham's views were studied with care.[117]

---

   [114] Emmen, "Heinrich von Langenstein," 625ff; and Binder, *Die Lehre des Nikolaus von
Dinkelsbühl*, 117ff.
   [115] See Appendix below.
   [116] The Stiftsbibliothek in Klosterneuburg, on the outskirts of Vienna, does own a
complete copy of the work, however (codex 296). For more on Wodeham and his work,
see Courtenay, *Adam Wodeham*, 223; Chapter 3 below; and Appendix below.
   [117] For the generation of students that followed, direct contact with Wodeham's works
is more difficult to establish. Courtenay has found quotations from Wodeham in works

Two other works also reach beyond the Viennese context to suggest intellectual contacts with Paris in spite of the Schism. The first is a copy of the commentary on the *Sentences* by James of Eltville (Jacobus de Altavilla), a work that many still mistakenly believe to be by Langenstein himself.[118] An angry remark, which Bremis directed to one of his scribes, suggests that he was having the text copied for his own use.[119] It is probable that he obtained this work through Langenstein, who was a close friend of James. Indeed before coming to Vienna, Langenstein had spent some time as the latter's guest at the Cistercian monastery in Eberbach.[120] The annotations and underlinings in the manuscript are light and sporadic, suggesting that Bremis had probably not completed his study of this text at the time of his death.

Even more suggestive, Bremis also owned an incomplete copy of questions on the *Sentences* by Aegidius de Campis (d. 1413), who had lectured on the *Sentences* in 1377–1378 and became a master of theology in Paris in 1383.[121] The scribe who copied this text was working with a defective original, as he noted in the colophon.[122] To date, this is the only known copy of the work, identified thanks to the scribe's marginal notes. Although the Aegidius selection is severely damaged, the first question ("Whether evangelical faith is compelling of the highest authority for any rational creature?") is decipherable. It reveals a bold work that Bremis read with considerable care, witness his many markings and underlinings.[123] The discussion is full of clever hypothetical situations that touch upon issues of burning relevance to the Church in the late 1370s and 1380s: e.g. "whether the pope can err?"[124]

---

by Arnold of Seehausen and by Peter of Pulkau's student, Peter Reicher of Pirchenwart (*Adam Wodeham*, 150ff). Given their heavy dependence on Henry of Oyta (see Chapter 4 below), it is likely that many of these citations were obtained at second hand.

[118] Damasus Trapp first made the correct attribution some thirty years ago in a footnote overlooked by much subsequent scholarship; see "Augustinian Theology," 252, n. 93. For further confirming evidence, see Appendix below.

[119] "Hic deficit unum folium quasi propter maliciam scriptoris pro precio" (ÖNB 4371, 132ᵛ).

[120] Falk, "Der mittelrheinische Freundeskreis," 517–528; Hartwig, *Henricus de Langenstein*, 57ff.

[121] On Aegidius de Campis (Gilles Deschamps), see de Launoy, *Regii Navarrae Gymnasii Parisiensis Historia*, 904–907; Glorieux, "L'Année universitaire 1392–1393," 469; des Mazis, "Deschamps, Gilles," *Dictionnaire d'histoire et de géographie ecclésiastiques*, XIV, 331–334; and Bernstein, *Pierre d'Ailly and the Blanchard Affair*, 109ff, 183ff.

[122] "Nota hic defectum ratione exemplaris" (ÖNB 4371, 246ᵛ).

[123] See Appendix below.

[124] "Si per papam intelligimus viatorem vicarium Christi Petri successorem, tunc omnia possunt dici de papa que dicuntur de ecclesia, tunc ista est igitur necessaria 'papa credit recte,' sicud hec est necessaria 'ecclesia credit recte' quia ly papa connotat quod sit

This hasty sampling of the issues that Bremis and his colleagues debated scarcely does justice to the document, but it already suggests a few conclusions. The four opponents in the *principia* disputation of 1388–1389 represented a variety of viewpoints, a state of affairs not unrelated to the fact that they had moved to Vienna from several other universities. The *Ripista* Lambert of Gelderen had studied in Paris. Bremis, with views that sound now like Henry of Ghent, now like Scotus, had spent most of his student years in Prague, where Lurtz, the natural philosopher, had also studied after several years in Pécs. As for Johann of Meigen, he was probably a product of the local *studium* in Vienna. Such diversity was by no means exceptional in the medieval university, which was par excellence a world of traveling scholars. Unlike the older universities, however, Vienna in the late 1380s clearly had not yet established a character of its own, into which it immediately expected to mold the students who flocked there. Pluralism permeated the Viennese academic climate in the early years. Few precedents had been set. And the daring theses that Lurtz and Bremis could discuss without censure before the entire university suggest that the senior members of the faculty of theology adopted an open-minded attitude toward the incoming students they needed in order to create a viable institution.

When the views of the individual *socii* are considered, it is not easy to decide where the university fits in the standard taxonomies of philosophical trends. The Scotist sympathies that transpire from Bremis's account of truth must be weighed against his understanding of the autonomy of theology and natural philosophy, and his reading of Wodeham. Lurtz's enthusiasm for logic and his appeal to the absolute power of God are illustrated in propositions reminiscent of John of Ripa. Traditionally "nominalist" stances occur side by side with traditionally "realist" views. Since the positions of these students emerged in the heat of a debate, they do not reveal the coherence and consistency that one expects from systematic treatises. The interest of the document lies precisely in the fact that it has preserved not the polished work of first-rate thinkers, but the wranglings of a group of late medieval theology students. Bremis's notebook lies close to the heart of academic activity in late fourteenth-century Vienna, and it reveals a strong pulse. Without more light on the subject, however, it is still difficult to identify the beast.

---

successor Petri et in omnibus etiam connotat quod sit vicarius Christi in fide [et] in omnibus; tamen hec est concedenda: 'papa potest errare' " (ÖNB 4371, 193ᵛ).

CHAPTER THREE

On Paralogisms in Trinitarian Doctrine (I):
The Early Fourteenth Century

Digne loqui de personis
vim transcendit rationis,
excedit ingenia;
Quid sit gigni, quid processus
me nescire sum professus,
sed fide non dubia.

ADAM OF ST. VICTOR,
Hymn *De Trinitate*
(mid-twelfth century)

THE BREMIS notebook discussed in the preceding chapter reveals in some detail the differing interests of four advanced theology students at Vienna soon after the revival of the university. The value of this document derives both from its specificity and its restricted time frame. But debates between four students during one academic year offer a very limited perspective on the intellectual life of an institution. One way of transcending this narrow picture is to adopt a developmental approach. The current state of research on the University of Vienna unfortunately precludes any definitive evaluation along these lines. The manuscript material relevant to such an inquiry is extensive, and much of it is unexplored.

As a preliminary effort in this direction, the following chapters trace the vicissitudes of one intriguing question among two generations of Viennese academics. The goal here is not to circumscribe an essentially Viennese outlook, but rather to explore changing trends within the institution and its context by focusing on one specific issue. Indeed the question selected here is not original with the University of Vienna. It stands out as unusual, however, on account of both its content and the amount of attention it received from theologians associated with Vienna. The question provides not only an entrée into their intellectual milieu, but also an important point of comparison with earlier trends in fourteenth-century thought. In the words of its proponents, the question reads, "Do Aristotle's rules of syllogizing suffice for the Christian to solve paralogisms in Trinitarian theology?"

Its specificity notwithstanding, this question touches upon broad controversial issues that go to the heart of late medieval thought, in particular the relation between knowledge obtained by natural means and the claims of Christian revelation. The late Middle Ages were keenly aware of the ground that had been covered since antiquity. As Henry of Langenstein remarked, "the greater part of human science has been discovered between the time of Aristotle and the present."[1] New knowledge was perhaps most obvious in theology, since the Christian revelation constituted the most conspicuous advance beyond the pagans. But strides forward were obvious in technology, natural philosophy, and also logic. Langenstein's predecessors and older contemporaries had forged logical tools that extended the power of existing analytical techniques beyond those of the Philosopher. Supposition theory, propositional analysis, the language of first and last instants—these and other conceptual implements sharpened the intellect, clarified thought, and served a critical purpose wherever they were applied, especially in theology and in natural philosophy.[2] In spite of these new directions, including a burgeoning interest in nonsyllogistic inferences,[3] Aristotle's rules of syllogizing generally continued to be seen as foundational. Thus William of Ockham, who was himself a creative logician, saw his work as a faithful exposition of the Philosopher's intentions.[4] Aristotle's syllogistic still undergirded most formal argumentation, and was virtually synonymous with natural reason itself.[5] It remained one of the primary tools of medieval academic thought, the omnipresent *organon* of the university disputation. In a culture that

[1] This statement justifies a premise in an intriguing argument against the eternity of the world in the last sermon Langenstein preached (25 November 1396). Since knowledge grows inexorably as a function of time, the world cannot be eternal, for we do not have infinite knowledge. For the Latin text, see A. Lang, "Die Katharinenpredigt Heinrichs von Langenstein," 147, lines 11–17. An analogous argument occurs in Aquinas, *De potentia Dei*, qu. 3, art. 17; see Aquinas et al., *On the Eternity of the World*, 50.

[2] See Moody, "The Medieval Contribution to Logic," 371ff; and Murdoch, "The Development of a Critical Temper," 53f.

[3] Stump, "Topics: Their Development and Absorption into Consequences," 286ff.

[4] Moody, *The Logic of William of Ockham*, 17.

[5] Duns Scotus, for example, understood Augustine to say that the first principles of the sciences and syllogistic forms were all known naturally (i.e. they did not require any divine illumination); see Brown, "Duns Scotus on the Possibility of Knowing Genuine Truth," 142–143.

followed Aristotle in identifying science with conclusions derived by demonstrative argument, the Aristotelian rules of syllogizing were a prerequisite for the acquisition of knowledge.

The Trinity, on the other hand, epitomized the mystery of Christian revelation. Together with the Incarnation and the sacrament of the Eucharist, the Trinity was one of the three "incomprehensibles" of medieval theology, and ipso facto a focal point of attempts to make sense of it. During the patristic period, Trinitarian theology developed as a response to the problem of reconciling the Old Testament references to the "Spirit of God" and its expressions of radical monotheism on the one hand, with the divine, or quasi-divine, claims made about Jesus in the New Testament on the other. But these solutions eventually became problems in their own right. In his *De Trinitate*, Augustine articulated the predicament as follows:

> The Father, the Son, and the Holy Spirit constitute a divine unity of one and the same substance in an indivisible equality. Therefore, they are not three gods but one God; although the Father has begotten the Son, and, therefore, He who is the Father is not the Son; . . . and the Holy Spirit is neither the Father nor the Son, but only the Spirit of the Father and the Son, and He Himself [the Spirit] is also coequal with the Father and the Son and belongs to the unity of the Trinity.[6]

With its language of threeness in oneness, of distinction and identity, Trinitarian theology faced a problem common to other forms of mystical thinking—how to express the inexpressible. Theologians thus frequently found themselves confronting paradoxes, particularly in the context of the later Middle Ages, when all students of theology received a solid training in logic. When arranged as the premises of standard syllogisms, orthodox Trinitarian propositions could generate unorthodox conclusions. Consider the following inference: 'every divine essence is the Father, the Son is the divine essence, therefore the Son is the Father'. For medieval theologians, the conclusion was false, even though the premises were true and the form of the argument was correct.[7] Since there had to be a flaw somewhere, an inference of this type was called a paralogism.

But where did the problem lie? Was the logic faulty? Were Trinitar-

---

[6] Augustine, *The Trinity* (bk. I, chap. 4), 10–11.

[7] Although Aristotle allowed only universal premises, late medieval logicians considered the introduction of singular premises to be formally consistent with Aristotle. See Ockham, *Summa logicae*, pt. III-1, chap. 8 (*OP*, I, 384–385); Bochenski, *A History of Formal Logic*, 232.

ian propositions inherently not amenable to logical treatment? Why
did the seemingly unimpeachable rules of logic clash with the equally
undeniable dogma of the Church? What criteria legitimately could be
brought to bear on the problem? Attempts to answer these questions
forced theologians and philosophers to examine critically the logical
tools they used. Were the rules that governed Aristotle's syllogisms
valid no matter what the meaning of the terms that filled their premises? Were these rules in fact universally applicable regardless of the
subject matter? Could one discover rules that would bring Trinitarian
paralogisms back within the boundaries of the accepted syllogistic?
Could one explain how such paralogisms were generated? Should one
turn to non-Aristotelian options? By raising such questions, the theologians of the late Middle Ages brought to a crux one of the chief pre-
dicaments of medieval philosophy—the relation between natural reason and revelation—but they did so in a narrowly circumscribed
context where linguistic precision and clarity of thought were at a premium. The discussions of these issues in late medieval Vienna took
place against a rich backdrop of lively debates in the late thirteenth and
early fourteenth century. Such an intricate history almost defies sum-
marization. Without a schematic overview of that background, however, the very language of the Viennese discussions—not to mention
their significance—would be lost.

·

   The tensions between Trinitarian propositions and the rules of logical discourse have a long history solidly rooted in the Church Fathers.
Augustine's *De Trinitate* opens with a warning against "the sophistries
of those who consider it beneath their dignity to begin with faith, and
who are thus led into error by their immature and perverted love of
reason."[8] It was in the later Middle Ages, however, that the Trinitarian
predicament came to the fore with particular urgency. In the eleventh
century, such figures as Peter Damian, Berengar of Tours, and Lanfranc of Bec debated the proper relation between critical methods and
the faith. The Trinity was of course a focal point of such debates. Peter
Abelard's theological works and his reputation of questionable orthodoxy illustrate the problems that a brilliant logician might encounter
in Trinitarian doctrine.[9] In the later twelfth century, with dogmatic

   [8] See Wolfson, *The Philosophy of the Church Fathers*, I, pts. 2 and 3; Augustine, *The
Trinity* (bk. I, chap. I), 3.
   [9] See Tweedale, "Abelard and the Culmination of the Old Logic," 155–156.

formulations still very much in flux, Joachim of Fiore (d. 1202) accused Peter Lombard (d. 1160) of having held that the divine essence somehow transcended the persons, thus implying a "quaternity."[10] In 1215, the issue was settled dogmatically, although not philosophically. Under the guidance of Pope Innocent III, a Paris-trained theologian, the Fourth Lateran Council condemned Joachim, and enshrined the Trinitarian formulation of Peter Lombard as the standard of orthodoxy for centuries to come:

> we believe and confess with Peter Lombard that there is some one highest thing, incomprehensible and ineffable, that is truly Father, Son, and Holy Spirit; three persons at once, and singly each of them; and therefore in God, there is only a Trinity, not a quaternity; since each of the three persons is that thing, namely substance, essence, or divine nature . . . , and that thing is neither generating, nor generated, nor proceeding, but is the Father who generates, and the Son who is generated, and the Holy Spirit who proceeds: so that the distinctions are in the persons, and the unity in the nature.[11]

The recovery of the Aristotelian corpus, the widespread teaching of dialectic in the universities, and the growing sophistication in logic served only to sharpen the issue.[12] The chief problem was to clarify the relation between the divine essence and persons in a way that would account for the requisite distinction between the persons, without, however, jeopardizing God's simplicity. The theologians of the late thirteenth century drew upon several distinctions that also served in philosophy proper. Hester Gelber has traced the vicissitudes of these distinctions through the latter third of the thirteenth century and into the early decades of the fourteenth century.[13] Two distinctions in particular set the boundaries of the Trinitarian problem, though they proved problematical to account for the difference between the persons and the divine essence specified by the Fourth Lateran Council. The first distinguished between separate or separable entities (e.g. a table and a chair). This distinction was variously called "real distinction" or "real difference." The second distinction, on the other hand, distin-

---

[10] Reeves, *The Influence of Prophecy*, 30ff.

[11] Denzinger and Schönmetzer, *Enchiridion symbolorum*, 261–262 (nos. 803–808).

[12] See, for example, John of Salisbury's *Metalogicon*, bk. II; Van Steenbergen, *Aristotle in the West*; Leff, *Paris and Oxford Universities*, chap. 4; Marrone, *William of Auvergne and Robert Grosseteste*, introduction.

[13] Gelber, "Logic and the Trinity," 9f. This chapter and the following owe much to Gelber's ground-breaking research.

guished artifacts of the conceiving mind; it therefore had no counterpart in reality apart from conceiving minds, and was called "difference
of reason," "rational distinction," and the like. To describe the differences between the persons of the Trinity and the divine essence, the
real distinction was clearly too strong, for it seemed to compromise
the divine simplicity. Conversely, to posit a rational distinction between them would suggest that this feature of the divinity had no ob-
jective reality (i.e. would disappear if all human minds were to disappear). Theologians therefore groped for some kind of middle ground,
either by positing new intermediate distinctions or by proposing new
varieties within the existing ones. From the outset, such distinctions
intersected a variety of issues in ontology (e.g. what kinds of entities
undergirded these distinctions), epistemology (e.g. how such distinctions pertained to modes of knowing and perceiving), and logic (e.g.
which terms could properly be predicated of each other and used in
various syllogisms).

Two examples will illustrate the terminological and conceptual hur-
dles involved in such endeavors. In the late thirteenth century, the
problem of God's simplicity emerged in several related contexts, such
as the attribution of diverse perfections (wisdom, goodness, etc.) to
God, and the attribution of personal properties (paternity, filiation,
spiration) to the divine essence. Although his typology is not always
clear, St. Bonaventure (d. 1274) in practice considered the differences
between the divine essence and the personal properties (which were
thought to be at the root of the distinction between the persons) to be
intermediate between a merely intellectual difference (*distinctio rationis*)
and a real difference (*distinctio a parte rei*). Indeed he classified under
both headings things that differed by a plurality of distinctions, but
were not diverse in essence. Although the function he assigned to his
distinction was intermediate between the real and rational distinctions,
Bonaventure called it a rational distinction. (For him, a real distinction
occurred only between separate essences; every other distinction was
in some sense rational.)[14] St. Thomas Aquinas (d. 1274), on the other
hand, took a relational approach to the problem. He thought that the
plurality of the divine perfections arose from a human inability to
comprehend God's perfection in one concept. Yet the terms that signified these diverse perfections were not synonymous; "wisdom" and
"goodness" had different meanings, or *rationes*, and were apprehended
as different by the human mind. Likewise, the persons, the personal

---

[14] Ibid., 15, 21; Jordan, "Duns Scotus on the Formal Distinction," 34–36.

properties, and the divine essence all had diverse *rationes,* as did the divine perfections, although they were ontologically one. With respect to the divine essence, there was only a rational difference between divine relations. But with respect to each other, "there is a real plurality, not merely of reason" between the persons.[15] For both Bonaventure and Aquinas, then, the distinction between the persons and the essence was in some sense "rational"—but they understood the term in slightly different ways. Indeed, as Alluntis and Wolter have noted, the term "ratio" can express "an intelligible feature or essential characteristic of a real or extramental thing (*ens reale*) as well as the formal content of the concept used to think about it (*ens rationis*)."[16]

·

The debate took a decisive turn in the work of the Franciscan John Duns Scotus (d. 1308). Like his immediate predecessors, Scotus focused on the problem of reconciling the simplicity of God with the plurality of persons. To a greater extent than his predecessors, however, he considered the Trinity to be, if not comprehensible, at least amenable to rational investigation. He saw no fundamental contradiction in the notion of a being that was one and three, and thought his arguments might not only enlighten the faithful but also persuade the infidel. Natural reason had its limits, to be sure, but it could do much to clarify the notion of infinite being, which distinguished God from all other beings.[17]

Scotus's use of the "formal distinction," which recently had entered the Trinitarian theology of the late thirteenth-century Franciscans, gave prominence to an element that was to dominate the discussions of the fourteenth.[18] In contrast to Bonaventure and Aquinas, Scotus found the various connotations of the term "ratio," and therefore of the rational distinction, problematical. Scotus tried to clear up this confusion by examining the way in which the divine attributes (wisdom, goodness, and so on), although one in God, were distinguishable. Not only did they have different definitions, but there was something in God that corresponded to these definitions. Thus the divine attributes had between them a *distinctio formalis a parte rei*—a "formal

---

[15] Gelber, "Logic and the Trinity," 15–25.

[16] Duns Scotus, *God and Creatures,* 506.

[17] Gilson, *Jean Duns Scot,* 216–217.

[18] See Grajewski, *The Formal Distinction of Duns Scotus*; and, most recently, Jordan, "Duns Scotus on the Formal Distinction," chap. 7, which provides a useful overview and typology of recent discussions of the formal distinction.

distinction on the part of the thing," where the last qualification asserts that the distinction holds in the order of things, apart from the activity of the conceiving mind.[19]

The same distinction could also be used to express the relation between the divine essence and the personal properties. Thus the divine essence was *formally* distinct from the divine paternity, where Scotus took the qualifier "formally" to diminish the force of the term "distinct."[20] Initially, he developed the formal distinction (or nonidentity) to deal with "distinct property-bearers within what is really one and the same thing." It is important to emphasize that Scotus thought the formal distinction was a useful *philosophical* concept in its own right. Quite apart from its utility in understanding Trinitarian distinctions, it could also illuminate the problem of universals, the soul and its power, or the principle of individuation, for example.[21] Since the formal distinction was not merely an artifact of the perceiving mind, there were some "non-identical entities within what [was] really the same thing," called (among other names) "formalities."[22] In addition, Scotus appealed to special kinds of predication that paralleled this distinction. Thus, when said of God, the proposition 'wisdom is goodness' is false according to formal predication (since wisdom and goodness are formally distinct), but true according to predication by identity, because wisdom and goodness are the same in God.[23]

From a logical point of view, the formal distinction or nonidentity played an important role in Scotus's thought. It salvaged the principle of contradiction by explaining why the personal properties, which were all predicable of the divine essence, were nevertheless not predicable of each other—even though God was one most simple being. Likewise, it also accounted for the failure of true Trinitarian premises to produce a true conclusion. In particular, the formal distinction between the persons and the divine essence introduced a lack of unity into the syllogism. Thus Scotus argued that in the premises 'the es-

---

[19] See Copleston, *A History of Philosophy*, II, 508ff; Gelber, "Logic and the Trinity," 97; Jordan, "Duns Scotus," 61ff.

[20] Gelber, "Logic and the Trinity," 90–92.

[21] Adams, "Universals in the Early Fourteenth Century," 415; idem, "Ockham on Identity and Distinction," 73; Duns Scotus, *God and Creatures*, 507; Jordan, "Duns Scotus," chap. 5.

[22] Adams, "Universals," 415.

[23] Duns Scotus, *God and Creatures*, 507. For the sake of brevity, the developmental aspects of Scotus's thought are omitted here: see Gelber, "Logic and the Trinity," 96–102; Adams, "Ockham on Identity and Distinction," 25–27, n. 67; Jordan, "Duns Scotus," chap. 4.

sence is the Father' and 'the essence is the Son', the identity between 'essence' and the personal terms was only essential, not formal. The lack of unity between the extremes ('Father' and 'Son') and the middle term 'essence' thus introduced into the syllogism a specific kind of fallacy (the fallacy of accident, on which more below), which made it illegitimate to conclude that the Son was the Father. Indeed Scotus's chief contribution, in Gelber's view, was his reorientation of the Trinitarian debate from epistemological to logical issues.[24] In doing so, he set the tone for much of the discussion in the century that followed.

The formal distinction and the assumptions associated with it were found wanting when they came under the scrutiny of some of Scotus's younger contemporaries. One of Scotus's most persistent critics was his fellow Franciscan, William of Ockham (d. 1349). Ockham rejected most of Scotus's views on the formal distinction for a combination of logical and ontological reasons. He argued that all distinctions reduced to three kinds: namely, distinctions between two things, between two concepts (or "beings of reason"), and between a thing and a concept. Yet the formal distinction was none of these. Ockham was correspondingly less enthusiastic than Scotus about the usefulness of the formal distinction. Whereas Scotus drew upon the formal distinction at a number of points within philosophy proper, Ockham in his own *Ordinatio* allowed it validity for only one reason: "It must not be posited except where it follows evidently from the traditions held in Sacred Scripture or the determination of the Church, on account of whose authority every reason must be taken captive."[25] The last sentence paraphrases II Corinthians 10:5 ("We destroy arguments and every obstacle that rises up against the knowledge of God and reduce every thought to captivity to follow Christ"), a text that, by the early fourteenth century, had a venerable history of usage in arguments about the limits of natural reason.[26] With this scriptural allusion, Ockham unambiguously expressed the subjection of reason to the Church's formulation in this specific case. He did not reject the formal distinction outright, for he evidently thought that the official Trinitarian formulations required, and were consistent with, some such distinction. But it was to be used only in this one case, when the requirements of the faith forced the hand of reason.

Ockham emphasized this point on several different occasions. Else-

[24] Gelber, "Logic and the Trinity," 88, 102, 207.

[25] Ockham, *Ordinatio,* bk. 1, dist. 2, qu. 1 (*OT,* II, 17–18); Guelluy, *Philosophie et théologie chez Guillaume d'Ockham,* 322ff; Adams, "Universals," 417.

[26] Gelber, "Logic and the Trinity," 281–282.

where in his *Ordinatio*, for example, he noted that the "formal distinction or nonidentity . . . is most difficult to understand and should not be posited except where faith compels."[27] In question 11 of the same distinction, Ockham was even more explicit. Although 'the Father is the Son' is false, yet 'the Father is that which is the Son' is true, since the Father is that essence which is the Son. Whenever a case of this type occurs, the formal distinction is permissible. "But," adds Ockham,

> such is never the case except in God, and therefore it [the formal distinction] is to be posited in God alone. Hence I say that there can be no formal distinction, nor can such a contradiction be verified, except where there are really distinct things that are nevertheless really one thing, which is possible only of the divine persons. . . . And hence, it is not possible that in creatures several really distinct things be one thing, therefore in creatures such a distinction ought not be posited, nor should it ever be posited where religious beliefs (*credita*) do not demand it.[28]

The Trinitarian formulation was therefore the only domain in which Ockham allowed the use of the formal distinction. He denied its validity even in other treatments of the Godhead, such as the relation between the divine essence and the divine attributes (wisdom, goodness, etc.).[29] In the *Summa logicae*, which postdates the *Ordinatio*, he repeated his claim that such a distinction could not apply to creatures "because among creatures it is impossible to find a numerically one thing which is really more than one thing and is each of those things, as is the case with God."[30] The word "impossible," which Ockham does not normally use loosely, is especially noteworthy here. The inappropriateness of the formal distinction for creatures was evidently a matter not of contingency (e.g. a failure to have discovered some trinitarian creature), but of necessity: there could be no creature like God in this way.[31] God was the only entity with the property of being "one nu-

[27] Ockham, *Ordinatio*, bk. I, dist. 2, qu. 3 (*OT*, II, 78).

[28] Ockham, *Ordinatio*, bk. I, dist. 2, qu. 11 (*OT*, II, 374); see also bk. I, dist. 2, qu. 1 (*OT*, II, 19–20). Also see the *Reportatio*, bk II, qu. 2 (*OT*, V, 41).

[29] "And therefore, since all traditions (*tradita*) in Sacred Scripture and the determination of the Church and the sayings of the saints can be saved without assuming it [the formal distinction] between essence and wisdom, therefore I simply deny that such a distinction is possible here, and I deny it universally in creatures . . ." (*Ordinatio*, bk. I, dist. 2, qu. 1 [*OT*, II, 18]).

[30] Ockham, *Summa logicae*, bk. II, pt. 2, chap. 2 (*OP*, I, 253–254); trans. in Freddoso and Schuurman, *Ockham's Theory of Propositions*, 90.

[31] In this respect, the *Summa logicae* marks a shift from the *Ordinatio* (bk. I, dist. 2, qu.

merically" yet "really several things and each of them." Indeed, as the Church had long held and as the Fourth Lateran Council had reaffirmed, the divine nature was incomprehensible. Ockham conceded that the formal distinction offered a way of stating that incomprehensibility. And for that very reason, he ruled the distinction out of order in every other domain.

Ockham's statements about the formal distinction have generated a number of different interpretations. According to Boehner, the formal distinction was for Ockham the "safeguard of the formality of Logic." Ockham used this distinction, in spite of his distaste for it, to avoid endangering "logic and the highest principle of reason, the principle of contradiction." Boehner concedes that a "careless reader" might misinterpret some passages in Ockham as denials of the principle of contradiction, pointing in particular to a passage from *Ordinatio*, bk. 1, dist. 1, qu. 5 (very similar to *Ordinatio*, bk. 1, dist. 2, qu. 3 quoted above). Here Ockham states: "It is most difficult to understand that some contradictories are verified of the same thing, nor should this be posited except because of faith alone; therefore this should not be posited except where faith compels it."[32] Boehner bristles at the thought that Ockham might have taught "arrant nonsense" to the effect that the statement 'contradictories are verified of the same thing' "might mean that the same in exactly the same sense is denied and affirmed in God."[33] It is, however, difficult to escape the conclusion that Ockham worried about some such thought. If he had thought it possible to

---

1). In the later question, after denying the formal distinction "universally in creatures," Ockham adds: "although it could be held in creatures as well as in God. Thus I believe that it is easy to hold the trinity of persons with a unity of essence in creatures as in God on account of some reasons in *oppositum*, for I believe that in this state of affairs, it could be shown with equal satisfaction with credible reasons that there are not three persons in one essence in creatures as well as in God" (*OT*, II, 18). Here the proposition that some creatures may have a trinitarian structure seems to be undecidable. Since the *Ordinatio* antedates the *Summa logicae*, however, it seems reasonable to take the term "impossible" in its strong logical sense in the latter work. Indeed, the author of an anonymous *Logica* (formerly attributed to Richard of Campsall) saw in Ockham's *Summa logicae* a denial of the formal distinction, which he considered to stand in contradiction with Ockham's *Ordinatio*. See Synan, "The Universal and Supposition in a *Logica* Attributed to Richard of Campsall," 184. For Synan's argument against Campsall's authorship of this post-Ockhamist *Logica*, see the introduction to his edition of the *Logica* in *The Works of Richard of Campsall*, II, 52ff.

[32] Ockham, *Ordinatio*, bk. 1, dist. 1, qu. 5 (*OT*, I, 455).

[33] Boehner, "The Medieval Crisis of Logic," *Collected Articles*, 367. Guelluy (*Philosophie et théologie*, 324) takes a position similar to Boehner's, in this case, by deemphasizing the importance of the single case in which Ockham allows the formal distinction.

meet the problem with a solution that faith did not force upon him, he surely would not have stressed his warnings as often as he did.

Ockham never denied outright that the principle of contradiction held for Trinitarian propositions. But to later critics such as Gregory of Rimini, Ockham seemed to have taken all but the final step.[34] The interpretation is forgivable. For Ockham, the ultimate criterion for re-jecting something as impossible in the created order was the principle of contradiction: not even by His absolute power could God do some-thing that involved a contradiction.[35] Conversely, the only reason for conceding the formal distinction was its agreement with dogma. For it was, "no easier to accept [this distinction] than the trinity of persons with the unity of essence."[36] In Marilyn McCord Adams's words, "So far from affording an intelligible account of anything, the formal dis-tinction signals for Ockham a step outside the bounds of rational dis-course."[37]

This view is consistent with other pronouncements in the *Summa logicae*, in particular Ockham's discussions of the topical and exposi-tory syllogisms. The premises of the topical syllogism, following Ar-istotle, were "necessary [propositions]—neither principles nor conclu-sions of demonstration—but which on account of their truth appear [to be true] to all, or many, etc." The articles of faith therefore did not meet the preceding criterion, for "they appear false to all, or to the majority, or to the wisest."[38] The Trinity undoubtedly figured prom-inently on Ockham's list. Ockham also discussed a number of Trini-tarian inferences. He had strong words for some theologians who ap-parently denied that validity of the expository syllogism. He defined the expository syllogism as an argument "from two singular premises, in the third figure" (i.e. arranged so that the middle term is the subject of both premises: 'A is B, A is C, therefore C is B'), with the additional requirement that the subject of these singulars "supposit for something that is not several things, nor really the same as something that is sev-eral things."[39] Like most fourteenth-century philosophers, Ockham

---

[34] Boehner, "Crisis of Logic," *Collected Articles*, 371; and below.

[35] Ockham, *Summa logicae*, pt. III-4, chap. 6 (*OP*, I, 779–780).

[36] Ockham, *Ordinatio*, bk. I, dist. 2, qu. I (*OT*, II, 17). In other words, Ockham's position suggests that if he had been asked whether God *de potentia absoluta* could create a trinitarian creature (i.e. one that required the formal distinction to give an account of it), he would have answered in the negative, on the grounds that God cannot do some-thing that involves a contradiction.

[37] Adams, "Ockham on Identity and Distinction," 74.

[38] Ockham, *Summa logicae*, pt. III-1, chap. I (*OP*, I, 360); trans. in Moody, *The Logic of William of Ockham*, 211.

[39] Ockham, *Summa logicae*, pt. III-1, chap. 16 (*OP*, I, 403).

took the validity of this syllogism to be self-evident, the implicit foundation upon which Aristotle's syllogistic rested (since all other figures
and moods could be converted to it). He thus considered it a waste of
time to argue with theologians who denied its validity. Ockham disagreed with those who thought that a demonstrative adjective or pro-
noun in the middle term sufficed to make the premises singular. Indeed
the restrictions that Ockham placed on the supposition of the singular
terms in his definition had the effect of ruling Trinitarian terms out of
the domain of the expository syllogism. In an earlier discussion, Ockham gave an example that left no doubt about his meaning: "the following is not an expository syllogism: 'this essence (referring to the
divine essence) is the Father, this essence is the Son, therefore the Son
is the Father'. The reason is that the essence in question is more than
one distinct thing."[40] Here again one can see the tension between formality and self-evidence, on the one hand, and Trinitarian dogmatic
requirements on the other.

Ockham argued that the above inference was not an expository syllogism because it was flawed by a fallacy of accident. In the late thirteenth century, this fallacy was identified with a variation, or "lack of
unity," in the middle term, which therefore made it improper to predicate one extreme of the other in the conclusion. Later, Scotus extended the range of this fallacy to include a lack of unity in the middle
term or the extremes. This lack of unity was tied to a concept of predication that distinguished "essential" from "nonessential" (or accidental) types of predication. In a tradition that extended back to Boethius,
with roots in Aristotle himself, essential predication designated cases
in which the predicate defined or included the subject ('man is an animal'). In nonessential types of predication, there was only an accidental
connection between subject and predicate (e.g. 'this animal is a man',
'man is brown'). Only in cases of essential predication were the subject
and predicate connected in conformity with Aristotle's rule about universal predication. This rule came to be called the *dici* (or *dictum*) *de
omni et nullo*. In Aristotle's own words, it reads:

> That one term shall be included in another as in a whole is the same as for
> the other to be predicated of all of the first. And we say that one term is
> predicated of all of another, whenever no instance of the subject can be
> found of which the other term cannot be asserted: 'to be predicated of
> none' must be understood in the same way.[41]

[40] Ockham, *Summa logicae*, pt. II, chap. 27 (*OP*, I, 337); trans. in Freddoso and Schuurman, *Ockham's Theory of Propositions*, 176.
[41] Aristotle, *Prior Analytics*, 24b, 27–30.

Fallacies of accident thus were thought to occur when the predicates in syllogistic premises were connected with the subjects in nonessential ways. It was this nonessential connection which introduced a lack of unity into the syllogism and vitiated the inference. Thus the fallacy of accident was classified as one of the fallacies that was dependent not "on speech" (*in dictione*), but on something "outside of speech" (*extra dictionem*). Interpreted in an essentialist vein, this distinction eventually mapped onto the distinction between words and things. This view seemed to imply that proper form therefore was not sufficient to determine whether an inference was legitimate. One also had to know something about the ontological relation between predicate and subject. Together with Campsall, Ockham took a completely different approach to the problem. Since all inferences and types of predication necessarily involved terms, it was specious to claim that fallacies outside of speech involved things. There was, however, a difference between the words used in spoken and written language (which signify by convention and can be equivocal) and the terms of mental language (which are nonconventional and univocal). Ockham thus identified the fallacy of accident as a flaw in the formal structure of an argument at the level of mental language (where the problem of "lack of unity" does not occur). The middle term was never varied in such fallacies, unless some other fallacy (e.g. the fallacy of equivocation) was also present.[42]

In spite of his strong concern for formality, Ockham made an exception for the Trinity. Such inferences as 'the essence is the Father, the Father is not the Son, therefore the essence is not the Son' involved such a fallacy of accident, but only where the terms signified the divine persons: "in such inferences composed of terms signifying creatures, there is never a fallacy of accident."[43] Although he could offer no general rule for all fallacies of accident, for Trinitarian paralogisms Ockham appealed to the so-called Rule of Anselm ("where the opposition of relation does not stand in the way, what is conceded of one person ought to be conceded of the other").[44] Gelber rightly sees Ockham's reliance on the fallacy of accident in Trinitarian syllogisms as a counterpart to his use of the formal distinction.[45] In neither case, however,

---

[42] For a thorough discussion of these issues, see Gelber, "Logic and the Trinity," chap. 7; and especially her "The Fallacy of Accident and the *Dictum de Omni*" (forthcoming). I am grateful to Hester Gelber for a preview of this paper.

[43] Ockham, *Summa logicae*, pt. III-4, chap. 11 (*OP*, I, 822).

[44] Ibid.; trans. in Gelber, "Logic and the Trinity," 223–224.

[45] Gelber, "Logic and the Trinity," 226.

did these exceptions receive genuine explanations; rather, they had an ad hoc character, which drew attention to the fact that the accepted rules of logic seemed to break down in the case of a being that was numerically one and each of three things. For Ockham, this being and the attendant logical problems were genuine singularities.[46] Yet by leaning on the fallacy of accident as on a crutch, Ockham lamely could claim that the expository syllogism was formal and universally valid. When Trinitarian terms replaced the variables in such a syllogism, the inference may have looked deceptively like an expository syllogism, but it was in fact a paralogism on account of the fallacy of accident.

Ockham's rejection of the formal distinction in every context but the distinction between persons and the divine essence suggests that he worried about its threat to the principle of contradiction. He banned the distinction in discussions of the created order, and even argued that it should not be allowed in non–Trinitarian theological contexts. In the case of the Trinity, the distinction played a strictly ad hoc role. Ockham did not explicitly deny the formality of Aristotelian logic in Trinitarian theology, but he took a step in that direction.

.

Where Ockham feared to tread, however, others would push ahead. A *Centiloquium theologicum* written before the mid–1330s took a less ambiguous position on these issues than Ockham, who once was thought to be its author. Hester Gelber has given good reasons for attributing the *Centiloquium* to Robert Holcot's fellow Dominican Arnold of Strelley (d. after 1347).[47] Of the treatise's hundred conclusions, three focused specifically on the relation between theology and Aris-

[46] "Just as it is unique (*singulare*) in God that three things are one thing numerically . . . , so it is unique (*singulare*) and beyond all understanding that this does not follow: 'the essence one numerically is the Son, the Father is not the Son, therefore the Father is not the essence'. And therefore this singularity (*singulare*) must not be posited except where the authority of Scripture requires it" (Ockham, *Ordinatio*, bk. 1, dist. 2, qu. 6 [*OT*, 11, 175]).

[47] Ernst Borchert inferred several conclusions about Ockham's theology from the *Centiloquium*; see his *Der Einfluss des Nominalismus*, 62ff, 75ff. Soon thereafter, Boehner argued that the author had affinities with Holcot; see Boehner, "The *Centiloquium* Attributed to Ockham" (pt. 1), 64. Gelber has shown why this cannot be the case ("Logic and the Trinity," 289ff) and has recently suggested that the author is Arnold of Strelley, O.P. See her *Exploring the Boundaries of Reason*, 45–46, nn. 28–29 (in n. 29, the reference to proposition 58 of the *Centiloquium* should read "59"; communication from the author). Also see her "Ockham's Early Influence: A Question about Predestination and Foreknowledge by Arnold of Strelley, O.P.," (forthcoming). I thank Hester Gelber for a preview of this paper.

totle's syllogistic. Conclusion 55 proposed that "one most simple and completely indivisible essence is three really distinct persons." The author's first comment on this thesis was an archetypal statement of fideism: natural reason was useless in attempting to make the proposition credible; it had to be believed on the basis of Catholic faith alone as something that "transcends all sense, all human understanding, and every reason altogether."[48] The objections to this thesis included the standard arguments against Trinitarian formulations: namely, that the expository syllogism was valid, yet yielded false conclusions when used with Trinitarian terms; that the three persons were three things, therefore the essence was three things; that if the thesis were true, there would be several Gods; moreover, contradictories with respect to each other would be true with respect to the same *significatum*.

Strelley answered each objection in turn. He argued that the expository syllogism held "in created and natural matter, but not in uncreated matter, and especially in propositions or terms of the divine Trinity."[49] Strelley and Ockham were clearly worried about the same problem—the formality of the expository syllogism. Ockham had defined this syllogism, which he considered self-evident, in a way that excluded Trinitarian terms.[50] Strelley did not restrict the definition, and therefore argued that the syllogism was invalid for Trinitarian terms. Instead of appealing to the fallacy of accident as Ockham had done, Strelley explained the problem by drawing upon historical considerations. Since Aristotle had not succeeded in finding terms that invalidated his inferences, he claimed that the latter were valid without exception. But following the revelation of the doctrine of the Trinity, about which Aristotle had known nothing, one could indeed find terms that invalidated his syllogisms.[51] Modern logicians had new information; logic had to change accordingly. Conclusion 56, which followed up the problems raised in the preceding conclusion, entered the territory that Ockham had studiously avoided: "no inference (*discursus*) that Aristotle or any other of the ancients posited is formal." Again the argument is straightforward. No inference is formal if it is possible to

[48] Boehner, "*Centiloquium*" (pt. VI), 267.

[49] Ibid., 269.

[50] Moody claims that his definition also excluded middle terms with common supposition; *The Logic of William of Ockham*, 217.

[51] Boehner, "*Centiloquium*" (pt. VI), 269. This position constitutes a clear disagreement with Ockham, who specifically inveighed against unnamed "modern theologians" by accusing them of denying the self-evident expository syllogisms. See *Summa logicae*, pt. II, chap. 27, 336; and *Ockham's Theory of Propositions*, 174.

find terms such that their substitution for the variables of a similar inference yields true premises and a false conclusion. But every one of Aristotle's inferences is of this sort, hence his inferences are not formal.[52]

The fact that one type of syllogistic was not formal, however, did not imply that no logic whatever was formal. Thus in conclusion 59, Strelley suggested a way of remedying the defects of Aristotle's syllogistic by making the conclusions conform to the formulations of the Fourth Lateran Council. He proposed a paraphrase of the conclusion to turn the paralogisms into valid syllogisms, together with a rule that tied the paraphrases to gender. The terms that stood for the essence should be neuter, he argued, and those that stood for the persons should always be masculine or feminine.[53] This ploy in effect translated into gender-specific terms the earlier Scotist distinction between formal predication and predication by identity, while the gender-specific paraphrase preserved, as it were, the memory of the middle term in the conclusion. Thus, given the following premises of an expository syllogism 'this divine essence is the Father, this divine essence is the Son', natural reason would conclude 'therefore the Son is the Father'. But enlightened by Strelley's circumlocution, the faithful would infer 'therefore something that is (*aliquid quod est*) the Son is the Father', a true statement since the essence is something that is the Son and also the Father. If, in violation of Strelley's rule, the subject of the conclusion were masculine ('someone who is', *aliquis qui est*), the conclusion would be false.[54] Appeals to circumlocutions as the key to solving Trinitarian paralogisms were not new. Walter Chatton had championed a route of this sort. Even Strelley's specific solution based on the gender of predicates owes a debt to Scotus.[55]

What is especially noteworthy is the sharp line that Strelley drew between Aristotle and the new rules on the basis of formality. The *Centiloquium* treated these modifications as outside the scope of Aristotle's syllogistic, and incommensurable with them. Indeed, conclusion 59 ended with the remark that "no natural *discursus*, that is, one discovered naturally, is formal, but some supernaturally discovered *discursus* is formal."[56] There were, in other words, natural as well as supernatural inferences, and formality was one of the properties that

---

[52] Boehner, "*Centiloquium*" (pt. VI), 272; idem, "Crisis of Logic," 357ff.
[53] Gelber, "Logic and the Trinity," 284–285; idem, "Ockham's Early Influence."
[54] Boehner, "*Centiloquium*" (pt. VI), 273–274.
[55] Gelber, "Logic and the Trinity," 285.
[56] Boehner, "*Centiloquium*" (pt. VI), 274.

distinguished them. Even if Strelley wrote the *Centiloquium* as a some-times playful exercise in the genre of *sophismata* rather than as a set of serious theses,[57] its importance remains undiminished both as an artic-ulation of early fourteenth-century assumptions about the role of logic in theology and as a possible stimulus to the growth of further ques-tions about that role throughout the later fourteenth century.

Views similar to those of the *Centiloquium* were expressed by the Dominican theologian Robert Holcot (d. 1349).[58] In a famous passage from his questions on the *Sentences* (ca. 1330), Holcot took a sharp stand. In book 1, question 5 ("Whether God is three distinct per-sons?"), after listing sixteen arguments for the negative, Holcot stated: "To this question I answer yes, since this is the Catholic faith revealed to the holy fathers, as is clear enough in various credal formulae (*sym-bolis*), for to prove this surpasses the capacity of human reason. It is therefore not only presumptuous, but also senseless, to attempt to prove them [= the formulae]."[59]

Furthermore, Holcot rejected outright the use of the expository syl-logism in cases involving an entity that was one and three. To empha-size his seriousness and consistency, he argued that the syllogism 'this God creates, this God is the Trinity, therefore the Trinity creates' was formally faulty, even though the premises and the conclusion were all true, and arranged according to the correct pattern of the expository syllogism. From this he concluded:

> Likewise it is not inappropriate (*inconveniens*) that natural logic should be defective in matters that pertain to faith. And hence, just as faith is above natural philosophy in positing that things are produced by creation (which natural philosophy does not reach), so the moral teaching of faith admits some principles that natural science does not concede. In the same way the rational logic of faith must be other than natural logic.[60]

Holcot went on to explain that Averroës, of whom he was otherwise suspicious,[61] had claimed that there was "one universal logic for all

---

[57] Gelber, "Ockham's Early Influence."

[58] Holcot studied at Oxford and was associated with the court of Richard of Bury, the bibliophile and Bishop of Durham.

[59] Holcot, *In quatuor libros Sententiarum quaestiones*, fol. f1ʳb.

[60] Ibid., fol. f2ʳa. The passage is edited on the basis of three manuscripts in Gelber, *Exploring the Boundaries of Reason*, 26–27, n. 72.

[61] See Hoffmann, *Die theologische Methode des Oxforder Dominikanerlehrers Robert Hol-cot*, 105ff.

sciences and [other] logics proper to each science." Holcot did not elaborate the nature of this "universal logic," which encompassed all others. But the Commentator's position did justify rules that were valid only in the logic of faith. As an example of such a rule, he cited a paraphrase of the Rule of Anselm, to which Ockham also had appealed. These considerations led Holcot to a bifurcate definition of formality. In his view, Aristotle's logic was not formal if formality signified validity in every realm. But it was formal if formality signified "that which admits no counterexample (*non capit instantiam*) in natural inquiry into things known to us by the senses."[62] According to the last definition, formality was not a strictly logical concept, but was linked to epistemological considerations: the way in which a statement had come to be known intimately affected the way it would function in a syllogism. For Holcot, the Trinity was not the only exception, however. Responding to the seventh argument *contra*, Holcot noted that "in arguments about Christ, one ought to have a peculiar logic, since in this case it is necessary that contradictories be conceded of the same *suppositum* with the specification of different natures."[63]

Holcot's understanding of the relation between natural and revealed knowledge had a counterpart in his understanding of how people came to believe. In answering the question "Whether any infidel can be compelled to believe?" Holcot listed several means. First, some miracles could bear witness to the truth of the faith—for example, if the preaching of the faith should lead to the resurrection of dead people, who would in turn testify to the truth of the preaching. But assent would also be compelled by a multitude of men "truthful in word, and honest in life, and experienced and circumspect in things known naturally." They too could induce infidels to believe in matters beyond the pale of natural reason.[64]

To Holcot, the consensus of otherwise reliable witnesses was of paramount importance in the formation of beliefs. In a striking argument, he proposed the following scenario. Given a straight line with a segment drawn from any point on it, two angles are formed, which are equal to the sum of two right angles. Yet if the entire multitude of geometry students were to assert that he is deceived, and that the opposite is true, Holcot admitted that he would begin to doubt his for-

[62] Holcot, *Quaestiones*, fol. f2^{r}a.
[63] Ibid., fol. f2^{r}a–b.
[64] Ibid., fol. a6^{r}b.

mer belief and assert the opposite. This analogy had important consequences for the faith: "And therefore I believe that in these modern
times, an important cause of assent to matters of faith for many faithful
is that they know that men of such experience and truth who neither
could have been fallible, nor have wanted to be fallible, have believed
these things."[65] Judgments about truth, on the one hand, and authorities and group consensus on the other, are linked here by a process that
has nothing to do with demonstration.

Several of Holcot's quodlibetal questions on the nature of God analyzed the same issues in more detail and, in some cases, with modifications of his views.[66] In the quodlibetal question "Utrum haec sit concedenda: Deus est Pater et Filius et Spiritus Sanctus,"[67] he claimed that
arguments against the faith ought to be countered by "Catholic rules."
In the case of the Trinity, he reiterated his appeal to the Rule of Anselm
("that all are one in divinity, where the opposition of relation does not
stand in the way") and urged apologists to assent to the premises, and
yet to deny the conclusion on the grounds that "the syllogistic form
admits counterexamples in these [Trinitarian] terms."[68] What is more,
according to Holcot, the faithful Catholic needed to know nothing
more than the Church's position in dealing with infidels:

> In conceding or denying either propositions or consequences, the Cath-
> olic needs to use no logic but the determination of the Church, nor other
> rules discovered by man such that these rules be "necessitive" of his
> concessions or negations in matters of faith. This is evident, since in such
> matters natural logic is deficient. For sometimes in an expository syllo-
> gism it is necessary to concede both premises and yet deny the conclusion;
> and yet according to natural logic, this inference is universal—indeed per-
> fect (*optimus*)—nor does it have any counterexample.[69]

As his last sentence indicates, Holcot here did not consider the expository syllogism to be formal. Although he did not contrast the two
logics in so many words, he retained the expression "natural logic"
(which suggested that there was another kind). But he explicitly contrasted "rules known naturally" with "rules of faith," "Catholic rules,"
and "theological rules." Moreover, sometimes a pair of propositions

---

[65] Ibid., fol. a6ᵛa.

[66] Gelber, *Exploring the Boundaries of Reason*, 26–27.

[67] Quodlibet I, qu. 2, according to Gelber's classification, *Exploring the Boundaries of Reason*, 5.

[68] Ibid., 33, lines 58–63.

[69] Ibid., 35–36, lines 102–110.

seemed contradictory when examined according to the former. But at other times, when examined according to the latter, the propositions were not contradictory; "and thus," he added, "I *believe* that they are not contradictory." The Church had never determined that contradictories should be conceded, Holcot noted carefully, but he also allowed that in matters of belief, there was no way of distinguishing contradictory from noncontradictory propositions. In this same quodlibet, Holcot turned Ockham's razor against Ockham's concession of a formal distinction between the essence and persons. In Trinitarian propositions, the syncategorematic term "formally" clarified nothing, nor did it avoid the contradiction that it was alleged to avoid. Far from being a solution, the use of "formaliter" (and similar terms) was for Holcot little more than a jargonized redescription of the original problem: namely, that "something is predicated of the essence, which is not predicated of the Father."[70]

In his *Quaestiones*, Holcot had denied that one could construct an expository syllogism with terms that signified a thing that is three and one. In the quodlibet "Utrum cum unitate essentiae divinae stet pluralitas personarum," he took up this point in detail.[71] With great clarity, he outlined the requirements for the expository syllogism. Like Ockham, he ruled out terms signifying one thing that is both several things and each of them. Such terms introduced a fallacy of accident into the inference, which was therefore not an expository syllogism at all.[72]

---

[70] Ibid., 33, 36–39, esp. lines 59, 106ff, 177–187 (emphasis added), 193–196; and 49–50, lines 406–414, 423–428.

[71] In the 1518 edition of the *Quaestiones*, this question is determinatio 10, which Gelber cautiously renumbers as quodlibet I, qu. 24, while conceding the possibility that it may not belong to quodlibet I (ibid., 20–21, line 117).

[72] Ibid., 79–81, lines 368–420. Gelber argues for a shift in Holcot's position between the *Quaestiones* and the quodlibets (ibid., 26–27). The views in the two quodlibetal questions discussed above differ in subtle but significant ways, particularly with respect to the expository syllogism and the fallacy of accident. In the first (qu. 2), the expository syllogism is treated as nonformal for Trinitarian terms. Holcot allows that the premises are true, though the conclusion is false. Yet he calls the inference not a paralogism, but an expository syllogism, in contrast to the *Quaestiones*, where he denies that there can be an expository syllogism with terms that signify three and one. He does not mention the fallacy of accident. In determinatio 10, or quodlibet I, qu. 24(?), he follows the *Quaestiones* in refusing to call the fallacious inferences expository syllogisms, and in addition he appeals to the fallacy of accident. Since the *Quaestiones* share with question 2 the antithesis between natural and theological rules, might it be that the chronological order of these views is as follows: quodlibet I, qu. 2; *Quaestiones*; determinatio 10, where the latter does not belong to quodlibet I at all (n. 71 above)?

The character of Holcot's position remains a hotly debated topic. The earlier historiography called him a skeptic or a fideist, charges that more recent interpreters have tried to temper.[73] The post-Enlightenment connotations of such a term as "skepticism" are certainly out of place in the context of the late Middle Ages. Yet by comparison with Duns Scotus's confidence in reason, Holcot's views do have a fideist ring. Beryl Smalley has shown that Holcot's philosophical and theological views were not restricted to his formal theological treatises. His fideism, she argued, also permeated his Biblical commentaries. His widely read *Commentary on Wisdom* rejected rational proofs for the existence of God, the immortality of the soul, and the resurrection of the body. In the same work, Holcot upbraided laymen for expecting theologians to undergird their faith "as if we could prove by demonstration what they believe only by faith." To emphasize his point, he recounted how a lay brother succeeded in converting a heretical clerk (he doubted the immortality of the soul) by confronting the skeptic with a wager like the one Pascal made famous.[74]

In one of his early articles, Heiko Oberman placed Holcot in the left wing of nominalism, which emphasizes logic and the omnipotence of God, and "leads to skepticism."[75] A few years later, however, after taking a second look at Holcot's position, he criticized Smalley's interpretation. Even though Holcot denied "that man unaided by grace can with his natural reason prove the existence of God, or grasp the mysteries of the Holy Trinity and of the Incarnation," such positions represented only a very mitigated skepticism.[76] Fritz Hoffmann's monograph is the most extensive recent attempt to rehabilitate Holcot from charges of fideism and skepticism. For Hoffmann, what appears to be "fideism among some masters of the fourteenth century must be understood as resistance to the foreign influence of philosophy on theological thinking."[77] Whatever one may choose to call Holcot's position, it is clear that he had a keen sense of the limits of human understanding. He placed the propositions of faith and the dogmatic pronouncements of the Church well beyond these limits—out of easy reach. If some aspects of Christian belief were officially acknowledged

[73] For a summary of the historiography, see Gelber, "Logic and the Trinity," 268ff.

[74] Smalley, *English Friars and Antiquity*, 183ff, esp. 187.

[75] See Oberman, "Some Notes on the Theology of Nominalism," 54.

[76] Oberman, *Harvest of Medieval Theology*, 247; idem, "Facientibus quod in se est," 317ff.

[77] Hoffmann, *Die theologische Methode*, 11.

to be incomprehensible, one should not be surprised if they stood in tension with the rules of understanding.

Accordingly, like Ockham, Holcot added little to the pronouncements of the Fourth Lateran Council on the incomprehensibility of the Trinity. He did, however, translate that incomprehensibility into the precise and unambiguous language of fourteenth-century logic. Even though Holcot claimed to believe in the unity of truth, the sharpness with which he drew his boundary lines and stated his positions was not always easy to accept. Others therefore continued to work toward a solution of the Trinitarian dilemma that would reduce the tensions between two sets of cherished beliefs.

In typologies of medieval philosophy and theology, Robert Holcot and Adam Wodeham, O.F.M. (d. 1358) are often mentioned in the same breath. Both men were careful students of Ockham's work, and both men went beyond that work in ways that earned them a classification as radical nominalists.[78] But their kinship is not always close on all issues. On the relation between logic and the Trinity in particular, they share some affinities, but they also differ in several noteworthy respects. To judge from his conclusions, Wodeham was troubled by the aspersions that had been cast on the adequacy of Aristotle's syllogistic—notably the suggestion that it required supplementation, or that it admitted exceptions, indeed that it was not formal. Ockham's appeals to the formal distinction and fallacy of accident, for example, had an exceptional character. In each case, Ockham tied the exception to the unique nature of God, a being that was three beings and each of them. Could one construct a solution that would be general, universally valid, and philosophically cogent while being accessible to unaided reason? To a surprising extent, Wodeham succeeded in meeting the dilemma with a solution that blended his own originality with the best work of his predecessors—a tour de force, as Gelber has called it.[79]

Wodeham defended his views in his Oxford commentary on the *Sentences* (1330–1332), of which Henry of Oyta wrote a summary called the *Abbreviatio* one generation later. Since Wodeham's views will reemerge in connection with Henry of Oyta in the next chapter, they

---

[78] For the first point, see Copleston, *A History of Philosophy*, III, 134; Gilson, *La Philosophie au moyen âge*, II, 658ff. For the second point, see Oberman, "Some Notes on the Theology of Nominalism," 54. For biographical details, see Courtenay, *Adam Wodeham*; and Murdoch and Synan, "Two Questions on the Continuum: Walter Chatton (?), O.F.M., and Adam Wodeham, O.F.M.," 212ff.

[79] Gelber, "Logic and the Trinity," 259.

are presented here in summary fashion. To begin, Wodeham admitted no distinction in God but the distinction between the persons, the minimum required by the official dogmatic statement. Like Holcot, he therefore rejected the formal distinction, even in the exceptional case allowed by Ockham, on the grounds that it remained a distinction, the qualifier "formal" being a modification, but not a negation, of the term "distinction." Thus, whatever was not distinguished was not formally distinguished. The persons and personal properties were formally *the same as* the essence. At the same time, he insisted that the principle of contradiction was unshakable, angrily upbraiding those who cast doubts on its universal validity, especially in God.[80] The target of these criticisms is not certain. But the stance of Wodeham's opponent shares a certain affinity with an uncharitable interpretation of Holcot's contrast between the natural and theological ways of examining contradictory propositions in quodlibet I, question 2.[81]

With respect to the problem of fallacies, Wodeham agreed with Ockham and Burleigh that the fallacy of accident could arise for reasons other than the variation, or lack of unity, in the middle term. Indeed such a fallacy could arise simply because of an improper relation of the conclusion to the premises, as in the standard example of such a fallacious inference from true premises: 'this dog is yours (*tuus*), this dog is a father (*pater*), therefore this dog is your father (*tuus pater*)'.[82]

Wodeham's own solution (in bk. I, dists. 33–34) answered the question "Whether there is a rule or art by which paralogisms made in Trinitarian matters can be solved consequently?" in the affirmative.[83] Paralogisms occurred for two reasons—they were defective in matter and/or in form. Faith or scripture regulated the former; logical rules and the art of solving *sophismata* covered the latter. Since the *dici de omni et nullo* was the rule that governed correct syllogisms in all moods of the three figures, paralogisms in Trinitarian theology arose from a failure to be so regulated. For Wodeham, this rule applied not only to universal premises, but also to the singular premises of the expository

[80] Ibid., 236, 239–246.

[81] See above. Another possible candidate is the "Magister Abstractionum," whom Ockham occasionally criticized, e.g. *Summa logicae*, pt. III-1, chap. 4 (*OP*, I, 367). Boehner thought he was Francis of Mayronnes, but Jan Pinborg made a more convincing case for Richard Rufus of Cornwall; see Pinborg, "Magister Abstractionum," 1–4.

[82] Gelber, "Logic and the Trinity," 227–233.

[83] "Utrum sit aliqua regula vel ars per quam consequenter solvi possunt paralogismi facti circa materiam trinitatis et talibus similes" (Wodeham-Oyta, *Abbreviatio*, 81ʳa).

syllogism, thereby reducing Ockham's exception to Aristotle's rule. The premise 'this A is B' could be universalized as the proposition 'all that is A is B', which could then be tested for conformity with the *dici de omni*. Thus, 'this essence is the Father' (which is true) is not equivalent to 'all that is the essence is the Father' (which is false, since 'Son' and 'Holy Spirit' are also predicable of essence, but not of 'Father').[84] Wodeham believed that he could account for all paralogisms with a procedure that did not require an appeal to revelation. Against the view that Aristotle's syllogistic would have been different if he had known about one thing being several things—a view that echoes Holcot, for example—Wodeham argued that the Philosopher had known about the Platonic hypothesis of "common quiddities" and had constructed a formal logic that took such a picture into account.[85] One of the most striking characteristics of Wodeham's work on these issues was his examination of problems in the broadest possible terms—for example, by using putative infidels to test the universality of a rule, or by considering the compatibility of Aristotle's logic with Platonic assumptions.

Gelber does not see sharp differences between the positions of Wodeham and Holcot on the relation between logic and Trinitarian theology: "There was no basic discrepancy between Holcot's use of two logical systems and Wodeham's and others' attempts to reformulate Aristotelian principles."[86] Indeed both men were responding to a similar problem, and both professed to believe in a single overarching logic. But Holcot did not say what such a logic might be, while Wodeham clearly thought that Aristotle's logic was the only one necessary. Wodeham strove for coherence and synthesis; Holcot was willing to live with more tension.

Like the preceding figures, Gregory of Rimini, O.E.S.A. (d. 1358) was trained in theology, reading the *Sentences* at Paris in 1343–1344,[87] in an environment permeated by the debates of the previous decade. One of the first loci for his views on logic and the Trinity occurs in his commentary on the *Sentences*, bk. I, dist. 5, qu. I ("Whether the divine essence can generate or be generated?"). At the head of a list of pro forma arguments for the positive, Gregory placed the inference 'every

---

[84] Ibid., 81ᵣa–b.

[85] Ibid., 81ᵥa.

[86] Gelber, "Logic and the Trinity," 316.

[87] On Gregory of Rimini, see Oberman, *Gregor von Rimini*, introduction; and the contribution by Marcolino, "Der Augustinertheologe an der Universität Paris," 168ff, which treats Gregory's Parisian sojourn in detail.

father has generated, the divine essence is the father, therefore the divine essence has generated' (syllogism A). The second argument (syllogism B) appealed to the expository syllogism 'this Father generates, this Father is the divine essence, therefore the divine essence generates'.

Before turning to his own answer to syllogism A, Gregory first discussed the response of *quidam*, whom the editors have identified as the Franciscan Robert Cowton.[88] According to this master, syllogism A was fallacious on two separate counts: a fallacy of figure of speech (*figurae dictionis*) and a fallacy of accident. In the first case, in the major premise 'every father generates', the verb was predicated formally (like all verbs) and not by identity; but in the minor premise, 'the essence is the Father' the predication was by identity. Hence the conclusion did not follow.[89] The language here is Scotist, but Wodeham too had found the distinction between these two types of predication attractive.[90] In the second case, Cowton argued as follows: that the Father generates is accidental to the Father, insofar as 'Father' is predicated of 'essence'. Therefore, since the middle term 'Father' was insufficient to conclude of the essence that it generates, the inference involved a fallacy of accident.

Rimini rejected both arguments. First, he argued, modes of predication did not have to be the same in order to yield correct conclusions, a point that he illustrated with a counterexample. In the second case, one could likewise find counterexamples. Thus if Cowton's objection were true, the syllogism 'every animal is white, every man is an animal, therefore every man is white' would also involve a fallacy of accident. Here, however, insofar as 'animal' was predicated of 'man', the former was white accidentally, but in a fashion that was far more accidental than generation was accidental to the Father.[91] In Gregory's view, Cowton's definition of "accident" (as anything extraneous to the *ratio*, or meaning, of the subject) would introduce a fallacy of accident into many proper demonstrations. Gregory therefore rejected it, taking the position that "if 'father' has the same supposition in both prem-

[88] Gregory of Rimini, *Lectura super primum et secundum Sententiarum*, I, 451, n. 3. The editors consulted Cowton's views in ÖNB 1397 (the specific reference should read 47ʳa–b, instead of 47ᵛa–b).

[89] Rimini, *Lectura*, I, 451.

[90] Wodeham, *Sentences*, I, dist. 33, qu. 1, art. 2; transcribed by Gelber, "Logic and the Trinity," 244, 635 n. 20. On inherent predication and predication by identity, see the present chapter above.

[91] Ibid., 451–452.

ises, and in both cases is taken substantively, no fallacy is involved."[92] The implication here seems to be that the fallacy of accident can be tied to variation in supposition of the middle term.

Gregory of Rimini then turned to the treatment of the same distinction by one of his contemporaries: "Another concedes that such a mode of arguing holds in all things, except in divinity. And the reason is that in no other instance can three things, none of which is another, be one thing numerically."[93] As Gregory's contemporaries knew, the last sentence came from Ockham's *Ordinatio*.[94] Gregory vehemently opposed such a position, for very interesting reasons:

> But this answer is irrational through and through, for in so speaking every way of proving or reproving something in divinity disappears. Indeed when Catholics want to prove something against heretics, it could be said at will that the argument and every inference are invalid, even admitting that they are regulated perfectly. To speak in this way is nothing less than to admit that our faith and Catholic doctrine are plainly contrary to certain reason, and hence false, and thereby to assert by our own admission that they ought to be condemned. . . . It was easy indeed to say that contrary reasons, though they may have been valid in this, yet they were not valid in that, which is completely frivolous.[95]

Coming from the pen of a figure associated with the Augustinian revival that sought to dissociate pagan philosophy from theology, these angry words are striking.[96] Apologetics is possible only if the rules of reasoning hold also in divinity. Arguments against heretics stand no chance of success if Christians concede at the outset that the accepted rules of reasoning break down in theology.

This interpretation of Ockham may not have been an accurate reflection of the latter's intentions. But Gregory's perspective on the issue clearly cannot be rejected out of hand, as Boehner wishes to do.[97] For one thing, Gregory took seriously Ockham's concern for consistency, and very pointedly pushed out the logical implications of the latter's arguments. Gregory of Rimini's outburst shows how intensely

[92] Ibid., 452.

[93] Ibid.

[94] Ockham, *Ordinatio*, 1, dist. 5, qu. 1 (*OT*, III, 46).

[95] Rimini, *Lectura*, I, 452–453. The same point appears in Johann Brammart's commentary on the *Sentences*. See Xiberta, *De scriptoribus*, 426; and de Wulf, *Histoire de la philosophie médiévale*, III, 115.

[96] For example, Schüler, *Prädestination, Sünde und Freiheit bei Gregor von Rimini*, 22, passim; and Leff, *Gregory of Rimini*, chap. 6, esp. 234.

[97] Boehner, "Crisis of Logic," 367.

he worried about the consequences of Ockham's claims for apologetics, which they appeared to undermine completely.

Gregory concluded his response by arguing that, in syllogism A, either the major premise ('every father has generated') was false or the syllogism was not regulated by the *dici de omni*. Following Averroës's commentary on the *Prior Analytics*, Gregory argued that there was a difference between a universal proposition and one governed by the *dici de omni*. A proposition was universal when the predicate was verified of the subject in such a way that each of its singulars was true (e.g. 'every leaf is green' is universally true if 'this leaf is green' and 'this leaf is green' and so on for all leaves). But the *dici de omni* required in addition that the predicate be verified of whatever the subject was verified. Thus, in 'every father has generated', the proposition is universally true, but does not meet the *dici de omni* requirement; for 'has generated' is not truly predicated of everything that is the Father (e.g. the divine essence, of which 'has generated' is not truly predicated).[98] Since syllogism A was not governed by the *dici de omni*, it was useless.

With respect to syllogism B ('this Father generates, this Father is the divine essence, therefore the divine essence generates'), Gregory offered a choice between two different answers. The first appealed to a nonstandard definition of the expository syllogism. Any term in it, he claimed, had to be so singular that it could not be predicable of many. The syllogism would be defective in form unless this criterion were met. The term 'essence' did not do so, Gregory argued.[99] For although "logically speaking" the term 'essence' is singular (since it supposits for a unique thing), it is nevertheless predicable of several things, namely the persons.[100] Since this argument relied on a questionable definition of the expository syllogism, it is perhaps not surprising that Gregory preferred his second argument. It constitutes a clear rejection of Ockham. "The expository syllogism is not evident per se and most perfect, but must be perfected by the *dici de omni* and *dici de nullo*, as is the case with other imperfect syllogisms." Gregory then brought up two examples from the *Prior Analytics* to show that according to Aristotle's intention "every good syllogism is reduced to perfect syllogisms of the first figure and is regulated by those principles; consequently this expository [syllogism], which cannot be regulated thus,

---

[98] Rimini, *Lectura*, I, 455.

[99] The standard definitions of the expository syllogism make the *subject* in each premise singular, but do not discuss the predicate; see Ockham, *Summa logicae*, pt. III-1, chap. 16 (*OP*, I, 403–404).

[100] Rimini, *Lectura*, I, 455.

is useless; such are the aforementioned syllogisms."[101] The reverence accorded to the expository syllogism was misplaced; the standard was not the third figure with singular premises, but the first-figure syllogism with universal premises. Rimini was one of those theologians whom Ockham could not have countenanced because they denied what was self-evident.

These arguments reveal several interesting points. Clearly Rimini was disturbed by the ad hoc character of Ockham's use of exceptions to the rule. Implicitly he was working with a strong definition of formality, for he was willing to sacrifice the expository syllogism for its failure to provide a consistent Trinitarian inference. At the same time, there was a pragmatic side to Gregory's argumentation, particularly in his appeal to an unusual category of inference—the useless. Inferences had a purpose to serve; if they failed in this respect, they were not worthy of further consideration. Gregory of Rimini did not mention his purpose explicitly here; but the harangue against Ockham suggests an important clue. Utility appears to have been closely tied to the defensibility of the faith.[102]

.

These early fourteenth-century debates developed a variety of options and approaches to the bewildering problem of handling the Trinity logically. Scotus's concern with the problem of contradictory predicates shaped the discussion by focusing on logic as the key to a solution. His own proposal drew upon the concept of a formal distinction and various kinds of predication. Whereas the formal distinction had philosophical integrity in Scotus's system, for Ockham it became a singularity, permissible only in dealing with the divine essence and persons, and only under the compulsion of faith. One exception justified another, so he used a new definition of the fallacy of accident to explain Trinitarian paralogisms in inferences that otherwise admitted no such fallacy. Figures such as Holcot and Strelley flirted with divisions between natural and revealed logic. Wodeham tried to explain all paralogisms with one Aristotelian rule. Rimini rejected Ockham's ex-

---

[101] Ibid., 455–456.

[102] Gordon Leff overstates his point when he claims that fourteenth-century theology—and Gregory of Rimini in particular—"allowed no place for apologetics" (*Gregory of Rimini*, 218). Even when fourteenth-century theologians gave up the scientific status of theology (and a *demonstrative* apologetic), they did not immediately give up all means of defending the faith, as Gregory himself illustrates here and as Holcot does elsewhere (e.g. Gelber, *Exploring the Boundaries of Reason*, 36, lines 119–123).

ceptions, and denied the self-evidence of the expository syllogism. Circumlocutions, supplementary rules, gender-specific or other types of predication—these and other techniques not discussed were also brought into play.

Although the various masters argued their positions as if their lives were at stake, their divergences on the whole do not seem to have made an impact beyond the confines of the university. When Wodeham pointed out that a rejection of Aristotle's syllogistic in theology would turn the faith into the laughingstock of the infidels, he probably did not have any particular infidels in mind. He took the hypothetical objections of the infidels seriously, however, and tried to rehabilitate Aristotelian logic as a universal language that was independent of, though compatible with, the perspective of the faith. In Wodeham's view, it should be possible—in theory at least—to discuss with infidels not merely the created order, but faith as well. In Paris and Oxford, this may have been a moot point; in Vienna, as we shall see, it was not.

CHAPTER FOUR

Trinitarian Paralogisms Come to Vienna:
Henry of Oyta and Henry of Langenstein

> Wollt ihr nach Regeln messen
> was nicht nach eurer Regeln Lauf,
> der eig'nen Spur vergessen,
> sucht davon erst die Regeln auf!
>
> RICHARD WAGNER,
> *Die Meistersinger von Nürnberg*
> (Act 1, Scene 3)

By THE mid-fourteenth century, a substantial body of writing had focused on the relation between logic and the Trinity. Since the many suggested solutions outlined earlier in the century involved conflicting assumptions about not only logic, but also ontology, epistemology, and theological method, it is not surprising that the debate about Trinitarian paralogisms continued to flourish. During the 1370s, these issues remained lively in Paris, in other universities, and in the theological *studia* of the various orders.[1] In the 1380s, the Schism scattered both the German masters and the seeds of

---

[1] Conrad of Ebrach, O. Cist., treated the question "Utrum principia forme syllogistice regulativa teneant in divinis" in his commentary on the *Sentences*, bk. I, dists. 4–7, qu. 2, which he defended in Bologna ca. 1368–1370 (Lauterer, "Konrad von Ebrach," pt. 1, 179–181; pt. 2, 41). The Augustinian Dionysius of Montina, who read the *Sentences* in Paris in 1371–1372, raised the same question (Zumkeller, "Ein Manuskript," 83). Johann Brammart, O. Carm., also dealt with the issue at Paris ca. 1379, and phrased his question in terms identical to those of Conrad and Dionysius (Wilhering, Austria, codex 87, 75ʳ). Brammart almost certainly was influenced by Wodeham, and perhaps personally by Oyta, who had recently completed his own commentary on the *Sentences* (Courtenay, *Adam Wodeham*, 148; A. Lang, *Heinrich Totting von Oyta*, 66–68; Xiberta, *De scriptoribus*, 414ff). Brammart's Carmelite colleague Walter of Bamberg, who eventually came to Vienna, treated the question "An principia regulativa formarum syllogisticarum teneant in divinis," in Bamberg, ms. theol. 77 (Q.III.36), 53ᵛ–62ʳ; see Xiberta, *De scriptoribus*, 464. Pierre d'Ailly also discussed the issue between 1376 and 1381; see Maierù, "Logique et théologie trinitaire. Pierre d'Ailly," 253ff.

the debate to the east. At the University of Vienna in particular, the problem fell upon fertile ground: over a thirty-year period it flourished in the writings of at least eight masters who were at one time or another associated with the university. Since several of them had come upon the problem before their arrival in Lower Austria, the flurry of activity around logic and the Trinity in Vienna may not be indigenous to the area. Nevertheless the sustained discussion that the issue received in the Habsburg university is striking and deserves attention. The tight temporal distribution of these questions makes possible comparisons and contrasts between nearly contemporary answers.

Of the figures in the preceding chapter, Gregory of Rimini was the only one who is known to have visited Vienna. As the newly elected general of the Augustinian order, he had set out for Vienna on 13 October 1358, arriving at the local house of studies the following month (16 November). Four days later his last letter discussed the final burial arrangements for Thomas of Strasbourg, his predecessor at the head of the order, who had recently died in Vienna. Gregory's personal contact with the local Augustinian Eremites was very brief, however. By the end of the month, he too was dead, and his hosts decided to bury the two former generals in the same tomb.[2] Because of Gregory's standing in the order, it is plausible to assume that his writings were read with care in the Augustinian *studium* at Vienna. But it is still unclear what role the Augustinians played in shaping Viennese theology after the university acquired its own faculty.[3] Once the university got underway, the secular clergy seems to have dominated the faculty of theology, while the Dominicans represented the only significant minority of regular clergy. To the extent that Gregory made an impact on the university, his intellectual appeal almost certainly took precedence over his Augustinian associations.[4] The discussions of paralo-

---

[2] Rimini, *Registrum generalatus 1357–1358*, 350, 371–376; Trapp, "La tomba bisoma," 5–17.

[3] They were presumably incorporated into the faculty of theology, as the Carmelites were in 1385; see Lickteig, *The German Carmelites at the Medieval Universities*, 183ff.

[4] Uiblein, "Zur Lebensgeschichte einiger Wiener Theologen des Mittelalters," 95–96; Ehrle, *Der Sentenzenkommentar Peters von Candia*, 167; and Chapter 1 above. Two fourteenth-century copies of Gregory of Rimini's commentary on books I and II of the *Sentences* have survived in the Nationalbibliothek of Vienna. One of them (ÖNB 1515) was acquired by Nicholas of Dinkelsbühl during a trip to Italy after 1402; see Uiblein, "Lebensgeschichte," 103. The other copy (ÖNB 4842) belonged to the library of the Collegium ducale, but its provenance is unclear. Other copies have survived in the sphere of influence of the University of Vienna: book I at Heiligenkreuz (codex 141, fourteenth

gisms in Trinitarian theology are more likely to have reached the faculty of theology at Vienna through its two leading professors. Both Henry of Oyta and Henry of Langenstein had been exposed to such questions in Paris and, in all likelihood, first treated them there as well. Their views will be discussed in turn.

.

After studying in Prague, teaching in Erfurt, and answering charges of heresy in Avignon, Henry Totting of Oyta taught theology in Paris in the 1370s, where he wrote the *Abbreviatio* of Adam Wodeham's commentary on the *Sentences*.[5] Oyta's *Lectura textualis* of the *Sentences*, dating back to his days in Prague, was an early work that stayed very close to the text of Peter Lombard. His *Quaestiones Sententiarum*, on the other hand, were thoughtful and philosophically sophisticated queries on the *Sentences*, most probably read first in Paris ca. 1378–1380. After the outbreak of the Schism, Oyta moved first to Prague, then on to Vienna by 1384, where he once again read his *Quaestiones*. Three of the best manuscripts of the *Quaestiones* were copied in Vienna, two of them in 1389.[6]

With respect to the problem of distinguishing paralogisms from syllogisms, Oyta's discussion reads like a review of the solutions proposed throughout the preceding half-century.[7] Since Oyta valued Wodeham's commentary on the *Sentences* highly enough to make it accessible in abbreviated form, it is not surprising that he leaned on it heavily for his own discussion. Wodeham's appeal lay in his moderation. Oyta had concluded his abridgment with the fervent prayer: "Grant, Lord Jesus, that we may keep to a middle road (*iter medium*) between Scylla and Charybdis. . . ." Likewise, his treatment of theological knowledge sought "to find a mean, in which there is virtue,"

---

century) and Klosterneuburg (codex 307, fourteenth century); book II and a complete copy at Melk (codices 40 and 178, respectively). See the introduction to the new critical edition in Gregory of Rimini, *Lectura super primum et secundum Sententiarum*, I, xxix–l.

[5] For biographical details, see A. Lang, *Heinrich Totting von Oyta*. Although Lang dated the *Abbreviatio* to Oyta's years in Prague sometime between 1370 and 1378, William Courtenay has recently given convincing reasons for revising the date and place to Paris between 1373 and 1378. See A. Lang, *Oyta*, 56; Courtenay, *Adam Wodeham*, 18, 146–147.

[6] A. Lang, *Oyta*, 63. The manuscripts are Munich, Bayerische Staatsbibliothek, Clm 17468 and 8867; and Graz, Universitätsbibliothek 639.

[7] The question appears in *Quaestiones*, bk. I, qu. 8, art. 2; see the analysis and edition in Maierù, "Logica aristotelica e teologia trinitaria. Enrico Totting da Oyta," 487–512.

between Henry of Ghent and Robert Holcot.[8] In some quarters the two men were evidently considered to be extremists.

Oyta's position on the use of logic in Trinitarian propositions strives for the same ideal of moderation. Like Wodeham before him, Oyta joined Richard of Campsall, Ockham, and Holcot in conceding some efficacy to the oft-cited Rule of Anselm ("in divinity, all is the same or one, where the opposition of relation does not stand in the way").[9] The chief advantage of this rule was that it provided a criterion by which to identify Trinitarian paralogisms. With Campsall and Wodeham, Oyta thus dismissed as unfounded Chatton's reasons for rejecting the rule altogether.[10] Just the same, however, the rule was incapable of specifying the logical reason for the defect. Oyta followed Wodeham in worrying about the implications of this state of affairs for the universality of logic: "Although the aforementioned rule [of Anselm] would suffice to some extent for the faithful among faithful, it would not suffice in general among infidels."[11] Since the rule was based on the data of revelation, it was not accessible to natural reason. Indeed Holcot once had identified this rule as belonging to the "logic of faith."[12] But even if it offered efficacious means for theologians (and the faithful) to separate syllogisms from paralogisms, it was useless beyond the confines of Christendom. Yet nonbelievers should provide the test for the universality of a logical rule. The Rule of Anselm was therefore inadequate as a general solution to the problem of Trinitarian paralogisms.

What then would constitute a satisfactory *general* solution, which would enable anyone to identify the specific cause of the paralogism? To set the stage for his answer, Oyta turned to a brief exposition of Plato's theory of forms. The importance of the theory lay in the fact that "according to this way of imagining (*modus imaginandi*), it could be conceded that Plato generates a son numerically consubstantial to himself and really distinct from himself, since the common essence, which belongs to both, neither generates nor is generated."[13] The rel-

---

[8] Wodeham-Oyta, *Abbreviatio*, 152ʳb; A. Lang, *Oyta*, 55, n. 21; idem, *Die Wege der Glaubensbegründung*, 225–226.

[9] Anselm, "De processione Spiritus Sancti," 180–181; Gelber, "Logic and the Trinity," 198f, 610 n. 105.

[10] Gelber, "Logic and the Trinity," 200–201.

[11] Maierù, "Logica aristotelica," 498, lines 56–58.

[12] Holcot, *Quaestiones*, fol. f2ʳa; Gelber, *Exploring the Boundaries of Reason*, 27, n. 72.

[13] Maierù, "Logica aristotelica," 499, lines 130–133. (In the quotation, "Plato" is of course a dummy variable, not the name of the philosopher.)

evance of this point to Trinitarian theology is already implicit in its language. But the connection emerges more explicitly in a corollary: "according to this 'imagination' (*imaginationem*), it is not completely untenable that one simple universal man is really three individual men, namely Sortes, Plato, and Cicero. This follows from the foregoing, and also because if a Platonist were to posit this, he could, it seems, defend himself from contradiction."[14] Interestingly, this hypothetical appeal to Plato, once again inspired by Wodeham,[15] occurs as a suggested solution to a problem that grows out of a logical and critical approach traditionally associated with nominalism. To be useful to the Trinitarian problem, the humanity that Sortes and Plato shared could not be merely the name given to a common abstraction; at the very least, it had to have no less an existence than individuals. For the sake of argument, the proposed solution posited a view that Ockham had discredited on nontheological grounds: if 'man' signified a self-subsistent entity common to Sortes and Plato, it would *be* Sortes and Plato, and therefore Sortes and not-Sortes—a flat contradiction. It was only because 'man' was a concept that contradictories could be verified of it: only as a concept could it stand, or "supposit," for different entities.[16]

Whatever its truth, this special Platonic mode of being implied three distinct ways of universalizing propositions: "it follows, by reason of this special mode of being which the aforesaid position posits in things, that three specifically distinct modes of universalizing propositions must be posited by those who rationally hold this position. This mode of being *in re* cannot be saved unless such a threefold mode of universalizing is conceded in the proposition."[17] Thus the proposition 'every universal man is Plato' could be universalized according to the three following modes.

The first was through the "singularization of the distributed term." In this case, the universal proposition above is equivalent to a conjunction of the following singular propositions: 'this universal man is Plato, and this universal man is Plato, and this universal man is Plato, and this . . . ,' to which is added the qualification 'and there is no universal man who is not Plato'. The type of distribution, according to

<hr>

[14] Ibid., 500, lines 143–147. I have retained the medieval "Sortes" throughout; the word had a life of its own as a disyllable.

[15] Gelber, "Logic and the Trinity," 262.

[16] See Guelluy, *Philosophie et théologie chez Guillaume d'Ockham*, 326; Ockham, *Ordinatio*, bk. 1, dist. 1, qu. 6 (*OT*, 11, 160 ff).

[17] Maierù, "Logica aristotelica," 500, lines 148–154.

Oyta, is called "distribution below the term" (*distributio infra ter-minum*). Under this particular mode of distribution, the universal proposition in the example is true.

The second mode adds to the first a different requirement, namely that the common term or terms be the same numerically as the subject: 'this universal man is Plato, and this universal man is Plato, . . . and there is no [one] thing which, or no one who, is a universal man with-out also being Plato'. This mode is known as "distribution outside the term" (*distributio extra terminum*).[18] Distributed in this way, the univer-sal proposition is false, since Cicero is someone who is also a universal man without being Plato.

Finally, the third mode adds to the "extrasumption" in the second mode the "extrasumption of complexes." Put more concretely, this mode adds to the second mode the clause 'and there are no [several] things which are this universal man without also being Plato'. Accord-ing to the third mode, the proposition 'every universal man is a sin-gular man' is denied, whereas it is affirmed in the first and second modes, since "no several things which are a universal man are one sin-gular man."[19]

Oyta's point in raising these issues was not that Plato's theory was categorically true, but that *hypothetically*, if it were true, then the three modes of universalizing would be distinct from a logical point of view.[20] When considered from the point of view of the three modes in turn, the same proposition might have different truth values. What mattered here was not the ontological point, but the logical one. Oyta conceded that from the common modes of being of creatures, it might not be possible to infer that the three modes of universalizing propo-sitions were distinct. But thanks to the *imaginatio* inspired by Plato, a rational man using the light of nature would be able to judge truly the possibility of their being distinct.[21] After all, it was as a pagan philos-

---

[18] The terminology of distribution *infra* and *extra terminum* parallels that of Albert of Saxony's *Sophismata*. See Maierù, "Logique et théologie trinitaire dans le moyen âge tardif," 199, n. 38; and Kretzmann, "Syncategoremata, Sophismata, Exponibilia," 233, n. 86. The analysis provided here is analogous to that given for terms such as 'totus' (the whole of), not surprisingly since the realist position was understood to take 'humanity' and 'animality' for parts of individuals; see Moody, *The Logic of William of Ockham*, 207. On such an assumption, 'omnis' would share features of 'totus."

[19] Maierù, "Logica aristotelica," 500–501, lines 155–183, 211–215; idem, "Logique et théologie trinitaire dans le moyen âge tardif," 190–191. See the detailed discussion of the three modes in Auer, "Aristotelische Logik," 48, n. 34.

[20] Maierù, "Logica aristotelica," 487.

[21] Ibid., 501, line 184ff.

opher that Plato by natural reason had developed this view. One could not accuse him of having concocted it ad hoc, simply to distinguish paralogisms from proper syllogisms in Trinitarian doctrine. This hypothetical venture hinged on one question: was the Platonic account indeed possible, i.e. not self-contradictory? Ockham had already answered in the negative. Oyta, on the other hand, did not feel compelled to answer, and without further ado concluded: "It follows that theologians can de facto rationally posit such a threefold mode of universalizing propositions in divinity."[22]

In this argument, the logical point draws upon historical considerations. The Platonic view had emerged prior to the Christian revelation; if the distinctions that Plato had posited could help solve Trinitarian paralogisms, any solutions derived from those distinctions would have a universality that transcended the specific requirements of the faith. And furthermore, if one could show that such distinctions were consistent with Aristotle's logic, the grounds for suggesting that there might be several kinds of logic would be undermined. Aristotle's logic would cover all syllogisms, Trinitarian or not, and would be accessible to believer and unbeliever alike.

As his second assumption, Oyta claimed that only a proposition universalized according to the third mode conformed to the *dici de omni* or *dici de nullo*.[23] The third mode thus represented the genuine Aristotelian interpretation of the *dici de omni*. The first corollary to this assumption is especially interesting, for it places the preceding discussion under the aegis of Aristotle: "The distinction of the aforementioned modes of universalizing may be rationally elicited from the sayings of the Philosopher."[24] Indeed, according to Oyta, the distinction between the first and third modes was found expressly in Aristotle's writings. As for the second mode, an experienced philosopher could derive it from Aristotle (by implication, therefore, it was Aristotelian even if Aristotle himself had not known it). Oyta's suggestion here may have been inspired by the passage in Gregory of Rimini's commentary on the *Sentences* (bk. I, dist. 5), where an appeal to Averroës justified a distinction between a universal proposition and a proposition governed by the *dici de omni*.[25] This subsumption of all three modes under Aristotle proved that it was not necessary to supplement the Philosopher.

---

[22] Ibid., lines 205–206.
[23] Ibid., 502, lines 218–220. On the *dici de omni et nullo*, see Chapter 3 above.
[24] Ibid., 502, lines 229–230.
[25] See Chapter 3 above.

Functionally the strong interpretation of the *dici de omni* in Oyta's "third mode" served an exclusionary purpose. It ruled out most Trinitarian premises as false while preserving the formality of the inference. But this move did not have the arbitrary character of other solutions, for it relied on a general rule that was not only consistent with Aristotle's syllogistic, but also applicable to such non-Aristotelian ontologies as Platonic realism and Trinitarian theology. A commitment to Platonic realism or to Trinitarian theology was not necessary to appreciate these distinctions. Like physicists who derive real solutions by using imaginary coefficients that play no role in their personal mathematical or physical ontologies, Wodeham and Oyta could point to the positive results they had reached by bracketing the truth of Plato's theory. Here was another instance in which hypothetical arguments *secundum imaginationem* could be brought to bear on difficult conceptual problems.[26]

In the second conclusion, the purpose of Oyta's endeavor became abundantly clear. Concurring with Wodeham, he quoted verbatim a thesis from the *Abbreviatio*: "The rule of Aristotle that pertains to syllogistic form, along with ordinary logic, scripture, and what is believed by faith, suffices for knowing every paralogistic defect one can make in divinity."[27] The argument adduced to support this view recalls Wodeham as well: a syllogism is defective on account of either its "matter" or its form; faith regulates the former, Aristotle the latter.[28] Theologians did not need to be defensive about their inferences, for "with respect to their form, all syllogisms in divinity can be sufficiently regulated by the *dici de omni* or the *dici de nullo* . . . from which it follows that in answering the Philosopher, the Catholic ought not claim that the syllogistic forms are defective in divinity." To do so would expose the Catholic faith to the blasphemy of infidels, for both Truth and the Philosopher agreed that the syllogism did not need to be supplemented.[29] Here, too, the agreement with Wodeham was complete. Aristotle's syllogistic was both universal and formal.

When conclusions antithetical to the faith seemed to have been reached from true premises, a specifiable mistake had been committed. Indeed, like Wodeham and Ockham, Oyta thought that most paralogisms in theology were instances of the "fallacy of accident." But

---

[26] Murdoch, "The Development of a Critical Temper," 53; idem, "From Social into Intellectual Factors," 292ff.

[27] Murdoch, "From Social into Intellectual Factors," 502–503, lines 254–257.

[28] Wodeham-Oyta, *Abbreviatio*, 81ʳa; Gelber, "Logic and the Trinity," 254, 642 n. 43.

[29] Maierù, "Logica aristotelica," 504, lines 309–317.

whereas Wodeham had followed Duns Scotus in conceding some efficacy to the distinction between formal predication and predication by
identity as the key to the fallacy of accident, Oyta—influenced perhaps
by Rimini's criticisms of Cowton on this very point—discreetly
avoided taking a position on the issue. He defined the fallacy of accident as "a deception arising from the fact that the extremes, because of
a conjunction or disjunction with the middle term, are believed to be
correspondingly (*proportionaliter*) conjoined to, or disjoined from, each
other, or to be predicated of the middle conjunctively, of which they
[the extremes] were predicated divisively [in the premises], even
though such a conjunction or disjunction is not true, or does not follow from the argument."[30] This definition has an Ockhamist flavor;
there is no appeal here to a "lack of unity" in the middle term. Indeed
in some particulars the definition parallels the *Summa logicae*.[31] Oyta
also emphasized the fact that the term "accident" in the expression
"fallacy of accident" had nothing to do with the counterpart to "substance," nor did it have any connotation of fortuitousness. Rather, it
simply meant "a relation (*habitudo*) of the middle to the extremes,
which does not suffice to infer the conclusion." Following Aristotle's
advice in *On Sophistical Refutations*, then, the answer that applied to all
paralogisms of accident was that the conclusion did not necessarily follow from the premises.[32] Oyta devoted the third article of his question
to the solution of specific paralogisms (this section follows the *Abbreviatio* very closely). He also followed Wodeham's lead in rejecting circumlocutions of the subject as a means of avoiding problems in universal as well as expository syllogisms.

But Oyta differed from Wodeham on at least two important issues—
the formal distinction and the expository syllogism. Where Wodeham
held to a real distinction between the persons and essence, Oyta accepted a formal distinction.[33] And on the question of the expository
syllogism, Oyta cast his lot with Gregory of Rimini. Wodeham had
argued that the expository syllogism had to be regulated by the *dici de*

[30] Ibid., lines 320–330.

[31] On Wodeham, see Gelber, "Logic and the Trinity," 244; on Oyta and the two types
of predication, see Maierù, "Logique et théologie trinitaire dans le moyen âge tardif,"
194, 208 n. 4; on Oyta and Ockham, compare Maierù, "Logica aristotelica," 504–505,
lines 330–340, with Ockham, *Summa logicae*, pt. III-4, chap. 11 (*OP*, I, 823–824, esp.
lines 165–188).

[32] Maierù, "Logica aristotelica," 505, lines 340–356; Gelber, "Logic and the Trinity,"
222.

[33] Maierù, "Logique et théologie trinitaire dans le moyen âge tardif," 188, 205–207.

omni, but Rimini had gone a step further: since this syllogism had to be perfected by the *dici de omni*, it was not self-evident. Oyta cited Rimini by name on this point. It evidently seemed preferable to sacrifice the self-evidence of the expository syllogism than to make an exception to the universality of the rule. Oyta, too, incurred Ockham's posthumous contempt,[34] but the *dici de omni et nullo* reigned supreme.

From all of this, Oyta inferred that "to distinguish syllogisms from paralogisms in divinity, it is necessary to posit neither some new syncategorematic term nor some genus of universalization that cannot be elicited virtually from the sayings of Aristotle."[35] In short "the *dici de omni* and *dici de nullo* suffice for formal syllogisms in every [subject] matter." Oyta's treatment concluded that "if Aristotle had known the mysteries of our faith, he could have distinguished true syllogisms from paralogisms without changing the syncategorematic terms and the modes of universalizing propositions that he posited."[36] Aristotle's conversion would not have affected the formal structure of his arguments, only the truth values he would have assigned to the premises or the conclusions.

Wodeham clearly cast a long shadow over the entire question. Oyta's treatment of paralogisms in Trinitarian theology followed his predecessor's in aiming for a general unified solution to such problems. Even Oyta's desertion of Wodeham for Gregory of Rimini in the case of the expository syllogism was consistent with these aims. If the *dici de omni et nullo* was to be a credible universal criterion for evaluating correct inferences, one could not allow exceptions, however cherished, to stand in the way.

.

Henry of Langenstein, who had been Oyta's friend and colleague in Paris and later again in Vienna, also touched on the relations between logic and the data of revelation in his *Tractatus de dici de omni in divinis*.[37]

---

[34] Maierù, "Logica aristotelica," 511, lines 590–593; Chapter 3 above.

[35] Ibid., lines 594–597. Whereas categorematic terms have definite signification in and of themselves (e.g. 'dog', 'brown'), syncategorematic terms do not. Rather, they are "determinations of other terms or propositions, having no signification when taken alone, but exercising their signification only as co-predicates, which is the literal translation of syncategorema," e.g. 'every', 'not', etc. (Boehner, *Medieval Logic*, 22). See also Kretzmann, "Syncategoremata, Sophismata," Exponibilia, 211ff.

[36] Maierù, "Logica aristotelica," 512, lines 615–618.

[37] At present, seven manuscripts of the work have survived: Paris, Bibliothèque nationale, Fonds latin 14580, 82ᵛb–86ʳa, and Bibliothèque de l'Arsenal 522, 106ʳb–109ᵛa; Erfurt, Ampl. Q 150, 93ʳ–104ᵛ; Graz, Universitätsbibliothek 1145, 10ᵛ–15ᵛ; Klosterneuburg 820, 108ʳ–114ʳ; Tortosa, Archivo de la Catedral 143, 61ʳ–64ʳ; and Vatican City, Vat.

Although the date of composition is not certain, the treatise almost certainly postdates the beginning of Langenstein's theological studies, for the Parisian theologians in particular did not look kindly upon the attempts of mere masters of arts to meddle in divinity.[38] Given both the flurry of debates on the issue in the Paris of the 1370s and the parallelism between the conclusions of Oyta and Langenstein, the French university is a very likely site of composition. The treatise opens with the following question: "Does the *dici de omni*, according to the intention of the philosophers and Aristotle, suffice in general for Catholics to make syllogisms in divinity?"[39] Since attention to the *dici de omni et nullo* was not new, the inspiration for the treatise could have come from several quarters. The origins of the *dici de omni* went back to Aristotle and Boethius, through a lively history in the late thirteenth and early fourteenth centuries.[40] Ockham had discussed the rule explicitly in the *Summa logicae* (pt. III-1, chaps. 4–5 in particular). Holcot's *determinatio* 10 (or quodlibet 1, qu. 24 [?]) ended with an allusion to the *dici de omni*, and a cross-reference to Ockham's *Summa logicae*.[41] But Ockham had linked his treatment of the *dici de omni* to his discussion of the fallacy of accident, which Langenstein did not address. It therefore seems unlikely that the Ockham-Holcot connection was the primary stimulus behind Langenstein's treatise. More likely, the immediate inspiration came from the work of Wodeham and Oyta, not only because they had treated the *dici de omni* extensively, but especially because they had raised it to the status of fundamental rule.

The *Tractatus de dici de omni* is not notable for its transparency.

---

lat. 3088, 10ʳb–14ʳa. (The discovery of the Tortosa manuscript was made possible by the microfilming project of the Hill Monastic Manuscript Library, St. John's University, Collegeville, Minn.) In the secondary literature and catalogues, the authorship of the *Tractatus de dici de omni* has been attributed to both Langenstein and Nicole Oresme. Although Kern (*Die Handschriften der Universitätsbibliothek Graz*, II, 245) and Hohmann ("Initienregister der Werke Heinrichs von Langenstein," 410, 425) attribute the work to Oresme, no manuscript does. On the contrary, the colophons of the Erfurt, the Tortosa, and the two Paris manuscripts all attribute the work to Langenstein (Henricus de Hassia). Several theology students in early fifteenth-century Vienna, who were in a good position to know, attributed the *Tractatus de dici de omni* to "our master"—clearly not Oresme; see Chapter 5 below. A critical edition of the text is nearing completion. The citations in the notes are based on all but the Erfurt codex, which I have not seen. The foliation of the Graz manuscript (hereafter G) is provided for reference purposes only.

[38] See, for example, Buridan's questions on Aristotle's *Physics*, bk. IV, qu. 8, trans. in Grant, ed., *Sourcebook in Medieval Science*, 50–51.

[39] "Inquisiturus de dici de omni secundum intentionem philosophorum et Aristotelis, an videlicet sufficiat generaliter catholicis ad syllogizandum in divinis" (G 10ᵛ).

[40] Gelber, "The Fallacy of Accident and the *Dictum de Omni*" (forthcoming).

[41] Gelber, *Exploring the Boundaries of Reason*, 112.

Strings of three or more adjectives, adverbs, and even dependent clauses abound while specific examples are in short supply. Even when the stylistic obstacles can be overcome, problems remain. Apart from the main question it addresses, the text offers few clues about its immediate intellectual context. Langenstein cites no authorities or opponents by name. His only foils are unidentified *aliqui*. The language and the key concepts, however, suggest that the text was drawing upon contemporary discussions about the mental counterpart of the spoken or written proposition.[42] The purpose of the following pages is not to analyze the work in detail, but to characterize Langenstein's early views on the relation between Aristotelian logic and theology.

In this treatise, Langenstein's approach to the *dici de omni* differs from that of Oyta in his question on the rules of syllogizing. Instead of emphasizing inferences, Langenstein turned his attention to supposition theory (a late medieval approach to analyzing the way terms function in sentences) and to the distribution of terms in universal propositions. Although supposition theory traces its roots back to the twelfth century,[43] it flourished primarily in the thirteenth and fourteenth centuries. At the heart of the theory lies the insight that terms do not always stand for what they signify. When uttered or written, alone or in a sentence, 'dog' brings to mind a hairy four-legged creature, which is what 'dog' signifies. But in the sentences 'dog is a three-letter word' and 'dog is a species', the term 'dog' stands, or "supposits," for something other than what it signifies—in the first case for a word, in the second for a class.[44] Thus, instead of dealing with Trinitarian paralogisms from the point of view of formal inference, the approach via supposition theory focuses on the particular ways in which terms "supposit" in the premises. Langenstein was not the first to take this path; the tradition goes back to the early years of the fourteenth century, and indeed has a counterpart elsewhere in Oyta's *Quaestiones*.[45]

As a preamble to his discussion of the varieties of supposition and distribution used in Trinitarian theology, Langenstein opened the work with a typology of the distinctions he allowed. Although their

---

[42] Nuchelmans, *Theories of the Proposition*, 197ff; Ashworth, "Theories of the Proposition," 83ff.

[43] De Rijk, *Logica modernorum*, II, pt. 1.

[44] For a good summary of supposition theory roughly contemporaneous with Langenstein's work, see Scott's introduction to Buridan, *Sophisms on Meaning and Truth*, 29ff.

[45] Maierù, "La Doctrine de la supposition en théologie trinitaire," 221ff.

intended use was clearly theological, Langenstein presented his definitions in general terms, and structured his dichotomous schema as
follows:

I. the rational distinction
II. "the distinction whose extremes hold on the part of the thing—
as opposed to concepts and terms"
   A. the formal nonreal distinction
   B. the real distinction
      1. the real essential distinction
      2. the real nonessential distinction

The rational distinction distinguishes concepts and terms by which
the same thing is conceived, such as the divine will and intellect. In
other words, such a distinction has no counterpart in the order of
things, but is introduced by the conceiving mind. At the other end of
the spectrum, the real distinction reflects differences between individual objects. The real distinction must meet two requirements: each of
the extremes must exist; one extreme must not be the other. The intermediate category is the most revealing: the formal distinction, Langenstein claimed, intervenes "only where the extremes may be verified
of each other, yet in contradictory fashion something is affirmed of
one extreme and truly negated of the other, which happens only in the
case of the divine essence and persons." This last restriction clearly
places Langenstein in the Ockhamist rather than the Scotist camp. To
illustrate, Langenstein provided one of his rare examples: although the
proposition 'the Father is the divine essence' is true, and 'the divine
essence generates' is false, yet 'the Father generates' is true. Thus given
a true minor premise and a false major premise, the conclusion is true.
Conversely when the major is negated, thereby making it true, the
conclusion becomes false. Langenstein noted that this state of affairs
"appears to be unimaginable, unless there be some kind of distinction
on the part of the thing (*ex natura rei*), which does not suffice to verify
a negative simply of the extremes, and which is therefore not real."[46]

---

[46] "Distinctio formalis non realis est solum ubi extrema licet de se invicem verificen-
tur, tamen contradictorie aliquid vere affirmatur de uno extremo et vere negatur de re-
liquo, et hoc solum reperitur de divina essentia et personis, quia quamvis hec sit vera
'pater est divina essentia', tamen hec est falsa 'divina essentia generat' et hec vera 'pater
generat', quod inymaginabile videtur nisi sit aliquis modus distinctionis se tenentis ex
parte rei, que distinctio non sufficiat verificare negativam simpliciter de extremis, et ideo
non est realis" (G 10ᵛ). For a similar notion, see the view that John Baconthorp expressed
in the 1330s, in Gelber, "Logic and the Trinity," 292.

Langenstein conceded the pertinence of an objection: the fact that contradictories are verified of A and B does not imply that there is some distinction *ex natura rei* in proper form between A and B. Indeed it would be sufficient that A be really distinct from something that is B. But Langenstein brushed the objection aside—he would not deal with it here. Ockham himself had raised this objection in an argument against the formal distinction in creatures.[47] Together these definitions and the objection demonstrate that Langenstein was interacting with Ockham's thought, either mediately or immediately.[48]

In the following sections, Langenstein went on to explore the mental underpinnings of the universal proposition. The context of his discussion owes a debt to the debates generated by the *complexe significabile* (literally, the "complexly signifiable")—the notion that there was "an eternal being, neither mental nor physical nor yet identical with God, which was at once the significate of an indicative sentence, the bearer of truth and falsity, and the object of knowledge and belief."[49] Although the view has its roots in Wodeham, it was popularized by Gregory of Rimini, and remained a hotly debated issue into the sixteenth century.[50] The relevance of this theory to Trinitarian paralogisms becomes apparent upon realizing that vocal or written syllogisms were believed to be the conventional counterparts of mental syllogisms, which signified naturally. To take only one example, how did the premises and conclusions of such syllogisms function at the level of mental language—as wholes or as the sum of their parts? What role,

---

[47] "Verum est quod aliquis posset dicere, non sequitur 'de A et B verificantur contradictoria, igitur inter A et B in propria forma est aliqua distinctio ex natura rei vel ex parte modi essendi in re', sed quod sufficeret ad huiusmodi verificationem quod A distinguatur ab aliquo realiter quod est B, quod pro nunc non curo reprobare" (G 10ᵛ). Langenstein's reference to this objection recalls Ockham's discussion of the Franciscan Henry Costesy's view. See Ockham, *Ordinatio*, bk. 1, dist. 2, qu. 1 and 11 (*OT*, 11, 14ff, 373ff); and Gelber, "Logic and the Trinity," 183–185.

[48] Langenstein's care in specifying the conditions under which the formal distinction legitimately could be used may be related to the intellectual climate of Paris during Langenstein's student days. In 1362, the year before Langenstein received his bachelor's and master's degrees, the faculty of theology at Paris condemned Louis of Padua, a disciple of John of Ripa, for abusing the formal distinction, specifically for holding that "something may be God according to his real being and yet not be God according to his formal being." Louis subsequently rejected the formal distinction altogether; see Combes, "Présentation de Jean de Ripa," 190–193.

[49] Ashworth, "Mental Language and the Unity of Propositions," 69; idem, "Theories of the Proposition," esp. 88–99; Nuchelmans, *Theories of the Proposition*, 227ff.

[50] Gál, "Adam's Wodeham's Question on the 'Complexe Significabile,' " 66ff; Ashworth, "Mental Language and the Unity of Propositions," 61ff.

if any, did such syncategorematic terms[51] as 'all/every' or 'no/none' play in mental propositions? Langenstein's language suggests that, at the very least, he was aware of contemporary discussions on the subject, whereas his arguments imply that he was reacting to some aspects of the *complexe significabile*.

After examining various ways of understanding the "complex apprehensions" involved in universal propositions such as 'every animal is a man', Langenstein made a case for the view that such propositions were resolved copulatively into singulars. It was the singular proposition which undergirded the universal, not the other way around. "Universalization," he concluded, "asserts something more than merely a universal term serving as subject in a mental enunciation."[52] Turning next to the elements of universal propositions, Langenstein argued that there was no such thing as a naturally signifying mental syncategorematic term. Every prospective candidate turns out to be either a proposition or a categorematic term, in other words, something suited to being a subject or a predicate in a proposition—not a syncategorematic. "From this follows the intended conclusion, namely that to vocal terms of the type 'all/every', 'none', etc., nothing corresponds in the mind unless it be some copulative *complexum* constituted by singulars of the universal term to which such an utterance [= 'all/every', 'none'] is added, like this *complexum* 'this man and this man, etc.' or this 'Sortes and Plato and Cicero'."[53] The implication was that for the human mind, at least, the distribution of common terms

---

[51] See n. 35 above.

[52] "Talismodi apprehensio complexa ubi subicitur terminus universalis de sui natura magis debet ab humano intellectu resolvi copulative quam disiunctive, cui etiam consonat quod infinita valet universalem et non ita particularis quasi signum particulare sit nota disiunctionis. Concluditur ergo ex hiis quod universalisatio dicit aliquid ultra subiectionem precisam termini universalis in mentali enuntiatione, quod fuit in isto capitulo inquirendum" (G 11ʳ).

[53] "Si dicatur quod illud sincathegorema significet equipollenter isti complexo copulato 'iste homo et iste homo et iste homo', tunc etiam significaret equipollenter isti complexo 'iste homo'; et per consequens esset terminus natus supponere in propositione mentali ut illud complexum vel sicud istud copulatum 'iste homo et iste homo', igitur non esset sincathegorema sed cathegorema. . . . Unde videtur quod omnis mentalis terminus complexus vel incomplexus naturaliter significans est propositio vel cathegoricus, id est per se natus subici vel predicari in propositione, quia de omni termino pro omni quod representat, vel ad quod intellectum obiective terminat, aliquod predicatum potest enuntiari. Patet ergo ex hiis conclusio intenta, videlicet quod huiusmodi terminis vocalibus 'omnis', 'nullus', etc., in mente nichil correspondet nisi quoddam complexum copulatum ex terminis singularibus termini universalis, cui talis vox additur, ut istud complexum 'iste homo et iste homo etc.', vel istud 'Sortes et Plato et Cicero' " (G 11ʳ).

in a proposition rested on the formation of singular concepts.[54] This view marks a definite disagreement with Gregory of Rimini's understanding of the *complexe significabile*, which posited that what the proposition signified was not the same as what its parts signified.[55] In contrast, Langenstein's approach was more atomistic and analytical.

After thus justifying the resolution of universal propositions into singulars, Langenstein defined the distribution of a term with respect to a predicate as the act of enunciating "the predicate of a subject constituted by the copulation of all singular terms inferior to the subject." Based on these conclusions, he argued that "it is not rationally imaginable how there might be several species of distribution of such a sort, unless the one would be affirmative distribution, and the other negative. The affirmative is denoted by 'all/every', or some equivalent sign, and the negative by 'no/none', or some similar conventional sign."[56]

There were, according to Langenstein, only a few categories of distributable terms: (1) common simple categorematic terms such as 'man', 'animal', etc.; (2) complex terms constituted by the preceding terms, joined to a commoner or inferior term by means of 'that is', e.g. 'the thing that is man', 'the being that is animal', etc.; (3) complex terms like those in the preceding category, but in the plural, such as 'the things that are man', 'the persons that are the divine essence', etc. Any type of distributable term that one might choose, however, was adequately distributed by the two aforementioned kinds of universal syncategorematics; no others were required. Therefore, since there were only two kinds, "it is fanciful to assume that because of the position of the Christian faith, it is necessary to find new kinds of syncategorematic terms and distributions, which investigation according to the light of nature has neither considered nor understood."[57] Although his arguments differed from those of Oyta, Langenstein clearly

---

[54] The restriction to the human is intentional, for Langenstein notes that one concept for an angelic intellect may be equivalent to many for us.

[55] Ashworth, "Theories of the Proposition," 91.

[56] "Ex quibus ulterius deducitur quod non sunt nisi due species sincathegorematum absolute universaliter distributivorum, quoniam ex iam dictis descriptionibus distributionis non est rationabiliter ymaginabile quomodo plures species talismodi distributionis esse possent nisi una affirmativa distributio et una negativa, quarum affirmativa denotatur per ly 'omnis' vel aliquod signum equivalens, et negativa denotatur per ly 'nullus' vel aliquod consimile ad placitum significans" (G 12^r).

[57] "fictitium est ponere quod propter positionem fidei Christiane novas species sincathegorematum et distributionum necesse sit inveniri quas naturalis luminis investigatio non consideravit nec intellexit" (G 12^r).

endorsed the same fundamental program as his friend: there was no need to go beyond the fundamental tools of Aristotelian logic, or to introduce new ones that were inaccessible to unaided reason.

What were these "new syncategorematics" that Langenstein considered to be superfluous? One interpretation might be that he meant such terms as 'formally,' 'really,' and so on, which earlier theologians had added to standard subject-predicate propositions with Trinitarian terms. In fact, Ockham and Holcot had called such terms syncategorematics, and clearly they were not part of Aristotle's syllogistic.[58] Yet such an interpretation does not seem fully consistent with Langenstein's concession of a formal distinction (even restricted to God) in his introductory remarks. A second possibility is that Langenstein was responding to positions similar to those that Elizabeth Ashworth has found in Pierre d'Ailly and several sixteenth-century logicians—specifically, to the notion that propositions themselves have syncategorematic meaning[59] (hence, by extension, universal propositions would be universal syncategorematics). Yet, this view does not quite mesh with Langenstein's counterarguments, which seem to be directed at syncategorematic terms in a more traditional sense.

In any event, if novel syncategorematics and modes of distribution were unnecessary, something new nevertheless was required. As the notion of supposition is a correlative of the concept of distribution ("for distribution occurs only with respect to that thing, or those things, for which the term is said to supposit"), Langenstein proceeded to discuss supposition. His goal was to develop categories of supposition that would resolve the problems associated with the use of Aristotle's syllogistic in theology. "Supposition is nothing other than a term serving as subject or predicate on behalf of that which is signified by it [the term], or on behalf of those things which are apprehended by it; and [that which is signified or apprehended] can be the term itself, or other terms, or things [that are] not signs."[60] Following a more common rule, a given term supposits for something if that term

---

[58] Ockham, *Ordinatio*, bk. I, dist. 2, qu. 11 (*OT*, II, 375): "when it is said that 'essence and relation are distinguished formally,' the term 'formally' is here a pure syncategorematic, like 'per se,' 'necessarily,' or 'contingently,' or 'all.' . . ." On Holcot, see Gelber, *Exploring the Boundaries of Reason*, 47, lines 363–365; 98–99, lines 896ff. See also Maierù, "Logique et théologie trinitaire dans le moyen âge tardif," 195.

[59] Ashworth, "Theories of the Proposition," 107–114.

[60] "suppositio nichil aliud est quam subiectio vel predicatio termini pro eo quod per ipsam importatur, vel eis que per ipsam apprehenduntur et hoc potest esse ipsemet / terminus vel alii termini vel res non signa" (G 12ʳ–12ᵛ).

can be predicated truly of it. Thus, according to this rule, in 'the Father is not the Son', 'Father' does not supposit for 'Son' since 'this Son is the Father' is false.

Langenstein divided supposition into two overarching categories: formal-and-proper supposition, on the one hand, and real-common supposition on the other. Formal-and-proper supposition he defined as "the acceptation of some term in a proposition for everything, or all things, relative to the proper singular concepts of which this term is truly enunciated by means of the copula of the proposition qualified by the word 'formally'."[61] The suggestion here seems to be that the copula 'to be' should sometimes be parsed as 'to be [formally]'. On this reading, 'formally' becomes an implicit part of the copula, where it can nevertheless affect the truth of the proposition. These definitions thus place the burden of ambiguity on the copula.[62]

Formal-and-proper supposition in turn subdivided into formal-essential and formal-notional.[63] Langenstein restricted the first to essential terms in divinity, which he identified with "the terms that are commonly verified of the three persons, such as 'goodness', 'eternity', 'will', 'intellect', etc." Formal-notional supposition, on the other hand, pertained to "notional and personal terms,"—for example, the terms that are not verified of all persons, such as 'Father', 'Son', 'spiration'.[64]

---

[61] "suppositio quodammodo dividi potest in duas species, scilicet in suppositionem formalem et propriam, et in suppositionem realem communem. Formalis et propria est acceptio alicuius termini in propositione pro omni eo vel eis de quorum propriis conceptibus singularibus iste terminus vere enuntiatur mediante copula propositionis determinata per ly 'formaliter' " (G 12ᵛ). These categories and definitions do not coincide with any of the known taxonomies, although they share a superficial terminological similarity with those of Burleigh and Campsall; see Maierù, *Terminologia logica*, 360ff.

[62] This marks a departure from Ockham's *Summa logicae*, which had pointed to the dangers involved in making 'to be' equivocal at will (bk. II, chap. 4), and approximates the formal predication favored in the Scotist tradition (see Chapter 3 above).

[63] This nomenclature draws on the distinction between "essentials" (the divine properties that the three persons have in common) and "notionals" (the properties specific to one or two of the persons); see the glossary by Alluntis and Wolter in Duns Scotus, *God and Creatures*, 525. It also parallels Wodeham's language: "subiectum potest sumi notionaliter . . . vel essentialiter," upon which Oyta evidently drew as well; see Maierù, "La Doctrine de la supposition en théologie trinitaire," 226, 236 n. 11.

[64] "Adhuc suppositio formalis subdividitur in suppositionem formalem essentialem et formalem notionalem. Suppositio formalis essentialis est solum terminorum essentialium in divinis, id est terminorum qui communiter verificantur de tribus personis, ut ly 'bonitas' 'eternitas' 'voluntas' 'intellectus', etc. Suppositio vero formalis notionalis est terminorum notionalium vel personalium, ut sunt termini qui non de omnibus personis verificantur, ut 'pater', 'filius', 'spiratio', etc." (G 12ᵛ). These distinctions parallel those of Wodeham; see Maierù, "La Doctrine de la supposition en théologie trinitaire," 226.

Interestingly, Langenstein defined real-common supposition nega-
tively, as "the acceptation of a term for that thing, or those things,
relative to the singular nonproper concepts of which the copula of the
proposition *not* determined by the word 'formally' is verified."[65] The
distinction between these two main categories of supposition thus involved not merely the absence or presence of 'formally' after the copula, but also the "propriety" (or absence thereof) of the singular concepts involved in the supposition. According to this view, the universal
proposition 'every divine essence is the Father' is true according to formal-and-proper supposition, but false according to real-common supposition. Although Langenstein did not explain why the proposition
is true in the first case, the reason seems to be that according to formal-
and-proper supposition, 'divine essence' can supposit only for that
which is the Father in the divine essence. Indeed, the definition of formal supposition allows only those terms which are formally identical
to be predicated of each other.[66] In the second case, the reason why the
proposition is false is more manifest. When the universalized subject is
distributed according to real-common supposition, the singulars are
not true (e.g. 'this Son who is the essence is the Father', 'this thing—
pointing to the Holy Spirit—is the Father'). In passing, Langenstein
noted that "the formal distinction alone does not suffice to syllogize
formally in every matter." He made no case for his assertion, stating

[65] "Suppositio vero realis communis est acceptio termini pro omni eo etc., de cuius
vel de quorum conceptibus singularibus non propriis mediante copula propositionis non
determinata per ly 'formaliter' verificatur, vel ipsa suppositio in genere vocetur realis
communis in quantum est acceptio termini pro omni etc., de cuius terminis singularibus
propriis et impropriis vel quibuscumque mediante copula propositionis verificatur non
determinata per ly 'formaliter' " (G 12^v).

[66] This point may be clarified by reference to an interesting text, "De modo predicandi
ac sylogizandi in divinis," discovered by Alfonso Maierù in Munich, Clm 17290, and
soon to appear in the Jan Pinborg memorial volume. For an overview of its contents,
see Maierù, "Logique et théologie trinitaire dans le moyen âge tardif," esp. 192ff. The
anonymous author argues that when a term has a single formal *suppositum*, the syllogism
holds not on account of the distribution of the subject, but because it functions as an
expository syllogism (in which the subject of each premise is singular): "omnis syllogismus in quo distribuitur aliquis terminus habens solum unum suppositum formale, non
tenet virtute distributionis eiusdem termini, id est, quod conclusio non probatur virtute
distributionis precise, sed tenet ut syllogismus expositorius, verbi gratia, iste syllogismus 'omnis essentia divina est pater, et sapientia est essentia divina, igitur etc.' non tenet
virtute distributionis huius termini 'essentia', sed ratione singularitatis divine essentie
. . . verbi gratia nec plus nec minus probatur per dictum syllogismum quam per istum:
'ista essentia divina est pater, et bonitas est ista essentia, igitur' " (139^r). I thank Alfonso
Maierù for sending me a copy of his transcription.

only that the point was obvious, presumably on the grounds that the formal distinction falls under the purview of real-common supposition (since formal-and-proper supposition handles only instances of formal *identity*).[67]

For formal syllogisms, the universalized subject term must be distributable according to the threefold manner outlined earlier; any of these modes must be understood below the term associated with the universal sign. In a universal enunciation, in fact, the predicate must be predicable of whatever the subject is predicable. And this is what Aristotle meant by the *dici de omni*.[68] Clearly Langenstein's point—although reached by a more convoluted route—is very close to that of Oyta's three modes of universalizing propositions.

Indeed the parallelism between Langenstein and Oyta pervades the following sections. First, in order to undergird his analysis of universal propositions and their distribution, Langenstein outlined four ways of descending to singulars from a nonplural term (e.g. 'man'). The descent can proceed (1) to vague singulars such as 'this man, this man' (*ut sunt ly iste homo, ista homo*), where the first 'this' is masculine, the second feminine (this combination of a feminine demonstrative with a masculine noun is well attested in all manuscripts);[69] (2) to proper and

---

[67] "Ex isto potest videri quomodo ista universalis propositio 'omnis essentia divina est pater' secundum formalem suppositionem et propriam est vera, et secundum realem communem est falsa. Sequitur ulterius quod sola distinctio formalis non sufficit ad formaliter syllogizandum in omni materia; manifestum est hoc. Si dicatur secundum quam istarum suppositionum magis de virtute sermonis ly 'essentia' debet dici supponere et distribui in ista propositione et consimilibus, potest dici quod secundum suppositionem formalem; tum quia doctores communiter istam universalem concedunt, et hoc non potest esse secundum suppositionem realem communem, quia secundum istam est manifeste falsa, quia iste singulares eius 'iste filius qui est essentia est pater', 'ista res (demonstrato / spiritu sancto) est pater', etc." (G 12ᵛ–13ʳ).

[68] "Huic est quod omni universali oportet intelligi distributionem fieri secundum suppositionem realem communem, que includat simul formalem et non formalem; et distributio secundum istam suppositionem est distributio simpliciter de omni necessario requisita secundum philosophos ad formaliter syllogizandum in omni materia. Et ita patet quod ad formaliter syllogizandum secundum philosophicam doctrinam, requiritur quod triplex distribuibile predictum in capitulo quinto distribuatur ex parte termini qui subicitur. Patet quia secundum predicta, in enuntiatione universali denotatur secundum philosophos quod de quocumque et quibuscumque verificatur subiectum, verificetur predicatum. Igitur necesse est quodlibet dictorum trium distribuibilium intelligi sub termino cui additur signum universale; hoc enim importat apud Aristotelem dici de omni et dici de nullo etc."(G 13ʳ).

[69] Langenstein evidently was treating the term 'homo' in the generic sense of human being (*anthropos*). 'Omnis homo' would then distribute over all men (*iste* homo) and women (*ista* homo). The distribution might be construed as vague because of the differ-

determinate singulars; (3) to proper determinate singulars to which one has added some determinations: 'this man who is matter and form', 'this white and cold man'; (4) to singulars taken vaguely under some common term added to the term that was distributed, such as 'this thing that is man', 'this duality that is man'.[70] These four modes provided a structure against which to analyze universal propositions and to assign truth values to them. In a manner reminiscent of Oyta, Langenstein argued that descents which yield true singulars under the first three modes fail to do so under the fourth mode.[71] Thus 'every divine essence is the Father' is false according to the *dici de omni*. The reason is familiar, namely that the *dici de omni* requires not merely that each singular proposition subsumed under the universal be true, but that in addition no term be verifiable of some singular in the subject without also being verified of the predicate.[72]

---

ence between the masculine gender of the universalized term, on the one hand, and the two genders of the singulars on the other. For a possible analogue, see Kretzmann, "Syncategoremata, Sophismata, Exponibilia," 230, n. 75.

[70] "Terminus universalis singularis numeri distribuitur pro quadruplici manerie singularium (primo pro) singularibus propriis vagis ut sunt ly 'iste homo', 'ista homo' etc.; secundo pro singularibus propriis determinatis quia sub quolibet termino universali sunt possibiles conceptus singulares essentiales, ut patuit ex secundo capitulo; tertio distribuitur pro singularibus predictis adiunctis eis quibusdam determinationibus ut 'iste homo qui est materia et forma', 'iste homo albus et frigidus', etc.; quarto modo distribuitur pro singularibus vagis sumptis sub quocumque termino communi adiuncto termino qui distribuebatur tamquam determinatione cuiusmodi sunt termini singulares 'hec res que est homo', 'ista dualitas que est homo', 'isti Sortes et Plato existentes homo', 'hoc animal album quod est homo', etc. Ad istas quatuor maneries singularium fit descensus sub termino distributo secundum suppositionem realem communem vel suppositi suppositione reali communi" (*G* 13ʳ). These views drew criticism from Langenstein's students (see Chapter 5 below).

[71] "Non equivalet descendere sub termino distributo ad singularia tertii modi et quarti. Patet aliqualiter in ista universali 'omnis homo naturaliter est corruptibilis' ubi descendendo ad singularia istius termini 'homo', primorum trium modorum omnes eius singulares sunt vere. Notandum est de hoc de primis duobus modis intelligendo de homine viatore. Similiter de tertio modo manifestum est quod iste singulares omnes sunt bone 'iste homo qui est dualitas materie et forme est naturaliter corruptibilis', 'Sortes qui est albus et frigidus est naturaliter corruptibilis, etc.' Descendendo vero ad singularia quarti modi, multe singulares essent false. Patet quia hec est falsa: 'ista dualitas materie et forme que est homo est naturaliter corruptibilis', 'iste binarius numerus qui est homo est naturaliter corruptibilis' " (*G* 14ʳ).

[72] "Ex quo sequitur quod hec est falsa de dici de omni syllogistico: 'omnis essentia divina est Pater'. Patet quia non est ita sicut per eam denotatur quia de ly 'trinitas' verificatur ly 'essentia' et tamen non ly 'pater' igitur. Sequitur ulterius quod terminus communis distributus non distribuitur pro omni de quo denotatur in propositione universali predicatum verificari, quia ut apparuit, denotatur verificari indifferenter pro commu-

Finally, the treatise concludes with words nearly identical to those used by Oyta—and here it is at present impossible to say with certainty who depends on whom: "To save syllogisms in divinity, it is not necessary to posit or discover some new syncategorematic terms or species of universalization other than those that Aristotle posited, or could have posited."[73] The syncategorematic terms 'omnis' [all/every] and 'nullus' [none/no] and the like "are sufficient for formal syllogisms in any subject matter whatever." What is more, this conclusion is valid for pagans and Christians alike:

> If Aristotle had been made a Christian, he would have conceded the following syllogisms without any variation of the syncategorematic terms and modes of universalizing that he held: 'every God is one person, Father and Son are God, therefore Father and Son are one person', but he would have termed the major premise false. Likewise he would have denied that 'every divine essence is a trinity' because he would have noted according to his aforementioned *dici de omni* that 'trinity' should be verified of every complex or incomplex term of which 'divine essence' is verified, and thus he would have thought that the Son and Father were a trinity.[74]

---

niori eo et aliis. Terminus enim distributus bene verificatur de communiori se, ut homo de substantia. Sequitur tertio quod ad veritatem universalis non sufficit quamlibet eius singularem proprie dictam esse veram, quia alias hec esset vera: 'omnis essentia divina est', sed oportet quod nullus terminus verificetur de singulari aliquo subiecti eius quin de eodem verificetur predicatum" (G 15ʳ).

[73] "Ad salvandum syllogismos in divinis non oportet aliquod novum sincathegorema poni nec inveniri, nec aliquas species universalizationis quas Aristoteles non posuit vel posuisset" (G 15ʳ).

[74] "Item apud Aristotelem et omnes philosophos dici de omni, ut predictum est, et dici de nullo sufficienter denotabantur per ista sincategoremata 'omnis', 'nullus', etc. Et illud ad formales syllogismos sufficit in omni materia, quia hec 'omne A est B' apud Aristotelem et philosophos denotabatur B inesse omni termino complexo vel incomplexo inferiori vel superiori respectu A, qui de aliquo respectu ipsius A verificaretur vel de quo significative sumpto verificaretur ipse terminus A. Et ergo Aristoteles si factus fuisset Christianus sine variatione suorum sincathegorematum et modorum universalizationis quos posuit, concessisset istos syllogismos 'omnis deus est una persona, pater et filius sunt deus, igitur pater et filius sunt una persona', sed negasset maiorem. Similiter, negasset istam 'omnis essentia divina est trinitas' ratio quia denotasset sibi secundum suum dici de omni predictum quod de omni termino complexo vel incomplexo verificaretur ly 'trinitas' de quo verificatur ly 'essentia divina', et per consequens representasset sibi quod pater et filius essent trinitas.

Item notum est quod concessisset istum syllogismum 'omnis homo est animal, Sortes et Plato sunt homo, igitur Sortes et Plato sunt animal' virtute sui dici de omni, igitur utique illud dici de omni suum sibi denotabat illud quod dictum est, videlicet predicatum universalis enuntiari de omni complexo / vel incomplexo, etc., de quo enuntiatur su-

Aristotle's hypothetical conversion would have given him the ability to distinguish between true and false premises, but would not have required fundamental changes in his logic. Fourteenth-century Christians were in a similar position—with this difference, that they had a superior understanding of supposition theory.

In any event, Christian theology in general, and its Trinitarian component in particular, made no extraordinary demands on logic: "It appears therefore that the Catholic is not compelled because of the advent of the Catholic faith to change syncategorematic terms and to find modes of universalizing other than those which Aristotle and others have used. And if we can thus save and defend what pertains to the faith, we must not concoct such superfluities, by which we are more ridiculed by those on the outside than we are protected from them."[75]

These concluding words encapsulate Langenstein's position. Additional syncategorematic terms were worse than superfluous. They were positively harmful, for they elicited ridicule from the very infidels who were to be brought into the fold. For all of these reasons, Catholics were not to tamper with the Aristotelian rules of syllogizing.

In the end, then, Langenstein and Oyta were in complete agreement. They concurred that Aristotle's syllogistic was formal and universal, and therefore valid also in Trinitarian theology. The two men differed in the path they had used to reach their conclusions. Oyta's dependence on Wodeham is both unambiguous and extensive; Langenstein was interacting with similar sources, but his direct debts are not so clear. Oyta was explicit about the relationship between Plato and Aristotle—the insights of Plato's ontology made possible a useful logical distinction between three modes of universalizing propositions that could not be instantiated in creation. Yet the result was said to be deducible from Aristotle. Unlike some of their predecessors, both men adopted a conciliatory attitude toward Aristotelian logic. Given their close association in Paris, there is every reason to assume that Langenstein and Oyta discussed these issues at some length. Indeed, the examples that Langenstein cited in the last section of his treatise also appear in the concluding paragraph of Oyta's question. Finally, both

---

biectum, quia virtute nullius alterius potuit dicere illam conclusionem ex illis premissis sequi etc." (G 15ʳ-15ᵛ).

[75] "Apparet ergo quod propter adventum fidei catholice non cogitur catholicus mutare sincathegoremata et alios modos universalizationis invenire quam Aristoteles et alii usi sunt; et si ita possumus salvare et defensare ea que sunt fidei, non debemus fingere talia superflua, quibus magis derideamur ab hiis qui foris sunt quam ab eis defensemur" (G 15ᵛ).

texts reflect an awareness of the apologetic implications of their positions. In Oyta's case, this emphasis derived directly from Wodeham, where the infidel entered the fray as an instrument to test the universality of a given position. Langenstein, on the other hand, made apologetics the focus of his concluding sentence, as a plea to keep matters simple so as to avoid the well-deserved censure of the infidels. Just as the absolute power of God served to test for contingency, so the unaided rational powers of the infidel served to test formality and universality.

How long did the agreement between Langenstein and Oyta last? It is not known whether Oyta ever reexamined his position. As the next chapter will show, however, Langenstein, by the end of his life, had rejected the conclusions of his *Tractatus de dici de omni*. In a dramatic reversal of his Parisian position, he argued that there was no reason to expect Aristotle's logic to function in an area about which the Philosopher had only the knowledge of the pagans.

CHAPTER FIVE

On Paralogisms in Trinitarian Doctrine (II): The Viennese Students

> But what becomes of logic now? Its rigor
> seems to be giving way here.
>
> LUDWIG WITTGENSTEIN,
> *Philosophical Investigations*

THROUGHOUT THE 1380s and 1390s, the drawing power of the University of Vienna was closely tied to the presence of its most prominent theologians, Henry of Langenstein and Henry of Oyta. It is not surprising, therefore, that the views of the two professors found a particularly attentive audience among the students they attracted. A definitive account of the extent of their influence must await detailed studies of indigenous Viennese writings. Even a limited examination of the attitudes toward the relation between logic and Trinitarian theology, however, shows that the impact of Langenstein and Oyta was notable.

The two men exerted their influence upon two groups of students: first, the older students who took up theology soon after the revival of the university, but who in most cases had studied in faculties of arts elsewhere; second, the younger generation of students who for the most part had received their arts training in Vienna, and subsequently went on to study theology there as well. Each group responded to its professors in a slightly different way. The comparison between them is complicated by the asymmetry in the sources that preserve their views. For the first group, the generation of 1389, as it were, fragments of a *principia* debate and short treatises survive, but no commentaries on the *Sentences*. Although commentaries on the *Sentences* survive for the second group, the generation of 1402, only incomplete sets of *principia* have been found.[1] This asymmetry notwithstanding, the

---

[1] Uiblein, "Zur Lebensgeschichte einiger Wiener Theologen," 105ff.

comparison is revealing, for it bears witness to a momentous shift in the attitude toward the use of Aristotle's syllogistic in Trinitarian theology at Vienna—a shift from openness to skepticism, if not outright rejection. As will become clear, the central figure in this shift was not a young maverick, but the dean of Viennese theologians, Henry of Langenstein himself.

·

According to the information in one manuscript, Henry of Oyta's questions on the *Sentences* were reread ca. 1389 at Vienna, where they generated much interest.[2] One careful reader outlined key theses from the latter's text, complete with folio references to the codex he was using.[3] The list of students who took an interest in these questions surely includes Johannes Bremis and his colleagues, who in 1388–1389 were clarifying their own theological views while commenting on the *Sentences* for the first time. Several of the theses that Bremis defended in his first *principium* clearly reflect the conclusions of Oyta, especially his refusal to emend logic on theological grounds and his statements about the universality of the expository syllogism and of the first-figure universal affirmative syllogism (*barbara*).[4] Bremis devoted almost half of his first *principium* to the proposition that the Trinity surpassed all other profundities of theological truth.[5] Among other theses, he argued that traces of the Divinity could be found in creatures, but that God's triune being could not be proved by necessary reasons.[6] His views did not go unchallenged. Lambert of Gelderen objected that the sacrament of the Eucharist and the article of the Incarnation were even

[2] The colophon of Munich, Bayerische Staatsbibliothek, Clm 8867 is dated 1389 and claims that the *Quaestiones* were "noviter pronunciate"; Clm 17468 and Graz, Universitätsbibliothek 639 are also dated 1389. Clm 18364 is dated 1398. A. Lang, *Heinrich Totting von Oyta*, 63–64. Klosterneuburg 294 is undated, but written in the hand of Johann von Retz, who was in Vienna during the last decades of the fourteenth century (see Appendix below).

[3] ÖNB 4708, 188ʳ–203ᵛ; fol. 110ᵛ of the same manuscript is dated 1390, but neither the hand nor the paper resembles those of the notes.

[4] See Chapter 2 above. Apart from these doctrinal similarities, ÖNB 4371 contains direct evidence of Bremis's interest in Oyta's work. The first is a faint marginal note "vide viᵗⁱˢ(?) H. Oyta" in Bremis's first *principium* (17ʳ); the second is the presence in the manuscript of a fragment from Oyta's *Abbreviatio* of Adam Wodeham's commentary on the *Sentences* (18ʳ–21ᵛ), with the same red annotations found in Bremis's hand throughout the remainder of the notebook (see Appendix below).

[5] See Chapter 2 above.

[6] "Quamvis hec veritas multipliciter vestigiata sit in creaturis, tamen deum talem esse nec potest, nec potuit rationibus convinci necessariis" (ÖNB 4371, 24ʳ).

less accessible to human understanding than the Trinity. He alleged, for example, that it was most difficult for a philosopher to be convinced that the entire quantity of Christ is entirely in every part of the wafer. But Bremis did not find this so incredible, since he could think of a natural-philosophical counterpart to this claim. According to the philosophers, the intelligence governing the orb of the moon was entirely in every part of it.[7] Lambert claimed in addition that faith in the Trinity was a consequent of natural law, which Bremis interpreted to mean that his opponent took the truths of the Trinity to follow from those of natural law. But this was a trivial point, Bremis argued, for the necessary follows from anything. Not even angelic spirits would know how to deduce the truths of the Trinity from natural considerations with being shown beatifically—i.e. by direct revelation—how to do so.[8]

In his own first *principium*, Hermann Lurtz defended for the sake of argument the proposition 'the Father is distinguished from the Son by a distinction greater than that between a man and an ass'. He was taking a direct aim at Bremis's thesis that "of all distinctions, the distinction between the divine persons is the least."[9] Lurtz proposed two arguments to show that an infinite distinction separates the Father from the Son: (1) the Father in divinity is distinguished from the Son by Himself (where 'Himself' refers to 'Father'), the Father is [something]

---

[7] "Sed quod magister meus dicit quod sit difficilius philosophum manuduci ad [[credendum]] *(interl* credendum) intelligendum quod [[totus Christus]] tota quantitas Christi sit in qualibet parte hostie tota quam quod deus sit trinus et unus, hoc non est verum cum reverentia, cum etiam philosophi puri crediderunt quod intelligentia orbis lune sit in qualibet eius parte tota, ita potuissent faciliter fuisse manuducti ad credendum de corpore glorificato vel sic qualificato sicud est corpus Christi" (ONB 4371, 70ᵛ).

[8] "Ad propositiones autem magistri mei ⟨Lamberti⟩ quas adiungit, quarum prima est quod fides trinitatis est consequens legis naturalis, si intelligit, ut videtur intelligendum esse, quod necessarie veritates de trinitate quas ex fide credimus sequuntur ex veritatibus legis naturalis, quis dubitat cum necessarium sequatur ad quodlibet? Sed nulli viatori sequitur evidenter; ymmo fortasse angelici spiritus licet videant misteria trinitatis, non tamen scirent ex naturalibus ea deducere nisi ⟨interl ex speciali gratia⟩ eis ostenderetur beatifice" (ÖNB 4371, 70ᵛ). Although rejected by Peter of Spain, the rule "The necessary follows from anything" was generally accepted in the fourteenth century. It was discussed by Pseudo-Scotus (see Boh, "Consequences," 309) and Ockham, *Summa logicae (OP,* I, 730–731), among others.

[9] ". . . contra ultimum corollarium secunde conclusionis quarti articuli mei quo dixi quod omnium distinctionum distinctio personarum divinarum est minima, posuit magister meus ⟨Lurtz⟩ ultimam suam propositionem, videlicet octavam, quod pater distinguitur a filio maiori distinctione quam homo et asinus distinguuntur" (ONB 4371, 8ʳ). Lurtz's original argument is on 76ʳ. Bremis's thesis has a Scotist ring; see Gelber, "Logic and the Trinity," 98.

infinite, therefore [the Father is distinguished from the Son by something infinite]; (2) the distinction of the Father from the Son is the divine essence, the latter is infinite, therefore [the distinction of the Father from the Son is infinite]. In contrast, a man and an ass are distinguished by a finite distinction only, since in themselves each is something finite.[10] And if this were the case, a greater *real* distinction would separate Father and Son than would separate two species.

By the fourth *principium*, Bremis had become irritated with Lurtz, who "rather impertinently impugns a contradiction in my statements" about these distinctions. In response, Bremis counterattacked and concluded: "I posit an infinitely small distinction, which is the real distinction of the divine persons, and yet another is smaller, such as the formal distinction between property and essence; nor is this a contradiction, or close to a contradiction."[11]

Discussions of logic and the Trinity at Vienna were not restricted to *principia* debates, however. Beyond his remarks on the subject against Bremis, Hermann Lurtz also wrote a *Tractatus de paralogismis consuetis fieri in divinis*. Although it is not certain whether Lurtz composed the treatise in Vienna, or after his move to Erfurt in 1395, there can be little question that the discussions in Vienna influenced his outlook.[12]

---

[10] "Probo propositionem sic: pater in divinis distinguitur a filio distinctione infinita sed ⟨homo⟩ distinguitur ab asino igitur etc. Argumentum probatur quia pater in divinis distinguitur a filio se ipso et ipse est infinitus, igitur. Similiter distinctio patris a filio est essentia divina et illa est infinita igitur, et quod homo et asinus distingwantur distinctione finita solum patet quia seipsis et quilibet est quid finitum igitur. Confirmatur: vel pater et filius in divinis distingwuntur finite vel infinite; ⟨si infinite⟩ habetur propositum; si finite ergo duo finita sunt in divinis, ergo aliquod finitum est in divinis, sed quicquid est in divinis est deus, quod est absurdum" (ÖNB 4371, 76r). The argument resembles Holcot's discussion of finite and infinite distinctions in bk. 1, qu. 5, where the distinction between man and ass is mentioned as well: "Preterea si tres persone distinguuntur, quero utrum finite an infinite? Si finite, igitur duo finita sunt in Deo; et ultra: igitur aliquid finitum est in Deo, et omne quod est in Deo est Deus; igitur aliquid finitum est Deus. Si infinite, ergo non magis differunt Deus et Diabolus quam Pater et Filius; nec homo et asinus magis differunt quam Pater et Filius" (*Quaestiones*, bk. 1, qu. 5, fol. e8va).

[11] "magister reverendus satis impertinenter impingit contradictionem in dictis meis . . . [[Ex quo]] sequitur quod pono unam distinctionem infinite modicam qualis est distinctio realis divinarum personarum; et tamen aliam esse minorem distinctionem ut est formalis distinctio inter proprietatem et essentiam, nec est contradictio nec prope contradictionem" (ÖNB 4371, 51r).

[12] See Meier, "Contribution," 456ff. For an outline of Lurtz's biography, see Kleineidam, *Universitas Studii Erffordensis*, pt. 1, 265–267. Alfonso Maierù is preparing an edition of the *Tractatus de paralogismis*, which exists in at least ten manuscripts. The Vienna manuscript (ÖNB 4948, 109r–126r), from which subsequent citations are drawn, is a fifteenth-century codex that originally belonged to the monastery in Rinkau and there-

A cursory glance at the work shows that Langenstein's *Tractatus de dici de omni* was evidently one of the principal sources upon which Hermann Lurtz drew for his own *Tractatus de paralogismis.* Thus the typology of distinctions that opens Lurtz's work is identical to that of Langenstein. Lurtz's definitions and preambles likewise follow those of the *Tractatus de dici de omni* very closely. Even if the content of the latter some day turns out to be derivative rather than original with Langenstein, it is almost certainly a prominent source of Lurtz's work. The fourth preamble, for example, deals specifically with the *dici de omni* and *dici de nullo* in terms that are reminiscent of Langenstein's own treatment of the subject.[13] The rules that Lurtz developed from the preambles have close affinities with the pronouncements of Wodeham, Langenstein, and Oyta: to deny the validity of syllogistic forms in divinity gives infidels the opportunity to blaspheme against the faith; such forms hold in every matter; every form that is not valid on account of its syllogistic form is not regulated by the *dici de omni,* and so on.[14] Lurtz's conclusions were as unambiguous as they were unoriginal: he, too, held that "it is not necessary to imagine new syncategorematic terms on account of syllogisms in divinity." Again he argued his case in terms identical to those of Wodeham, Oyta, and Langenstein. New syncategorematics would expose the faith to the derision of the infi-

---

fore is not directly connected with Lurtz's stay in Vienna. As it was copied on poorly sized paper, which behaved like a blotter, the reader is urged to check my transcriptions carefully against the forthcoming Maierù edition.

[13] Compare the *Tractatus de dici de omni* (Chapter 4, n. 56, above) with the fourth preamble: "Quartum preambulum est de dici de omni et de dici de nullo, pro quo dico primo quod non est ymaginabile quod sint plures propositionis distributiones vel(?) quod plures species distributionis possint esse quam due, scilicet una affirmativa, alia negativa" (ÖNB 4948, 110ʳa).

[14] "Prima regula: dicere quod forme syllogistice non valent vel ⟨non⟩ tenent in divinis est erroneum et minus in loyca sapientium; patet quia est dare infidelium occasionem blasphemandi fidem. Secunda regula: quod forme syllogistice tenent in omni materia. Tertia regula: quod forma syllogistica est sicut rectum quod est iudex sui et obliqui et nullo alio indiget ut sit evidens. Quarta regula: si aliqua forma non valet in divinis, tunc nec valet in aliis terminis. Quinta regula: Omnis forma que non valet ratione forme syllogistice non regulatur per dici de omni vel per dici de nullo. . . . Sexta: quod regula qua tenet omnis bonus syllogismus quoad omnes modos trium figurarum est dici de omni et dici de nullo. Septima: adhuc syllogismus sit regulatus per dici de omni non sufficit proponi de omni esse universalem sed cum hoc oportet quod per eam denotetur quod de quacumque verificatur subiectum quod de eodem verificatur predicatum. . . . Decima regula: secundum Aristotelem(!) ⟨= Ariminensem⟩ syllogismus expositorius non est evidens nisi reguletur vel possit regulari per dici de omni vel dici de nullo ut iste syllogismus 'Sortes est albus et Sortes est musicus, igitur musicum est album, etc.' qui autem non potest sic regulari est inutilis coniugatio et hoc de illo" (ÖNB 4948, 112ʳa).

dels. The rules that regulated the *dici de omni* and *dici de nullo* were quite capable of dealing with all syllogisms regardless of their subject matter, including the Trinity. Lurtz was very confident of his position, for it had the consensus of the age: "Almost all modern doctors agree in principle."[15]

Another protagonist in the Bremis debate was Johannes Meigen, the vice-chancellor of the university in the late 1380s. He is very probably the author of a short, eleven-folio incunabulum, *Tractatus distinctionum* ascribed to a "Johannes Meyger" and printed in Vienna in 1482.[16] His justification for writing the treatise lay in the fact that "distinctions are necessary to investigate the quiddities of things." He couched much of his discussion in philosophical terms, without explicitly tying it directly to theological problems. The treatise nevertheless is of passing interest to the relation between logic and the Trinity, for two reasons: first, because it dealt with the status of the formal distinction (particularly in contrast to the real distinction); second, because it eventually brought Trinitarian examples to bear on the discussion.[17] In his *principia*, Meigen's statements had a strong "essentialist" flavor, which is also apparent in this work. Like the Scotists, he accepted the formal distinction as a valid tool for dealing with extra-theological problems; he also used the language of "formalities,"[18] devoting most of the trea-

---

[15] ". . . tales circumlocutiones non sunt [⟨necessarie?⟩] ad solvendum paralogismos in divinis, ut etiam predelatum(!) ⟨= predillatum⟩ fuit corollarie contra Burley, nec oportet fingere nova sinkathegoremata propter syllogismos in divinis, ut declaratum fuit ibidem. Tales enim dictiones novarum sinkathegorematum et circumlocutionum exponunt fidem nostram derisioni infidelium. . . . Dico ergo quod per dici de omni et per dici de nullo regulantur omnes syllogismi et sic in omni modo et figura circa materiam trinitatis sicut [. . . ?] in aliis materiis. In principio concordant quasi omnes doctores moderni" (ÖNB 4948, 116ᵛa).

[16] *Inc*: "Quia verum quidtitates(!) volentes investigare. . . ." Expl.: ". . . distinctionum divinarum attributorum ac proprietatum personalium in summa ac simplicissima trinitate quae sit benedicta per infinita secula seculorum." The Österreichische Nationalbibliothek and the monastery at Göttweig appear to own the only surviving copies. The work is also extant in two manuscripts (ÖNB 4951, 154ʳ–163ʳ; ÖNB 4963, 119ʳ–127ʳ). For the few biographical details, see Chapter 2 above; and Aschbach, *Geschichte*, I, 410–411.

[17] "Verum est dicere quod trinitas non differt a tribus personis realiter, quia sic trinitas esset quaternitas, quod falsum est. Sed eius supposita differunt realiter et formaliter, quia pater differt realiter per paternitatem a filio; et filius per filiationem a patre, ergo illa que sunt distincta formaliter fatiunt differre realiter" (Meigen, *Tractatus distinctionum*, 4ᵛ).

[18] "Distinctio formalis est cuius distincta ponuntur in diversis diffinitionibus. Et illo modo distinguuntur subiectum et sua propria passio, anima et sue potentie, inferius et superius. . . . Dico quod formalitas est quedam ratio obiectalis reperta in re per intellectum quam non oportet semper intellectum movere" (ibid., 1ᵛ, 3ʳ).

tise to such issues. Two questions—"Whether those things that are formally distinguished are really distinguished?" (4ᵛ) and "Whether formality and reality in the same simple thing are distinguished?" (8ᵛ)—fill half the treatise. From these moderate Scotist sympathies,[19] we may infer that Meigen almost certainly did not hold that Trinitarian paralogisms undermined the formality of Aristotelian logic.

Bremis, Meigen, and Lurtz, all of whom were in direct personal contact with Langenstein and Oyta, generally agreed with the views of their teachers on the relevance of Aristotle's syllogistic to Trinitarian propositions. Indeed, if anything, their emphasis may have had a more pronounced Scotist bent than that of the older professors. As for Lambert of Gelderen, it seems unlikely that as a follower of Ripa he would have disagreed with his colleagues on this point.

·

The discussions of the professors and students of the late 1380s set the stage for the younger theologians of the following decade, a group composed predominantly of indigenously trained students. A cursory examination of their commentaries on the *Sentences* at first sight tends to confirm Albert Lang's judgment that, from a doctrinal point of view, Henry of Oyta was the most influential among the early Viennese theologians.[20]

The views of four students in particular will concern us here: Nicholas Prunczlein of Dinkelsbühl (d. 1433), Peter Czech of Pulkau (d. 1425), Arnold of Seehausen (d. after 1424), and Johann Berwart of Villingen (d. 1411). Dinkelsbühl first matriculated at Vienna in the spring of 1385, becoming a master of arts in 1389. He served as dean of the faculty of theology in the summer semester of 1410, and again in

---

[19] Meigen at one point cites the *formalizantes* as an alien group, which suggests that he did not belong to the followers of John of Ripa. On the *formalizantes*, see Combes, *La Théologie mystique de Gerson,* I, 58; II, 568ff; and idem, "Présentation de Jean de Ripa," passim.

[20] A. Lang, *Oyta,* 241. The influence of Henry of Oyta's questions on the *Sentences* extended beyond the Vienna circle. In the late fourteenth and early fifteenth centuries, several theologians from the Holy Roman Empire show the imprint of his views, including—among others—Marsilius of Inghen, Johannes Brammart, and Walter of Bamberg. See de Wulf, *Histoire de la philosophie médiévale,* 115; A. Lang, *Die theologische Prinzipienlehre,* 204; and Möhler, *Die Trinitätslehre des Marsilius von Inghen,* esp. 26ff. Although Möhler is unaware of the similarities, his description of Marsilius's views places the latter squarely in the Wodeham-Oyta tradition. See Ritter, "Studien zur Spätscholastik I," 141ff; and Xiberta, *De scriptoribus,* 414ff, 461ff.

1427.[21] Johann Berwart of Villingen matriculated in the fall of 1385 and became a master of arts with Dinkelsbühl. Although he did not serve the faculty of theology in an official capacity, he held posts as dean of the faculty of arts and as rector of the university on several occasions.[22] Peter of Pulkau matriculated in the fall of 1387, and became a master of arts in 1391, a *baccalarius sententiarius* in 1403, and a master of theology in 1409. He became dean of the faculty of theology in the winter semesters of 1410 and 1412.[23] Arnold of Seehausen first matriculated at Vienna in the spring of 1401 as "frater Arnoldus de Sehawsen." At the time, he was already a Carmelite and an advanced student, for he moved through the ranks rapidly, becoming a master of theology in 1405. He served as dean of the faculty of theology in the summer semester of 1408.[24] All four men were active in university affairs, especially the first three. After Seehausen's departure for Prague and Villingen's murder in 1411 (while carrying the university *rotulus* back from Rome),[25] Dinkelsbühl and Pulkau eventually became dominant figures in Viennese theology and academic life. Their commentaries on the *Sentences* share several similarities, if not identities. In the question of the prologue to book I of the *Sentences*, ("Whether theology is a science?"), their texts are so closely related that a composite edition would be the most efficient and informative way to handle their relationship. Likewise large tracts of other questions deal with the same material, organized in almost identical fashion, with lengthy segments of text taken verbatim from Oyta.

One such question is familiar: "Whether the rules of the philosophers and Aristotle about syllogisms generally suffice for Catholics to

[21] He also served as dean of the faculty of arts in the winter semester of 1392 and the spring of 1397, and as rector of the university in 1405 (*MUW*, I, 18; *AFA*, I, 35; *ATF*, I, xxv–xxvi). For additional biographical details, see Madre, *Nikolaus von Dinkelsbühl*, 7–43.

[22] Johann Berwart of Villingen served as dean of the faculty of arts in the summer semester of 1393, the winter semester of 1401, and the summer semester of 1401; he became rector of the university in the winter semester of 1401 and in the summer semester of 1403 (*MUW*, I, 18; *AFA*, I, xx, xxii, 35).

[23] He served as dean of the faculty of arts in the summer semester of 1396, as well as in the winter semesters of 1400 and 1405, and as rector of the university in 1407 and 1411. See *MUW*, I, 24; and Girgensohn, *Peter von Pulkau*, 9ff.

[24] *MUW*, I, 60; *AFA*, I, 499; *AFT*, I, xxv. Arnold's name appears variously in the secondary literature as Seehusen, Seehausen, and Sehnsen. See Xiberta, *De scriptoribus*, 471–476 (from numerous citations of Aquinas and Bonaventure in books III and IV of Arnold's commentary on the *Sentences*, Xiberta conjectures that he was a realist); and Lickteig, *The German Carmelites*, 188–191.

[25] Lickteig, *The German Carmelites*, 191; Aschbach, *Geschichte*, I, 251, n. 4.

syllogize in divinity?"[26] On this issue, Johann Auer was the first to point out the intellectual filiation between Oyta and later members of the faculty of theology at Vienna. He postulated a three-generational connection: Nicholas of Dinkelsbühl drew upon Oyta's question, but modified it by adding a *dubium* that undermined the original conclusion; then, in 1422, a Johannes Wuel de Pruck in turn reproduced Dinkelsbühl's version, to which he contributed a few editorial changes of his own.[27]

In fact, the picture is considerably more complex. Nicholas of Dinkelsbühl wrote two commentaries on the *Sentences*. The first, known as the *Quaestiones communes*, dates to the last years of the fourteenth century. It survives in an autograph manuscript with significant marginal additions.[28] During the course of his teaching, however, Dinkelsbühl again commented on the *Sentences* and modified his earlier text. These *Quaestiones magistrales*, as they have come to be called, date from the years 1408–1412 and contain a question on the rules of syllogizing that is not found in his *Quaestiones communes*. He evidently deemed the issue important enough to warrant inclusion as a separate question in his new lectures.[29] In the years between these two versions, three other *baccalarii sententiarii*—Peter of Pulkau, Arnold of Seehausen, and Johann Berwart of Villingen—read the *Sentences*. All three had debated their *principia* to the *Sentences* against each other ca. 1402,[30] and all three included in their commentaries questions about the place of Aristotle's syllogistic in Trinitarian theology. Each of these questions included at least part of the *dubium* that Auer had ascribed to Dinkelsbühl. Clearly the *dubium* antedates the latter's *Quaestiones magistrales* by several years, and is therefore not original with Dinkelsbühl. What is more, the form of the text that Auer edited and attributed to Johannes Wuel de Pruck is identical to the question found in the commentary on the *Sentences* by Arnold of Seehausen, who must therefore be considered its rightful author.[31] Nicholas of Dinkelsbühl's *Quaestiones magis-*

---

[26] Auer, "Die aristotelische Logik," 475.

[27] Ibid., 457–459.

[28] Vienna, Schottenstift 269 (274); see Madre, *Dinkelsbühl*, 72ff.

[29] According to Madre (*Dinkelsbühl*, 79ff) the *Quaestiones magistrales* also exist in two versions: *reportatio* A, whose exemplar is ÖNB 4820; and *reportatio* B in Vienna, Schottenstift 254 (230).

[30] The fourth participant in the debate was Johannes Langheim, O. Cist.; see Uiblein, "Lebensgeschichte," 106.

[31] See Munich, Bayerische Staatsbibliothek, Clm 7456A, 147^v–155^v. The explanation of this confusion is simple. In ÖNB 5067, the colophon at the end of book 1 reads: "finitus per Johannem wul de prukk" and, in another hand, ". . . legendo Anno etc.

trales are related to the preceding texts in a revealing way. With a few exceptions, the new version of his commentary parallels that of his good friend Peter of Pulkau, from whom he seems to have drawn much of his text. The intellectual relationship between the two men was evidently a symbiotic one. For several other questions in book I, on the other hand, Peter of Pulkau appears to have drawn on the earlier *Quaestiones communes* of Dinkelsbühl.[32]

All four students broached the issue of formality in their questions on the adequacy of the Aristotelian syllogistic to solve Trinitarian paralogisms. Seehausen and Villingen did so implicitly by proposing a counterexample to the formality of Aristotle's syllogistic in their arguments *contra*. Pulkau and Dinkelsbühl did so explicitly, by prefacing the counterexample with a positive claim in the arguments *pro*, to the effect that syllogisms regulated by the Aristotelian rules of syllogizing "are commonly formal, and therefore syllogisms similar in form hold in any subject matter whatever."[33]

From the outset, the four theology students interacted with the views of Henry of Oyta and Henry of Langenstein. Soon after opening their questions along the lines of Oyta, they introduced the views of "some venerable modern doctor" (*quidam venerabilis doctor modernus*) on the regulation of the three figures of the syllogism by the *dici de omni* and *dici de nullo*, and hence on the modes of distribution. A rapid comparison shows that the definitions are taken verbatim from Langen-

---

vicesimo secundo" (280ʳ). See Unterkircher, ed., *Katalog der datierten Handschriften in Österreich*, IV, pt. 1, 204, and pt. 2, fig. 528. Although Auer interpreted this note as the author's own remark, he himself pointed out that the matriculation date for Johannes Wuel de Pruck (14 April 1420; *MUW*, I, 126) is late for someone who, as Auer alleged, completed his commentary on the *Sentences* in 1422. This discrepancy led Auer to postulate that Pruck was an ordained priest at the time of his matriculation; see Auer, "Die aristotelische Logik," 458, 496. A more plausible suggestion, advanced by the editor of the above *Katalog*, is that Pruck was merely a scribe.

[32] The case is especially clear for the traditional question on the prologue to book I, "Whether theology is a science?" If ÖNB 4668 is indeed Pulkau's autograph, as is traditionally claimed, he seems to have integrated into his own running text materials that appear only as marginal additions and on small scraps of paper in Dinkelsbühl's autograph in Schottenstift 269 (274). Although Dinkelsbühl's marginalia cannot be dated with certainty, the priority of his commentary over Pulkau's by almost a decade strongly suggests that Pulkau used Dinkelsbühl, and not vice versa. In ÖNB 4820, on the other hand, Nicholas of Dinkelsbühl included in the body of his text fragments that appear only as marginalia in ÖNB 4668.

[33] ÖNB 4668, 133ᵛ; ÖNB 4820, 55ʳ. From the sentences that follow, it is clear that the words "commonly formal" function as a single expression, which suggests that other kinds of formality were discussed in these circles; for example, see Maierù, *Terminologia logica della tarda scolastica*, 43.

stein's *Tractatus de dici de omni*, only to be criticized as false.[34] After dismissing the latter's account of distribution, the four students systematically reproduced with minor changes the arguments that Oyta had advanced in his question on the rules of syllogizing. In one or two cases, they suggested counterarguments to Oyta's position after presenting it. For example, they argued that under complete distribution (according to Oyta's third mode), propositions of the type 'every angel is an angel' would be false, since the last element in the lengthy conjunction that constitutes this distribution ('all things that are an angel are an angel') is false. Secondly, assuming that the first criticism is correct, then two contradictories would be simultaneously false. Thus 'every angel is an angel' is false, as demonstrated above; but its contradictory would also be false under the disjunctive distribution of the subject required in such cases (since the disjunction 'some angel, or some thing that is an angel, or some things that are an angel, is not or are not an angel' is false). The argument is later answered by claiming that the distribution of the universal affirmative should be understood disjunctively, rather than conjunctively, to prevent the falsity of 'every angel is an angel', and that the entire disjunct should be distributed.[35] Other objections surfaced in a similar vein.

After Oyta's question ended, however, they went on to raise, in a lengthy *dubium*, a much more serious question about one of Oyta's central conclusions.[36] One portion of this addendum is particularly noteworthy. Oyta's fifth conclusion (the second in the version of his students) had argued that Aristotle's syllogistic rules were sufficient for the Christian to syllogize in divinity.[37] Against this thesis, the four students raised a common objection. If the conclusion were true, then the following third-figure syllogism (*in disamis*) should hold: 'the Father in divinity generates, every Father in divinity is the divine essence, therefore the divine essence generates'. Even with the subject of the minor premise completely distributed according to the strong interpretation of the *dici de omni* (Oyta's third mode),[38] however, it was not possible to identify the defect. Yet each of the premises was true, and the conclusion was false and heretical.[39] Nor would Platonists concede the following syllogism of the same form: 'Sortes generates; every Sortes, or thing that is Sortes, or things that are Sortes, is or are the

---

[34] Auer, "Die aristotelische Logik," 476–477, lines 20–62.
[35] Ibid., 486, lines 427–454; 491, lines 654–662.
[36] Ibid., 490ff, line 616ff.
[37] See Chapter 4 above; and Auer, "Die aristotelische Logik," 482ff, line 264ff.
[38] See Chapter 4 above.
[39] Auer, "Die aristotelische Logik," 492, lines 703–709.

common man; therefore the common man generates'.[40] In addition, following Gregory of Rimini, the four students rejected the claim that a difference in predication (formal in the major premise, identical in the minor) caused the paralogism.[41] In other words, contrary to Oyta's claim, this particular inference failed both for the Christian theologian and the Platonic realist.

At this point, Dinkelsbühl, Pulkau, Villingen, and Seehausen all added a remarkable comment:

> For this and similar reasons, it appeared to our master that the responsive conclusion [of Oyta] was false, as he has written and also lectured in school, although he wrote the opposite in a *Tractatus de dici de omni* before this became clear to him. Consequently he claimed that the rules of Aristotle, along with scripture and faith, do not suffice to distinguish paralogisms from syllogisms in divinity.[42]

The passage is significant for at least two reasons. First of all, it conclusively resolves the dispute about the authorship of the *Tractatus de dici de omni* in favor of Langenstein. In the introduction to his edition of the question by Oyta and "Johannes Wuel de Pruck," Johann Auer had identified this unnamed master with Nicholas of Dinkelsbühl.[43] But this attribution cannot hold, for two independent reasons. In one version of Dinkelsbühl's *Quaestiones magistrales*, the scribe has written "Hassya" in the margin. Arnold of Seehausen's commentary on the *Sentences* likewise confirms this attribution with another marginal note, "M. h. de h."[44] Over the years, the *Tractatus de dici de omni* has also been attributed to Nicole Oresme.[45] But the preceding passage occurs in the writings of at least three students who had known Langenstein in Vienna and who in all likelihood had studied under him as well. The "our master" who wrote the *Tractatus de dici de omni* can be no one but Henry of Langenstein.

But the passage is even more important because a witness to the genesis of a contemporary idea is a rarity in the academic literature of the Middle Ages. In a formal theological treatise in particular, it is unusual to find departures from the standard atemporal references to authorities, which are cited *pro* or *contra* a given position. These refer-

---

[40] To these examples, Arnold of Seehausen adds yet another *in bocardo* (the major premise and the conclusion are negative); ibid., lines 713–717.

[41] Ibid., lines 717–722; and Chapter 3 above.

[42] Ibid., lines 723–729.

[43] Ibid., 459, 470–471.

[44] ÖNB 4820, 59ʳ; Munich, Bayerische Staatsbibliothek, Clm 7456A, 154ʳ.

[45] See Chapter 4, n. 37, above.

ences to Langenstein's change of mind in formal commentaries suggest that his about-face made a lasting impression on his students, and with good reason.

The reversal was indeed momentous. In his *Lectures on Genesis* Langenstein had argued that although the writings of the Philosopher were not completely free from error, their presence on the curriculum of the universities was nevertheless a "sign of divine favor." After being cleansed of their mistakes, they were a valuable tool not only for the acquisition of knowledge but also for apologetic purposes, as a means of undermining the "errors or doubts of the pagan philosophers."[46] Langenstein's original position in the *Tractatus de dici de omni* had placed no restrictions on the validity of Aristotelian logic, which was both universal in scope and formal in character. This attitude was consistent with Langenstein's general attitude toward Peripatetic philosophy, and indeed was commonplace. The overwhelming majority of fourteenth-century theologians agreed. The small minority that flirted with the notion that Aristotle's syllogistic was not formal included Holcot and Strelley. But even they cannot be counted unambiguously as gainsayers of formality, for Holcot eventually softened his position, and Strelley seems to have expressed his position as a kind of *sophisma*.[47] Now Langenstein was stating explicitly that Aristotelian logic was *not* universally satisfactory. Langenstein's shift was nothing less than an about-face on a fundamental controversial issue of medieval philosophy and theology.

Judging from his students' reports, Langenstein defended his change of mind by answering a standard objection, which Adam Wodeham had raised, Henry of Oyta had repeated, and Langenstein knew by heart: in arguing with infidels, the rejection of Aristotelian logic would expose the Christians to ridicule.[48] Langenstein responded to this charge by denying that Aristotle had the final word in logic. The authority of Plato could, he claimed, be used to support an alternative to Aristotle.[49] What were the grounds for resorting to this solution?

Since the mysteries of the Most Blessed Trinity, of the Incarnation of the Son and many other beliefs of our faith surpass purely natural human

---

[46] Steneck, *Science and Creation in the Middle Ages*, 38.

[47] See Chapter 3 above.

[48] See Wodeham-Oyta, *Abbreviatio*, 81rb; Maierù, "Logica aristotelica," 504, lines 312–317.

[49] The appeal to Plato to understand the Trinity has a long history. See, for example, Augustine, *The City of God*, bk. x, chaps. 23–24; Abelard, *Theologia Christiana*, bk. I, chap. 68ff (*OT*, II, 100ff); Abelard's criticism of Platonic analogies to the Trinity in his *Dialectica*, ed. L. M. de Rijk, 558–559; and Henle, *Saint Thomas and Platonism*, 407.

investigation, why is it disturbing (*inconveniens*) that one philosopher re-
lying on natural inquiry did not discover rules sufficient for us with respect to everything according to the tradition of our faith?[50]

In short, Aristotle did not have all of the relevant data at his disposal
when he established his logical rules. (This criticism takes seriously the
inductive basis of Aristotle's procedure in the *Prior Analytics*. If he had
known about other true sentences like the Trinitarian ones, he would
have been forced to come up with other rules.) Under these circumstances, Langenstein argued, we would place the faith in even greater
subjection to the force of natural inquiry, threaten it even more with
derision "if we were to subject the faith in all things to the claims of
those who even have held in some points the opposite of the articles
[of faith]," such as the eternity of the world, for example. The incon-
sistencies between Christian theology and Aristotle's position in natural philosophy demanded that Christians distance themselves from
Aristotle, and also cast doubts on the utility of the latter's logic for
dealing with specifically Christian problems. In no field was the Philosopher's word to be considered final—not even in logic. And, the
students added, presumably still quoting Langenstein: "Did not Isaiah
foretell this in saying, 'Unless you believe you shall not understand?' "[51]

An additional sign of weakness in Aristotle's syllogistic was its failure to solve *insolubilia*, those logical or semantic puzzles that medieval
logicians used to illustrate their analytical methods, and on which they
sharpened their logical skills.[52] Langenstein was thinking of the var-

[50] Auer, "Die aristotelische Logik," 492, lines 731–736. Compare Langenstein's remarks with those of Francis of Mayronnes, who some seventy years earlier had introduced mixed and modal propositions to obviate the problems of contradiction in Trinitarian syllogisms: "Sed obiceres, quod Aristoteles et alii philosophi non posuerunt istam
logycam de mixtionibus istis et ideo videntur ⟨esse⟩ fictiones. Dico, quod Aristoteles
circa divina non vidit ista genera propositionum, quas sancti docent formari in divinis,
et ideo non mirum ⟨si non⟩ adinvenit illas mixtiones" (Roth, *Franz von Mayronis*, 342;
the emendations indicate variants in a manuscript of the text bound with Munich, Universitätsbibliothek, Incun. 1166). On Mayronnes, see Gelber, "Logic and the Trinity,"
143ff. Langenstein knew parts of Francis of Mayronnes's work, for he criticized the
aspersions the latter had cast upon St. Bernard of Clairvaux in the matter of the Immaculate Conception (Roth, *Franz von Mayronis*, 221ff). He also cited Mayronnes at least
once in his commentary on the *Sentences* (Damerau, ed., *Sentenzenkommentar*, bk. II [vol.
15], 31).

[51] Auer, "Die aristotelische Logik," 492–493, lines 736–741, reading "articulorum" for
"Aristotelicorum" at line 738. For "non intelligetis," the Vulgate reads "non permanebitis" (Isaiah 7:9), i.e. "you shall not endure." The source of this alternative translation
is probably Augustine; see Chapter 7, n. 107, below.

[52] Kretzmann, "Syncategoremata, Sophismata, Exponibilia," 211ff.

iants on the "liar's paradox" in such works as the *Rules for Solving Sophismata* by William Heytesbury.[53] If Aristotle's syllogistic could not handle *insolubilia*, why should it be so surprising that it could not shed light on the highest and most difficult theological statements?[54]

As for the failure of the argument in *disamis*, the specific counterexample that reportedly had triggered Langenstein's outburst, the students went on to point out that faith could account for the defect. The paralogism was caused by the formal distinction between the divine essence and each person of the Trinity, "which distinction Aristotle probably would have denied, just as he argued against the opinion of Plato, which is relevant to the matter at hand."[55] Aristotle's putative rejection of the formal distinction proved that his logic was not suited to its theological task. Wodeham and Oyta had drawn comfort from their argument that Aristotle's logic (including his rule about the *dici de omni*) was general enough to take Plato's ontology into account.[56] It was precisely this contention that Langenstein rejected.

Dinkelsbühl, Pulkau, and Seehausen also dealt with an objection to Langenstein's position: namely, that if his position were correct, it would be possible to find counterexamples in some of the four moods of the first figure as well. (Villingen concluded his text after the first part of the objection.)[57] But, they argued, an invalid argument in moods of the second or third figure (e.g. *bocardo* or *disamis*) did not necessarily imply a lack of validity in the moods of the first figure to which they could be reduced (*barbara* and *darii*, respectively).[58] When this happened, however, one of the premises usually turned out to be false:

> From these claims of our master, it appears that the rules of Aristotle and other philosophers do not suffice to solve paralogisms in divinity, since according to the complete distribution by which some want to solve pa-

[53] The *Loyca Hesbri* [Logic of Heytesbury] figures among the works scheduled to be read at Vienna in the winter semester of 1390 (*AFA*, I, 54, lines 10–11), by which Heytesbury's *Regulae solvendi sophismata* were surely meant; see Wilson, *William Heytesbury*. Spade (*The Mediaeval Liar*, 78–79) lists *Quaestiones et propositiones de insolubilibus* of 1393, by Ludolf Meistermann, in ÖNB 5252. Meistermann (or Mestermann) was in Vienna between 1385 and 1387; see *AFA*, I, 4–14, passim.

[54] Auer, "Die aristotelische Logik," 492–493, lines 741–745.

[55] Ibid., 493, lines 746–755. As the sympathetic attitude toward Plato suggests, this is probably one of Langenstein's arguments, not that of his students.

[56] Maierù, "Logique et théologie trinitaire dans le moyen âge tardif," 191–192. The argument parallels those of Burleigh and Ralph Pigaz, whom Wodeham had mentioned; see Gelber, "Logic and the Trinity," 262.

[57] Villingen's question (Klosterneuburg 41, 57ʳ) ends at line 779 of the Auer edition.

[58] Auer, "Die aristotelische Logik," 492–493, line 764ff.

ralogisms in divinity (as has been discussed earlier), one or both of the
premises are frequently and almost always false when syllogizing in the
first figure, as is clear to anyone who looks into the matter.[59]

Dinkelsbühl and Seehausen raised an additional objection. Even if one
were to concede the threefold distribution suggested by Oyta, syllogisms of the third figure would not be solved and "therefore, according to this distribution, syllogistic arguments in divinity would be of
almost no use or force." Yet, perhaps one could find a way out, by
considering that Aristotle often formulated his premises as 'A belongs
to all of that to which B belongs', thus suggesting that he allowed circumlocutions. And if one were to add circumlocutions such as 'the
being that' or 'the thing that' to the middle and extremes, syllogisms
of this sort would be universally valid. Even so, the students conceded,
this did not imply that, with theological terms such as 'Father', 'essence', and 'Son', one could construct valid syllogisms without adding
further qualifications beyond the standard syncategorematic terms.[60]

The three remaining masters concluded their text with an attempt
to save Oyta's second conclusion from Langenstein's criticisms. The
suggestion was evidently advanced first by Peter of Pulkau: his account
is in the first person. Nicholas of Dinkelsbühl and Arnold of Seehausen
both reported the argument in the third person.[61] The burden of this
section was to argue that the inference in *disamis* on which Langenstein
had based his refutation ('the Father in divinity generates, every Father
in divinity is the divine essence, therefore the divine essence generates')
was not a proper argument "in that the major extreme is not concluded
of the minor in the conclusion." The case rested on a distinction between adjectival and substantive kinds of predication, and on a conversion of predicates to make the distinction explicit. The argument thus
concluded that the predicate in the major premise was actually 'the
Father generating', whereas the predicate in the conclusion was 'the
essence generating'. Since the predicate was not the same in the major
and the conclusion, the inference was not a proper syllogism in *disamis*.

It is difficult to judge with certainty how much stock the students
placed in this solution. The concluding arguments betray a palpable
hesitation on their part. After formulating Langenstein's objections,
they hinted that circumlocutions might provide a way out, yet they

[59] Ibid., 494, lines 785–790.
[60] Ibid., lines 791–806.
[61] Pulkau reads *suppono* (ÖNB 4668, 141ᵛ), where Dinkelsbühl and Seehausen read
supponitur (ÖNB 4820, 60ʳ) and *supponit* (Auer, "Die aristotelische Logik," 495, n. 123),
respectively. Arnold reports the argument as the view of *quidam de magistris meis*, a reference to one of his colleagues.

simultaneously conceded that, in theology, additional syncategore-matics might be required—the very reason why Langenstein had re-jected his original view. And they remarked that their colleague Pul-kau "tried" to save Oyta's conclusion, without stating explicitly that he had done so. All of this wavering and wringing of hands suggests that the students were not sure of their own views. But there can be no doubt that they were struck by Langenstein's change of mind, which forced them to reexamine the issue with care and to try to re-solve the tensions between the views of Langenstein and Oyta.

•

So far the evidence for Langenstein's arguments has been limited to secondhand reports. But the substance of these views is corroborated by two texts—a commentary and a lecture. The first is Langenstein's commentary on the *Sentences,* in which he touched on the relations between logic and the data of revelation, and on the value of Platonic notions. The work raises several problems of chronology, which re-quire attention before proceeding further. Notwithstanding a venera-ble tradition to the contrary, only one version of Langenstein's com-mentary appears to have survived. A so-called *Lectura Eberbacensis,* allegedly written in Eberbach after Langenstein composed an early commentary in Paris, is in fact the work of his host James of Eltville, the abbot of the Cistercian monastery at Eberbach. Langenstein may indeed have *read* the work at Eberbach, but he did not write it.[62]

The remaining version (misleadingly called *Lectura Parisiensis* in the secondary literature) is not without its share of problems. Only two manuscripts have been located thus far.[63] Both the date of the work and its place of composition remain contested issues. Albert Lang has

---

[62] About the tradition of Langenstein's two commentaries, see Appendix below.

[63] They are ÖNB 4319; and Alençon, Bibliothèque de la ville, codex 144. The most complete of the two copies is Alençon 144, which probably dates to the early fifteenth century, for the scribe knew that Langenstein had died: "Expliciunt questiones quarti sententiarum et per consequens totius lecture magistri henrici de hassia, doctoris subtilis et ingeniosi valde cuius anima et omnium fidelium defunctorum requiescant in pace . . ." (Alençon 144, 140ᵛa). The manuscript presents at least two disturbing peculiarities. The first is a marginal annotation: "Responsio Gregorii," which occurs in the text facing the author's first-person remark "Ad primam nego consequentiam . . ." (24ᵛa). The sec-ond is the *explicit* of book II, which contains a puzzling date: "Expliciunt questiones secundi libri sententiarum per eundem anno domini 1334" (113ᵛa). The copy is not com-plete: some arguments stop abruptly in mid-sentence (e.g. 11ᵛa and the scribal note on 48ᵛa: "Nota quod non plus inveni in exemplari et ergo non plus scribo in isto articulo . . ."). The hand is very similar to that of Johann of Retz, who also copied Henry of Oyta's commentary on the *Sentences*; for a sample, see Unterkircher, ed., *Katalog,* II, pt. 2, fig. 26, and Appendix below.

suggested that it belongs to the Vienna years. Konrad Heilig and Justin Lang, on the contrary, set it in Paris—the former between 1373 and 1375, the latter between 1375 and 1381. Justin Lang concedes that it reads like a mature work, and may have been read in Vienna at a later date. Rudolf Damerau thinks it was read in Vienna after parts of the commentary had been written in Paris.[64] Several clues point to a work from Langenstein's Viennese period. Both copies are late. Michael Suchenschatz, who copied ÖNB 4319 in Vienna some fourteen years after Langenstein's death, went to much trouble to obtain an original, presumably from Langenstein's own notes.[65] The commentary refers on two occasions to Henry of Oyta's *Rapularium*, a lost notebook known to contain records of disputations from Oyta's Viennese years.[66] Both the fact of the reference and its character—a passing allusion to a recent volume by his colleague—make little sense in the Parisian context. Although inconclusive in isolation, the added qualifier in a reference to the "Cancellarius Parisiensis," which would have been unnecessary in Paris, further reinforces the presumption that the commentary had a Viennese audience.[67]

To these internal clues must be added an interesting external one: Hermann Lurtz clearly did not know about Henry of Langenstein's change of mind when he wrote the *Tractatus de paralogismis*. At that time, Lurtz thought that his own position represented the consensus of almost all doctors. Although Lurtz did not name all of his sources, he showed no reticence about citing his opponents by name, and his *principia* confirm that he did not have a shy personality.[68] Langenstein's arguments against Aristotle would have constituted an important objection to the view that Lurtz was defending. Lurtz could not have avoided confronting it if he had known that Langenstein had publicly disavowed the position of the *Tractatus de dici de omni*. As will become clear, the surviving version of Langenstein's commentary on the *Sen-*

---

[64] A. Lang, *Die Wege der Glaubensbegründung*, 213, n. 3; Heilig, "Kritische Studien zum Schrifttum," 164; J. Lang, *Christologie*, 65; Damerau, ed., *Sentenzenkommentar*, bk. II (vol. 15), xxix.

[65] The colophon of ÖNB 4319, whose text is even less complete than that of Alençon 144, suggests that the work was not readily available: "Expliciunt questiones . . . Henrici de Hassia . . . cum difficultate et magno labore recollecte et conscripte . . ." (ÖNB 4319, 237ᵛ). J. Lang provides a list of the questions and compares the two manuscripts in his *Christologie*, 59–67.

[66] A. Lang, *Oyta*, 111–112.

[67] Damerau, ed., *Sentenzenkommentar*, bk. II (vol. 15), 38, line 2.

[68] The treatise mentions the names of at least twenty-five people, mostly contemporaries; see Meier, "Contribution," 460–468. See Chapter 2 above for Lurtz's interaction with Johannes Bremis.

tences shows that he was beginning to distance himself from his earlier treatise. Since Lurtz did not become a *baccalarius formatus* until 1390, it is most unlikely that his treatise on Trinitarian paralogisms predates that year. Hence Langenstein's change of mind and his commentary presumably postdate 1390.

In the first question of this commentary, devoted to the prologue to book I ("Whether the truths of human science are repugnant to the conclusions of Christian theology?"),[69] Langenstein examined the relation between natural and revealed knowledge. Following a discussion of truth that confirms his familiarity with, but distaste for, the language of the *complexe significabile*,[70] in his second article he focused on the reasons why contradictions might appear between theological truths and the tenets of natural knowledge.

Langenstein began with the traditional premise that no two true propositions were contradictory or contrary. When apparent conflicts between two truths did arise, it was on account of errors committed by people inexperienced in science.[71] Another problem that led to the appearance of conflict between two truths was that certain propositions pertaining to natural knowledge had been given a status that did not legitimately belong to them. Both the eternity of the world and the dictum that nothing comes from nothing were conclusions not of natural philosophy, but rather of some tradition of philosophical opinion.[72] Langenstein went on to criticize Aquinas and Giles of Rome for holding that Aristotle was in fact doing natural philosophy when he claimed to have proven the eternity of the world.[73]

---

[69] "Utrum veritates scientie humane repugnent conclusionibus christiane theologie" (Alençon 144, 9ʳa).

[70] Langenstein was of the opinion that it is more correct to consider the complex *significata* of the proposition as indistinct from the *significata* of the terms, which he preferred to call "adequate significata." (This expression appears in Burleigh, as well as in later figures such as André de Neufchâteau; see Nuchelmans, *Theories of the Proposition*, 221, 231, 256.) This view is consistent with his position in the *Tractatus de dici de omni*; see Chapter 4 above.

[71] "Secundo modo vero recipiendo vel considerando / scientiam sic contingit ipsos imperitos in scientiis errare et si illi ex defectu ipsorum et errore contradicant veritati nostre secte, ex hoc tamen non est dicendum scientiam scientie contrariari nisi reciperetur scientie valde inepte pro quocumque ab aliquo in tali scientia vel arte, quod facere non expedit nec est necesse" (Alençon 144, 9ᵛb–10ʳa).

[72] "Primo infertur ex istis quod iste conclusiones 'mundus fuit ab eterno, idem in numero non potest reverti, ex nichilo nichil fit' non sunt conclusiones naturalis philosophie sed cuiusdam traditionis vel opinionis philosophice, puta Aristotelis vel peripatheticorum" (Alençon 144, 10ʳa).

[73] "Etiam apparet quod tam Egidius quam Sanctus Doctor minus bene glosant Aristotelem in rationibus quibus nititur probare eternitatem mundi, dicentes quod arguat ibi

Of particular interest for our purposes is the fact that Langenstein's discussion turned quickly from natural philosophy to methods of proof and the status of logic:

> I infer that if the philosophers and Aristotle assert that syllogistic forms (i.e. *barbara* etc.) do not suffer, or cannot suffer, counterinstances in any matter, they have done more than the deduction of natural reason or investigation permitted or demanded of the intelligence, if they believed that distribution within a term is necessarily equivalent in all things to the distribution outside the term, and thus that syllogisms of this sort are universally valid.[74]

The language here recalls Oyta's three modes of universalizing propositions. Unlike Oyta, however, Langenstein evidently doubted that Aristotle understood these three modes as distinct. He thus raised doubts about the formality and universality of Aristotelian logic. But he did not explicitly deny either point, for his thesis was a conditional proposition. He did claim, however, that from the vantage point of natural reason, Aristotle's assertions had gone too far: the latter had pushed claims about logic beyond their proper boundaries. Langenstein obviously had in mind a specific criticism of Aristotle's views on logic, but he also worried more generally about Aristotle's excessive confidence in natural reason:

> Aristotle did not exercise the care that he could and should have in asserting this conclusion 'the world was from eternity', 'motion will be eternal', and other falsehoods of this sort, since if he had discussed them with utmost care, he never would have thought that they were knowable by nat-

---

secundum viam naturalis philosophie; patet quia alias naturalis philosophia nostre veritati contradiceret, quod est falsum" (Alençon 144, 10^{r}a). These views (and nearly identical phrasings) also appear in Johann Brammart's commentary on the *Sentences*, bk.. 1. See Xiberta, *De scriptoribus*, 427.

[74] "2° infero quod si philosophi et Aristoteles formas syllogisticas, scilicet barbara etc., in nullis rebus simpliciter instantias pati vel posse pati asserunt {plus}, plus fecerunt quam deductio naturalis rationis seu investigationis iussit vel petebat intelligentie, si crediderunt distributionem in termino necessario equivalere in omnibus distributioni extra terminum, et sic syllogismos huiusmodi valere universaliter" (Alençon 144, 11^{r}b). The first part of this excerpt is identical to a passage in the commentary on the *Sentences* by a Carmelite named Walter: see A. Lang, *Die Entfaltung*, 51–52, n. 80, quoting Bamberg, Staatsbibliothek, Cod. theol. 77, fol. 35^{v}b; also idem, *Die Wege der Glaubensbegründung*, 187. According to Xiberta (*De scriptoribus*, 463), contrary to a seventeenth-century cataloguing note in the manuscript, the author is Walter of Bamberg—not Walter Disse, a near-contemporary Carmelite who studied theology in Cambridge. For definitions of distribution "below" and "outside" a term, see Chapter 4 above.

ural investigation, but [that they were] matters of opinion or that the intellect should adopt an indifferent stance with respect to them.[75]

The interest of these statements lies in their forthright relativization of Aristotle. The Philosopher had overstated his case by giving scientific status to propositions that were only matters of opinion. Such an evaluation of Aristotle's natural-philosophical propositions was commonplace in the fourteenth century. With respect to his logic, however, Langenstein's position was much more unusual.

Inevitably Langenstein also touched upon the relation between apologetics and the indemonstrability of the Trinity. In an earlier corollary, he had taken the view that "all arguments against the teachings of our faith are flawed and thus are humanly answerable." But his thesis faced a number of objections. One argument claimed that if the corollary were true, then the Trinity would be demonstrable. For if such arguments against the faith were answerable and solvable, the conclusion against which they were directed would thereby be shown to be possible. But Langenstein disagreed: to discredit arguments against a conclusion did not prove that the latter was possible, as counterexamples could easily show.[76] As he noted one folio later: "It is easier to untie than to tie, and to tear down than to build up."[77]

[75] ". . . Ex quo ulterius sequitur 4º quod Aristoteles not fecit diligentiam quam potuit facere et debebat asserendo isti conclusioni: mundus fuit ab eterno, motus erit eternus, et huiusmodi falsis, quia si diligentem discussionem ultimate circa eas habuisset, numquam putasset eas debere sciri naturali investigatione, sed opinari vel indifferenter se debere habere intellectum respectu illorum" (Alençon 144, 11ᵛa).

[76] "Nunc consequenter videndum est de alio argumento quod fiebat in lectione precedenti, contra secundum corollarium conclusionis prime istius questionis, in quo corollario dicebatur quod omnia argumenta contra nostre fidei doctrinam sunt peccantia et sic possunt habere responsiones ab homine. Et fuit primo argutum sic: tunc posset trinitas in divinis demonstrari, quia quando solvitur sufficienter aliqua ratio, ostenditur conclusio contra quam erat non esse impossibilis etc. 2º Propositum fidei non potest sufficienter probari nec intelligi, igitur nec defendi. Item facta bona forma arguendi vel consequentia que tenet universaliter in omnibus aliis rebus, si debet solvi oportet hoc esse per interemptionem et sic oportet instantiam dari extra propositis, quod erit impossibile in pluribus, ut in articulo de trinitate, igitur.

"Prima propositio: Veraciter solvere aliquam rationem factam contra aliquam conclusionem non ostendit illam esse possibilem; apparet manifeste quia plures rationes magne apparentie facte contra aliquas conclusiones impossibiles sunt veraciter et artificialiter solubiles. . . .

"Ex illis sequitur quod ista consequentia non valet de forma que fiebat in argumento primo, videlicet 'omnes rationes facte contra articulum trinitatis sunt vere solubiles ab homine, igitur iste articulus non est impossibilis'; sed bene valeret si adderetur in antecedente 'et eius oppositum est particulariter(?) repugnans respectu veritatum et eviden-

Langenstein was not one to dismiss out of hand the powers of the human intellect, however. His criticisms of Aristotle notwithstanding, he continued to believe that "every good syllogistic form that is valid among creatures is also valid in divinity, where the terms and distributions of terms are used according to the usual procedure in the sciences of human origin." And even though human reason could not hope to demonstrate the truth of the Trinity, it could still show, for example, whether a given reason was sufficient to have knowledge of a particular conclusion, or whether it was necessary to assent to it. One could know, furthermore, when arguments were mistaken, even if one could not know wherein the mistake lay.[78] The theologian played a special role in these matters, for he was in a position to give "the cause and reason that must suffice according to the light of nature for every destructive argument that can be made against the Christian faith."[79] Langenstein then went on to elaborate several specific rules pertinent to the logical distribution of terms in universal propositions. What is perhaps most interesting is that Langenstein eventually admitted that—in this specific context at least—he was a partisan of Platonic realism:

> With the Platonists, I concede real universals and [I concede] that the universal man, or the real human species, is Sortes and is likewise Plato quidditatively and essentially, and yet that Sortes the father is not Plato his son, but really distinct from him by reason of individual and personal properties.[80]

---

tiarum naturalis luminis'. Et ratione illius additi sequitur articulum ne⟨gan⟩dum esse possibile sed de facto verum" (Alençon 144, 12ʳb).

[77] "Facilius est dissolvere quam ligare, et destruere quam construere" (Alençon 144, 13ʳa).

[78] "Omnis bona forma silogistica que valet in creaturis etiam valet in divinis, utendo terminis et distributionibus terminorum modo consueto in scientiis humanis. . . . Secunda propositio est quod ex humana doctrina potest ostendi de qualibet ratione an sufficiat ut per eam conclusio sciatur vel sine formidine ei debeat assentiri. . . . Homo potest certus esse de multis rationibus quod sunt peccantes, quas tamen numquam suo studio sciet solvere; patet de simplicibus fideliter credentibus articulos fidei" (Alençon 144, 13ʳa–13ʳb).

[79] "Septima propositio: expertus / in theologia potest dare causam et rationem debentem sufficere lumini naturali omnis interemptionis quam oportet fieri in argumentationibus contra fidem Christi" (Alençon 144, 13ʳb-13ᵛa).

[80] ". . . concedo cum Platonicis universalia realia et quod universalis homo vel species realis humana sit Sortes et similiter sit Plato quidditative et essentialiter etc., et quod tamen Sortes pater non sit Plato filius eius, sed distinctus ab eo realiter ratione proprietatum individualium et personalium" (Alençon 144, 13ᵛb).

After all, Langenstein argued, Aristotle never gave scientific or demonstrative reasons why Plato's theory was false. Parenthetically, Langenstein recorded his amazement that Aristotle was indeed able to make so many suggestions that went beyond natural reason, since "it is not easy to imagine how he would have done so, except with respect to the power of God, of which he in no way could have known to what extent, and how, it ultimately could act and could be."[81] This passage is remarkable: in the same breath with his admission of sympathy for Platonic realism, Langenstein acknowledges the power of God as a tool of natural philosophy. From the context it is clear that Langenstein meant the absolute power of God, the *potentia Dei absoluta*, the characteristic means with which fourteenth-century intellectuals explored the world of possibility and tested the noncontradictory character of their assumptions.[82] This conjunction strikingly illustrates the need for caution in adopting early fourteenth-century categories to circumscribe the thought patterns of later thinkers.

Langenstein was convinced that Aristotle had proceeded carelessly when he investigated logic (*ars prioristica*), for there were indeed modes of syllogizing available to natural reason such that "in no case would the rules and modes of syllogizing be subjected to counterexamples." The logic of the Platonists was just such a logic, "sufficient and universal in created as well as uncreated things."[83]

These arguments from the commentary on the *Sentences* already display strong affinities with the report of Langenstein's students. But he articulated the breach with Aristotle even more clearly in a series of theology lectures that he delivered a few months before his death. They are preserved in ÖNB 4718, a manuscript copied by his scribe

[81] "Iuxta istam declarationem pono talem conclusionem quod Aristoteles non potuisset demonstrare nec convincere quantum ad naturalem modum sciendi istam sufficienter ymaginationem vel consimilem esse impossibile vel in nullis rebus posse reperiri, tum quia supponit multa esse possibilia simpliciter et ultra naturam, sicut patet in libris suis; et hoc non potest ymaginari bene quomodo hoc fecisset nisi respectu divine potentie, de qua potentia divina nullo modo scire poterat quantum et qualiter ultimate posset et se haberet . . ." (Alençon 144, 13ᵛb).

[82] Sylla, "Autonomous and Handmaiden Science," 357ff; Oberman, "Some Notes on the Theology of Nominalism," 46ff.

[83] "Ex quibus sequitur corollarium, quod Aristoteles tradidit minus caute et complete artem prioristicam investigando modos et species syllogismorum, quamvis fuerint sub naturali lumine tradibilis complete et sufficienter, sic videlicet quod in nullis rebus regule et modi syllogismorum instantias paterentur. Tum quia ars prioristica Platonicorum vel tradibilis secundum eorum ymaginationem et philosophiam de rebus fuisset sufficiens et universalis tam rebus creatis quam increatis, ut patet ex precedentis" (Alençon 144, 14ʳa).

Peter Lewin (perhaps from dictation), but corrected and annotated in Langenstein's own hand.[84] The relevant passages occur not long before a marginal annotation that indicates the end of the lecture for 2 September 1396.[85] As will soon become apparent, the language of this lecture is very similar to the secondhand report by the four bachelors of theology, so similar that it is almost certainly the presentation that three of the students had heard. Plato had figured prominently in the commentary on the *Sentences*, and he reappeared in the lecture as the pagan with the wondrous insight:

> . . . aids to the clearest understanding of high truths can be taken not only from the true opinions of the ancients, but from some of their false "imaginations" as well. Of these "imaginations" of the ancients, there was that marvelous "imagination" of the Platonists concerning the real universal distinct from singulars—that the same [thing] according to number was several singular men and yet each of them. How could human understanding come closer to conceiving of the uncreated Trinity, in which one essence is common identically to three really distinct persons? Surely if the human mind could grasp the first and hold it as a matter of opinion, it could grasp the second [and] at least see that it is not untenable.[86]

Although Langenstein termed the Platonist concept of the universal a "false imagination," he nonetheless gave it his blessing. From a long-term historical perspective, the point is ironic. Various kinds of Platonism had long inspired Western theologians—one need only point to the long shadow of Augustine. When the Fourth Lateran Council crystallized a millennial tradition of Trinitarian formulations in the early thirteenth century, Aristotle had yet to make his deepest inroads among medieval theologians. The congruence of Platonism with Trinitarian

[84] See my "Academic Benefices and German Universities," 42, n. 2.

[85] "finis lectionis diei Sancti Antonii etc lxxxxvi^ti" (ÖNB 4718, 48^v). NOTE: ÖNB 4718 has been erroneously foliated. Folio 62 is followed not by folios 63, 64, and so on, but by folios 3, 4, and so on. In this and subsequent citations of the manuscript, the folios belong to the *second* set of numbers.

[86] "Potest iam videri ex hiis primo quomodo non solum ex veris antiquorum opinionibus, sed etiam ex nonnullis falsis ipsorum ymaginationibus summi possent manuductiones ad concipiendum declaratius altas veritates; de istis ymaginationibus veterum fuit et illa mirabilis yma / ginacio Platonicorum de universali reali distincto a singularibus, quod idem numero essent plures singulares homines et quilibet eorum. Quid humana intelligentia propinquius potuit concipere Trinitati increate, in qua una essentia est communis ydemptice tribus personis realiter distinctis? Profecto si humanum ingenium potuit primum concipere et opinative tenere, potuit concipere et secundum saltem ⟨mg potuit⟩ videre quod hoc non est inopinabile" (ÖNB 4718, 27^v–28^r).

formulations, which so amazed Langenstein, has a historical explanation that eluded him.

Conversely, Aristotle's rules presented serious problems for Christians. In some instances, according to Langenstein, it was impossible to avoid contradictions when using unadulterated Aristotelian syllogistic forms. Thus if one conceded the following string of inferences— 'this is God, therefore He is immortal'; 'this is immortal, therefore [this] is nonmortal'; 'this is nonmortal, therefore [this] is not mortal'; 'this is not mortal, therefore [this] in no way is mortal'—"then the copulative proposition 'this Son of God is immortal and this same Son of God is mortal' unavoidably reduces to a contradiction, notwithstanding the fact that the Son of God is not mortal and immortal in the same respect."[87] Many inferences that were perfectly acceptable according to natural philosophy had to be rejected as incompatible with the special mode of being in God: namely, that one thing is three really distinct things as well as each of them. Among the examples that Langenstein cited were 'the Son of God is immortal or nonmortal, therefore the Son of God is not mortal' and 'this essence is three persons, this essence is the Father, therefore the Father is three persons'. Hence:

> There is no doubt that if Aristotle were alive today and were asked whether the syllogistic forms that he once posited were valid (assuming that the aforesaid mode of existence obtains in divinity), he certainly would answer no, but that something would have to be added or considered in greater depth if the modes of syllogizing were to hold universally.[88]

This passage seems to leave open the possibility that additions or modifications of the received syllogistic could save the day. But Langenstein had apparently given up on that traditional option as well:

[87] ". . . hoc supposito quod iste commune sint bone 'Iste est deus, igitur est immortalis', 'iste est immortalis igitur non est mortalis', 'Iste est non mortalis, igitur iste non est mortalis', 'Iste non est mortalis, igitur nullo modo est mortalis', manifestum est quod concessis huiusmodi consequentiis, concedens hanc copulativam 'Iste filius dei est immortalis et iste idem filius dei est mortalis' reducitur inevasibiliter ad contradictionem, non obstante quod filius dei non secundum idem sit immortalis et mortalis nec similiter" (ÖNB 4718, 28ᵛ–29ʳ).

[88] "Non est dubium si Aristoteles hodie viveret et interrogaretur an, supposito quod in divinis sit dictus modus essendi, valerent forme sylogismorum quos olim posuit, diceret utique quod non, sed / quod aliquid oporteret addi aut ⟨*mg* in hac materia⟩ profundius considerari si modi sylogizandi debeant universaliter teneri" (ÖNB 4718, 29ᵛ–30ʳ).

And it would certainly be consonant with [Aristotle's] statement that the most astute Christian logicians and philosophers have worked on this for the longest time, and no mode has been found that suffices. On this issue, the most powerful mode that has been found thus far relies on the full *dici de omni* or full universalization, taking [distribution] within and outside the term in the singular and in the plural.[89]

But this too had failed. Langenstein went on to mention specifically the same third-figure syllogism in *disamis* that his students had cited as a counterargument to Oyta's solution: "Why indeed should it be surprising if no mode could be found with which to save in divinity all forms of syllogizing handed down by the philosophers according to the requirements of the modes of being of dependent things, from which the highest God is infinitely different and dissimilar?"[90] Langenstein's students indeed had heard him correctly. They had understood very clearly that he was rejecting with one sweep his own earlier position, that of his colleague Henry of Oyta, and Aristotle's syllogistic with it.

The tensions that Johann Auer discovered in the students' text he edited persuaded him that Dinkelsbühl had also rejected Oyta's position. To account for the shift, he tried to link it with innate intellectual proclivities tied to geographic origins. The Frisian Oyta was the scholar and theoretician who saw theology as a deductive, scientific enterprise; the Franconian or Swabian Nicholas of Dinkelsbühl, by contrast, was more practically oriented, and therefore more interested in the revelation that grounded the faith than in the process of understanding it.[91] Apart from its improbability a priori, this geographic

---

[89] "vel forte diceret ⟨Aristoteles⟩ quod si ita est qualiter secundum traditionem Christiane religionis patefactum est desuper circa divina et humana, de facto esse et posse esse, forte inveniri non potest vel vix modus aliquis quo sylogismi secundum modos et conditiones essendi creaturarum positi teneant universaliter. Et certe consonaret dicto modo suo quod iam a philosophis et logicis acutissimis Christianorum diutissime laboratum est super hoc et nondum inventus est modus aliquis qui sufficiat. Unde potior modus circa hoc ⟨h⟩actenus inventus est recurrendo ad plenum dici de omni seu ad plenum universalizari, sumendo intra et extra terminum singulariter et pluraliter" (ÖNB 4718, 30r).

[90] ". . . non valet sylogismus ille in disamis qualitercumque / universalizatur minor 'pater divinus generat, omnis pater divinus est essentia divina, igitur essentia generat'. Quid etiam mirum si nullus modus inveniri possit quo salventur in divinis omnes forme sylogizandi a philosophis traditi secundum exigentiam modorum essendi rerum dependentium ex quo deus ipse ⟨*mg* summus⟩ infinite dispariter et dissimiliter se habet in [[essendo]] conditionibus et essendi modis causati entis" (ÖNB 4718, 30r–30v).

[91] Auer, "Die aristotelische Logik," 472.

determinism is vitiated a posteriori both by the diverse origins of the four students (from Austria, Swabia, and Saxony), and also by the fact that Langenstein, who had but one birthplace, held both views in succession. Indeed, it is not clear that the four students were as secure or as unambiguous in their rejection of Oyta's position as Langenstein was, and as Auer would have it. But there can be no doubt that they were considering the option with great seriousness.

The consensus in the students' presentation of this issue is nevertheless striking. The general agreement—and often identity—between the texts from the generation of 1402 at first sight suggests a complete lack of originality and critical sense. Taken in the aggregate, however, this is surely not the case. The four versions of the question demonstrate that the students subjected the views of their teachers to a searching critical evaluation. In fact, they were forced to do so, for the two most respected professors on the faculty of theology held irreconcilable positions. When compared, the similarities between the four questions seem to reflect not the regional origins of the authors, but the homogenizing tendencies of the new university. By the time they committed their views to paper, Nicholas of Dinkelsbühl, Peter of Pulkau, and Johann Berwart of Villingen had spent almost two decades together, first in the faculty of arts and later in the faculty of theology, a lengthy period of close interaction within a small institution. On the other hand, Arnold of Seehausen was, by comparison with his three colleagues, an outsider. He not only matriculated too late to come under the direct influence of Langenstein and Oyta (1401), but he also belonged to the regular clergy. Under the circumstances, his verbal agreement with Dinkelsbühl, Pulkau, and Villingen is surprising. Indeed one hint suggests that Arnold's conformity was perhaps grudgingly exacted. The final lines of his question express a distinct lack of conviction about its results: "There are several other ways of answering in this matter, from which each should choose what to him seems most appropriate. For I think that the doctors who discovered the various modes of universalizing did not posit them without extensive examination and mature consideration."[92]

Although the variants in the texts examined above offer no clues about the way Arnold might have come so quickly to agree with his three colleagues, the records of the faculty of theology are more suggestive. In 1404, Nicholas of Dinkelsbühl, Peter of Pulkau, and Johann Berwart of Villingen together brought to the faculty accusa-

---

[92] Ibid., 496, lines 875–878.

tions against Arnold on account of views he had expressed in a sermon before the university community.[93] The Acts of the Faculty of Theology unfortunately give no details about the views that drew this concerted censure. The collusion of just these three masters against Arnold raises questions about the extent to which they brought pressure to bear on the latter's official theological statements. In any event, the conformity of the four men on this one issue contrasts sharply with the diversity of opinion expressed in the *principia* of the Bremis notebook some fifteen years before. By the early fifteenth century, the theological pluralism of the first student generation clearly had begun to fade.

[93] *ATF*, i, 9.

CHAPTER SIX

Langenstein and the Viennese Jews

'Tis evident, that all the sciences have a relation, greater or less, to human nature; and that however wide any of them may seem to run from it, they still return back by one passage or another.

DAVID HUME,
A Treatise of Human Nature

THE THEOLOGIANS who revived the University of Vienna began their careers optimistic about the ability of Aristotelian logic to handle Trinitarian paralogisms. But the first generation of their indigenously trained students was not so sure, and subjected the theses of their teachers to careful scrutiny. As argued in the last chapter, the pivotal figure who forced this reevaluation was Henry of Langenstein, who in the last months of his life rejected in Vienna the conviction he had defended earlier in his career.

But why did Langenstein change his mind? Certainly, there is no reason to suspect him of being particularly tradition-bound or dogmatic. If anything, he had an interest in unusual views. In 1364, he had raised against the standard astronomical system of epicycles and eccentrics a number of objections based on empirical evidence as well as internal consistency. He even made vague proposals of an alternative system to replace it.[1] His conciliar arguments of 1379, although not original, offered timely suggestions for an early solution to the Great Schism. Finally, Langenstein is known to have changed his mind on the controversial question of the Immaculate Conception, shifting from a proposed moratorium on discussions of the issue to a position of explicit support.[2] But critical attitudes and intellectual flexibility do not account for the shift in his position on logic. By rejecting the for-

---

[1] Kren, "A Medieval Objection to 'Ptolemy,' " 378–393; idem, "Homocentric Astronomy in the Latin West," 269–281.

[2] Emmen, "Heinrich von Langenstein," 638ff.

mality of Aristotelian logic in Trinitarian theology, Langenstein was adopting a view superficially similar to Robert Holcot's early position and to Arnold of Strelley's *Centiloquium*.[3] But whereas Holcot and Strelley in the end made their peace with Aristotle's syllogistic, Langenstein gave up on it, and decided to set his hopes on a "Platonic logic." No other instance of such a position readily comes to mind. Moreover, by the time he arrived in Vienna, Langenstein was already an elderly man. Indeed, his old friend Johannes of Stralen, who wrote to him about exchanging a prebend in 1387, assumed that Langenstein was looking for a relaxing retirement site, presumably far from the pressures of academic responsibility.[4] One would not have expected Langenstein at such a point in his life suddenly to throw out assumptions that had guided his life work.

The internal logical considerations that Langenstein's students used to justify his about-face reduce to a few counterexamples, and his theology lectures of 1396 corroborate such an interpretation. Firm believers in a specific fundamental position normally do not dismiss it because they are suddenly confronted with some exceptions. The attempt to find arguments or examples against any given position was part of the usual dialectical give-and-take in university disputations. Although the counterexamples no doubt played a role in Langenstein's decision, they certainly were not sufficient to motivate it. Unlike his predecessors, Langenstein was giving up all hope of finding a satisfactory solution along Aristotelian lines. In rejecting his own earlier position, Langenstein was turning against the consensus of the day, as Hermann Lurtz had described it in his *Tractatus de paralogismis*.[5] This consensus included not only a number of earlier doctors, but also a respected friend and associate such as Henry of Oyta. What could have driven Langenstein to reopen a question he had once settled to his satisfaction, to give up hope in a new solution, to turn against the received wisdom, and to adopt a position that was rather startling even in the context of the iconoclastic fourteenth century?

Several important events intervened between Langenstein's Parisian writings and his change of mind in Vienna during the 1390s. The most momentous was surely the Great Schism, which had both immediate

---

[3] See Chapter 3 above.

[4] See the letter from Arnold of Emelisse to Langenstein, edited in Shank, "Academic Benefices and German Universities," 40, esp. lines 2–3, 9–11. Although Langenstein was elderly by medieval standards, he was probably not as old as the widely accepted birthyear of 1325 would imply (ibid., 42, n. 2).

[5] See Chapter 5 above.

and longer-ranging consequences for Langenstein and his colleagues. After the initial shock caused by its outbreak, the Schism resulted in much soul-searching throughout Europe. The final court of appeal for theological orthodoxy had always been the pope, even if university theologians sometimes considered themselves better qualified for the task.[6] But now there were two competing highest courts of appeal, each excommunicated by the other. In such a context, what were the criteria of orthodoxy? Which of the two popes held the power to make binding decisions in matters of faith? Although political expediency quickly proposed to answer such questions unambiguously, no thinking churchman could have been satisfied with these solutions. The Schism thus gave an unsettling immediacy to questions of authority, and raised on a pragmatic level the issue of standards of truth, which had already been the focus of many theoretical arguments.[7] These considerations cannot have avoided influencing Langenstein, whose sense of urgency about the Schism drew him into the earliest efforts to bring it to an end.

In the early 1380s, the dissensions surrounding the Schism forced the departure of the German students and masters from the University of Paris, many of whom returned to their home towns. Following his own exodus, Langenstein spent a few months in the Cistercian monastery at Eberbach, where his friend James of Eltville was abbot. Several scholars have pointed to this visit as a turning point in his thinking. But Langenstein's alleged shift at Eberbach to a more "Augustinian" theological position tinged with mystical tendencies was predicated on the existence of two different versions of his commentary on the *Sentences*. Since the more Augustinian of the two commentaries is now known to be by his Cistercian host, a convincing case for such a shift will require new documentation based on Langenstein's genuine writings.[8] The Schism and Eberbach no doubt deserve prominent places in any exhaustive account of Langenstein's intellectual biography, which

---

[6] See, for example, Lytle, "Universities as Religious Authorities," 76.

[7] André Combes has articulated forcefully the tensions that thoughtful churchmen faced during the later years of the Schism. See his "Facteurs dissolvants et principe unificateur," 299–310; also see Oberman, *Harvest of Medieval Theology*, 323f.

[8] This is not to deny either an Augustinian strain or a mystical element in Langenstein's writings following his visit to Eberbach. The crucial question is whether these elements were new. See Heilig, "Kritische Studien zum Schrifttum der beiden Heinriche von Hessen," 164–165; J. Lang, *Christologie*, 16ff; and Lhotsky, *Die Wiener Artistenfakultät*, 57–58, for the correlation with Eberbach. For arguments against the standard two-version theory of Langenstein's commentary, see Trapp, "Augustinian Theology in the Fourteenth Century," 253, n. 93; and Appendix below.

is, however, not the purpose of this study.[9] The aim of the following pages is rather to explore one specific facet of Langenstein's change of mind, which does not exclude others but complements them—his move to, and thirteen-year residence in, new urban surroundings. Langenstein's relocation in Vienna constituted a decisive change of context, which cannot be overlooked in evaluating his rejection of Aristotle's logic in Trinitarian theology. From a social and religious point of view, one of the notable differences between Paris and his new situation was the presence in Vienna of a relatively large Jewish community, which gave the city an unusual religious and cultural pluralism—in fact if not in intent. This chapter examines Langenstein's interaction with the Jewish community in Vienna and suggests that this encounter was one of the stimuli that prompted him to reconsider the universal validity of Aristotelian logic in Trinitarian theology.

·

Whether or not the small Jewish settlements in Austrian territories already existed in Roman times, several of them certainly date back to the late twelfth century, when Duke Leopold v of Babenberg tried to stimulate commerce in his realm. The duke had a Jewish master of the mint whose name was Schlom and who owned four houses near the synagogue. The names of two Vienna rabbis have survived for this period.[10] These few data already imply the presence of a community. In 1236, the Holy Roman Emperor Frederick II issued a privilege that removed the life and property of the Jews from the jurisdiction of general law, placing them under the immediate control of the emperor. To respond to the problem of ineffectual protection under common law,

---

[9] Since the crisis of authority generated by the Schism affected an entire era, specific evidence from Langenstein's writings will be necessary before the Schism can be said to explain his shift away from Aristotle. Other areas that deserve to be investigated for their potential influence on Langenstein's about-face include contemporary discussions of evidence and proof in canon law, in the "practical sciences" such as ethics and politics, and in conciliar theory—not to mention theology and natural philosophy. In addition, a host of more specific questions suggest themselves: for example, whether Langenstein was responding to contemporary attacks on attempts to demonstrate the Trinity (e.g. the Dominican Nicholas Eymeric's attacks on Lull; see Madre, *Die theologische Polemik gegen Raimundus Lullus*, 106–109).

[10] Schwarz, *Das Wiener Ghetto*, 29–30; Vienna, Haus-, Hof-, und Staatsarchiv, Urkunde Bischof Wolgers von Passau (30 March 1204), cited in Lohrmann, "Die Juden im Wirtschaftsleben," 185; Scherer, *Die Rechtsverhältnisse der Juden*, 119. (According to Grunwald, who does not cite his source, Schlom and fifteen coreligionists were murdered by crusaders passing through Vienna; see his *Vienna*, 4–5.)

and to exploit the situation for his policy of centralization, Frederick II
placed the Jews in the Empire under his personal jurisdiction as *servi
camerae nostrae*, "servants of our chamber."[11] For their justification, the
new statutes drew upon the *Sachsenspiegel*. According to this early thirteenth-century lawbook, the Jews had become the slaves of Emperor
Vespasian after the fall of Jerusalem in A.D. 70. But the latter granted
them protection after Josephus cured Titus of the gout. As the political
successor of Rome, the Holy Roman Emperor lay claim to the same
rights and obligations, both in terms of the servitude it implied and the
protection it required.[12]

The same statute legalized the position of the Jews in Austrian territories, and became the model for similar documents throughout
Eastern Europe. The very first article of the privilege proclaimed: "we
receive the Jews in Vienna as servants of our chamber under our protection and favor."[13] The privilege promised imperial protection, for-
bade forcible baptisms as well as the use of force in exacting testimony
from Jews, and delineated the procedure for settling legal complaints
between Jews and Christians. It also authorized Jews to sell wine, dye-
stuffs, and medicine to Christians.[14] The extent to which such transactions in fact occurred is uncertain, for there is little independent evidence for Jewish involvement in Austrian trade during these years.
The authorization to do so is nevertheless significant. In any case, the
privilege assumed that moneylending was the dominant economic activity of Jews. It gave secular legal sanction to a state of affairs that
violated the prescriptions of canon law.[15] In 1244, a second privilege
more specific than the first was issued for Habsburg territory.[16]

The protection that the Habsburgs as imperial vassals extended to
the Jews in their duchy was for the most part effective.[17] In the late
1340s, the outbreak of the Great Plague had disastrous consequences

---

[11] Kisch, "The Jews in Medieval Germany," 143ff.

[12] Kisch, *Sachsenspiegel and Bible*, 170, n. 31.

[13] ". . . Nos Judeos Wienne seruos Camere nostre sub nostra et Imperiali protectione
recipimus et fauore." For the complete text, see Scherer, *Rechtsverhältnisse*, 135–137.

[14] "Praeterea uinum suum, Pigmenta et antidota possunt uendere Christianis" (ibid.,
136).

[15] Lohrmann, "Die Juden im Wirtschaftsleben," 185; Scherer, *Rechtsverhältnisse*, 147.

[16] For the Latin text, see Scherer, *Rechtsverhältnisse*, 179–184; English translation in
Marcus, *The Jew in the Medieval World*, 28–32.

[17] A notable exception was the accusation of host desecration in Pulkau in 1338. Even
Pope Benedict XII saw through these charges: he attributed them to the jealousy and
hatred of the populace, and interpreted them as pretexts to rob the Jews of their money;
see Browe, "Die Judenbekämpfung im Mittelalter," 224.

for many Jewish communities throughout Europe, especially in the Holy Roman Empire. Accusations of well poisonings quickly gave way to raids, expulsions, and massacres. In Habsburg territories, however, only one such incident is reported, in Krems in 1349.[18] Indeed there were a few voices on the side of moderation. In discussing the plague epidemic of that year, the former rector of the Bürgerschule in Vienna, Conrad of Megenberg, was skeptical about the rumor of well poisonings:

> Whether some Jews did this or not, I do not know. . . . But I know this full well, that they were as numerous in Vienna as any city I know in Germany, and that they also died there to such an extent that they had to expand their cemetery considerably and buy two houses for this purpose. Had they poisoned themselves, what a folly that would have been![19]

When persecutions did break out, Duke Albert II's retribution of instigators and participants proved swift and harsh, earning him the epithet of "defender of the Jews" (*fautor Judaeorum*) in a contemporary monastic chronicle.[20]

As *servi camerae*, the Jews heretofore had stood under the protection of the emperor. Duke Rudolph IV (1358–1365) modified their legal status in the "Privilegium Maius" (1358/1359). In this clever forgery, which alleged that the Holy Roman Emperor had granted several major privileges to the Habsburgs in the thirteenth century, Rudolph assigned himself the right to "hold, without harm or offense to the Empire, Jews and public usurers whom the common people call *Gawertschin*."[21] This ruse worked, for in 1360, Emperor Charles IV gave his ambitious son-in-law some ground. Although he denied Rudolph the right to keep the *Gawertschin* (Christian usurers from Cahors)—a privilege no other prince-elector possessed either—he did authorize his son-in-law to "keep Jews." What once had been an exclusive imperial prerogative now became a ducal one as well. Rudolph's inter-

---

[18] See Guerchberg, "La Controverse sur les prétendus semeurs de la 'Peste noire,' " 3–40. Without giving his source, Gerson Wolf claims that during these years, on the advice of its Rabbi Jona, the Jewish community of Vienna committed suicide in the synagogue to avoid being massacred; see *Die Juden*, 15.

[19] Pfeiffer, ed., *Das Buch der Natur von Konrad von Megenberg*, 112. For a more detailed passage to the same effect, see Conrad's *De mortalitate in Alamannia*, edited by Krüger in her "Krise der Zeit," 867–868.

[20] Vielmetti, "Die Juden in Österreich während des Mittelalters," 182. This judgment also finds an echo in a Jewish chronicle of the sixteenth century (ibid., 181).

[21] Wattenbach, "Die Österreichischen Freiheitsbriefe," 112–114, esp. 113. See also Grunwald, "Lombards, Cahorsins and Jews," 393–398.

action with the emperor on this issue suggests what a coveted right this was: Charles IV made his concession only on the condition that Rudolph would neither take in nor protect any Jews from the territories ruled by Charles and his brother John.[22] Rudolph soon translated his ambitions into specific benefits. The possessions of the "servants of his chamber" formerly had stood under the direct control of the emperor. Backed by the "Privilegium Maius," Rudolph now intended to treat them as his own. Several documents show that he and his successors did not consider this an empty claim: they took full advantage of a clause that granted them the possessions of fugitive Jews.[23]

For the Jews, these privileges were therefore two-edged swords. They offered security, to be sure. But the dukes were not averse to exacting tribute in exchange for renewing the protection clauses of the privilege. In the event a Jew fled the country, they demanded that the coreligionists who had remained behind post bail for the fugitive. In 1367, for example, six men were ordered to collect the enormous sum of 20,000 guldens for two fugitives.[24] For members of the nobility with large debts, the temptation to "produce" fugitives must have been difficult to resist, particularly since the duke often remitted debts in such cases. Several feudal lords were in fact heavily indebted. In 1373, for example, Hans von Schönberg (in the Kamptal) borrowed 900 *Pfund* from David Steuss, a Viennese Jew. By 1380, he owed 2,300 *Pfund* and had to give up his castle and dependencies. Albert III then took possession of these territories. In Albert's hands, the indebtedness of his vassals became a powerful tool, which he used very effectively to manipulate the nobility and keep it under his control.[25] David Steuss—fortunately for him—lived in Vienna, where the duke was in a position to enforce his privilege. Jews in the provinces presumably found it more difficult to make good on their immunities.

The flight of creditors was not the sole occasion for the remission of debts, however. Rudolph IV and his successors also used this stratagem to reward the loyalty of their vassals or to repay them for services rendered. From 1365 to the death of Albert III in 1395, at least 3,700 guldens were remitted, including one enormous debt of 2,983 guldens.[26] In other instances, the interest on a debt might be suspended for a number of years. In 1382, "considering the great and heavy indebtedness in

---

[22] Scherer, *Rechtsverhältnisse*, 375–376.

[23] Trusen, *Spätmittelalterliche Jurisprudenz und Wirtschaftsethik*, 97–98.

[24] Scherer, *Rechtsverhältnisse*, 388.

[25] Stowasser, "Zur inneren Politik Herzog Albrechts III. von Österreich," 145–146.

[26] Staudner, "Die Wiener Juden als Geldgeber im Mittelalter," 133–135.

which the city of Vienna lies," Albert III granted the entire city a three-year reprieve.[27] Another ploy involved the confiscation of Jewish goods, while allowing the creditors to retain their records, thereby ensuring a renewable source of income. One massive confiscation of this sort took place in the 1370s.[28] This method of generating revenue proved effective for political as well as economic reasons. It not only provided additional income for the duke from the pockets of his subjects, but also shunted off the anger of the populace in the direction of the Jews, who became in effect the unwitting agents of an underhanded scheme of indirect taxation. And ironically the Christian majority was probably pleased to see a heavy penalty imposed upon the Jews, who often symbolized decadent living in the moralizing literature of the Latin Middle Ages.[29]

These hardships notwithstanding, by the late fourteenth century the Jewish community of Vienna was one of the largest in the Holy Roman Empire.[30] At the time of Langenstein's arrival in the city, that community had all the appearances of an established group that served a specific economic function. The Jewish quarter constituted a well-defined section of the city, surrounded by walls and accessible through four gates. It consisted of sixty-nine buildings, including a synagogue, a hospital, and facilities for butchering and ritual bathing.[31] In spite of several earlier upheavals, the Viennese Jews had lived in relative peace since the *Handfest* of 1377.[32] Their long-standing presence in Austria was an acknowledged fact, which found expression in the historical myths of the time. Thus the "Österreichische Chronik der 95 Herrschaften," a late fourteenth-century chronicle composed by Leopold Stainreuter of Vienna (d. ca. 1400), began its list of Austrian rulers

---

[27] Tomaschek, ed., *Die Rechte und Freiheiten der Stadt Wien*, 197.

[28] The event is variously reported in three different chronicles as occurring in 1370, 1371, and 1377; see Scherer, *Rechtsverhältnisse*, 392, n. 2; the appendix to "Germanicum Austriae Chronicon" and the "Fragmentum historicum de IV. Albertis Austriae ducibus," in Pez, *Scriptores rerum Austriacarum*, I, col. 1160, and II, col. 383, respectively; and the "Kleine Klosterneuburger Chronik," edited by Zeibig in *Archiv für Kunde Österreichischer Geschichtsquellen* 7 (1851) 235.

[29] See Shachar, *The Judensau*, 4ff, 12f, 17f, for associations between *gula* and *luxuria* on the one hand, and the *Judensau* motif on the other; and the Oyta sermon "Ecce salvator tuus venit. Ysaiae 62. Pro sancti spiritus impetranda gracia . . ." in Sommerfeldt, "Aus der Zeit der Begründung der Universität Wien," 296–297.

[30] See Conrad of Megenberg (n. 19 above). A recent estimate sets the Jewish population of Vienna at about 500 in the late fourteenth and early fifteenth centuries; see Perger, "Beiträge zur Wiener Verfassungs- und Sozialgeschichte," 14.

[31] Schwarz, "Geschichte," in *GStW*, v, 26–27.

[32] Scherer, *Rechtsverhältnisse*, 395ff.

with a Jew. The first name of Austrian territory was Judeisapta (= *Judeis apta*, "suited for Jews"), ruled by Abraham of Temonaria, who had been driven from Terra Ammirationis ("Land of Admiration") by his overlord Sattan von Alygemorum. As these names suggest, Stainreuter's account takes place in mythical time, and the tone is Biblical: "[Abraham] came to a country by the Danube that long ago was named Judeisapta by a Jew, although the latter never traveled there. And he walked about until he found a city that pleased him. Then he built himself a house and lay down, and named the city Anreytim, which today is called Stockerau."[33] The chronicler clearly believed in a very ancient, pre-Christian Jewish presence in Austria. In other localities, such a view coincided with the recognition that the original settlers did not share the traditional blame for the crucifixion of Christ.[34] It is difficult to know whether the Viennese population as a whole shared Stainreuter's outlook. But the Habsburg court in the 1380s probably assumed with him that the Jews had a long-standing claim to residence in Austria, for Stainreuter was not just any chronicler. He was the court chaplain of Albert III, for whom the chronicle was written.[35]

If the social situation of the Viennese Jews was moderately secure by comparison with that of their coreligionists elsewhere in Europe,[36] the prospects associated with their economic function were less promising. Like Habsburg territories in general, Vienna in the 1380s was still beset with serious problems—the legacy of Rudolph IV's large expenditures for military purposes, not to mention additional military debts incurred during twenty years of feuding between his brothers Albert

[33] "Er cham in ain Land bey der Tunaw, daz vor langer zeit ain Jud het gehaissen Judeisapta, der selb Jud doch nie in das land cham, und gieng als lang, bis er vand ain stat, die im wol geviel. Da machet er im selber ain hauz und lie sich da nider und nant die stat Anreytim, die yczund haisset Stocharaw" ([Stainreuter], "Österreichische Chronik der 95 Herrschaften," bk. 1, chap. 42, 26). Although the chronicle was anonymous when first edited, its author has now been identified; see Heilig, "Leopold Stainreuter," 225–289.

[34] See Schwarz, "Geschichte," in *GStW*, v, 3–4; and Stowasser, "Zur Geschichte der Wiener Geserah," 110. Before attributing excessive goodwill to Stainreuter, it is well to recall that Abraham's overlord was named Satan.

[35] Heilig, "Leopold Stainreuter," 262, passim.

[36] The "Chronicle of the Four Alberts" claims that in the 1370s the dukes intended to burn all the Jews. The plan was thwarted, however, allegedly on the advice of "doctors of theology" who suggested that "the Jews not be killed, but subjected to hard servitude." This proposal was then followed by attempts to convert them. See Scherer, *Rechtsverhältnisse*, 392–393. If the approximate date of 1370–1377 is indeed correct, these theologians may have been the teachers in the *studia* of the local orders.

and Leopold.[37] The Habsburgs resorted to the expedient of tampering
with the silver content of the *Wiener Pfund*.[38] Then, in 1384, Duke Albert III sought to revive the university. He allocated funds for sizable
pensions to attract the prized professors Langenstein and Oyta eastward, and effected further expenditures to establish his new Collegium
ducale.[39] The duke's craving for revenue was so well known that his
subjects assumed any new venture had financial motivations. Thus in
his new university privilege, Albert had to defend himself from the
suspicion that he had revived the Viennese *studium* for economic gain.[40]
The town in general was subjected to unusual taxes in an attempt to
replenish the Habsburg treasury, and this at a time when the city itself
was borrowing more than half of its budget. The populace, too, was
heavily in debt. In most cases, the creditors were members of the Jewish community.[41] Undermined by past military expenditures, epidem-
ics, bad weather, and poor vintages, the economic situation deterio-
rated even further throughout the 1380s. It was during these years that
Langenstein pleaded for more support from the duke. But the latter
was in such dire straits that he decided to run the risk of an interdict by
dipping into Church funds.

Under these circumstances, it would have been impossible for Langenstein to come to Vienna and remain oblivious of its Jewish community. As a university administrator competing for scarce capital, he
must have been keenly aware of the pitiful state of city as well as ducal
finances, and of the role played by Jewish creditors. As a resident of
the city, he could not have avoided noticing this visible minority with
its distinctive, pointed "Jewish hat."[42] As a theologian, he could not

---

[37] Between June 1368 and the end of 1369, for example, the dukes paid 20,000 guldens
to Freiburg im Breisgau, 116,000 to the Bavarian dukes for Tyrol, and promised another
32,000 to Freiburg. In November, they lost a war with Venice, which adversely affected
the trade with the Adriatic and further deprived the Habsburgs of much-needed revenue.
See Scherer, *Rechtsverhältnisse*, 391–392.

[38] Brunner, *Die Finanzen der Stadt Wien*, 24.

[39] See Chapter 1 above.

[40] ". . . ne fortassis de exiguo avaricie arguamur, aut huiusmodi Studium suspicemur,
pecuniarum acquirendarum animo erexisse . . ." (Kink, *Geschichte*, II, 54).

[41] Goldmann, ed., *Das Judenbuch*, introduction.

[42] Although no dress regulations for late fourteenth-century Vienna appear to survive,
the practice of wearing the pointed hat had been specified in a provincial ecclesiastical
council held in Vienna in May 1267; see Scherer, *Rechtsverhältnisse*, 331. It seems to have
been habitual, and is confirmed by legal documents from Germany, Austria, and Bohemia from the mid-thirteenth century; see Kisch, "The Yellow Badge in History," 107,
129 (documents 4 and 5). Indeed, the Austrian iconography of the period portrays Jews
with the *Spitzhut* or *Judenhut*; see, for example, the fourteenth-century stained-glass

have failed to know that their beliefs differed from his, and that they were not subject to ecclesiastical control.

・

This confrontation with an alien culture made a vivid impression on Langenstein.[43] Numerous references to the Jews are scattered throughout his theological writings. In addition, he wrote two works that dealt extensively with aspects of Jewish life and culture: a treatise on the Hebrew language (*De ideomate Ebraico*, 1388) and a treatise on contracts (*Tractatus de contractibus*, 1390–1391), which discussed social and economic relations between Christians and Jews.[44]

Some aspects of Langenstein's interest in the Jews dated back·to his

---

windows depicting Moses and the brass serpent in St. Stephen's Cathedral (reproduced in Grunwald, *Geschichte der Wiener Juden*, plates 1, 8–9), and Jesus among the doctors of the law, in the ambulatory of the Klosterneuburg monastery on the outskirts of Vienna (Baldass et al., eds., *Gotik in Österreich*, fig. 27). The best example for our purposes is an illustrated *ketuba*, or marriage contract, from Krems in 1391–1392, in which the groom wears the *Spitzhut* (ÖNB Cod. Hebr. 218, published in [Schubert], ed., *Judentum im Mittelalter*, fig. 42b; and Metzger and Metzger, *Jewish Life in the Middle Ages*, 228). Other illustrations are found in Blumenkranz, *Juden und Judentum*; expanded in *Le Juif médiéval*. In some localities, the Jews were required to wear distinctive dress and to trim their hair according to established rules; see, for example, the Cologne ordinance of 1404 (*Monumenta Judaica* [Cologne, 1963], B.313), quoted in Rubens, *A History of Jewish Costume*, 98–102. For a different tradition, see Mellinkoff, "The Round, Cap-Shaped Hats Depicted on Jews," 155–166 (I thank Mary Garrison for this reference).

Panofsky has observed that the late Middle Ages tended to Christianize classical forms, and to present classical themes in contemporary form—his "principle of disjunction"; see Panofsky, *Renaissance and Renascences*, 84. The same point might be made about ancient religious themes. It is therefore especially striking to see the strong Jewish elements in early fifteenth-century depictions of the *Marienleben* by the Meister des Albrechtsaltar (late 1430s) and the Meister von Schloss Lichtenstein (ca. 1455); see Baum, *Katalog des Museums Mittelalterlicher Österreichischer Kunst*, 39–47, figs. 19–21. The iconography thus further corroborates the cultural visibility of the Jews in Austrian lands. By contrast, a more painstaking observer such as Dürer would be far more fanciful in his representations of the Jews than were the Lower Austrian artists. Thus, the lunar crescent on the headdress of Dürer high priests (e.g. in his *Marienleben* woodcuts) derives from a specific literary tradition rather than from observation; see Boeke, *Rondom het Paradijsverhaal*, 129–146 (I thank Jane Carroll for this reference).

[43] Langenstein was not alone in this. A Christmas sermon attributed to Henry of Oyta ("Ecce salvator tuus venit. Ysaie 62. Pro Sancti Spiritus . . .") in ÖNB 4427, also discusses the Jews. See Sommerfeldt, "Aus der Zeit der Begründung," 295–297.

[44] The environment of Vienna also affected Henry of Oyta, who also wrote a *Treatise on Contracts* (published with Langenstein's in the 1484 Cologne edition of Jean Gerson's *Opera omnia*, IV) and a *Disputatio Catholica contra Judaeos* (see A. Lang, *Heinrich Totting von Oyta*, 108ff).

years in Paris. In *De ideomate Ebraico,* Langenstein mentioned that he had learned Hebrew from "converted Jews and others in Paris and Vienna."[45] Indeed his *Epistola concilii pacis,* written in Paris in 1381, reveals some reflection about the relations between Christians and Jews, and in particular a keen awareness of the special problems that faced converted Jews. In chapter 17 of the *Epistola,* which confronts the ecclesiastical authorities with a battery of hard questions about reform, Langenstein asks:

> Why are the necessities of life not mercifully given to converted Jews from their property, instead of their being compelled by extreme poverty to apostatize and accuse Christians of ungodliness? Why is it not ordained that Jews must not remain among Christians unless they earn their livelihood by becoming servants to the Christians or by cultivating the fields or working as artisans and not by practicing usury, which for themselves is committing sin and for Christians means extortion?[46]

These proposals implied that recently converted Jews should be granted the right to live temporarily from the fruits of usury. In other words, the Church should consider making an exception to its general ban on lending at interest. As Langenstein realized, this concession was a pragmatic compromise required by a system that forced the Jews into one single economic activity. His second rhetorical question attacked the problem at the root. The unconverted Jews should be integrated into society as servants, peasants, and artisans. These estates represented the lower echelons of society, to be sure. But the upper levels were completely closed to non-Christians: the nobility was hereditary, and Church careers were obviously out of the question. The fact that

---

[45] ". . . longo tempore a iudeis conuersis et aliis parisius et Wyenensis fui eruditus." See the partial edition in Walde, *Christliche Hebraisten Deutschlands,* 10. One possible candidate is Themo Judaei, whose career at Paris probably overlapped briefly with Langenstein's. He too was a member of the small English-German nation and shared Langenstein's interest in astronomy. Themo, who served as receptor of the nation between 1357 and 1361, is last mentioned in its records on 10 November 1360; see the *Auctarium,* col. 261. Peter Ceffons mentions contacts with Jewish astronomers in Paris during the 1340s, but it is not clear from the context whether they had converted to Christianity; see Trapp, "Peter Ceffons of Clairvaux," 101, n. 2.

[46] Von der Hardt, *Magnum oecumenicum Constantiense concilium,* II, pt. 2, cols. 54–55. I have emended slightly the Cameron translation in Spinka, ed., *Advocates of Reform,* 136. This theme also occurs in the sermon attributed to Henry of Oyta; see n. 29 above. Dr. Georg Kreuzer has prepared a new edition of the *Epistola concilii pacis* in his Augsburg *Habilitationsschrift,* which I have not seen.

Langenstein did not specifically mention commerce as a possible activity is curious—perhaps the reflection of a traditional social outlook.

Langenstein may have had contacts with unconverted Jews in Paris, but this is not very likely. Since the Jews had only recently been allowed to return to France by the time Langenstein probably arrived in the city, the community could have been neither very numerous nor well established.[47] The Hebrew teachers he knew in Paris were almost certainly converted Jews. Indeed the fourteenth century as a whole was not propitious for French Jewry. One scholar has called the expulsion of 1306 under Philip the Fair "a deathblow," followed by a slow agony until the final expulsion in 1394.[48] Paris was the scene of a massacre in 1321 (probably followed by an expulsion in 1322), an edict of expulsion in 1365, and anti-Jewish riots in 1380 and 1382.[49]

In Vienna, by contrast, the Jews claimed a nearly unbroken presence reaching back at least to the privileges of 1238 and 1244. Whatever might be said of individuals, as a group they presented a very different sociocultural profile from that of their Parisian counterparts. Sporadic confiscations and threats notwithstanding, they were established, tolerated, relatively numerous, and indispensable to the duke's economic policies. For all of these reasons, Langenstein would have had occasions both to be very aware of the Jews in Vienna and to encounter them.

Langenstein's involvement with the Viennese Jews almost certainly went beyond the personal contacts and the instruction in Hebrew mentioned in his treatise *De ideomate Ebraico*. Before his arrival in the city, Langenstein already had a strong predisposition for open debate

---

[47] Langenstein obtained his bachelor's and master's degrees in 1363 (*Auctarium*, cols. 279, 284–285). The Jews had only been readmitted to Paris in 1359; see Baron, *A Social and Religious History of the Jews*, x, 70–71.

[48] See Loeb, "Les expulsions des juifs de France au xivᵉ siècle," 39. King Charles v (1364–1380) had named Rabbi Mattathias chief rabbi of France. A succession controversy arose when Mattathias's son Johanan took over his father's functions, again by royal appointment; see Lauer, "R. Meir Halevy aus Wien," 1, and Kohn, "Royal Power," 133ff. This episode implies that in spite of expulsion edicts some Jews remained in or had returned to France, perhaps primarily in the south. Also, the papal documents about Jewish matters deal especially with southern France; see Eubel, "Zu dem Verhalten der Päpste gegen die Juden," 29–42. Kohn dates one return to ca. 1380; see "Royal Power," 133.

[49] Kahn, *Les Juifs à Paris depuis le vrᵉ siècle*, 25–32; Chazan, *Medieval Jewry in Northern France*, 201. In this context, see John Duns Scotus's assertion around 1300: "secta Judaeorum non manet in vigore" (prologue to the *Ordinatio*, pt. 2, qu. 1; *Opera omnia*, 1, 76), which may be a general post-diaspora remark, rather than a specific comment about his own times.

as the proper method of settling differences. In 1379, his arguments for a conciliar resolution of the Great Schism rested on the premise that the truth would eventually emerge from the process of the disputation. Thus in his *Epistola pacis*, he wrote:

> Does not the exercise of disputation always detect concealed falsehood and fraud in the end? Is this not why Mohamet forbade disputation on those matters that pertained to his laws, knowing that the fine and exact winnowing-sieve of the disputation could not long hide fraud and falsehood? Very great therefore is the judgment of truth of the Christian law, because in this [law] all things for a thousand years have been exposed, and daily are exposed, to the most rigorous scrutiny, and yet they endure.[50]

True Christianity had nothing to fear from debates with schismatics or Muslims. This attitude of open-minded superiority, with its unshakable confidence in the disputation as the method for separating truth from falsehood, suggests that Langenstein not only did not fear, but would have welcomed, the opportunity to debate with Jews. At the very least, the writings from his Viennese years prove that he often had the Jews on his mind. Even works with a likely literary inspiration convey a sense of immediacy that transcends the written word. One of these is an early excerpt from his monumental *Lectures on Genesis*, specifically his commentary on Genesis 1:26 ("Let us make man in our image and likeness"). In this verse, he argued, the use of the verb in the first person plural implied a plurality of persons in God, even though the number of persons was not specified. Langenstein followed the Church Fathers in seeing here an obvious allusion to the Trinity in the Old Testament:

> The Jews and the Arabs, and especially the former, contradict him who claims that the plurality of persons in God can be inferred from the writings of the Old Testament. And I therefore want to proceed some against both, but first and especially against the Jews [at this point in Langenstein's autograph, "Jews" is crossed out, and followed by "those utterly blind Jews"]. I want to show how the plurality of persons and the unity of the Deity can be deduced even from the Old Testament.[51]

---

[50] Bernstein, *Pierre d'Ailly*, 36, n. 46, citing C. E. DuBoulay, *Historia Universitatis Parisiensis*, IV, 577, lines 3–9.

[51] "Contradicunt Iudei et Arravi et maxime primi [[harum]] iam dictarum conclusionum dicentes quod ex scripturis veteris testamenti pluralitas personarum in Deo concludatur ⟨*mg* fortiter resistunt ex cecitati Iudei⟩. Et ideo contra utrosque volo procedere aliquantulum primo et principaliter contra [[Iudeos]] illos excecatissimos Iudeos, volo

Langenstein offered four arguments. The first appealed to the fact that the most frequently used designation for the divinity in the Hebrew scriptures is *elohim*, a plural form, which almost always appears in conjunction with a singular verb (e.g. *bereshit bara elohim* in Gen. 1:1). What could possibly have been intended here if not a statement about a plurality of persons in one God? Indeed for Langenstein this was confirmed by the fact that the tetragrammaton YHWH, a singular form, was used elsewhere to refer to "God absolutely, according to His intrinsic properties."[52]

Why this difference in words, if not to make different points? According to Langenstein, the Jews responded by arguing that *elohim* did indeed signify some kind of plurality, but a plurality of attributes such as the power, wisdom, and goodness by which God created all that is. Langenstein retorted that these qualities also existed in human creators, where they are more distinct than in God, and yet in such cases a singular subject is used with a singular verb.

The broad outlines of this argument were not new. In the early fourteenth century, the Franciscan Nicholas of Lyra, whom Langenstein occasionally quoted, had raised the issue of plurality and unity in his own commentary on this passage. In his *Postilla super totam Bibliam*, both Nicholas's exegesis of Genesis 1:26 and the Jewish counterarguments he mentioned differ from those in Langenstein's account. Nicholas emphasized the creation of the soul in this passage.[53] The Jews claimed that the plural *faciamus* was the word of God to the angels—an impossibility for Nicholas, since the angels could not cooperate in the creation of man's soul.[54] But in the *Quodlibetum de adventu Christi* of 1309 (sometimes called the *De Iudeorum perfidia*), Nicholas of Lyra presented arguments from which Langenstein may have drawn inspira-

---

ostendere quomodo pluralitas personarum et unitas deitatis deducitur(?) potest etiam ex veteribus scripturis" (ÖNB 4651, 100ᵛ–101ʳ).

[52] ". . . tetragrammaton quod significat deum absolute secundum proprietates suas intrinsecas absque comparatione ad extra" (ÖNB 4651, 101ʳ).

[53] " 'Faciamus' in plurali ad denotandum pluralitatem personarum in divinis; verumtamen quia ita pluralitas stat cum unitate simplicis essentie, ideo postea subdicitur in singulari 'et creavit deus hominem ad imaginem suam.' Imago autem dei consistit in anima quantum ad proprietates naturales scilicet memoriam, intelligentiam et voluntatem. . . . Iudei autem in glosa super Psalmos ponunt imaginem in anima quantum ad quasdam alias proprietates. Primo quod sicut anima replet totum corpus, ita deus totum mundum. Item quia sicut deus unicus est in suo seculo, sic anima in suo corpore. Item sicut deus videt omnia et non videtur" (*Postilla fratris Nicolai de Lyra . . . super Genesim . . .* , I, fol. Ac8ʳ).

[54] Hailperin, *Rashi and the Christian Scholars*, 148, 294 n. 93.

tion. The "ancient Hebrew doctors," Nicholas argued, conceded that there might be some plurality in God, while "later Jews distort, saying that divine knowledge, goodness, and power are those properties in which God created the world."[55]

The problem of understanding plural verbs with singular subjects (and vice versa) was not restricted to exegetical studies, however. It had also made its way into mid-fourteenth-century discussions of logic and the Trinity. In arguments directed against Ockham and others, Holcot in one of his quodlibetal questions had warned about the deceptive implication of plurality when compound expressions made of two terms signifying one thing were the subject of a plural verb (e.g. 'the sun and the sun are one' (*sol et sol sunt*), 'the divine essence and the relation are the same', 'the essence and the Father are formally distinct'). Such propositions were either false, unintelligible, or misleading.[56] Against such a background, it is not surprising to hear Langenstein drawing ontological conclusions from such an unusual combination as a plural subject with a singular verb in the revealed text.

A few lines later, after discussing some problems of translation, Langenstein noted:

> It is a great deficiency in the Church that there is no instruction in various languages, namely in Hebrew, Greek, etc. . . . And because of this deficiency, the Jews boldly raise their horns; and when they answer clerics before laymen and the simple people, they dare implicitly to impugn our translations, saying that [a given passage] does not read thus in their Bible.[57]

Once again, this plea for the study of Biblical languages was not new. The issues that had occasioned the first such calls had become timely once again. Already in the thirteenth century, the general of the Dominican order had established a school for the teaching of Hebrew,

[55] Nicholas of Lyra, *Biblia*, VI, 276B; trans. in Cohen, *The Friars and the Jews*, 182.

[56] Gelber, *Exploring the Boundaries of Reason*, 25; 41, lines 217–229; 42–43, lines 254–283; 48, lines 378–385.

[57] "Magnus est in ecclesia defectus eo quod non est in ea eruditio in diversis linguibus, scilicet in ebraica, greca, etc ut alii [. . . ?] de ecclesia salubriter provisum fuit per illam(?) clementinam. Unde propter illum defectum Iudei erigunt audacius cornua sua et coram laicis et simplicibus respondendo clericis audent dicere impingendo implicite in nostras translationes se non habere sic in biblia. Ex quo quia nemo super hoc eos convincit multi scandalizari possunt" (ÖNB 4651, 102ʳ).

Arabic, and Aramaic to members of his order.[58] Other advocates of the study of Hebrew included Ramón Lull and Roger Bacon. In 1312, at Lull's instigation, the Council of Vienne (Isère, France) gave official sanction to their suggestions by proposing chairs in these languages at five universities, including Paris and Bologna. Some professorships were evidently established in years that followed.[59] By the late fourteenth century, however, such chairs had apparently disappeared, for Langenstein's own statement suggests that he knew nothing of their existence. Indeed, one potential teacher of Hebrew was starving in early fifteenth-century Paris.[60]

Langenstein's rationale for proposed instruction in Hebrew was very defensive. His anxiety focused primarily on the "simple" and lay people. He worried that their faith might suffer from seeing their leaders confounded by Jewish arguments that relied on knowledge of the Hebrew originals. For Langenstein, concern for the simple folk was a recurrent theme. It was an important element in the verdict of the faculty of theology on the controversial theses of Johann Müntzinger, a verdict in which Langenstein played a decisive role.[61] It also surfaced in Langenstein's discussion of a telling question: "Whether the faithful may return the greeting of a Jew who greets him?" Langenstein decided for the negative, in part "lest weaker Christians suspect those who show the Jews honor of knowing and holding something of their sect."[62]

The tone of Langenstein's dialectical presentation, with its arguments and counterarguments in close succession, differs noticeably from that of the dispassionate academic commentary, or even from the polemical writings of Nicholas of Lyra. In Paris, where Lyra had presented and revised his treatises, there were no Jews with whom he might have disputed.[63] In Vienna, by contrast, discussions of apologetics could not long retain the aloofness of Parisian pronouncements, which could comfortably remain untested. Like the debates preserved

---

[58] See Moore, "Christian Writers on Judaism," 202–203; Thiel, "Grundlagen und Gestalt der Hebräischkenntnisse," esp. 4–15.

[59] *Chartularium*, II, no. 695, 154–155; Altaner, "Die Durchführung des Vienner Konzilbeschlusses," 226–236 (see also his "Zur Kenntnis des Hebräischen im Mittelalter," 288–308).

[60] Jourdain, "De l'enseignement de l'hébreu," 233ff.

[61] A. Lang, "Johann Müntzinger," 1213.

[62] "An fidelis honorantem se Judeum licite rehonorare possit(?) . . . Iudei non sunt a Christianis publice in vicis verbo vel gestu honorandi vel rehonorandi propter rationes factas. Etiam ne Christiani infirmiores scandalizentur suspicantes eos qui Iudeos reverentur aliquid de secta eorum sapere ac tenere" (ÖNB 4677, 196ʳ–196ᵛ).

[63] Cohen, *The Friars and the Jews*, 188.

in the Bremis notebook, Langenstein's account follows the form of an actual discussion (statement, reply, counterargument, rebuttal, etc.). What is most striking, however, is the emotional intensity of his remarks. Their vehemence, which is preserved in the very erasures of his autograph manuscript, suggests that Langenstein himself may have lost face before some laymen. The first part of the passage, on the other hand, shows that the Trinity lay close to the heart of Langenstein's concern about Jewish arguments. Even more specifically, these views raised questions about the distinctions between the persons in the Trinity, and the relation between those distinctions and such attributes as power, wisdom, and goodness.[64]

Significantly, this portion of the lecture on Genesis antedates Langenstein's treatise on the Hebrew language (1388), which presumably was a response to his urgently felt need for instruction in Hebrew.[65] The first part of the work was an elementary introduction to the Hebrew letters, whereas the second half turned to the mystical meaning of those letters.[66] In the first part, after discussing the value of knowing Hebrew for resolving ambiguities in the Latin text of the Bible (especially the confusion between the letter combinations *ni, ui, in, iu*, and *iv* in manuscripts), Langenstein remarked: "Erudition in the foregoing [Hebrew language] is of no mean worth in order to defeat and confute the perfidy of the Jews, which they brashly corroborate with false and frivolous excuses from these scriptures of theirs before unlettered Christians."[67] Langenstein's repetition of this rationale underscores the seriousness of his concern, but also gives further credence to the hypothesis of public confrontations between Christians and members of the Jewish community.

[64] Oyta's *Disputatio Catholica contra Judaeos* further hints at interest in the issue at the time; see A. Lang, *Oyta*, 108.

[65] His own knowledge of the language was probably elementary. The autograph of the first volume of his lectures on Genesis preserves samples of Langenstein's Hebrew calligraphy sometimes as part of the text (ÖNB 4651, 101^v–102^r), sometimes simply for practice. Langenstein's recommendations for the study of Hebrew are also discussed briefly in Oedinger, *Über die Bildung der Geistlichen*, 35ff.

[66] Walde, *Christliche Hebraisten Deutschlands*, 28. Walde quotes extensively from the first part. The second, available only in one manuscript, which I have not seen (Erfurt, Ampl., Q 125), suggests that Langenstein looked into aspects of the Kabbalah, or such sources as the "Book of Creation"; see Scholem, *Major Trends in Jewish Mysticism*, 75ff, 133ff.

[67] "Valeat eciam non parum erudicio in predictis ad conuincendum et confundendum iudeorum perfidiam, quam falsis et frivolis suarum scripturarum allegacionibus coram christianis harum ignaris audacissime confirmant" (Walde, *Christliche Hebraisten Deutschlands*, 10).

In his treatise on contracts, Langenstein delved into a number of other issues concerning the Jews. The work reportedly was produced at the request of the city council in order to settle a legal dispute between the duke and the city.[68] It provided justifications for a Jewish presence among Christians. The first was based on Jesus' Parable of the Tares (Matthew 13:24ff)—the tares in the wheat field should not be uprooted until harvest time, lest some of the good grain be destroyed as well. The tone was ominous, but the argument implied that the final word was reserved for God. Another justification claimed that faith was greater when one believed in an environment filled with many contradictors.[69] This argument is especially intriguing because it suggests that the Jews were anything but passive in discussions of matters of faith.[70] The treatise contained an extensive discussion of contracts, along with their use and abuse by Christians to derive financial benefits from the high interest rates that the Jews were allowed to charge. Langenstein's critique of usury returned to some of his earlier concerns. Chief among these was that usurers did not work: the Jews therefore escaped the state of labor, which had been divinely ordained for all. Even more infuriating, their laziness gave them too much time to devote to the rebuttal of Christian arguments and to the deception of the simple.[71] This statement was firmly grounded in the local context. Indeed it was not the Viennese rabbis, but their wives, who most frequently entered their names in the records of monetary transactions in the late fourteenth century. Meanwhile, their husbands devoted themselves to full-time scholarship[72]—not unlike the theologians themselves.

Langenstein also upbraided Christians for participating in usury by entering with Jews into contractual agreements that circumvented the prohibition against outright moneylending.[73] Usury was a multifac-

---

[68] Trusen, *Spätmittelalterliche Jurisprudenz*, 18–20. Other works on Langenstein's economic theory include Winter, *Rudolph IV. von Österreich*, II, 264ff and 247n; and Noonan, *The Scholastic Analysis of Usury*, 68–69. I have not seen the dissertation by Sommerfeld, "Ökonomisches Denken in Deutschland vor der frühbürgerliche Revolution."

[69] Langenstein, "Tractatus de contractibus," in Gerson, *Opera omnia*, IV, 197^{v}a.

[70] "With respect to doctrinal issues, it was the Jewish side that usually took the offensive" (Berger, *The Jewish-Christian Debate in the High Middle Ages*, 13).

[71] "non sic studerent quomodo in calumniam vere fidei scripturas perversa intentione glosare possent et christianorum rationibus et observantiis calide et colorate ad corruptionem simplicium laicorum et clericorum respondendo obviare" (Langenstein, "Tractatus de contractibus," 198^{r}a).

[72] Spitzer, "Das Wiener Judentum," 144.

[73] "Iam per eos tam publica facta et communis quod a quibusdam christianorum avaris

eted evil, not only in its direct effects (particularly the impoverish-
ment of the common people, as Langenstein noted with empathy), but
in terms of its side effects, which hindered the conversion of the Jews
to Christianity and gave them the leisure to bolster their polemical arguments.

·

The work that sheds the most light on Langenstein's final thoughts
and looks back on his activities is the sermon he preached on 25 November 1396, only a few months before his death in February 1397.[74]
The occasion was one of the most solemn academic anniversaries, the
feastday of Saint Catherine of Alexandria, the patron saint of the faculty of arts.[75] Saint Catherine's fame derives from her legendary sin-
gle-handed conversion of fifty pagan philosophers to Christianity by
the force of her argumentation.[76] For Langenstein, the sermon thus
became the occasion for a lengthy discussion of his ideal for the university, and of his understanding of the relation between the various
fields of study. As befitted both his concerns and the anniversary, he
set the homily within the context of apologetics, the use of rational
argument to convert infidels.[77] The text around which Langenstein or-

---

vix peccatum esse reputatur hec iniquitas tamdiu iudeis permissa est et in eis a potentibus
defensa quod iam plurimum in christianos redsidavit(!) magnos et parvos clericos et lai-
cos. Unde est a iudeis iam tantum derivata / in christianos inter quos ex usuris vivere
permittuntur quod quidam christiani manifeste dant ad usuras quidem iudeis pecunias
concedunt et usuras cum eis dividunt quidam palleatis usurarie iniquitatis contractibus
et modis variis sine labore student divitiis abundare. De istis ergo Christianorum usu-
rariis in hoc peioribus iudeis dicendum est consequenter ubi quia Christianorum avaricia
usuras subtiliores sunt iudeis et eo acutius student hanc palleare iniquitatem quo apertius
et universalius prohibita est Christianis quam iudeis" (Langenstein, "Tractatus de contractibus," 198ʳb–ᵛa).

[74] The sermon, which exists in a single manuscript (ÖNB 5352), has been edited by
A. Lang, "Die Katharinenpredigt Heinrichs von Langenstein," 123–159, regrettably
with several omissions. It is there analyzed (233–250) as well as in his "Die ersten Ansätze
zu systematischer Glaubensbegründung" (361ff).

[75] The provisions for the Feast of St. Catherine were outlined in the first ordinance of
the 1389 statutes of the faculty of arts. See Lhotsky, Artistenfakultät, 226.

[76] The account goes back to Basil II's Menologion (ca. 1000). See Beatie, "Saint Katharine of Alexandria," 788–789, 799–800.

[77] It is noteworthy that St. Catherine was an important figure in the planning and
iconography of St. Stephen's. A statue of St. Catherine from the second quarter of the
fourteenth century graces the left-central portion of the choir. A chapel dedicated to St.
Catherine, housed in the base of the gigantic south steeple, faced the Bürgerschule and
was in use when Langenstein preached his sermon; see Zykan, Der Stephansdom, 90.
Most interesting of all, the tympanum of the so-called Bischofstor on the northwest face

ganized the sermon was "Doctrix est disciplina Dei" (Wisdom of Solomon 8:4), which he applied to Saint Catherine according to a threefold structure. Catherine was the "teacher of God's knowledge": first, by the erudition of science and learning in others; second, by her exemplary demonstration of morals and virtues; and third, by her castigation of vice and her suffering of many torments. Significantly, Langenstein opened his exposition of the text with a citation from the popular *Commentary on Wisdom* by Robert Holcot, whose outline he followed for part of the sermon.[78]

The first point in the exposition stands out as particularly salient. Langenstein began by noting that Catherine was first educated in the liberal arts, then divinely inspired about the truths of theology. Inspiration notwithstanding, Langenstein marveled at the fact that such a young woman—not only a member of the fragile sex but also single—dared to argue with so many barbarian men, all so well trained in the science of the world. Yet she succeeded in leading them to "a way of life that is completely contrary to the traditions of gentile philosophers, that is so very remote from the natural way of knowing, as are the articles of our faith."[79]

From the outset, then, Langenstein confronted his audience with the disjunction between natural and revealed knowledge. In his analysis, he carefully noted that conversion did not proceed univocally: "some infidels are converted to faith by prayers, others by arguments, some by prayers and arguments together."[80] But there were prerequisites to conversion:

> First of all, the infidel must be willing to acquiesce in the probable and persuasive reasons possible in moral matters, reasons that ought to move any rational man. He must concede this if he is a rational man, since demonstrative certainty should not be sought in all matters, least of all in moral matters.[81]

---

of the cathedral depicts Rudolph IV and his wife Katharina at the center. On the left side, they are flanked by a statue of St. Catherine holding her wheel and standing on the cowering bust of a man, undoubtedly a "pagan philosopher" but in this case dressed in the standard attire of a medieval Jew, with the beard and the hat (Zykan, *Stephansdom*, 65 [fig. 27] and 72). See also Kosegarten, "Zur Plastik der Fürstenportale am Wiener Stephansdom," 74–96.

[78] A. Lang, "Katharinenpredigt," 133, lines 8–13.

[79] Ibid., 134, lines 41–44.

[80] Ibid., 135, lines 7–9.

[81] Ibid., 136, lines 33–37. Interestingly, Buridan's commentary on Aristotle's *Ethics* claimed that ethics as a practical science required a special moral logic; see Wieland, "Aristotle's *Ethics*," 668. For Buridan's understanding of moral science and its relation

Langenstein's criteria of rationality included the willingness to give up demonstrative certainty for probable and persuasive reasons. Such a view was consistent with his rejection of the scientific status of theology—in the Aristotelian sense that science represented the conclusions of correct syllogisms with premises that were self-evidently true. Apologetics thus became a moral matter. These views were also consistent with Langenstein's acknowledgment that the Aristotelian syllogistic could not handle Trinitarian paralogisms.

According to Langenstein, however, the refusal to give up demonstration presented insuperable obstacles to the conversion process:

> If the infidel does not concede this assumption, then he is obstinate even in the sciences of the infidels; therefore, he cannot be persuaded by the path of reason. And this is why the Jews cannot be persuaded by arguments, because they are stubborn.[82]

Langenstein did not specify what arguments failed to persuade the Jews. But it is significant that he saw a direct connection between the refusal to concede this assumption and Jewish stubbornness. In any case, the Jewish opponents in Langenstein's sermon were clearly unwilling to give up demonstration easily.

There are good reasons to believe that Langenstein's "obstinate Jews" were not merely faceless *exempla* plucked from any number of Christian polemical texts to spice up a long sermon. By the later fourteenth century, Vienna, Krems, and Wiener Neustadt had become centers of Jewish learning that attracted students from France and the Rhineland, as well as from southern Austria and northern Italy.[83] Two rabbis in particular were active in Vienna during these years, Meir ben Baruch Halevi and Abraham Klausner.[84] Both men—but especially Rabbi Meir ben Baruch Halevi—had a keen sense of their worth as

---

to demonstrability, see Krieger, *Der Begriff der praktischen Vernunft nach Johannes Buridanus*, 66–85.

[82] A. Lang, "Katharinenpredigt," 138, lines 6–9. Langenstein made a similar point in his lectures on Genesis: ". . . legalis et rationabilis homo non exspectat ut evidenter scripturis aut rationibus communicatur ad credendum hec vel illa. Homo qui hoc exspectaret in omnibus credendis protervus esset et incivilis humane societati quod sine fide non potest [. . . ?] congruens. Quomodo enim staret hominum politica conversatio quin nullus credere vellet quod ille sit vel fuerit·pater suus aut quod sit legitimus aut baptizatus et huiusmodi nisi hoc evidenter sibi ostendatur?" (ÖNB 4679, 177ᵛ).

[83] Güdemann, *Geschichte des Erziehungswesens und der Cultur der Juden*, III, 26ff.

[84] See Gastfreund, *Die Wiener Rabbinen*, 23–29. Goldmann has found independent evidence for their presence in the lending records of the period; see *Das Judenbuch der Scheffstrasse*, xxxi–xxxii.

scholars and teachers. They valued, used, and conferred on their students the title of *morenu* ("our teacher"), which may have been a self-conscious counterpart to the title of doctor at the university.[85] Indeed, they appear to have elicited a grudging respect from the local theologians.[86] Apart from the circumstantial clues suggested by Langenstein's remarks, there is at present little direct evidence for the attitude of the Viennese rabbis toward Greek philosophy and Aristotle in particular. If the Viennese rabbis were familiar with the polemical tradition of Maimonides, Langenstein's rejection of demonstrative certainty would have struck them as irrational. They presumably followed the perspective of medieval Jewish philosophy, which espoused the traditional Aristotelian hierarchy of demonstrative, dialectical, and rhetorical methods outlined in Averroës.[87]

Although many questions remain to be answered about the philosophical interests (or lack thereof) of late medieval Jewish communities, rationalist attitudes and criticisms did surface in Spain during this period.[88] Indeed similar attitudes were not unknown in Central European Jewry. Within a hundred and fifty miles of Vienna, two rabbis from late fourteenth-century and early fifteenth-century Prague closely match the profile one would expect from Langenstein's remarks and emotional responses. Rabbi Yom Tov Lipmann Mühlhausen, who was in Prague before 1389 and remained active into the

[85] See Lauer, "R. Meir Halevy aus Wien," 1ff, for a summary and critical evaluation of this position. Although the title *morenu* was not introduced by Meir ben Baruch Halevi himself in late fourteenth-century Vienna, as Moritz Güdemann and others have claimed, it does go back to Meir of Rothenburg, who in the thirteenth century was a student of the Viennese rabbi Isaac ben Moshe. See Wellesz, "Isaak b. Mose Or Sarua," 129, 209–210.

[86] Arnold of Seehausen's claim that "multi sunt infideles sicut Judaei et heretici, qui sunt magni theologi, qui multis partibus theologiae dant fidem" takes on additional significance within the Viennese context, where it was written in the early fifteenth century; see Vooght, *Les Sources de la doctrine chrétienne*, 252 (quoting from Munich, Bayerische Staatsbibliothek, Clm 3546, 3ʳa).

[87] Altmann, "*Ars rhetorica* as Reflected in Some Jewish Philosophers of the Italian Renaissance," 3–5. Davidson ("Medieval Jewish Philosophy in the Sixteenth Century," 112) argues that the majority of Jewish "philosophic writers" in the fifteenth century favored a more conservative position than that of Maimonides, conceding to revelation a place above reason in the hierarchy of knowledge. According to Ben-Sasson, however, "despite the general view to the contrary, the scholars and leading personalities of Ashkenaz Jewry in those days [the later Middle Ages] were well acquainted with secular works and regarded with favour elements of culture and attitudes that are usually thought to be characteristic only of Spanish Jewry" (*A History of the Jewish People*, 624; I thank Mark Verman for this reference).

[88] Ben-Sasson, ed., *A History of the Jewish People*, 612ff.

1410s, had been a pupil of Meir ben Baruch Halevi of Vienna. He had a profound interest in philosophy, and he helped disseminate Maimonides' *Guide of the Perplexed* in Central Europe. Most interesting of all, he had a reputation as a formidable polemicist—apparently well deserved since he composed a *Sefer ha-Nizzahon*, which collected his polemical writings and "which he intended to serve as a handbook for the ordinary Jew compelled at times to wrestle with complex theological problems beyond his ability."[89] An unusual individual, he knew Latin, was familiar with Christian theological writings, and admired the ancients. Indeed he strongly urged the study of the Greeks as a source of wisdom: "Many of the degrees of wisdom can be found among the sages of Greece . . . and from this do not make the error that those degrees are forbidden, namely, natural philosophy and astronomy and philosophy, for these are branches of our faith and lead to the love of His Blessed Name and the fear of Him . . . and this is not Greek wisdom but the wisdom of all who are wise."[90] Since Mühlhausen traveled extensively and had Austrian contacts, it is very likely that both he and his work were known in Vienna, certainly among the local Jews but perhaps among the Christian theologians as well. Nor was he alone. Rabbi Avigdor Kara (d. 1439), also from Prague, likewise had a reputation as a skilled polemicist, and was presumed to have "had discussions with high Christian dignitaries." Kara reportedly was on good terms with King Wenceslas IV of Bohemia and influenced John Hus. He was a friend and colleague of Mühlhausen, with whom he shared an interest in both the Kabbalah and Maimonides.[91] Avigdor Kara's relative, Menahem ben Jacob Kara, wrote commentaries on Maimonides and al-Ghazālī.[92] Men such as these clearly had the interests, the skills, and the desire to argue with Christians.

Did Langenstein himself interact with Yom Tov Lipmann Mühlhausen, with whom he seems to have shared more than a few interests? Did Mühlhausen have Viennese counterparts? What impact, if any, did the latter's book make on the Viennese Jews? The answers to these

[89] Ta-Shma, "Mühlhausen, Yom Tov Lipmann," *Encyclopaedia Judaica*, xii, col. 501; Seligsohn, "Lipmann-Mühlhausen," *Jewish Encyclopedia*, viii, 97–98. The date of composition of the *Sefer ha-Nizzahon* varies widely from 1390 (Ta-Shma, 501) to "before 1410, for he expressed [in the book] a hope that the Messiah would arrive in that year" (Seligsohn, 98; citing the *Sefer ha-Nizzahon*, para. 385), to c. 1420 (Ben-Sasson, ed., *A History of the Jewish People*, 624).

[90] Ben-Sasson, ed., *A History of the Jewish People*, 624.

[91] David, "Kara, Avigdor ben Isaac," *Encyclopaedia Judaica*, x, cols. 758–759; Gladstein, "Eschatological Trends in Bohemian Jewry," 243ff.

[92] Horowitz, "Kara, Menachem ben Jacob," *Encyclopaedia Judaica*, x, col. 760.

questions are unclear. One thing is certain. Prague and Vienna in the late fourteenth century were not insulated intellectual centers. Since mid-century, when Prague had become the residence of the Holy Roman Emperor, the two cities were intensely aware of each other. Rudolph IV had made no secret of the fact that he had great ambitions for Vienna. He had chartered the University of Vienna as a counterpart to his imperial father-in-law's foundation of the University of Prague. Likewise, his plans for a monumental church of St. Stephen were in open competition with designs underway in the Bohemian capital.[93] This history did not disappear when Rudolph's brothers took charge. In the mid-1380s, when disenchanted students and masters from Prague swelled the enrollments of the University of Vienna, interest in developments at Prague remained high. On the Jewish side, rabbis such as Mühlhausen had Austrian contacts and traveled extensively. In a word, there is every reason to believe that there were frequent, if not necessarily cordial, contacts between the two cities.[94]

Jews in Vienna with interests like those of Mühlhausen and Kara would have been most unlikely to give up demonstrative arguments at the point where Langenstein wished they would. In his sermon, the procedure for converting infidels suggests one source of tension. If the infidel was rational, the following steps should be taken. First, one should present the first principle of the Catholic faith: namely, that there is only one God. Langenstein believed that this proposition could be demonstrated with at least as much certainty as the proposition 'prime matter exists', or any other conclusion of natural philosophy. But according to Langenstein, it did not matter whether or not this principle was demonstrable in the strict sense—it could be proved with the strongest reason that was humanly possible. As a second step, one should establish the *quid nominis* (or "nominal definition") of God. Third, once this was conceded, one should proceed to the attributes of God. Interestingly, the first attribute that Langenstein mentioned was freedom from contradiction, followed by perfection. Fourth, the infidel should be confronted with the proposition 'whatever is revealed by God is true'.

It is most unlikely that these arguments for the existence or the

---

[93] See Chap. 1 above.

[94] See, among other examples, the report in 1390 of a quarrel between a Viennese master and the faculty of arts at Prague—still under discussion nine years later (*AFA*, 1, 48, 166); the request made by the beadle of the faculty of arts for permission to visit Prague in 1393 (ibid., 94); or the thinly veiled criticisms of academic standards at Prague in 1397 (ibid., 146).

unicity of God would have become the focus of a heated debate. They
were not points of contention between Jews and Christians. Maimonides, for example, held that "these two principles, I mean the existence
of the deity and His being one, are knowable by human speculation
alone. Now with regard to everything that can be known by demonstration, the status of the prophet and that of everyone else who knows
it are equal; there is no superiority of one over the other. Thus these
two principles are not known through prophecy alone."[95] But, as happened frequently in the long history of the Jewish-Christian debate,
severe difficulties would have arisen in any discussion that attempted
to specify the nature of God any further, particularly to prove that the
Godhead included three persons, distinct yet one in essence.

It is easy to see why the Jews would have balked at this demand. The
suggestion of a plurality in God was the epitome of heresy. It was, in
fact, an argumentative move for which the rabbis had been prepared
by the Talmud and the Midrash.[96] As David Berger has argued,

> Jews were convinced that some of the central articles of faith professed by
> Christians were not only devoid of scriptural foundation but were with-
> out logical justification as well; to use Christian terminology, they lacked
> both *ratio* and *auctoritas*. The Trinity, which was an obvious target for
> logical questions, posed a peculiar problem for Jewish polemicists; they
> considered it so irrational that they had trouble in coming to grips with
> it.[97]

Yet it was precisely at this point that Langenstein wanted to give up
demonstrative certainty for moral certainty. To intimate, as he was
doing, that the Jews should give up fundamental rules of reasoning to
accommodate a view that was heretical, irrational, and philologically
senseless must have seemed preposterous. This theme is a familiar one
in the polemical literature of Spanish Jewry during the late fourteenth
century. Although accounts of the long Tortosa disputation (1413–
1414) can be used to argue that the Jews had lapsed into fideism or
irrationality, and did not have the logical sophistication to counter the
syllogistic arguments that confronted them, it is hazardous to gener-

[95] Maimonides, *The Guide of the Perplexed* (bk. II, 33), 364.
[96] See Rankin, *Jewish Religious Polemic*, 69ff, which mentions the Midrash Rabbah on
Genesis (I, para. 7; VIII, para. 9); and his translation of the fifteenth-century poem
"Memoir of the Book of Niẓẓachon of Rabbi Lipmann," the first three stanzas of which
(60ff) express very eloquently the disbelief that Langenstein must have encountered.
[97] Berger, *The Jewish-Christian Debate in the High Middle Ages*, 13.

alize from Tortosa to the rest of Europe during the late Middle Ages.[98]
Even in Spain in the decades before Tortosa, Profiat Duran (d. ca.
1414) explicitly appealed to syllogistic arguments against the Trinity.[99]
And the commentary on Duran by Joseph ben Shem Tov (ca. 1400–
ca. 1460) shows that the latter was fully aware of the circumlocutions
proposed by earlier fourteenth-century Christian theologians in order
to avoid unorthodox conclusions,[100] and that he used these in turn
against the Christians. Crescas' (d. 1412) refutation of the Trinity was
based on extensive arguments about the divine attributes and their relation to God's simplicity.[101] If the existence of God was demonstrable
with "the strongest reasons that are humanly possible," as Maimonides
claimed, why should a lower point on the chain of argument be even
less accessible to reason?[102]

Langenstein abandoned logical criteria when he reached the fourth
point of his scheme, the attempt to show the infidel that whatever God
has revealed is true: "Here we reach a major difficulty, for I think that
no man could ever be so bestial that he would not believe something if
he knew that God had said it."[103] Langenstein's position stands in stark
contrast to the position of Peter the Venerable in the twelfth century.
For Peter the Venerable, the natural endowments of the human race
were sufficient to perceive the truths of Christianity. Since the Jews did
not do so, it followed logically that they were not quite human.[104] The
St. Catherine's Day sermon proves conclusively that this was not Langenstein's attitude.

How then might one establish the credibility of the prophet, the medium through which God spoke? By considering the holiness of his

[98] Maccoby, *Judaism on Trial*, 87–88.

[99] Lasker, *Jewish Philosophical Polemics*, 90. I thank Talya Fishman for this reference.

[100] Ibid., 91f.

[101] Ibid., 69ff.

[102] Medieval theologians might have demurred when asked to rank the existence of
God and His triune nature in order of ontological priority. But when discussing the
organization of their theological principles, they did not hesitate to make the existence
of God prior to his triune nature. Thus Arnold of Seehausen wrote in the prologue to
his commentary on the *Sentences*: "that only one God exists is the first principle. How
indeed could anyone believe that God is three and one unless he believed first in time or
by nature that God is one. Such is the case with the Jews and many Gentiles" (Latin in
Vooght, *Sources de la doctrine chrétienne*, 252).

[103] A. Lang, "Katharinenpredigt," 139, lines 16–20.

[104] See his "Tractatus adversus Judaeorum inveteram duritiem," in *PL* 189, cols. 550–
551. Also see Kniewasser, "Die antijüdische Polemik des Petrus Alphonsi," 34–76;
Cohen, *The Friars and the Jews*, 24–25; and idem, "Scholarship and Intolerance," 602–
603.

life, the perfection of his doctrine, his marvelous works, and the trib-
ulations he has suffered. As Holcot had argued in the *Quaestiones*, it
was the character of the witness that guaranteed the truth of his pronouncements and justified belief.[105] For Langenstein as for Holcot,
logical criteria had disappeared. Only persons "of holy and honest life"
could undergird the credibility of the process. The remaining six
points in Langenstein's outline were all historically oriented. The first
three focused on the story of Israel—the worship of one God, the statements of the prophets, the promise of a savior. The next two points
claimed that the savior had come, and identified him as Jesus of Naz-
areth. Finally, his doctrine should be explained to the infidel.[106] According to Albert Lang, this scheme represented a new direction in
apologetics, particularly "where Christian belief as such came into
contact with unbelief or was threatened by unbelieving tendencies."[107]
In this regard, Langenstein's historical approach to apologetics contrasts with that of the early Henry of Oyta. Although the two men had
once shared similar presuppositions about the place of logic in theology, Langenstein's outline differed in at least one notable respect from
Oyta's, which was assembled some twenty years earlier. Oyta's apologetic scheme proceeded according to a deductive and systematic outline; the historical features of Langenstein's were altogether absent.[108]

As if to dispel any doubt that he was thinking specifically of the local
Jews throughout his discussion of apologetics, Langenstein proposed
a *dubium*: "But, someone might say, if it is so easy to convert an infidel
to the faith, why therefore have we not converted in this fashion all
infidels, and especially the Jews, who are so familiar to us?"[109] Of the
four reasons offered, two pertained to the Jews. First, they were stub-
born, the character trait symptomatized by their refusal to admit nondemonstrative arguments in apologetics. Second, they were accus-
tomed to delicate living and feared poverty, so that those who did
convert frequently fell back into their former ways. Unlike the impasse
over the issue of demonstrability, the second problem could be solved.
Langenstein proposed the foundation of a halfway house for converted
Jews, like that recently established for Viennese prostitutes.[110] This

[105] See Chapter 3 above.
[106] A. Lang, "Katharinenpredigt," 138–141; summarized in idem, *Die Entfaltung des
apologetischen Problems*, 209.
[107] A. Lang, *Entfaltung*, 208.
[108] Ibid., 203–205.
[109] A. Lang, "Katharinenpredigt," 141, lines 4–6.
[110] Ibid., 141, lines 13–15. See also Langenstein's remarks in the *Epistola concilii pacis*,
quoted above, to the effect that poverty forces converts to apostatize.

proposal was not the abstract suggestion of a scholar dealing exclusively with texts in isolation from the day-to-day world; it had the immediacy of an administrator groping for concrete solutions to a pressing problem. This is not to deny that some of Langenstein's remarks were commonplace in the polemical literature against the Jews. Early in the fourteenth century, for example, Nicholas of Lyra had cited three reasons for the obstinacy of the Jews: their cupidity (for their law promised them material goods); their long education in an anti-Christian frame of mind; and the difficulties of Christian dogma (especially the Trinity, the twofold nature of Christ, and the Eucharist).[111]

But Langenstein was thinking primarily of his own times and context. Thus he went on to argue that part of the blame for the failure to convert the Jews also rested with the Christians. It was not simply that they had not tried hard enough to convert the Jews. There were more fundamental reasons for the failure of apologetics:

> . . . we are deficient in holiness of life: our Church is in disarray and is in some sense answerable to no authority when we act against our law, since the infidels can argue from our perverse works that the things we preach to them are false and deceptive; nor do we believe the same articles with true and firm faith, since we constantly evince and carry out the opposite in deed.[112]

How then could the infidels be brought to the faith? Langenstein answered that if Christians lived in accordance with the law given by their savior, all who saw them would be moved to adopt their way of life. Apologetics had failed for more than strictly logical considerations. The moral inadequacy, indeed the ritual impurity, of the Christians—not merely as individuals, but as a collectivity—was also to blame. The source of the pollution was none other than the Great Schism. These bitter remarks recall Langenstein's own words twenty years earlier in the *Epistola concilii pacis*. Langenstein remained the reformer.

The failure of apologetics and the profound despair in the face of the Schism, illustrated in Langenstein's last sermon, parallel another disillusionment in his life during the early 1390s. The dismal condition of the Church, from the not-so-faithful in the pews to the two mutually excommunicated popes, suggested to Langenstein in the mid-1380s that perhaps the Apocalypse was at hand. Accordingly, Langenstein

---

[111] Hailperin, *Rashi and the Christian Scholars*, 140 (Latin text on 287, n. 37); Cohen, *The Friars and the Jews*, 185.

[112] A. Lang, "Katharinenpredigt," 141, lines 28–35.

turned his attention to writings devoted to the signs of the Last
Things. Two letters from ca. 1383–1384 show a keen interest in the
prophecies of Hildegard of Bingen and Joachim of Fiore. By 1390,
Langenstein was praising Joachim in public for his attempts to forecast
the Last Things from scripture.[113] The most intriguing aspect of this
fascination with Joachim of Fiore is the latter's link with two of Langenstein's chief concerns, the Trinity and the Jews. Joachim's schema
of history was Trinitarian through and through, moving from the Age
of the Father (Old Testament times) through the Age of the Son (from
the Incarnation to the near future) to the Age of the Spirit, when history would reach its culmination and the Jews would all convert to
Christianity.[114] By 1392, however, the hopes that Langenstein had
placed in Joachim had been dashed (he specifically mentioned the latter's erroneous views on the Trinity), and the old professor turned
with bitterness against the man he now saw as a false prophet. Langenstein still expected the Jews to convert after Christ would slay the An-
tichrist, but he had given up on a renewal of the Church before the end
of time.[115] Although the temporal and thematic congruities between
these two blighted hopes are intriguing, the precise connection between Langenstein's crushed millenarian expectations and his confession of failure in apologetics remains—for the present at least—an open
question. Even more intriguing, Langenstein was not alone in thinking
that he lived in momentous times: Yom Tov Lipmann Mühlhausen
expected the Messiah to come in 1410.[116]

Taken as a whole, the themes and allusions in Langenstein's writings
show a consistent preoccupation with Jewish life and thought for more
than a decade. Of Langenstein's intellectual struggle with his own version of the Jewish question, there can be no doubt. His writings in a
variety of genres and contexts strongly suggest that his involvement
went beyond the use of literary sources to include actual interaction
with Viennese Jews. The evidence is tantalizing, even though at present it derives from only one of the parties. Among other things, it

[113] Reeves, *The Influence of Prophecy*, 425–426. The letters are addressed to Bishop
Eckehard of Ders, and were edited by Sommerfeldt in "Die Prophetien der hl. Hildegard
von Bingen," 46ff and 298ff. Langenstein preached his sermon on Ascension Day 1390
(see ÖNB 4017, 146ᵛ–164ʳ; 4384, 18ᵛ–29ʳ). Langenstein's stay at Eberbach after leaving
Paris may be related to his exposure to these views, for Joachim had prophesied great-
ness for the Cistercian order, of which he had once been a member (Reeves, 14, 146).

[114] Reeves, *The Influence of Prophecy*, chap. 2. Pierre d'Ailly also was interested in such
views; see Pascoe, "Pierre d'Ailly: Histoire, Schisme et Antéchrist," 615–622.

[115] Reeves, *The Influence of Prophecy*, 426–427.

[116] See n. 88 above.

includes Langenstein's interest in Hebrew, which he studied with converted and unconverted Jews; the emotional intensity captured in his autograph of the *Lectures on Genesis*; his impatience with the practice of usury in Vienna, which allowed some Jews to devote time to the refutation of their opponent's arguments; his recurrent anger at the fact that Jews were initiating discussions with the simple folk; and finally Langenstein's last sermon, a confession of failure to convert the local Jews with apologetic arguments.

In any program of apologetics that tried to begin with first principles, the Trinity would have been the first stumbling block for the Jews. Indeed, Jewish polemicists were skilled at exploiting the logical difficulties in the Christian position—difficulties of which the Christians themselves were all too keenly aware. During the early years of the faculty of theology, the Viennese theologians and their students agreed that Aristotle's rules were sufficient for the purposes of syllogizing in this area. In spite of this consensus, to which Langenstein himself had contributed with his *Tractatus de dici de omni*, he came to reject his earlier view. It is perhaps not surprising that he did so in an environment in which polemical encounters between Christians and Jews were not only likely, but almost inevitable. As Jeremy Cohen has remarked about a different historical context, "The Scholastic synthesis did not rest in an ivory tower; it attempted to create a harmony between theory and practice, to apply the logic and conclusions of scholarship to social structures and individual lives."[117] Langenstein's last years in Vienna indicate that such a causal nexus was not unidirectional. After giving up on the universal validity of Aristotle's logic, the common language that Christian intellectuals shared with their Jewish and Muslim counterparts, Langenstein set his hopes on a vague Platonic logic, about which he knew little, save that it promised to preserve the ineffability of the Trinity. Once Aristotle's syllogistic lost its status of neutral language suited to discussing the highest tenets of the faith, yet another bridge between two polarized communities disappeared in the tense atmosphere of that other *fin-de-siècle* Vienna.

[117] Cohen, "Scholarship and Intolerance," 605.

CHAPTER SEVEN

"Unless You Believe,
You Shall Not Understand"

When something is firmly classed as anomalous
the outline of the set in which it is not a member
is clarified.

MARY DOUGLAS,
Purity and Danger

. . . moi, j'ai décidé d'être logique et puisque j'ai
le pouvoir, vous allez voir ce que la logique va
vous coûter. J'exterminerai les contradicteurs et
les contradictions.

ALBERT CAMUS,
Caligula (Act 1, Scene 8)

IN SEPTEMBER 1396, Langenstein explicitly rejected the conclusion
that Aristotle's syllogistic could deal with the highest truths of theology. Two months later, he outlined a program of apologetics that
relied less on logic than on the moral credibility of the apologist as a
witness to salvation history, publicly admitting the failure of earlier
attempts to convert the Jews. Whether Langenstein had always
thought that the two issues stood together is not certain, but they def-
initely fell together. The preceding chapter has emphasized one factor
in this change of mind—Langenstein's move to a new urban environment, which forced him to deal with infidels and apologetics in concrete rather than hypothetical terms. This encounter in the shadow of
the Great Schism was not only intellectual but, in all likelihood, personal as well.

Langenstein's rejection of Aristotle in Trinitarian theology pitted his
views against those of Henry of Oyta, the other leading theologian in
Vienna. The deaths of both men in 1397 soon bequeathed this intellectual breach to the following generation, along with the Schism itself.
As they sought to come to terms with both divisions, the theologians

in the generation of 1402 were on their own. But they were also at the beginning of their careers, and could think about the future in ways that neither Langenstein nor Oyta could. Although the younger generation had grown up under the Schism, it was no less appalled than its elders at the "monstrous bicephalous pestiferous beast that [was] devastating the Church of God," as one Viennese master called it.[1] One of the differences between the two generations lay in the means that they proved willing to use in order to solve their problems.

The early years of the fifteenth century were anything but idyllic. Nationalist currents, political turmoil, economic insecurities, and ecclesiastical tensions all contributed to the malaise of these stormy times. In such an environment, the rejection of Aristotelian logic in Trinitarian theology among a few academics seems little more than a straw in the wind. In a whirlwind, however, even straws can be deadly. The abstract positions of the theologians helped shape decisions and justify actions that left an indelible imprint on the lives of their peers, the leaders of the Hussite movement, and the Viennese Jews.

In Vienna, the fourteenth century drew to a close with the prospect of uncertain times ahead. Albert III died in 1395, Henry of Langenstein and Henry of Oyta within months of each other in 1397. These deaths marked the end of a decade of relative stability and continuity in Austrian politics and at the university. The Habsburg territories entered a new period of feuding among Albert's potential successors, his son Albert IV and his nephew William. Within the city, the ducal court enacted in 1396 a new privilege that gave legal sanction to a reorganization of the city council. Representatives of the patricians, the merchants, and the artisans were each to compose one-third of the council.[2] Whatever else it may have signified, this official redistribution of political power implicitly acknowledged that the old order was crumbling under the pressure of social change. At the university after Langenstein's death, one of the old mentor's dreams lived on. During the early years of the fifteenth century, Vienna continued to seek a solution to the Schism, the only *studium generale* of the Empire known to have done so consistently.[3]

The university also did its best to maintain its reputable record on heresy. Already in the early years of the university, Henry of Oyta had

---

[1] Graz, Universitätsbibliothek 443, 107ʳ. The context of the remark was a disputation on the comet of 1402, and its potential for producing monsters and plagues.

[2] Brunner, "Die Politik der Stadt Wien," 7; idem, *Die Finanzen der Stadt Wien*, 14; Schalk, "Zum Parteiwesen in Wien," 458–459.

[3] Swanson, *Universities, Academics, and the Great Schism*, 170.

emphasized the place of higher learning in controlling deviations from orthodoxy. The Church had established universities, he claimed, "in which to nourish, increase, and make acceptable, true and Catholic doctors who have the knowledge and the ability to extirpate heresy and sow sound doctrine."[4] Soon after Oyta's pronouncement, the university had occasion to put these Church-given talents to use. Authorities outside the realm appealed to Vienna in several questions of heresy. In a case brought by the Dominicans of Ulm, a commission of Viennese theologians (including Langenstein and Oyta) ruled that six propositions defended by a Johann Müntzinger were not in doubt "among those who understand and have their senses exercised in the faculty of theology." But they warned about preaching such things to the simple folk. Like atheism in the eighteenth century, theology in the fourteenth was not a matter to discuss before the common people.[5] Vienna was also one of the institutions that the University of Paris drew into the controversy surrounding propositions defended by the Dominican Juan de Monzón.[6] A third case involved the Beghard Nicholas of Basel, who allegedly had taught that he was perfect, demanded unstinting personal obedience from his followers, and claimed the power to make them revert to the innocence that preceded the Fall. An early fifteenth-century source claims that Henry of Langenstein—true to his apologetic instincts—tried to convert the man. Apparently he did not succeed, for Nicholas was burned at the stake in Vienna sometime between 1393 and 1397.[7] Several years earlier, in his *Lectures on Genesis*, Langenstein had warned his students about brash laymen, almost certainly burghers, who were not content with their estate and pried into matters reserved to the clergy.[8] Woe to the layman who did not trust "them that knew" and meddled in domains beyond his ken.

[4] Sommerfeldt, "Zwei politische Sermone," 321.

[5] See A. Lang, "Johann Müntzinger," 1211–1212; Becker, *The Heavenly City of the Eighteenth-Century Philosophers*, e.g. 31. Cf. Holcot's quodlibetal question "Utrum haec sit concedenda: Deus est Pater et Filius et Spiritus Sanctus," in Gelber, *Exploring the Boundaries of Reason*, 34.

[6] See the letters of 17 February and 25 March 1389 from George of Rain to the University of Vienna; *Chartularium*, III, nos. 1569–1570.

[7] Lerner, *The Heresy of the Free Spirit*, 152–153.

[8] "ruricole et mechanici imprudentes murmurant sepe contra clericos, milites et principes . . ."; ". . . inferiores, qui ausibus temerarii se intromittant de quibusdam factis proprie ad sacerdotes pertinentibus, ut predicare populo, exponere scripturas, discutere questiones et difficultates profundissimas in materia fidei et hiis similia" (Munich, Bayerische Staatsbibliothek, Clm 18146, 308^v, and Clm 18147, 121^r, respectively, as transcribed by Oedinger, *Über die Bildung der Geistlichen*, 1, n. 3, and 52, n. 2).

Heresy preoccupied not only the university, but also the political authorities. In the early 1390s, persecutions directed against the Waldensians of Italy stimulated their migration into Austria. In 1395, Albert III responded to the influx by ordering against them a full-scale inquisition, which his successors William, Leopold IV, and Albert IV pursued after his death. These efforts led to 1,000 arrests and to the eventual execution of 80 to 100 persons.[9] Around the turn of the century, heresy had begun to infiltrate the inner sanctum: accusations emerged within the faculty of theology itself. In 1397, Lambert of Gelderen, the dean of the faculty, denounced several false propositions advanced by the Minorite Johannes of Haderdorff.[10] On 13 February 1404, Nicholas of Dinkelsbühl and Peter of Pulkau brought charges against an Augustinian Eremite who had preached to the populace in the vernacular. Not two months later, the two men joined forces with Johann Berwart of Villingen to attack a university sermon by the Carmelite Arnold of Seehausen, who had been a debate partner of Pulkau and Villingen in the *principia* of 1402.[11]

Albert IV's death in 1404 was soon followed by the death of the regent William in 1406, precipitating another succession quarrel. Which of the uncles, Frederick, Leopold, or Ernest, would rule during the minority of Albert V? The question divided partisans of Leopold and Ernest in particular: in Vienna, the large landowners, the patriciate, the city administrators, and the clergy supported Ernest, who governed Styria; the nobility and the mass of the Viennese citizens favored Leopold, who ruled Austria, Carinthia, and Carniola.[12] The hostilities ran deep, turning into the most serious urban conflict in decades. In 1408, after their trial by a town council dominated by the patricians, five artisans were beheaded for conspiring to put Leopold on the throne. The following summer, their plot came to fruition posthumously. Leopold did take power and imposed an extraordinary tax on the city, which offered open resistance to the ordinance. He also avenged the deaths of his supporters with the execution of the burgomaster Konrad Vorlauf and two associates.[13]

While city strife smoldered, the tensions surrounding the Schism intensified. In 1409, the Council of Pisa convened in an effort to end

---

[9] Bernard, "Heresy in Fourteenth-Century Austria," 50–63, esp. 59–62; Kieckhefer, *Repression of Heresy in Medieval Germany*, 64–66; Koller, *Princeps in ecclesia*, 45, n. 40.

[10] Salvadori, *Die Minoritenkirche in ihrer ältesten Umgebung*, 81–82.

[11] *ATF*, I, 9; and Chapter 5 above.

[12] Schalk, "Zum Parteiwesen in Wien," 458–459.

[13] Brunner, "Die Politik der Stadt Wien," 16–17.

the divisions. In late March, the University of Vienna formally selected two representatives to the council, the Dominican theologian
Franz of Retz and the vice-chancellor Peter Deckinger. Conveniently
both men also served as the ambassadors for Duke Ernest of Austria.[14]
The gathering succeeded in reaching a hopeful consensus: it deposed
the two popes and chose a single replacement. But once Peter of Candia was elected as Alexander v, the two other popes refused to step
down. The two-headed monster had now become an unholy trinity.
A distressing situation was verging on the grotesque.[15]

Meanwhile, as the Council of Pisa struggled for unity, several decades of conflict were taking their toll on the University of Prague.[16]
The tensions between Bohemians and Germans that had boosted enrollments at the University of Vienna in the 1380s persisted into the
early fifteenth century. Here a complex convergence of issues involving social class, linguistic concerns, ethnic origins, philosophical pref-
erences, and ecclesiastical reform exacerbated the tensions. The
wealthier burghers were generally Germans, who played a prominent
role in city politics. At the university, the Bohemians frequently complained that the Germans received preferential treatment in the distribution of ecclesiastical benefices and academic appointments.[17] At the
same time, glaring abuses in the Church such as corruption, absenteeism, and immorality stood out for all to see. In a different context, one
anonymous wit suggested the following recipe to solve the Church's
problems: "Take twenty-three cardinals, as many archbishops, and an
equal number of prelates of any nation; and [take] as many curial officials as you can get; let them be immersed in the Rhine and remain
there for three days. This will be good for St. Peter's stomach and the
purging of its corruption."[18]

Not everyone was so cynical, however. Prague had been the scene
of various attempts at reform throughout the later fourteenth century.
By the last decade of the century, the tradition of reform combined
with strong Bohemian sentiments and a deep interest in the writings
of the English reformer, theologian, and realist philosopher John Wy-

---

[14] Leinweber, "Eine neues Verzeichnis," 224, 245–246 (a scribal mistake accounts for
the peculiar form of Deckinger's name in this reference). See also Frank, "Die Obödienzerklärung der österreichischen Herzöge," 53.

[15] Combes, "Facteurs dissolvants et principe unificateur," 301.

[16] The summary that follows is based on Spinka, *John Hus at the Council of Constance*,
30ff; Leff, *Heresy in the Later Middle Ages*, II, 620ff.

[17] See Chaloupecký, *L'Université Charles à Prague*, 125ff.

[18] Koller, *Princeps in ecclesia*, 20, citing ÖNB 5113, 1r.

clif (d. 1384). In the absence of legitimate authority within the schismatic Church, Wyclif had appealed to scripture as the "law of God." In addition, his realism led him to deny that the bread in the sacrament of the Eucharist, for example, could be annihilated, since bread, like any other created thing, participated in the being of God.[19] In the early fifteenth century, one of the leaders of the reform movement was John Hus, a master of arts at Prague who became taken with the philosophical ideas of Wyclif, most notably in such works as *De ideis, De materia et forma,* and *De universalibus.*[20] In 1402, soon after Hus's term as dean of the faculty of arts at Prague, the masters of the Czech nation elected him to the pulpit of Bethlehem Chapel, from which he exhorted his listeners to personal reform. Concurrently, at the university, the fascination for Wyclif's ideas was growing to such an extent that the German nation agitated for a condemnation of his views. The Germans, who were in the majority, pushed through a motion of censure against forty-five articles, which inevitably stimulated even more interest in the work of the English theologian.[21] Hus played an important part in the defense of Wyclif's philosophical views, two of his colleagues being responsible for the theological views. By 1405, Wyclif's writings on Church reform were making a noticeable impact on Hus's preaching at Bethlehem Chapel. Two years later, Hus had become the leader of the reform party. The spokesman for the Germans was Ludolph Meistermann, a bachelor of theology and former master of arts at Vienna.[22]

By late 1408, the efforts to bring the Schism to an end began to play into an already complex situation. King Wenceslas of Bohemia was persuaded to follow the conciliar path, which would elect a new pope after deposing the two schismatic ones as heretics. To retaliate against the German masters who refused to take this course, the king altered the traditional allocation of votes within the university. His decree of Kutná Hora dismissed the principle of "one nation, one vote" by giving three votes to the small Czech nation, while allotting only one vote to each of the other three.[23] Interactions between Czechs and Germans

[19] On Wyclif, see Robson, *Wyclif and the Oxford Schools*; Spinka, *John Hus at the Council of Constance,* 27ff; and Leff, *Heresy,* II, chap. 7.

[20] Leff, *Heresy,* II, 622ff.

[21] For most of the documents, see *Documenta Mag. Joannis Hus vitam, doctrinam, causam in Constantiensi concilio,* 327ff.

[22] See Chapter 2 above.

[23] Chaloupecký, *L'Université Charles,* 124–125; Spinka, *John Hus at the Council of*

had been strained for several decades already; the reforming zeal of Hus, with its Wyclifite overtones, had heightened the tension further. Now the Kutná Hora decree effectively severed relations between Germans and Czechs: in 1409, the German students stalked out of the city in protest. Most went northwest to Leipzig, where they established a new university; some traveled southeast to Vienna.

Disgruntled Germans were not the only wayfarers on the road to Vienna. In 1410, a close associate of Hus, one Jerome of Prague, began to preach in the regions surrounding Bohemia, including Austrian territory.[24] The timing of his trip was not propitious. Not only was Vienna suffering from a plague epidemic, but in addition the university was on the lookout for heretics. Already in June, as dean of the faculty of theology, Nicholas of Dinkelsbühl called attention to "some articles that were false or sounded bad, which three men had been accused of preaching in public from the pulpit before the common folk."[25] After Jerome's visit to the Vienna area, a tribunal drawn from the faculty of theology—Nicholas of Dinkelsbühl, Peter of Pulkau, and Lambert of Gelderen among them—formally charged him with heresy in August 1410.[26] Upon hearing that the university had slandered him, Jerome returned to Vienna, allegedly to rehabilitate himself. He was suspected of being a Wyclifite, and was therefore confronted first with the forty-five articles of Wyclif that had been condemned in Prague and London, then with twelve additional articles concerning his own alleged statements—almost all of which he denied.

The trial proceedings record some concern about the implications of Jerome's philosophical realism. These fears were expressed in a number of charges: Jerome had claimed that universals should be posited in the mind of God; he had owned a copy of Wyclif's *Logica* while in Paris; and, while in Heidelberg, he had called Ockham, Mauleveld, Buridan, Marsilius of Inghen, and their disciples "not dialecticians, but diabolical heretics."[27] Accusations such as these have been highlighted to emphasize the philosophical character of the dispute.[28] In the testi-

---

Constance, 35ff; and Šmahel, "The Kuttenberg Decree and the Withdrawal of the German Students," 153–161.

[24] On Jerome of Prague, see Bernard, "Jerome of Prague," 3–22; Šmahel, "Leben und Werk des Magisters Hieronymus von Prag"; and Kałuża, "Le chancelier Gerson et Jérome de Prague," 81–115.

[25] *AFA* I, 348, n. 11; *ATF*, I, 17. For a list of the deans, see *ATF*, I, xxv.

[26] See Klicman, *Processus iudiciarius contra Jeronimum de Praga*, 1.

[27] Ibid., 13, 22.

[28] Klicman, "Der Wiener Process gegen Hieronymus," 446–447.

mony presented at the Viennese trial, philosophical issues played a role, but by no means the only one. The specific attack on Ockham and his associates was reported by only one witness, who clearly was disturbed by Jerome's realism; but the prosecutor made little of this charge. Indeed, not all members of the Viennese faculty of theology were vehemently opposed to realism per se. Unless Lambert of Gelderen had reversed himself since his days as a bachelor of theology, he must have had at least some residual sympathy for realist theses. As a former (if not current) follower of the extreme realist John of Ripa, he should perhaps have shown some understanding for a man accused of holding that "there are in the divine mind several formalities formally and really distinct."[29] The thesis attributed to Jerome was not so different from Ripa's assertion of "immensely distinct formalities" in the divine essence.[30]

The importance of philosophy in the trial at the very least testifies to the thoroughness of the prosecutor, who left no stone unthrown. He called upon witnesses who had known or heard Jerome in Oxford, Paris, Heidelberg, and Prague. Most of them were German students who had left Prague in the wake of the Kutná Hora decree only a few months earlier, and their ensuing bitterness dominated the trial. One of the most frequent allegations against Jerome was that he had perjured himself by supporting the rise to power of the Czech nation at Prague. By fostering discord among the nations, therefore, he had violated his magisterial oath to promote unity within the university. As one witness candidly admitted, "he gladly would see [Jerome] prosecuted—insofar as compatible with justice—because he had worked toward the destruction of the University of Prague; otherwise not."[31]

Jerome realized that it would be very difficult for an outspoken Bohemian realist to receive a fair trial in an atmosphere so highly charged as that of Vienna in 1410. Although he had sworn that he would remain in town until the conclusion of the trial, he decided not to wait around for the obvious verdict. His flight did not endear him to his

---

[29] See Klicman, *Processus*, 1, 5; and Kałuża, "Le chancelier Gerson," 98–99, n. 32; Gilson, *La Philosophie au moyen âge*, II, 614; and Chapter 2 above.

[30] The position attributed to Jerome is closer yet to a corollary advanced by Ripa's disciple Louis of Padua, and later condemned by the faculty of arts at Paris in 1362: "Any volition by which God wants A to be is no less formally distinguished from the volition by which God wants B to be [than God] is really distinguished from prime matter." See Combes "Présentation de Jean de Ripa," 200; also see Vignaux, "Philosophie et théologie trinitaire chez Jean de Ripa," 224–227.

[31] Klicman, *Processus*, 24.

judges. Characteristically Jerome added insult to perjury by sending to the prosecutor a brash letter (gleefully signed "Yours always") from his hideout in Bohemia. The prosecutor posted a public notice summoning Jerome to appear, and several days later pronounced him "guilty of perjury, excommunicate, and vehemently suspect of heresy."[32] Word of the trial spread well beyond Vienna: on 24 May 1413, the faculty of arts received from the University of Cracow a request for a copy of the trial proceedings.[33] Meanwhile, the faculty of theology remained vigilant. On 8 March 1413, with Peter of Pulkau serving as dean, three members of the faculty who had "preached carelessly" received reprimands, and agreed to retract their views. The case eventually lasted almost nine months, as one of the accused later decided to fight the charges.[34]

Although Jerome of Prague's flight cut short any action against him, the Council of Constance (1414–1418) would soon provide the opportunity to overcome this difficulty, and indeed to stage other trials around which the various schismatic factions could unite. By the time the council began its deliberations, nearly all means of settling the Schism had been tried—including the very disappointing Council of Pisa a few years earlier. Under such circumstances, it is not surprising that the council was ready to take the view that a desperate situation required desperate means.[35] Representation at the council was broad. In addition to many ecclesiastical dignitaries, whose prestige as a class was not at its zenith, a notable proportion of academics also gathered in Constance. Indeed, the universities as institutions took an active interest in the work of the council. Some discussed the agenda; others sent delegates, whom they advised by letter.[36] The University of Vienna was especially well represented. It had elected Peter of Pulkau and Caspar Maiselstein as its official delegates. In addition, Nicholas of Dinkelsbühl and Henry of Kitzbühl traveled to Constance as personal representatives of Duke Albert v.[37] But these officials evidently accounted for only a small fraction of the participants from the university: Peter of Pulkau reported that the members of the Viennese *studium*

---

[32] Betts, "Jerome of Prague," 68–69. The documents are edited by Palacký, in *Documenta*, 416–420.

[33] *AFA*, I, 397.

[34] *ATF*, I, 24.

[35] Combes, "Facteurs dissolvants et principe unificateur," 300–303.

[36] Swanson, *Universities, Academics, and the Great Schism*, esp. 190ff.

[37] Girgensohn, "Die Universität Wien und das Konstanzer Konzil," 256.

were as numerous as the members of all other German universities combined.[38] The Viennese delegation thus had a preponderant influence on the position of the German delegation. And the Germans were especially eager to work for unity; as a group they felt that their honor depended on the success of the council. At the beginning of the council, Nicholas of Dinkelsbühl preached before Emperor Sigismund a sermon on the verse "Our fate is in your hands" (Gen. 47:25)."[39] The first person plural undoubtedly was meant to include all of Christendom. But the Germans empathized more keenly with Dinkelsbühl's text than any other group. This particular council had been convened at the instigation of the Holy Roman Emperor: one anonymous writer remarked in 1415 that the honor of the Empire would dissolve into ignominy were the council to fail.[40]

Early on, the council turned to the condemnation of heresy, particularly the views of Wyclif and Hus. Wyclif, long dead, was condemned on the basis of his writings. Hus came to Constance with the promise of a safe-conduct guaranteed by Emperor Sigismund. Primed by their own interaction with Jerome of Prague in Vienna five years earlier, Dinkelsbühl and Pulkau no doubt paid close attention to the proceedings against Hus, in which presuppositions about the role of logic in theology played a notable part. Jean Gerson, the chancellor of the University of Paris and one of the leaders in the council's proceedings, claimed two weeks after Hus's execution that some of the articles held by Wyclif and Hus were defensible in good grammar and logic, and even that they were possibly true in themselves. Yet this was not sufficient to make them sound:

> A general council can damn many propositions along with their authors, even though they might have true glosses, expositions, or logical senses. This was done in this council to many articles of Wyclif and John Hus, some of which could have been defended by the power of logic or grammar, as in articles that are taken indefinitely, or that make claims about possibility, insofar as logical possibility is excessively broad, or that can be taken in some true sense if posited distinctly.[41]

---

[38] Firnhaber, "Petrus de Pulka," 29–30; Girgensohn, "Die Universität Wien," 252. Among the other delegates were Berthold of Regensburg (dean of the faculty of theology), John Sindrami (dean of the faculty of law), Nicholas of Höbersdorf (dean of the faculty of medicine), Peter Deckinger, and Lambert of Gelderen; see *AFA*, I, 456, lines 10–13, n. 8.

[39] Von der Hardt, *Magnum oecumenicum Constantiense concilium*, II, cols. 182–187.

[40] Koller, *Princeps in ecclesia*, 18.

[41] Gerson, *Œuvres complètes*, V, 476. I have not yet seen the recent Stanford dissertation by Douglas Taber, "The Theologian and the Schism."

But Gerson went further. The decision of the council, in which he had played a leading role, was far from arbitrary. It rested upon a crucial distinction:

> Thus moral science, and theology likewise, has its own logic and a literal sense, other than [those of] the speculative sciences. This directive or law thus far has preserved the glorious University of Paris from many errors by commanding and compelling academics always to speak according to the certain rule of faith. If only this teaching were followed in other areas of study.[42]

The precedent from academic life harks back to Gerson's attacks on the *formalizantes*, or followers of John of Ripa, whose sin was pride—the attempt to understand matters that went beyond natural reason.[43] If excessive philosophy presented a serious problem, however, so did consistency with scripture if the latter was not taken in the proper frame of mind:

> A general council can and must damn many propositions or assertions of this sort, even though they cannot be reproved obviously from the bare text of Holy Scripture alone, excluding the expositions of the doctors, or the common usage of the Church, and so on. This was done during this council in many assertions of Wyclif and Hus, especially in the matter of the laity taking Communion under the species of bread and wine. The directive or law "prospers the way"[44] for the extermination of heresies and heretics, since the heretics that we saw submitted at the very most to its defense, since they did not want to recant [their] heresies absolutely, but only conditionally, namely if they could be convicted of erring from the rigor of the text of scripture, claiming that the expositions of the doctors, canons, and decretals are apocryphal and that one should pay no attention to them. But there is no one who does not understand how clearly this presumption leads to error.[45]

Gerson's statement was not an isolated claim, merely an example mentioned in passing, or a slip of the tongue uttered unthinkingly in the heat of the execution. Six months after Hus's death, on 3 December 1415, Gerson again emphasized that "Holy Scripture must not be explained according to the power of the logic or dialectic that serves the speculative sciences. The sophists who do so, shamefully deceive

---

[42] Gerson, *Œuvres complètes*, V, 476–477.

[43] Combes, *La Théologie mystique de Gerson*, I, 48–59.

[44] The text of the sermon was "May God prosper our way" (*Prosperum iter faciet nobis Deus*), from Vulgate Psalm 67:20 (68:19 in the modern).

[45] Gerson, *Œuvres complètes*, V, 477.

themselves. But scripture has its own logic and grammar, even as the moral sciences have rhetoric as [their] logic."[46]

Clearly there was more at issue here than logic. Gerson and Hus clashed on their understandings of the relative roles of scripture and tradition in determining the faith and practice of the Church. Such tensions had been endemic to the fourteenth century. Like Bradwardine and Wyclif, Hus favored a strict scripturalist view, whereas Gerson emphasized the place of tradition, like Ockham. This divide was a crucial one—according to Heiko Oberman, "the decisive late-medieval demarcation line."[47] For all of his opposition to the curialist faction of the Church, Gerson in this case preferred to side with the Curia than with the advocates of *sola scriptura*. It is nevertheless significant that Gerson chose to defend the place of tradition in the Church by appealing to the demarcation line between logic and rhetoric.

Prior to the council, such disagreements had been confined largely to academic disputations. Indeed this theme, to which Gerson kept returning at Constance, had already emerged in different contexts around the turn of the century. In the sermon *Contra curiositatem studentium* (November 1402), for example, although he emphasized the consonance of the articles of faith with natural philosophy, Gerson was unmistakably clear about the distinction between the two realms. Both philosophy and the teaching of faith had limits. Philosophy was limited by the divine will: to draw too many conclusions from natural necessity, or to attempt to answer such questions as the eternity of the world apart from the revealed will of God, would transgress the proper boundaries of reason. The doctrine of faith, on the other hand, was limited by the "sacred writings," beyond which "human conjectures and petty syllogisms" could easily lead one astray.[48] The sermon was already expressing much wariness about the interface between natural and revealed knowledge. At about the same time, Gerson expressed similar views in *De duplici logica* (ca. 1401):

Even according to the philosopher, logic is twofold: the first is subservient to the natural and purely speculative sciences. It is called by the usual word—almost by antonomasia—"logic." Peter of Spain describes it as the

---

[46] Gerson, "Réponse à la consultation des maîtres," in *Œuvres complètes*, x, 241; this speech is dated on 167. In the same passage, Gerson contrasted his position with that of the Jews, particularly on the issue of the literal sense.

[47] On the history of this bifurcation, see Oberman, *Harvest of Medieval Theology*, chap. 11, esp. 391.

[48] Ozment, *Homo Spiritualis*, 49, n. 2; Latin and English in Ozment, *Jean Gerson*, 26–45, esp. 30–37, 40–41.

road to all methods; others call it "verbal." The second, however, is the logic we appropriately designate as "rhetoric." It primarily aids, serves, and lends support to, the moral, political, and civil sciences, and pertains to the practical intellect.[49]

The context of these remarks was an attack on the "sophists" who questioned the truth of such verses as "And there went out to him [John the Baptist] *all the country of* Judea, and *all the people* of Jerusalem" (Mark 1:5). The detractors argued that such universal statements could not be true. Against them, Gerson made a case for understanding scriptural statements in terms of tropes, figures of speech, and figures of rhetoric. Gerson's distinction between the two approaches—the first speculative, the second practical—paralleled Buridan's distinctions between the logic appropriate to science and that appropriate to ethics.[50]

At Constance, however, these themes came to have consequences that went beyond the academic realm of logic. Gerson explicitly identified as heresy attitudes that he had criticized in the students of the University of Paris. Wyclif and John Hus in particular were guilty of transgressing beyond the proper boundaries of faith and philosophy. Yet at Constance, Gerson's views included an additional distinction. Neal Gilbert has pointed to "Augustinian similarities" in figures as diverse as Robert Holcot, John Wyclif, and Jean Gerson. All sought to condemn those among their colleagues who stressed dialectical skill over a Biblical focus. He finds in them "a basic reluctance to call any statement of scripture false *de virtute sermonis.*"[51] But in Gerson's views at Constance, there was also a deep reluctance to consider some conclusions logically derived from scriptural statements as true *de virtute sermonis.* Indeed his distinction between logic and rhetoric has an almost Petrarchan ring, misleadingly so. For Gerson did not argue that rhetoric and logic should be united (according to Petrarch's Ciceronian ideal), but rather that they should be distinguished clearly, a view more in accordance with Gerson's contemporary Salutati.[52]

Hus's evident failure to understand that scripture had its own logic was the last straw. Hus's ultimate fate is well known. Even prosecutors like Cardinal Zabarella conceded that some of the testimony against him was weak.[53] Jean Gerson played a leading role in the affair, which ended with Hus's condemnation to death at the stake. As Paul de

[49] Gerson, *Œuvres complètes*, III, x, 58.
[50] Wieland, "The Reception and Interpretation of Aristotle's *Ethics*," 668.
[51] Gilbert, "Ockham, Wyclif, and the 'Via Moderna,' " 120–121.
[52] Seigel, *Rhetoric and Philosophy in Renaissance Humanism*, chap. 1, and 69–70.
[53] Spinka, *John Hus at the Council of Constance*, 76.

Vooght has pithily summarized the proceedings, Hus was condemned to die for refusing to abjure ideas he never professed.[54] The sentence was executed on 6 July 1415.

Against Hus's wishes, his disciple Jerome of Prague also came to Constance in April 1415, and was taken into custody soon thereafter. When Hus's death unleashed a wave of protests in Bohemia, some leaders of the council hoped to secure a recantation from Jerome.[55] He was tried on 11 September 1415 and submitted a thorough recantation. He denounced the forty-five Wyclifite articles (as he had done in Vienna in 1410) and condoned the condemnation of the articles attributed to Wyclif and Hus.[56] Instead of being released, however, Jerome was returned to prison, a procedure that Gerson justified in a sermon preached on 19 October 1415.[57] By November, the German nation—for, following the practice of the universities, the council had organized itself to vote along regional lines—called for a new prosecution. Since the German nation included many members of the University of Vienna, it is not surprising that the commission placed in charge of the proceedings included one of their own, Nicholas of Dinkelsbühl, who could not be accused of impartiality.[58] On 23 May 1416, when accusers from each of the four nations confronted Jerome, the German representative was Lambert of Gelderen, another veteran of Jerome's Viennese trial.[59]

As he had done for Hus, Bishop Jacob Balardi of Lodi preached the sermon that preceded the execution of Jerome of Prague on 30 May 1416. It was an impressive piece of oratory, which ranged over the accusations—explicit as well as implicit—that justified Jerome's death.[60] In the list of "six disasters that you inflicted upon yourself in that public audience [of the trial]," one item stands out starkly:

Apparently you did not know the distinction between logic and rhetoric, since you said that the claims of the witnesses against you scarcely consti-

[54] Vooght, "Jean Huss et ses juges," 160.

[55] See Peter of Pulkau's letter of 24 July 1415 to the University of Vienna in Firnhaber, "Petrus de Pulka," 24.

[56] Betts, "Jerome of Prague," 80–81.

[57] Von der Hardt, *Magnum Concilium*, III, col. 39. Jerome was no stranger to Gerson, who had witnessed Jerome's stormy disputation in Paris in 1406; see Kałuża, "Le chancelier Gerson," 81–83.

[58] Madre, *Nikolaus von Dinkelsbühl*, 27; see also Watkins, "The Death of Jerome of Prague," 112.

[59] Betts, "Jerome of Prague," 84; Klicman, *Processus*, 1.

[60] On the treatment of heresy in the sermons pronounced at Constance, see Arendt, *Die Predigten des Konstanzer Konzils*, 156ff.

tuted a demonstrative argument. You do not know, it seems, that the
genus of demonstration is one thing in logic, another in rhetoric. For logic
demonstrates by immediate propositions and expository syllogisms.
Rhetoric, for its part, "remonstrates" by praise and reprimand. The natural philosopher demonstrates in one way, the ethicist and moralist in another. Thus the lawyer, canon as well as civil, demonstrates only by allegations and proofs. And so they are demonstrating against you by
legitimate allegations and most sufficient proofs about the truth. Who, I
ask you, can demonstrate against you more than you have demonstrated
against yourself?[61]

Balardi was rephrasing in a different framework the point of Gerson's
message from the previous autumn: natural philosophy drew upon
ways of reasoning different from those of the moral and ethical sciences. For the Bishop of Lodi and others at Constance, Jerome's lack
of clarity about the proper boundaries of logic and rhetoric was a serious, indeed a fatal, mistake.[62] But then, as the Italian bishop suggested, what could one expect from boors on the outskirts of civiliza-
tion?[63] To illustrate the distinction between natural philosophy and the
moral sciences, Balardi contrasted the former with law rather than
with theology, which Gerson had stressed. Just the same, he was accusing Jerome, a mere master of arts, of using the methods of his faculty in domains where they were not appropriate. Gerson, too, had
found the line between theology and the arts blurred in Jerome of
Prague, a master of arts who defended theological positions.[64]

    The irony of the Bishop of Lodi's appeal to rhetoric stands out most
clearly when contrasted with the account of Jerome's death provided
by the papal legate Poggio Bracciolini. Poggio's famous letter to Leo-

----

    [61] "Quartum fuit quia apparuit, ut nescires inter Logicam Rhetoricamque distingvere,
cum dixeris, dicta testium contra te demonstrativum argumentum minime facere. Nes-
cis quippe, quod demonstrationis genus aliud est in Logica, & aliud in Rhetorica. Logica
quidem demonstrat per propositiones immediatas & Syllogismum expositorium. Rhetorica vero monstrat per laudes & vituperia. Aliter namque demonstrat Physicus ⟨=
Philosophus⟩ Naturalis, & aliter Ethicus & Moralis. Unde Legista, Canonicus vel civilis,
non demonstrat nisi per allegata & probata. Itaque contra te demonstrant per allegata
legitima, & probata de veritate sufficientissima. Rogo te, quis magis contra te potest
demonstrare, quam tu ipse contra te & adversum temet demonstrasti?" (Von der Hardt,
Magnum Concilium, III, col. 61).

    [62] On the classical background of the bishop's categories, see O'Malley, *Praise and
Blame in Renaissance Rome*, chap. 2.

    [63] "Attendite, quaeso, *Catholici Domini*, ut homines viles, plebeji, infimi, ortuque ig-
noti, auderent nobile regnum Bohemiae totum concutere. . . . O quanti mali fuit radix,
horum duorum rusticorum ⟨Joannis Hus et Hieronymi⟩ praesumatio" (Von der Hardt,
Magnum Concilium, III, cols. 58–59; italics in the text).

    [64] Kałuża, "Le chancelier Gerson," 88ff and n. 14.

nardo Bruni (30 May 1416) not only saw diversity as the road to truth, but implicitly exculpated Jerome from charges of heresy. Jerome embodied the archetype of the classical orator, the reincarnation of Socrates facing death. In a striking reversal of the interpretations of Gerson and Jacob of Lodi, Poggio saw in Jerome a man who had successfully joined eloquence to wisdom, a genuine philosopher in whom articulate speech and argumentation had truly produced virtue.[65]

At the Council of Constance, the distinctions between the logic of natural philosophy, the logic of scripture, and rhetoric were discussed in a complicated forum that was ecclesiastical, homiletic, juridical, and also political, for the secular arm was closely involved in the proceedings and carried out the sentences. Since the setting was not academic and since distinct rules governed discourse, evidence, and inference in these diverse areas, one should not assume without further ado that the discussions of the proper role of logic in the conciliar context formed a seamless whole with the university debates about the place of logic in theology. Yet, during the Schism and at Constance in particular, the boundaries between university, ecclesiastical court, and pulpit were not as clear as they would have been in less desperate times. In the context of a divided Church, academics could participate in the proceedings *qua* academics in a way that would not have been possible under normal circumstances. When the chancellors, deans of faculties, professors of theology, and masters of arts came to the council, they did not put behind them their ways of thinking, arguing, and organizing themselves. Even the voting structure of the council, based on four geographical nations, was borrowed from the University of Paris.[66]

Strengthened by the consensus it had achieved in the condemnation of heresy, the council removed the three popes, by resignation or deposition, and elected Martin v in their stead. Upon learning of the news in Vienna, the duke ordered that all church bells in the city be rung simultaneously. Masses of jubilee were celebrated for two days.[67] The participants in the Council of Constance returned to their respective lands elated by the results they had obtained. After spending some four years in a council they had expected to last a few months, the theologians from Vienna returned to the university weary, but flushed with success and filled with a new sense of power. Unity had been restored,

[65] Watkins, "The Death of Jerome of Prague," esp. 119–120. For another contemporary's description of these events, see Guillaume Fillastre's "Diary of the Council of Constance," in Loomis, *The Council of Constance*, 282–284.

[66] Kibre, *Nations*, 105.

[67] Sommerfeldt, "Zwei politische Sermone," 324.

and they had played major roles in the historic proceedings. Lambert of Gelderen had participated in the prosecution of Jerome of Prague; Dinkelsbühl had preached before the emperor and had taken part in the successful election of Martin v—an unprecedented privilege usually reserved only for cardinals.[68] Peter of Pulkau had the honor of preaching sermons before the entire council.[69] The long-awaited resolution represented the almost universal consensus of Christendom, and had for all practical purposes brought the Schism to an end.[70] Having put the uppermost levels of its house in order, the Church could now extend the range of much-needed reforms to the lower echelons of the hierarchy. And the Viennese theologians, Dinkelsbühl in particular, had long been eager to take responsibility in this area. They now had a mandate not only from the duke, but from the entire Church.

Far from solving the Hussite problem, however, the Council of Constance succeeded only in fanning both the zeal of the reformers and the rage of the Czechs. Bohemian nationalism rallied around the martyrdom of John Hus and Jerome of Prague, and openly began to resist the Catholic authorities.[71] Vienna was intimately affected by the conflict in Bohemia, and not merely for reasons of geographic proximity. From the outset, Albert v had taken a very active role in the ecclesiastical affairs of his realm; not surprisingly, he also took a strong stand against the Hussite movement, both through his representatives at Constance and in his support of Emperor Sigismund.[72]

Under Albert v, the faculty of theology continued to remain vigilant. On 25 November 1415, the dean was notified that an *octonarius*[73] had made reckless claims while preaching at St. Stephen's. The offense involved upholding the following propositions without qualification: that the prayer of someone in a state of mortal sin was not valid, and that prayer for someone in such a state was not valid. Both proposi-

[68] Madre, *Dinkelsbühl*, 24–25.

[69] See Combes, *La Théologie mystique de Gerson*, I, 399.

[70] The Schism in fact lingered on until 1429, when the last successor of a schismatic pope resigned; see Swanson, *Universities, Academics, and the Great Schism*, 190.

[71] Kaminsky, "Hussite Radicalism," 108ff.

[72] See the letters in Palacký, ed., *Urkundliche Beiträge zur Geschichte*, I, passim; Koller, *Princeps in ecclesia*, 41–42, 73ff.

[73] In a major church or ecclesiatical community, the *hebdomadarius* was the prelate responsible for one week; see the *Lexicon Latinitatis Medii Aevi*, 435. The term *octonarius* presumably refers to a week-long assignment involving eight calendar days—for example, from Saturday noon to Saturday noon. I thank James Provost and Wilfred Theisen for clarifying this point.

tions had Wyclifite overtones.[74] But no action was taken on these charges, pending the return of some of the canons (presumably Pulkau and Dinkelsbühl). In 1419 and again in 1420, similar cases came to the attention of the faculty.[75]

The methods used at Constance to eradicate heresy and achieve ecclesiastical unity set a precedent that Pulkau and Dinkelsbühl had ample time to ponder during their lengthy stay at the council. After they returned, they may have had the opportunity further to discuss these matters with Gerson on their own turf, sometime before the summer of 1419. The duke evidently had offered a professorate in Vienna to Gerson, who acknowledged the compliment with a poem in the duke's honor.[76] Whether or not Gerson considered the offer seriously, he did travel as far as Melk and Klosterneuburg by mid-August 1418, and almost certainly visited Vienna as well.[77] But his stay must have lasted less than a year, for by June or July 1419 he was already on his way to Lyon.[78]

In any case, on their return to Lower Austria, the theologians turned their attention to the unfinished agenda of the council. Dinkelsbühl in particular took in hand the reformation of the monasteries that surrounded Vienna, beginning with Melk.[79] But the problem of Hussitism, which the Council of Constance had exacerbated, continued to fester. Already in 1416, the Viennese representatives at the council had sent a letter back to the university, warning them that the Hussites were being sent to surrounding areas to preach their errors.[80] Now there were infidels near Vienna, perhaps even within the city itself. The city was developing a siege mentality. The threat from the heretical

---

[74] See articles 4 and 15 from the list of condemned propositions; *Documenta*, 328–329.

[75] *ATF*, I, 33–34, 36, 39–40.

[76] See the "Carmen in laudem ducis Austriae," in Gerson, *Œuvres complètes*, IV, 169–170.

[77] A letter to his brothers written from "Neuenburg on the Danube" on 10 August 1418 indicates that he was probably staying at the monastery of the Augustinian Eremites in Klosterneuburg and was therefore within a half-day's march from Vienna (ibid., II, 216).

[78] Combes, *La Théologie mystique de Gerson*, II, 373.

[79] Koller, *Princeps in ecclesia*, 63ff, 88ff; Madre, *Dinkelsbühl*, 29ff; Girgensohn, *Peter von Pulkau*, 64ff. The spirit of reform had its limits, however. The university was keen on protecting its own interests at the expense of reform, particularly in the areas of absenteeism from parishes and the cumulation of benefices, which were standard practice among academics. At Constance, the university had lobbied effectively against the attempts to abolish these privileges. See Firnhaber, "Petrus de Pulka," 29.

[80] *AFA*, I, 469.

Bohemians on the outside began to merge with the threat from infidels on the inside.

For 1419, the Acts of the Faculty of Theology read like a litany of heresy accusations, interrupted now and then by records of academic events. On 5 May, a preacher from Passau appeared before the faculty on account of "some erroneous articles" he had uttered in a sermon. On the same day, the faculty decided that the dean and Peter of Pulkau should talk to some law students who had proposed some "erroneous articles" during their disputations.[81] By 22 May, the duke was so worried about tensions between Christians and Jews that he made a special effort to avoid altercations. In an unusual step, he assigned two city officials—the *magister civium* Zingk and the city judge—to notify the university that its members should refrain from insulting the Jews. The university took the matter so seriously that the deans were told to visit each of the student hostels to disseminate the injunction.[82]

On 9 June, another *octonarius* was brought before the faculty for having preached unspecified "injurious things about the faculty," almost certainly doctrinal in nature. In the same session, a Franciscan preacher was taken to task for "some erroneous things" he had stated in a sermon. He denied the charges and was told to put his recollections in writing. The next item reads:

> In the same meeting, there was talk about a plot by Jews, Hussites, and Waldensians; about the multitude of Jews; about their delicate life and their despicable books, which they keep as an insult to the Creator, and in blasphemy of Christ and all the saints, and to the greatest injury of all Christians. Because some masters were absent, however, this topic was postponed until their arrival and that of the prior of Gemnicus, who might prove useful in case the faculty should wish to bring this up with the duke.[83]

Prima facie, the charge of conspiracy sounds so unlikely that it is tempting to write it off as a paranoid rumor. Yet several Jewish sources reveal signs of interaction that go well beyond the encounters of daily life. Hussites in Prague were rumored to have sung hymns on the unity of God written by Rabbi Abigdor Kara (d. 1439).[84] Indeed, Ruth Glad-

---

[81] *ATF*, I, 36[r].

[82] *AFA*, II, 30[r]; Kink, *Geschichte*, I, pt. 2, 45. In Kink, after "iudeorum," add "vel talibus se miscerent sicud tamen factum noviter exciterat."

[83] *ATF*, I, 37. A "prior de Genickko" worked with Nicholas of Dinkelsbühl on the reform of the abbey of Göttweig in 1418; see Madre, *Dinkelsbühl*, 31, n. 136.

[84] See Güdemann, *Geschichte des Erziehungswesens und der Cultur der Juden*, III, 155. Apart from the Hussite issue, there is independent evidence for the Jewish use of Ger-

stein has shown that millenarian expectations, on one side, and messianic hopes, on the other, fostered a rapprochement between Jews and
Hussites. With their emphasis on reform, their opposition to images,
and eventually their open warfare with institutionalized Christendom,
the Hussites did not look like any of the Christians with whom the
Jews were familiar. Like his friend Yom Tov Lipmann Mühlhausen,
Rabbi Avigdor Kara seems to have thought that the coming of the
Messiah was at hand, for he composed a hymn on unity that reached
out to the Gentiles: "Jew, Christian, Arab! Understand! God has no
form that can be seen." Other stanzas alluded to opposition to images,
and made an unmistakable appeal to the conversion of Gentiles.[85] Most
striking of all, this hymn survives in Yiddish, the language in which it
evidently was sung in public with the hope of persuading Hussite listeners. This hope was so strong that in one instance it colored the
interpretation of the events at Constance. A remarkable early fifteenth-
century Jewish source describes Hus as a priest who had converted to
Judaism. The execution of Hus and his associates at the stake is called
Kiddush hashem ("sanctification of the divine name"). The use of this
term, reserved for Jewish martyrdom, proves that Hus was no longer
considered a Gentile.[86] Such a rapprochement added the volatile ingre-
dient of conspiracy in time of war to long-standing tensions between
Christians and Jews on matters theological and economic. Jewish
sources report official worries about charges of Jewish weapon shipments to the Hussites.[87]

In Vienna, such rumors worsened the already precarious situation of
the Jews, which had been deteriorating steadily for two decades. The
year 1397 had been a particularly tense one for Jews in the provinces.
According to the *Wiener Annalen*, a thousand Styrian Jews fled to Vi-

---

man poems and hymns on the unity of God; see Steiman, *Custom and Survival*, 106 (I
thank Talya Fishman for this reference). On the collaboration of heretics and Jews, see
Kurze, "Häresie und Minderheit im Mittelalter," 529–573, esp. 552 ff. Paul de Vooght
claims that Waldensian views were spread about by Nicholas of Dresden from ca. 1410;
see *L'Hérésie de Jean Huss*, 470.

[85] "The mystery of faith is nowhere found / Except among the Hebrews. / Forbidden
altars shall lie upon the ground. Hallelujah // The Kenite, Naʿamn—Obadiah too— /
Rahab, Naʿamah and Ruth of Moab / Entered the saving faith and true. Hallelujah!"
(Gladstein, "Eschatological Trends in Bohemian Jewry," 250). I thank Steven Marrone
for this reference.

[86] Ibid., 243–246. For evidence of Judaizing trends among the Hussites, see Newman,
Jewish Influence on Christian Reform Movements, 435–453.

[87] Kestenberg, "Hussitentum und Judentum," 18f.

enna, where the duke and the city reaffirmed their privileges, against the resentful wishes of the nobility and populace.[88] The same chronicle reports that in 1404 heavy taxes were levied on the clergy, the Jews, and the burghers.[89] Compounding the habitual insecurities of their status, the Viennese populace, on the night of 5 November 1406, ransacked and burned the Jewish quarter—for three days, by one account. According to one contemporary report, no one was injured, but the rampage destroyed many financial records, as well as goods estimated at more than 100,000 florins.[90] Students also participated in the riot, witness the request that the *Landmarshall* and the city judge made to the university on 18 November to "visit individual dwellings of university members because of the goods of the Jews." The faculty of arts agreed that the students should return anything they had taken, but suggested that its members clear themselves by swearing an oath as an alternative to having their residences searched. This counterproposal evidently satisfied the ducal representatives. All the members of the university who were present at the meeting took the oath immediately; the remainder did so on the following day.[91] Duke Leopold IV was still making modest attempts to enforce the provisions of his protection privilege.

The university as a whole was involved not only in the raid and in the ducal dressing-down, but also in issues (e.g. Jews and heretics) that one would expect to be the province of the theologians. In 1410, for instance, it was not the faculty of theology, but the faculty of arts that sent representatives to the citizenry to deal with the case of a Jew who had "relapsed" to his former faith. In the same year, it was the faculty of arts that offered to contribute financially to the prosecution of Jerome of Prague.[92] Early in 1413, at the other end of Europe, Pope Benedict XIII (Pedro de Luna) lent his support to a lengthy "disputation" at Tortosa, the main aim of which was the massive conversion of Spanish Jews. The debate, which never had reciprocity as a goal, finally concluded a year and a half later, in November 1414, the very month in which the Council of Constance officially started.[93]

---

[88] "Wiener Annalen (1349–1404)," 238.

[89] Ibid., 241.

[90] *Kleine Klosterneuburger Chronik*, 227–252, esp. 238–239; Ebendorfer von Haselbach, *Chronicon Austriae*, 303. In spite of its frequent lapses into speculation, the most extensive treatment in the secondary literature is Krauss, *Die Wiener Geserah von Jahre 1421*, chap. I; for a cautionary note, see Otto Stowasser's review in "Zur Geschichte der Wiener Geserah," 104–118.

[91] *AFA*, I, 267–268.

[92] Ibid., 349–350.

[93] Maccoby, *Judaism on Trial*, 82–94, including translations of Jewish and Christian

During the years of the Council of Constance, the economic condition of Austria did not see much improvement. By 1415, Albert V was in such dire straits that he pawned off his household silver. In January 1417, he decided to finance a debt by demanding 6,000 guldens from the Austrian Jews.[94] That same year, the duke renewed his privilege to the Jews for four more years, a grimly prophetic figure.[95]

By 1420, the mood in Vienna was one of pervasive suspicion that bordered on collective paranoia.[96] On 1 March 1420, Pope Martin V had declared a crusade against all "Wyclifites, Hussites, and other heretics, their supporters, abetters, and defenders."[97] Around Easter, charges of Host desecration were brought against a Jewish resident of Enns. All the Jews "above and below the [River] Enns" were imprisoned, including women and children.[98] On 1 May 1420, the university once again wondered what it should do about the Hussites.[99] On 10 May, the faculty of theology received a letter from the Archbishop of Salzburg requesting advice in the matter of "indiscreet preaching" in Judenburg.[100] The records of the faculty of theology for the first semester of 1420 are missing, but during the second semester other charges surfaced. On 17 October, the faculty reported that another *octonarius*, named Franz, had stated during a banquet "how the doctors and masters here preach heresies." The faculty was worried about its public image. On 10 November, the faculty enjoined yet another *octonarius*, named Peter, to retract the theses that "St. Paul had not sinned in persecuting the Church of Christ" and that "the crucifiers of Christ could be excused out of ignorance."[101] The first thesis evidently had Hussite overtones,[102] and the second sounded too lenient on the Jews.

During Advent 1420, Nicholas of Dinkelsbühl preached a series of

accounts from Solomon ibn Verga's "Shevet Yehuda" and from the Latin protocols (168–215); Ben-Sasson, ed., *A History of the Jewish People*, 587.

[94] Scherer, *Die Rechtsverhältnisse der Juden*, 408–409. In this one respect, the situation of the Austrian Jews was not unique. From 1414 to 1420, Emperor Sigismund put enormous "fiscal" pressures on the Jewish communities of the Holy Roman Empire. See Kerler, "Zur Geschichte der Besteuerung der Juden," 1–13.

[95] Schwarz, *Wiener Ghetto*, 9 and n. 11.

[96] See the suggestive comments linking the Schism, heresy, and fear of the Jews in Delumeau, *La Peur en Occident*, 273–278, 389ff.

[97] Palacký, ed., *Urkundliche Beiträge zur Geschichte*, I, 17–20. A letter on this issue from the papal legate Branda to Nicholas of Dinkelsbühl survives in Zwettl, codex 158; see Madre, *Dinkelsbühl*, 27 n. 125.

[98] See the report of the *Kleine Klosterneuburger Chronik*, 245.

[99] *AR*, 107v.

[100] *ATF*, I, 42.

[101] Ibid., I, 39–40.

[102] Ibid., II, 442, n. 297.

sermons to an audience that included several Jews.[103] The thrust of the sermons was heavily apologetic. Preaching on the messianic text "Blessed is he who comes in the name of the Lord" (Matthew 21:9), Nicholas raised as his first question "Whether this blessed one in the verse has now come, and whether it can be proved from scripture that the time of his first coming has now passed."[104] The text bears an uncanny resemblance to the antepenultimate step that Langenstein recommended in his scheme of historical apologetics in the St. Catherine's Day sermon:

> If there are some who do not understand the preceding points about the advent of the true Messiah the Lord Christ, if there are some—and especially men just converted to the faith from Judaism, for whose instruction I speak—they should not be moved or disturbed if they do not understand these things, and also some of the other mysteries of the Christian faith such as the Trinity, the sacrament of the Eucharist, and other things that transcend human reason. As they believe these things strongly, firmly, and in succession, they will understand to the extent that it suffices for their salvation and conforms to their status.
>
> They should heed such things because the order of gaining knowledge in human affairs and attaining understanding requires that students [first] believe their masters from the beginning, and then they will be able to reach understanding and the reason of the believer, as Aristotle teaches in the P[oste]rior Analytics, book I.[105]

[103] According to Madre (*Dinkelsbühl*, 130) the sermons were intended to convert the Jews. His evidence for this claim is not clear. This would have been a violation of the ducal privilege, which is of course no reason to assume that it did not happen. But the sermon itself states that Dinkelsbühl was preaching to recently converted Jews, who perhaps had been baptized under duress, and whose beliefs were not in tune with their new sacramental status: "aliqui et potissime homines nunc primo ex iudaismo conversi ad fidem propter quorum informationem predicta principaliter locutus sim" (ÖNB 4354, 11ʳ).

Although translated from the Latin here, the sermons also exist in a German version (Madre, *Dinkelsbühl*, 161ff). Such bilingual works were characteristic of the spiritual literature produced in Vienna since the time of Henry of Langenstein; see Hohmann, *Heinrichs von Langenstein 'Unterscheidung der Geister,'* 257 ff. Whether the Jews Dinkelsbühl wanted to persuade were converted or not, Latin would have been an unlikely language in which to address them. Indeed the sermons that exist both in Latin and the vernacular were usually preached in the vernacular. Since arcane academic sermons would have been of little interest to the populace, it would have been useless to translate them into German. On this issue, see Schäffauer, "Nikolaus von Dinkelsbühl als Prediger," 516ff.

[104] "An iste benedictus, de quo sermo nunc, venerit et an ex scripturis hoc probari potest, scilicet quod tempus sui primi adventus nunc transivit" (ÖNB 4354, 9ʳ).

[105] Presumably *Posterior Analytics*, bk. I, chaps. 1–2: "I call an immediate basic truth of syllogism a thesis when, though it is not susceptible of proof by the teacher, yet igno-

Given that this is so in human affairs, how much more ought the disciples (who must be taught by God their master where the supernatural
and matters exceeding common understanding are concerned) believe
simply from the beginning from the authority of God, and thereafter
reach the reason and understanding of the believer, which [is what] Isaiah
also meant when he said "Unless you believe, you shall not understand."[106]

This passage summarizes in a new context arguments that Langenstein
had made in his St. Catherine's Day sermon almost twenty-five years
earlier. The theory of knowledge represented here does not include
demonstration. Although Dinkelsbühl urged his listeners to follow
Aristotle's advice in the *Posterior Analytics*, he was appealing not to the
theory of demonstration, but to the notion that "all instruction given
or received by way of argument proceeds from preexistent knowledge." The analogy to the master-pupil relation is telling: there is no
hint here of the spirit of reciprocity that characterized Langenstein's
praise of the disputation, or even his treatise on the Hebrew language.
In his St. Catherine's Day sermon, Langenstein had laid part of the
blame for the failure of the Jews to convert on the dismal state of the
schismatic Church: the immorality of Christians presented an obvious
obstacle to the conversion of the Jews. With the Schism behind him,
Dinkelsbühl evidently considered that argument obsolete. The Jews
now had no excuse but their obstinacy. Hence Dinkelsbühl felt justified in assuming that the transfer of information should take place in
one direction only. The "student" was to receive knowledge from the
God-like master. Dialogue, disputation, or argumentation were out of

---

rance of it does not constitute a total bar to progress on the part of the pupil; one which
the pupil must know if he is to learn anything whatever is an axiom" (Ross, ed., *The
Works of Aristotle*, 1, 72a15ff).

[106] "Si hec superius dicta de tempore adventus veri Messie Christi domini et maxime
de duabus naturis in Christo et de modo unionis divine persone ad humanam naturam
aliqui et potissime homines nunc primo ex Iudaismo conversi ad fidem propter quorum
informationem predicta principaliter locutus sim, vel etiam si aliqua alia christiane religionis misteria ut de trinitate, de sacramento eukaristie, et ceteris humanam rationem
transcendentibus non intelligerent, non debet ex hoc moveri aut omnino turbari tantum
fortiter et firmiter ea credant et ipsa successive quantum eis ad salutem sufficit et statui
eorum competit intelligent attendant tales quod ordo addiscendi in humanis et ad intelligentiam perveniendi hoc exigit ut discipuli a principio magistris suis credant et tunc
poterunt postea ad creditorum attingere intelligentiam et rationem ut docet Aristoteles
primo P⟨oste⟩riorum. Et ex quo res ita se habet in humanis quanto magis discipulos a
magistro Deo de supernaturalibus et communem rationem excedentibus erudiendos
oportet a principio simpliciter ex ipsius dei auctoritate credere et consequenter ad creditorum rationem et intelligentiam pervenire quod etiam Ysaias intendebat cum dixit:
'Nisi credideritis, non intelligetis' " (ÖNB 4354, 11ᵛ).

the question. Dinkelsbühl's plea ended with the verse from Isaiah that he had copied into his *Quaestiones magistrales* a decade earlier, the very verse to which Langenstein had appealed when rejecting the validity of Aristotle's syllogistic in Trinitarian theology. The version of Isaiah 7:9 cited here was that used by Augustine, presumably from a pre-Vulgate translation.[107] Instead of "you shall not understand," the Vulgate read "you shall not endure" (*non permanebitis*). The semantic differences between the two translations would soon be pulverized in the crucible of expediency.

In some social and political contexts, and in some ethical frameworks, the demise of a logically oriented program of apologetics might have had only philosophical or theological implications. Vienna in the 1420s was not such a context, nor did Nicholas of Dinkelsbühl's ethical views constitute such a framework. His thoughts about ethics and argumentation appear in sharp focus in his commentary on St. Matthew, particularly in his discussion of the Sermon on the Mount. When he came to Matthew 5:21 ("You have heard that it was said to the men of old, 'You shall not kill,' But I say to you . . ."), Dinkelsbühl raised several *dubia*. After considering the permissibility of killing "plants and other irrational things," he proposed a second *dubium*: "Whether it is permitted to kill evil and sinful men?" He adduced two arguments for the negative. The first was the Parable of the Tares (Matthew 13), in which Jesus had urged that the tares not be weeded out before the harvest, lest some of the wheat be destroyed with it. This was the very text that Langenstein put at the top of his list of reasons why Christians had allowed the Jews to live in their midst.[108] Almost unavoidably, the second reason was the reference to the Mosaic commandment, "by which it appears at least that every killing of a man is forbidden."[109]

For the positive—his own view—Dinkelsbühl cited two other verses: "You shall not suffer evildoers to live" (Exodus 22:18) and "In

---

[107] Augustine, *De magistro*, 195, lines 35–36; idem, *De doctrina Christiana*, II, xii (43, lines 19–32).

[108] "Primo namque ut si forte granum aliquid adhuc paleis permixtum sit aut misceri contingat non pereat sed tandem in horeum domini cum ceteris colligatur" (Langenstein, "Tractatus de contractibus," chap. 28, in Gerson, *Opera omnia*, IV, 197ᵛa).

[109] As Nicholas did not write the *Commentary on Matthew* at one sitting, it is particularly difficult to date specific sections of the work. One question, about Matthew 4, dates back to 1401; another, on Matthew 7, to 1425 (Madre, *Dinkelsbühl*, 57 n. 6, 61). It is therefore impossible at present to state specifically how the events of Constance affected Dinkelsbühl's exegesis of Matthew 5. All references are cited from the autograph in Melk, Stiftsbibliothek, codex 504.

the morning, I kill all the sinners of the earth" (Psalm 100[101]:8).[110]
He then turned to a different argument:

> It must be noted that, concerning the aforementioned commandment
> "You shall not kill," there was a second heresy,[111] namely that of the Wal-
> densians who say that under the new law, neither the secular power, nor
> even the ecclesiastical power, nor anyone else, is allowed to kill a man,
> even an evildoer; nor is anyone allowed to do anything by reason of which
> the life of a man is shortened. But that this is heretical and a manifest error
> is clear from the fact that according to Acts 5, St. Peter carried out the
> death sentence against Ananias and his wife Saphira. And Paul carried out
> a sentence of blindness against Elymas the Magus (Acts 13). And in Ro-
> mans 13, the Apostle says that "the powers that be do not carry the sword
> without reason, for the minister of God is the wrathful avenger of the
> evildoer."[112]

Whatever else might be said about Dinkelsbühl's use of these Biblical
quotations, it is noteworthy that his tactic consisted in defending his
own position by making that of his opponent heretical. To undermine
the gradualist connotations of the agricultural imagery in the Parable
of the Tares, Dinkelsbühl turned to a surgical metaphor: "Likewise if
we see that the amputation of some member benefits the health of the
entire body, as when [a member] is rotten and corrupting the other,
such members are laudably and salubriously cut off."[113]

Nicholas had undoubtedly heard almost identical words at Constance. This was the very justification Jacob Balardi, Bishop of Lodi,
had used in his sermon before the solemn gathering of the entire coun-

---

[110] "Maleficos non patieris vivere" and "In matitutino interficiebam peccatores terrae."
The term *maleficus* can mean "evildoer" in a generic sense or "witch" in a more specific
sense. The context of Dinkelsbühl's parallel usage of the term *malefactor* later in the passage suggests that he had the generic sense in mind here. I translate from the Vulgate.

[111] The first was the Manichean heresy cited in the first *dubium*, to the effect that no
living thing should be killed (Melk 504, 308[r]).

[112] "Notandum quod circa dictum mandatum 'non occides,' fuit secunda heresis et /
adhuc est Waldensium dicentium quod in nova lege non licet potestati seculari vel etiam
ecclesiastice aut cuicumque occidere hominem etiam malefactorem nec licet aliud facere
ratione cuius vita hominis abbreviatur. Sed quod hoc sit heresis et manifestus error patet
ex hoc quod beatus Petrus ut habetur Acta 5° tulit sententiam mortis contra Ananiam et
Saphiram uxorem eius, et Paulus tulit sententiam cecitatis contra Elimas magum Acta
13°, et ad Romanos 13, dicit Apostolus quod potestas non sine causa gladium portat, dei
enim minister est vindex in iram ei qui male [[fecit]] agit" (Melk 504, 308[r]–308[v]).

[113] "Item videmus quod si saluti totius corporis humani expedit precisio alicuius mem-
bri ut cum putridum fuerit et corruptum aliorum laudabiliter et salubriter abscinduntur"
(Melk 504, 308[v]).

cil on 6 July 1415, the morning of Hus's execution. Preaching on the
text "Let the body of sin be destroyed" (Romans 6), a particularly
ironic text in view of Hus's emphasis on conformity to the dictates of
scripture, the bishop had appealed to Jerome's *Liber de expositione Ca-
tholicae fidei*: "Rotten flesh should be cut from the body lest the entire
body perish or rot."[114]

Yet this suggestion seemed to clash with the restraint implied by the
well-known argument from the Parable of the Tares. Dinkelsbühl
therefore could not proceed without explaining why the teachings of
Jesus did not apply in this case:

> the Lord teaches that it is preferable for the evil to live, and be reserved in
> the end for the Last Judgment, than for the good to be killed at the same
> time. When, however, the excision of the evil does not endanger the
> good, but involves instead protection, and salvation, and common peace,
> and utility, then the evil may legitimately be killed.[115]

For Langenstein in the 1390s, the Parable of the Tares had counseled
restraint by raising doubts about the ability of the reapers to discrimi-
nate between wheat and weed.[116] For Dinkelsbühl in 1420, it had the
opposite meaning. The tares were obvious: they lived in a separate
quarter of the city and could be identified by sight. How could there
be any question of confusing them with the wheat? Under those circumstances, the "excision of the evil" would not only be safe; it would
also contribute to the "protection, and salvation, and common peace,
and utility" of a city beleaguered by Jews conspiring with Hussites,
not to mention staggering economic problems.

Nicholas's arguments evidently did little to move those in his audience who could neither believe nor understand. On 12 March 1421,
the recalcitrant Jews were burned at the stake. As the *Kleine Klosterneuburg Chronik* reported laconically: "On Black Sunday they tortured
these same Jews [who had been imprisoned in 1420], all who showed
evidence of wealth buried in the ground. In Vienna alone, they burned
240 persons."[117] These figures did not include those who chose *Kiddush*

---

[114] Von der Hardt, *Magnum Concilium*, III, pt. 1, 1.

[115] "Unde dominus docet magis esse sinendum malos vivere et ultimo reservandum
usque ad extremum iudicium quam quod boni simul occidantur quando vero ex occi-
sione malorum non imminet periculum bonis sed magis tutela et salus ac communis pax
et utilitas, tunc licite possunt mali occidi" (Melk 504, 308ᵛ).

[116] See Chapter 6 above.

[117] Zeibig, "Kleine Klosterneuburger Chronik," 245. Another chronicle reports:
"Item anno vicesimo wurden die Juden gefangen in allen Lant ze Österreich an den ach-

hashem, the sanctification of the divine name, by killing one another or committing ritual suicide to avoid slaughter.

On 9 April 1421, the faculty of theology entrusted Nicholas of Dinkelsbühl and Peter of Pulkau with the task of "striving before the duke and elsewhere [to obtain] some books of the Hebrew tongue—at least better and more correct ones—in accordance with the advice of the doctors of law and others, according to what would seem to them best for the university and the theological faculty."[118] Three days later, the duke began distributing the spoils, which included all the property in the Jewish quarter. The first beneficiary was the burgomaster Hans Musterer, who received a substantial house (now at the corner of the Wipplingerstrasse and Stoss-am-Himmel) conveniently located around the corner from the town hall.[119] Albert v gave away seven other houses as well, including one to a recent convert from Judaism. He sold forty-five others: fifteen to individuals and thirty to the city, which in turn resold them during the following decade.[120] On 1 May 1421, therefore, with one threat behind it, the Faculty of Arts convened to ponder its course of action in the matter of the Hussites, and it decided "to hold a procession [or a fast, *stacio*] throughout the university to assuage the matter and to extirpate this evil sect."[121] Two weeks later, the university acceded to Albert's wish that solemn feast-day "stations" (i.e. partial fasts) and Masses be held "for the peace and tranquillity of the Christian populace and the security of the fatherland." The university decided to begin the series on Trinity Sunday at

---

ten Tag zu der Auffart, oder des Pfinzatag vor Pfingsten, ind Ir wurden vil getawft. Und dy sich nicht wolten bekehren, die hett man gefang uncz in die Vasten. Und an Mitichn Judica ward Sand Gregorii Tag, da verbrant man sew alle, Weib und Man" (*Anonymi Viennensis Breve Chronicon Austriacum ab anno* MCCCII *ad* MCCCCXLIII, in Pez, *Scriptores*, II, col. 550).

A grim medieval reminder of the event has survived to this day. On the façade of the house "Zum grossen Jordan" on the Judenplatz, a late Gothic low relief depicts the baptism of Christ by John the Baptist. An inscription that puns on the owner's name refers to the cleansing of bodies in the Jordan and how "the flame, rising furiously through the city in 1421, thus cleanses the terrible crimes of the Hebrew dogs. The world is now purified by the Deucalion-like waters." For the Latin text, see Siegris, "Die geplante Instandesetzung der Fassade," 32.

[118] *ATF*, I, 41–42. Wappler has misunderstood this passage to imply that the faculty of theology was already studying the Bible in Hebrew; see *Geschichte der theologischen Fakultät*, 24.

[119] Schwarz, *Wiener Ghetto*, 10 (map on 160–161).

[120] Ibid., 14ff; idem, "Geschichte der Juden in Wien," 39–40.

[121] *AFA* II, 36ʳ; printed incompletely and without ellipses in Kink, *Geschichte*, I, pt. 2, 22.

the Dominican convent, a date and a place laden with significance. The theologians were urged to concentrate their homilies on the Hussite threat.[122] The internal Jewish threat had passed.

On 31 July 1421, sensing perhaps that the mood was now opportune, the faculty of medicine suddenly saw fit to hear the case of

> a certain Caspar, a baptized Jew who practiced medicine [and to ask him] by what audacity and authority he practiced. He answered that we be patient with him for a little while, that he intended to travel home for some things he needed, and that after he returned he would obey the laws of the faculty, which [request] was granted to him for now.[123]

Surprisingly, on 23 January 1422, Caspar the empiric did return. The faculty of medicine threatened him with legal action if he did not stop practicing medicine within eight days. But the duke, apparently on his own initiative, stayed the order on 12 February. The case dragged on until September 1422, when the duke took upon himself the responsibility of adjudicating any complaints against Caspar's practice.[124] The episode suggests that Caspar was Albert v's personal physician—presumably a successful one—and therefore a competitor of Johann Aygel, the duke's university trained "personal physician."[125]

The participation of the university in the demise of the Jewish community of Vienna has left not only verbal but also material traces. On 22 December 1421, following a reminder by none other than Master Johann Aygel himself, the university acted on the duke's offer to use the stones from the demolished synagogue to put up a much-needed building. It approved the expenditure of funds to remove the stones from the ghetto to the construction site near the Dominican convent. A note in the Acts of the Faculty of Arts during the rectorship of Peter of Pulkau, reads: "Behold the wonder! The synagogue of the old law is miraculously transformed into the school of virtue of the new law."[126] Traces of this "wonderful transformation" have survived in the books of the period. Several manuscripts associated with the university

---

[122] *AR,* I, 112; transcribed in Koller, *Princeps in ecclesia,* 74, n. 163. For official worries about Hussite doctrine, see the letter from the papal nuncio to the university in Uiblein, *Ein Kopialbuch,* 73–74.

[123] *Acta Facultatis Medicae Universitatis Vindobonensis,* I, 46.

[124] Ibid., I, 48, 52–53.

[125] Scherer, *Rechtsverhältnisse,* 416. Aygel may have initiated the complaint. He had a keen sense of his status, witness his frequent disputes with members of the faculty of law about the relative positions of lawyers and physicians in the university's holiday processions; see Kühnel, *Mittelalterliche Heilkunde in Wien,* 64–65.

[126] *AFA* II, 46ᵛ; printed in Kink, *Geschichte,* I, pt. I, 140, n. 161 (the entry is dated 22 December 1421).

still have flyleaves and gathering reinforcements from dismembered Hebrew manuscripts.[127]

By 16 November 1421, the mood of suspicion had not abated. The entire university took an oath on the matter of heresy. On 22 November it discussed a letter from the Bishop of Passau, in whose see the university was located. He too remained very concerned about Hussites and Wyclifites in his diocese.[128] The mistrust that pervaded the city and university also placed restrictions on academic propriety and philosophical originality. On 23 March 1422, the dean of the faculty of arts (Stephen Marquart of Stockerau),[129] filed a curious complaint with the faculty. He was appalled that Christian of Traunstein's quodlibetal disputation included a controversial proposition:

> [Traunstein] had posited that . . . all truths and falsities and defects of paralogisms could be saved without assuming suppositions, ampliations, restrictions; from this he inferred that the disputations of masters concerning the same were phantasms, and the ruin of scholars, and fictitious terms. In the dean's opinion, this was an insult to the honor of the faculty and the older masters who had worked so fervently in that long-famous doctrine.[130]

Here was a master who wished to do away with the main tools of the "proprietates terminorum," including supposition theory. Traunstein had exceeded the bounds of the permissible. The faculty promptly enjoined him to apologize under penalty of exclusion from all academic functions of the faculty. On 14 April 1422, Traunstein complied.[131]

The incident was symptomatic of changes in the university since its revival. The bold theses that Johannes Bremis and Hermann Lurtz had discussed without censure in the late 1380s had long been forgotten. No one remembered, or dared to point out, that some older masters had had iconoclastic tendencies. The faculty of arts in the 1420s was taking itself so seriously that the freedom of the quodlibetal disputation was being curtailed. It was not sufficient for the other masters to criticize Traunstein's "excesses" in the forum of the disputation—the

[127] A partial list includes ÖNB 4632, 4654, 4659, 4668 (the presumed autograph of Peter of Pulkau's commentary on the *Sentences*), and 4795, as well as volume 2 of the Acts of the Faculty of Theology (see Uiblein in *AFT*, I, xiii). The library of the Schottenstift contains 23 manuscripts with Hebrew fragments, several of which were originally connected with the university; see Hübl, ed., *Catalogus manu scriptorum*, 578.

[128] See *AR*, 114^r, 115^r.

[129] *AFA* II, 44^v. Aschbach (*Geschichte*, I, 588) mistakenly calls him Johannes.

[130] Kink, *Geschichte*, I, pt. 1, 178–179, n. 215.

[131] Ibid.

pride of Christendom, according to Langenstein. Instead, the dean turned the matter into an official concern and a subject of threats.

The atmosphere of the university both reflected and shaped its environment. The times were unusually tense from several points of view. With the end of the Schism, the Church at last had recaptured some of the moral authority that Langenstein had considered so necessary for the conversion of infidels. The Church militant was developing a new sense of confidence, which the theologians probably felt as keenly as any other group. But the new assertiveness reemerged in a very explosive context. The Hussites were fighting a war on the fringes of Habsburg territory. Apart from the military situation, the threat of heretics who were also Bohemian nationalists remained a matter for serious concern within the university and the city. Severe economic problems threatened to paralyze both the city and the ducal court. All of these factors contributed to an extraordinarily defensive attitude in Vienna. The city drew inward. In Constance, the pursuit of unity had proved to be an all-encompassing end that justified unusual means but yielded the desired results. In Vienna, unity would perhaps solve other problems as well. All outsiders, for whatever reason they chanced to be on the outside, appeared very threatening. Jews, Hussites, foreigners—all threatened the unity of the faith, the cohesiveness of the city, and the integrity of the duchy. Even the Irish Benedictines of the Schottenstift, a religious institution established within the city for two centuries already, were replaced by Germans during the postconciliar reforms.[132] Under the circumstances, university theologians such as Nicholas of Dinkelsbühl and his colleagues might have played a moderating role, for which Langenstein had set a precedent.[133] Instead, they exacerbated the tensions by lending their authority to a course of events that was running headlong into disaster.

[132] Madre, *Dinkelsbühl*, 31; Rapf, *Das Schottenstift*, 26–29.
[133] See Chapter 6 above.

Conclusion

FROM ITS very beginnings, the University of Vienna was no ivory tower. Founded by an ambitious duke, revitalized by the latter's competitive brother, granted a faculty of theology by a pope in dire need of political support, the institution came into existence and thrived with the encouragement of powers that had in mind goals more tangible than learning.

Although conscious decisions in centers of power laid the foundation upon which the institution could grow, unanticipated events helped shape the character of the new university. Without the "blessed Schism" (as Langenstein once called it in a rare flight of optimism), the fledgling *studium* could not have grown as successfully as it did. Many of the academics who came to Vienna after its revival in 1384 found the new university attractive in large part because circumstances beyond their control had closed preferred options. Several professors of theology left Paris when the pressures on the German minority to endorse the pro-French pope became unbearable. And, in an era of rising Bohemian consciousness, dissatisfied masters left Prague after Germans clashed with Czechs in a predominantly German university. Vienna offered some respite from these conflicts, and capitalized on the influx of new students and masters.

But the University of Vienna was not merely an institution at the mercy of higher authorities, passively buffeted by external circumstances. It wielded influence in its own right. Spiritual and temporal rulers alike sensed that knowledge was power long before Bacon said so. The members of the university who controlled some of that knowledge played an increasingly prominent role at the Habsburg court—guarding the health of the dukes, providing spiritual counsel for their souls, guiding their children, representing their interests at home and abroad, advising their policies. Theologians were in the forefront of these activities. Henry of Langenstein, Henry of Oyta, Nicholas of Dinkelsbühl, and other colleagues passed judgment not only on abstract matters of concern to their peers or the papacy, but also on the conduct of civic life, including issues of social and economic import. In addition, as a Church institution charged—in intent, if not in fact—with the training of clerics and the preservation of orthodoxy, the university took an active role in attempts to settle the Schism and limit the growth of heresy, two circumstances that many considered to be intimately related.

The intellectual life of the university was no more insulated from its environment than were the lives of its members. In general, the immigration of individuals from diverse institutional and geographic backgrounds during the 1380s contributed to the pluralism that characterized the Bremis debate. But the local context also left its mark on specific areas of intellectual life. Like most of their colleagues in the fourteenth century, Henry of Langenstein and Henry of Oyta initially shared common presuppositions about the universality of Aristotelian logic. The rules of syllogizing were adequate to deal with the subject matter in all faculties of the university, including such problematical theological areas as the Trinity. During the course of their Viennese careers, the two men parted ways. Langenstein came to believe that Aristotle's syllogistic was not suited to treating the fundamental truths of the faith. Though the Philosopher's logic remained valid for creatures and for the framework of the faculty of arts, it failed to preserve truth when dealing with the Creator and revelation in the faculty of theology.

Almost all of Langenstein's predecessors had dealt with problematical Trinitarian inferences by supplementing, or otherwise modifying, Aristotle's rules of syllogizing or by identifying fallacies in the inferences. Instead of trying to salvage the syllogistic in theology, however, Langenstein rejected it outright near the end of a long professorial career. It is no coincidence that he reevaluated his earlier position, and eventually changed it, after his move to Vienna. In the arguments of Wodeham and Oyta, the "infidels" who put the universality of logical rules to the test inhabited the realm of pure possibility. In Vienna, they had faces and names, and actively participated in city life; they lived and lent, thought and taught in real space and time. Statements and clues scattered throughout the writings from Langenstein's Viennese years suggest that he was interacting not only with Jewish themes from the literary tradition, but also with the Jews of Vienna, some of whom taught him Hebrew. Concurrently with his rejection of the universality of Aristotelian logic, Langenstein adopted a historically oriented apologetics that emphasized the personal credibility of the apologist and admitted the failure of attempts to convert the local Jews. If there was one issue that not only raised difficulties for Christian theologians who tried to reconcile it with Aristotle's syllogistic, but also presented a most serious hurdle to apologetic efforts aimed at Jews, it was the Trinity. In this context, in which both Jews and Christians seem to have had polemical interests, Langenstein took a second look at a problem he had once solved to his satisfaction, and he changed his mind at the expense of Aristotle.

Langenstein's closest predecessors, Wodeham and Oyta, both thought that Aristotle's logic was compatible with Plato's ontology. Although they put no stock in Plato, the Philosopher's views illustrated the comprehensiveness and neutrality of his own syllogistic. Langenstein, in contrast, considered Plato to be incompatible with Aristotle: where the latter's logic had failed, perhaps the former would succeed. Although he did not develop his ideas on the subject, Langenstein's proposal illustrates a curious development in late medieval philosophical theology. By the end of the fourteenth century, questions sharpened by the critical use of logic associated with nominalism led one theologian to set his hopes on Plato.

By giving up Aristotle's syllogistic in theologically sensitive areas, Langenstein effectively removed the highest tenets of his faith from the public arena. When he lost hope in the universality of Aristotle, one of the few bridges between Christian and Jewish intellectuals in late medieval Vienna disappeared.

Langenstein's new position was striking, if not unprecedented. As heirs to both Oyta and Langenstein, his students were forced to confront the issue—whether or not they wanted to do so. The Council of Constance did little to quell their doubts, for the tide was turning against Oyta. At the council, the Viennese theologians Nicholas of Dinkelsbühl and Peter of Pulkau heard Jean Gerson and other ecclesiastical dignitaries emphasize the distinctions between the methods of theology and those of natural philosophy; logic was suited to the latter, rhetoric to the former. Both John Hus and Jerome of Prague were accused of having overlooked these distinctions at their peril. Hus had erred by insisting on being proven wrong from the text of scripture, and Jerome had demanded to be convicted by demonstrative arguments. It was futile to argue with heretics who failed to understand such a crucial distinction as this. The measures that the council took in this matter and in the reform of the papacy were drastic, but in the end they succeeded in mending the Schism. This historic accomplishment seemed to justify the means used to bring it about. Enpowered by their success, the participants at Constance could now take action to reform the Church and bring heresy under control.

In the late 1410s, however, this triumphalist attitude returned to Vienna in an atmosphere filled with tension. Although the Schism had ended, heretics and infidels seemed to be everywhere—the Hussites were overrunning Bohemia, and local Jews conspired with them. Expediency outweighed other considerations. When the common peace was at stake, Dinkelsbühl argued in his *Commentary on Matthew*, evil could legitimately be excised. This argument was nondemonstrative, but it had the backing of the temporal authorities. The secular arm, with which the university was so interdependent, had both the will and the power, in the words of Camus' Caligula, to "exterminate the contradictors and the contradictions." For Hussite heretics and Austrian Jews, argumentation abruptly came to an end.

APPENDIX

THE NOTEBOOK OF JOHANNES BREMIS

Vienna, ÖNB codex 4371 is a late fourteenth-century manuscript of 246 paper folios. The paper includes at least ten different types of watermarks and is filled with the writing of at least sixteen different hands.[1] When I first examined the manuscript in 1979, it was bound in a solid nineteenth-century binding, but the paper was in an advanced state of decay. The folios in the first two quires threatened to separate from the binding. The last several quires were very badly faded by dry rot and water damage, some of it very old indeed; large vertical cracks marred the center of each folio. After the historical significance of the manuscript became clear, Dr. Eva Irblich (manuscript department of the Österreichische Nationalbibliothek) scheduled the codex for

[1] The following folios either have watermarks or are the conjugates of such folios. The paper types listed here are given as a rough guideline only, closely resembling, but are not necessarily identical in all particulars to, those of the manuscript—FOLS. 1–12, 39, 58–59, 67, 69–70, 89–100: Briquet (*Les Filigranes*) 2898 "casque." FOLS. 13–14, 25–26, 64: Piccard, *Die Turm-Wasserzeichen*, 859. FOLS. 15–16, 23–24, 27–31, 34–38, 77–78, 80–84: similar to Briquet 3974/3941 "cloche." FOLS. 17, 22, 61–62: Briquet 11681 "monts." FOLS. 32–33: similar to Briquet 702/706 "arbalète." FOLS. 40–57: Briquet 13868 "sirène." FOLS. 71–76, 79, 85, 101–126, 180–192: variant of Briquet 5442 "croix grecque." FOLS. 127–179: similar to Piccard, *Die Ochsenkopf-Wasserzeichen*, 524/571. FOLS. 193–246: similar to Briquet 7341 "fruit" and Mošin-Traljić (*Filigranes*) 4255. FOLS. 18–21: unidentified watermark. FOLS. 60, 63, 65, 66, 68, 86: no watermark.

The hands are distributed throughout the manuscript approximately as follows—HAND 1 (Johannes Bremis): fols. 3, 9^r, 11^r, 13–17^r, 22^r–26^v, 28^v–30^v, 35–36, 40^r, 43^r–46^r(?), 48–52, 58, 61–62, 67, 69^v, 70, 77–80, 84^r–85^r, 86^v–87^r. HAND 2 (Bremis's scribe): 1–2, 3^v, 4^r–8^v, 9^v, 10^r–11^r, 28, 29^r–30^v, 31–34, 37, 38^v, 39, 59, 69, 79^r, 85^r–86^r, 89–100. HAND 3: 11^v–12^r. HAND 4: 18–21. HAND 5: 10^r–11^r(?), 27, 37, 46^v–48^r, 88, 153–167. HAND 6: 60, 68. HAND 7: 63. HAND 8: 64^v. HAND 9 (Johann of Retz): 65. HAND 10: 66. HAND 11: 71–76. HAND 12: 81–83. HAND 13: 101–124. HAND 14: 127–140, 168–192. HAND 15: 141–152. HAND 16: 193–246.

In addition, the following folios contain traces of Bremis's activity in the form of corrections, annotations, or red markings: 1^r, 2, 3^r, 4^r, 8^v, 10^r–12^r, 18–21, 27–28, 37–38, 40–52, 59–60, 72^r–76^r, 81–83, 88, 107^r–111^r, 113^v–117^r, 127^r–136^r, 146^r–150^r, 152^v–161^v, 162^v–192^v, 193^r–199^r, 203–206, 208^r–211^r, 213^v–218^r, 224–236, 238^r, 241^r–243^r, 246^r.

The quires are distributed as follows (Roman numerals indicate the number of sheets in a given quire, Arabic numerals indicate single folios, while the superscript indicates the number of the last folio in the quire): VI^{12} + VII^{26} + (V + 3)^{39} + IX^{57} + (IV + 5)^{70} + III^{76} + (V + 2)^{88} + VI^{100} + VII^{114} + VI^{126} + VII^{140} + VI^{152} + VII^{166} + (VII + 1)^{179} + VI^{192} + VI^{204} + VI^{216} + VI^{228} + VI^{240} + III^{246}.

restoration. The work of preservation was completed in 1984. Since the poor condition of the paper made rebinding inadvisable, the manuscript is currently preserved in six folders containing the unbound leaves of the codex (I: fols. 2–40; II: fols. 41–80; III: fols. 80a–120; IV: fols. 121–160; V: fols. 161–200; VI: fols. 201–247 [fol. 247 is in fact the original fol. 1, at which location it properly belongs]). Many pages are encased in semitransparent restoration paper, which sometimes has achieved permanence at the expense of legibility.

The descriptions and foliations in this appendix pertain to the manuscript in its bound, prerestoration condition, a record of which is preserved on microfilm (available through the ÖNB and the Hill Monastic Manuscript Library, Collegeville, Minnesota).

THE OWNER

Direct evidence that Johannes Bremis once owned the manuscript is provided by the text on fols. 81r–83v, which begins:

> Corollarium primum: quod non omnia individua eiusdem speciei sunt essentialiter eque perfecta, cuius oppositum dixit magister meus reverendus magister Jo. Premis contra me in corollario tertie propositionis principii sui tertii [81r].

In the manuscript, the main theses of the argument are underlined in red ink. In the margins, facing the statements attributed to "Magister Johannes," a cursive hand has added remarks in the first person, also in red ink: "prima ratio contra me" (81r), "contra rationem meam" (81r), "respondi" (81v), "ad rationes meas" (82v), "contra me" (82r, 83r). Similar red markings extend to large portions of the manuscript. Many folios in the first third of the manuscript are entirely in Bremis's hand; only a few folios show no traces of his activity.

THE CONTENTS OF THE MANUSCRIPT

Whatever the cause of Johannes Bremis's premature death in 1390,[2] it probably saved his theological notes from destruction at his own hand. Had he lived longer, he presumably would have revised his *principia*, included them in the definitive version of his commentary on the *Sentences*, and discarded the rough drafts now preserved in ÖNB codex 4371. According to a provision in Rudolph IV's privilege of 1365, the next-of-kin of a deceased university member was allowed a year and a day to claim his relative's possessions. After this period, the rector was instructed to place the books of the deceased in the university library.[3] Judging by the disarray of the manuscript, this last is precisely what happened. Bremis's loose notes were haphazardly gathered into quires and bound together with several long fragments of commentaries on the *Sen-*

---

[2] *AFA*, I, 51. See Chapter 2 above.
[3] See the text of the Rudolphine privilege in Lhotsky, *Die Wiener Artistenfakultät*, 217.

tences in his possession. The volume was then presumably added to the small library of the Collegium ducale, of which Bremis was a member.[4]

These circumstances would also account for the survival of the only other presently known fragment of Bremis's writings—a single folio that serves as the back flyleaf in the first autograph volume of Henry of Langenstein's *Lecturae super Genesim* in ÖNB codex 4651. The leaf, which is bound recto for verso, is badly worn; but the hand is clearly that of Bremis. The contents attest to his activity in the faculty of arts: they consist of notes on natural philosophy, including the question "Utrum necesse est in omni motu absque movente medio esse cum re mota simul indistanter" (128^v), which is inspired by John Buridan's *Questions on the Physics* (bk. VII, qu. 4).[5]

THE *Principia* TO THE LECTURE ON THE *Sentences*

Whereas the latter part of the manuscript consists of several lengthy texts, the numerous hands, types of paper, and short fragments in the first eighty-eight folios bear no obvious relation to each other. This confusion is only apparent, however. With the exception of a few folios, most of these texts belong to a single theological debate. The following list of contents tentatively reconstructs the order in which the debate took place:

Bremis's *principium* to book I of the *Sentences*: 13^r–17^v, 22^r–26^v, 61^r–62^v, 68^{r-v}

Lambert of Gelderen's (?) *principium* to book I: 31^r–34^v

Hermann Lurtz's *principium* to book I—against Bremis: 71^r–76^v

Bremis's *principium* to book II—against Lambert of Gelderen: 58^{r-v}, 70^{r-v} (first draft, incomplete); against Hermann Lurtz: 2^r–4^v, 9^r, 59^{r-v}, 69^{r-v} (first draft) and 5^r–8^v (second or only draft); against Johann of Meigen: 11^v–12^r

Bremis's *principium* to book III—introduction: 77^r; against Lambert of Gelderen: 78^r; against J. of Meigen: 84^r; against H. Lurtz: 86^v–87^r

Johann of Meigen's *principium* to book III—against Bremis: 60^{r-v}, 68^{r-v}

H. Lurtz's *principium* to book III—against Bremis: 81^r–83^v

Bremis's *principium* to book IV—*collatio*: 40^r–42^v; against L. of Gelderen: 43^r–48^v; against H. Lurtz: 48^v–51^r; against J. of Meigen: 51^v–52^v

According to its statutes, the faculty of theology at Vienna required its candidates for the degree of *sententiarius* to finish their lectures on the *Sentences* of Peter Lombard within "one or two years, as determined by the faculty."[6] In

---

[4] This hypothesis not only accounts for the fact that ÖNB 4371 once bore the call number "Univ. 808," but is also consistent with Henry of Langenstein's attempts to build up the university library; see his letter to Duke Albert III in 1388, edited and misdated by Sommerfeldt, "Aus der Zeit der Begründung der Universität Wien," 306. For the correct date, see Denifle, *Die Entstehung der Universitäten*, 622, n. 1636.

[5] On Langenstein's autographs, see Shank, "Academic Benefices and German Universities," 42.

[6] Kink, *Geschichte*, II, 115.

Paris and Bologna, the institutions in which most of the Viennese professors had studied theology, the usual lecture on the *Sentences* appears to have lasted one year.[7] The optional two-year term mentioned in the Viennese statutes evidently was intended to cover exceptional cases. Presumably, then, Johannes Bremis and his three associates held their *principia* debates during a single academic year.

These debates must have taken place sometime between 1387, the earliest known date of Johann of Meigen's tenure as vice-chancellor, and 1 July 1390, the date on which the faculty of arts reported Bremis's death.[8] Several other considerations suggest a further restriction of this interval. The frequent use of academic titles during the debates makes it highly probable that if one of the four *socii* had been rector during the course of the *principia*, this fact would have been mentioned, as was Johann of Meigen's title of vice-chancellor on several occasions. But this is not the case, even though Hermann Lurtz and Lambert of Gelderen served as rectors during the spring semester of 1387 and the fall semester of 1389, respectively.[9] Furthermore, since Lambert was away as a *rotulus* envoy between early February and early July 1390,[10] only two academic years remain as possibilities: 1387–1388 and 1388–1389.

Finally, one other circumstance makes the second academic year more plausible than the first. On 17–18 May 1388, the general chapter of the Dominican order convened in Vienna. The occasion was marked by a festive *lectura pro forma* of the *Sentences* by Franz of Retz, O.P., the second known graduate of the Viennese faculty of theology.[11] But mid-May was the specified date for holding the *principium* to the fourth book of the *Sentences* in the *studia* of Bologna. The Bologna statutes treat the *principia* regulations in more detail than those for any other university, and are also known to have influenced the Vienna statutes.[12] If Bremis and three of his *socii* had been ready to complete their

---

[7] Ehrle, *Sentenzenkommentar Peters von Candia*, 49–50. A year-long *lectura* was also standard in thirteenth-century Oxford; see Little, "The Franciscan School at Oxford in the Thirteenth Century," 826, and Courtenay, *Adam Wodeham*, 49, n. 21. For early fourteenth-century Paris, see Maier, "Der literarische Nachlass des Petrus Rogerii," 335–336, n. 10. On the timing of the *principia* in the Bologna *studia*, see Ehrle, ed., *I più antichi statuti*, 22 (variant 13). Although this variant is found in the 1440 version of the statutes, it probably codifies earlier practice since there are few ways to divide the academic year into four roughly equal parts.

[8] *AFA*, I, 51, 533.

[9] *AR*, I, 10ʳ, 17ᵛ; *AFA*, I, xix, 16 n. 4. This last reference cites *AR*, I, 7ᵛ, but folios 7–9 seem to be missing from the manuscript.

[10] *AR*, I, 22ʳ: "Hec acta sunt tempore magistri Hermanni de Treysa quando fuit rector substitutus in absentia magistri Lamberti de Gelria." This note falls between an entry on 9 February 1390, under Lambert's rectorate, and a 13 February entry under Hermann Lurtz. See also *AFA*, I, 46, 51–52.

[11] Häfele, *Franz von Retz*, 320.

[12] Ehrle, ed., *I più antichi statuti*, clxxx and 22 (variant 13); Uiblein, "Zu den Beziehungen der Wiener Universität," 178.

principia to the fourth book of the *Sentences* at the time of the Dominican convention, would the young faculty of theology have missed such a splendid
opportunity to display its vigor? No grandiose disputation is recorded, however—only the solitary *lectura* by Franz of Retz. Such negative evidence is not
compelling, to be sure. But until information to the contrary is uncovered, the
academic year 1388–1389 remains the most plausible date for these *principia*.[13]

FORMAT AND CONTENT

The rough state of the manuscript does not make easy reading. It does, however, offer insight into Johannes Bremis's style of work. Not surprisingly, his
first *principium* shows signs of hesitation and caution. It is in Bremis's hand,
and the theses are separated by blank spaces intended for addenda and missing
arguments. This format meets the requirements of the Viennese statutes,
which discouraged excessive reliance on written arguments, but allowed the
use of brief notes for mnemonic purposes.[14] Two items are consistent with the
hypothesis that Bremis was the bachelor who opened the debate: none of the
names of his partners (*socii*) appear in his first *principium*; nor has the fourth
principium survived for any of his partners. As the Bologna statutes suggest,
the order adopted for the first *principium* seems to have been maintained in the
last three as well.

Two drafts survive for a major section of the second *principium*. The first is
in Bremis's hand, with slight revisions and corrections. The second, which
was written by his scribe, incorporates the revisions and contains only minor
spelling corrections in Bremis's hand. The text of the fourth *principium* implies
that Bremis had grown more confident, for it seems to have been drafted but
once. It is written partly in Bremis's hand (with corrections and rephrasings in
sequential order in the text rather than above the lines) and partly in the hand
of a scribe, to whom the text was probably dictated.

If this collection is typical, scribes evidently played an important role in the
mechanics of the debate. Bremis relied on scribes not only to take down his
dictation, but also to recopy the drafts of his arguments. In addition, the fragments of Hermann Lurtz's second and third *principia* as well as Johann of Mei-

---

[13] In the *AR*, the record of Lambert's election as rector on 17 October 1389 does not
mention him as a *baccalarius formatus* (I, 17ᵛ). This is probably an oversight. In Vienna,
this title was normally conferred upon completion of the *principium* to the third book of
the *Sentences* (see the statutes in Kink, *Geschichte*, II, 110). We know, however, that Lambert is named in Bremis's fourth *principium* (e.g. 43ʳ), but that he had not returned from
Rome before the latter's death. Thus if the omission of the title of *baccalarius formatus* in
the *AR* was deliberate (because Lambert had not completed his third *principium*), the four
socii would have had to complete their *principia* to the third and fourth books of the
Sentences, as well as their *lectura* on the third book, between mid-October 1389 and early
February 1390. Such an odd schedule is not impossible a priori; it nevertheless seems
very unlikely.

[14] Kink, *Geschichte*, II, 116.

gen's third *principium* were all written by scribes. Since these last three texts deal only with Bremis's arguments (those of the other *socii* against each other are missing) and since they begin at the top of a folio, the scribes presumably were hired specifically to copy this part of the debate. Several misreadings of abbreviations prove that these fragments were not taken down aurally at the time of debate, but were copied from written notes. Thus Vienna evidently followed the Parisian custom that required students to provide their debate partners with copies of their arguments.[15] The surviving texts are probably the very ones Bremis received from Meigen and Lurtz.

In general, these *principia* conform structurally to the prescriptions of the statutes, even though the customary subdivisions are not always obvious. The statutes, for example, intended the *collatio* as a speech in praise of theology or Peter Lombard's *Sentences*.[16] Although it is not easy to identify on the basis of this criterion, a marginal note on 23[r] mentions a foregoing *collatio*.[17]

THE SMALL FRAGMENTS

In addition to the *principia*, several short texts were also bound with the debate, most of them single folios without apparent connection at the level of content. Their placement in the codex seems to have been dictated by the convenience of the binder.

Fragment 1

> *Inc.*: Utrum homo ex puris naturalibus prescise possit tam bene agere moraliter quam male agere ex eisdem. Et arguitur quod sic [27[r]].
> *Expl.*: . . . potest eque bene morale ex puris naturalibus integris fieri saltem repugnantia non est, ex quibus patet responsio ad questionem etc. [27[v]].

The single-folio text is in a scribal hand (HAND 5), which Bremis has corrected on several occasions.[18] A fourteen-letter blank left in the text by both the scribe and Bremis suggests that the latter is not the author.

Fragment 2

> *Inc.*: Utrum Christus secundum hominem meruit sibi et nobis gloriam et immortalitatem. Arguitur quod non [37[r]].

---

[15] At Paris, Peter Ceffons was also in a position to quote the exact words of his *socius*; see Trapp, "Peter Ceffons of Clairvaux," 104.

[16] Kink, *Geschichte*, II, 93–127.

[17] "Patet ex hiis que tacta sunt in collatione" (23[r]). This portion of the debate was perhaps not taken as seriously as in former times.

[18] Thus, *rationem* has been changed to *recte* (27[r]), and *naturalium* to *virium* (27[v]).

Expl.: quod Christus quamvis esset comprehensor quoad aliquid, erat tamen nescior(?) quantum ad aliquid etc mereri potuit [37^v].

The text begins in HAND 5, then changes to HAND 2 (37^v). Bremis has made annotations in the margin. The bottom quarter of 37^v is blank, suggesting that the question may be complete in its present form.

Fragment 3

Inc.: Utrum propter catholice credenda sint regule et principia humane scientie varianda. Licet tytulus questionis posset se extendere universaliter ad omnia catholice credenda [28^r].
Expl.: et tamen nichil de materia prima corrumpitur aut annichilatur [28^v].

The text is in HAND 2. Below the explicit, Bremis has added fourteen lines dealing with the "physics of the Eucharist" (problems of containment, commensurability, interpenetration of bodies, etc.).

Fragment 4

Inc.: Utrum quodlibet divinum vel propheticum promissum sit impletum vel implendum [65^r].
Expl.: consequentia tenet per suppositiones; antecedens probatur quia alias necessitet [*illegible*] Ex istis sequitur [65^v].

Below the explicit, the same hand has written: "Hec reverendissime pater et doctor humiliter s⟨unt?⟩ dicta cum vestra [*illegible*]." Like the adjoining folios, this one has been badly damaged by water; only the center is legible without the aid of ultraviolet light. Neither the corrections nor the margins bear any trace of Bremis's hand. This question, which may be complete, evidently belongs to a disputation. It is written in a hand having no counterpart in the manuscript, but strikingly similar to that of Johann of Retz, O.E.S.A. (d. after 1404).[19]

For several independent reasons, Johann of Retz may be considered the author as well. Near the end of the question, a corollary has been crossed out and replaced with a different wording, added in the lower margin in the same hand;[20] several other small revisions appear on 65^v. Also, the text at one point

---

[19] See ÖNB codex 4151, 243^r reproduced in Unterkircher, ed., *Katalog der datierten Handschriften in Österreich*, II, pt. 2, fig. 26.

[20] The original third corollary, now crossed out, reads: "voluntas potens necessitare quamlibet creaturam ad esse non potest esse necessitas antecedens ad quamlibet creaturam esse." Following a crossed-out quolibet, the revised version reads: "quamvis voluntati divine nichil possit resistere, non tamen potest esse necessitas antecedens ad aliquam cr⟨eaturam esse⟩" (65^v).

argues "secundum Hugolinum [de Orvieto, O.E.S.A.] ordinis nostri" (65ʳ); this remark is significant not only because it identifies the author as an Augustinian, but also because Hugolinus was a decisive influence on the thought of Conrad of Ebrach, the mentor of Johann of Retz.[21] Finally, one of the crossed-out lines on 65ʳ mentions a "dominus magister meus reverendus presidens in lectura sua super primo Sententiarum questio ultima articulo ultimo in principio"; this line follows a lengthy quotation from "Helyphat" (Robert Halifax) on four ways of defining revelation.

Henry of Oyta's questions on the *Sentences* contain the same passage from Halifax at the specified location. For the purpose of the preceding identification, the most readily accessible copy of Oyta's work was Klosterneuburg, Stiftsbibliothek, codex 294. Much to my surprise, it was written in a very familiar hand, readily identifiable as that of Johann of Retz.[22]

In ÖNB codex 4371, Fragments 3 and 4 appear to be completely unrelated. They share an interesting kinship, however: both questions are found contiguously in the same hand in Munich, Bayerische Staatsbibliothek, Clm 27034 (98ᵛb–101ʳb), as part of a series of questions that Damasus Trapp associates with book III of the *Sentences*.[23] Fragment 3 above closely resembles its Munich counterpart, but both versions contain mistakes that identify them as independent copies.[24]

The two versions of Fragment 4 reveal some notable differences. In ÖNB 4371, the argument is very detailed and is clearly part of a disputation. Clm

[21] Johann of Retz himself mentioned Hugolinus's influence on Conrad of Ebrach's commentary on the *Sentences* in the graveside eulogy he delivered for Conrad. In the same address, Retz acknowledged Conrad's formative influence on his own life and thought: "sibi dicere possum: 'Manus tue fecerunt me et plasmaverunt me' Job 10" (see Lauterer's edition of the funeral oration in his "Johannes von Retz," 36). See also Lauterer, "Konrad von Ebrach" (pt. 2), 60–120, esp. 109 ff; and Zumkeller, "Der Wiener Theologieprofessor Johannes von Retz" (pt. 2), 118–184, esp. 183. According to Zumkeller, a concrete trace of Conrad's influence on Johann of Retz is Oxford, Bodl., Can. misc. 573, which contains a copy of the former's commentary on the *Sentences* in the latter's hand (dated Prague, 1385).

[22] To judge from a comparison with the handwriting sample mentioned at n. 19 above, Klosterneuburg, Stiftsbibliothek, codex 294 is also in Retz's hand. (At 109ʳb, a seemingly new hand with a sharp pen takes over the copying. But by the time we reach the explicit on 243ʳb, the "new" hand has insensibly changed back into the old; hence Johann of Retz must have copied the entire manuscript.)

[23] Trapp, "Clm 27034," 332. I thank the director and staff of the manuscript department of the Bayerische Staatsbibliothek in Munich for permission to examine this limited-access manuscript, and for providing a microfilm of key passages.

[24] Clm 27034 has *finitus* on several occasions (101ʳa) when the context requires *factus*, as ÖNB 4371 correctly reads (28ᵛ). On the other hand, the latter has *noᵐ* (for *novum?* 28ʳ), where *nullum* is clearly correct (Clm 27034, 100ᵛa); has *formulare* (28ʳ) for *formidare* (100ᵛb); and omits a line (28ᵛ) supplied by Clm 27034 (*licet ab eterno . . . 3ᵃ conclusio,* 101ʳa).

27034, however, records only the outline of the argument (propositions, corollaries, conclusions). But the second half of this argument has no counterpart in ÖNB 4371, thus suggesting that it was later expanded, perhaps as a sequel to the disputation itself.[25]

Although these observations shed less light than desired on the relationship between the two manuscripts, a few tentative conclusions may nevertheless be drawn: (1) Fragment 4 above was composed and written by Johann of Retz, O.E.S.A. (2) It is probable that Fragment 3 above, and the other questions "In Tertium" found in Clm 27034, 82ʳ–141ᵛ (and perhaps those "In Quartum" 142ʳ–149ʳ) are also by Johann of Retz, since Trapp's arguments for unity of authorship remain very plausible.[26] (3) A distinction must be drawn between the author of the preceding questions and "D" [= *Discipulus Henrici de Oyta*]. According to Trapp, "D" is the scholar who assembled Clm 27034 and is the author of several other texts in the same manuscript, including a so-called *Lectura Oxoniensis*.[27]

[25] Clm 27034 contains only the revised version of the corollary in n. 20 above.

[26] Trapp, "Clm 27034," 332.

[27] *Ibid.*, 324–327. Several coincidences make it tempting simply to equate Johann of Retz and "D." Beyond the former's authorship of texts that Trapp attributes to "D," one can point (a) to the fact that Retz is indeed a disciple of Oyta and has close contacts with the Viennese theologians of the first generation, as Trapp has inferred for "D"; (b) to the presence in Clm 27034 of texts by Conrad of Ebrach, whom Johann of Retz admired; (c) to the use of Berthold of Regensburg (later also an Augustinian like Retz) as a scribe; and (d) to the fact that Johann of Retz was a bachelor of theology by 1391 and a master by 1394, dates that fit smoothly into the chronology and contents of the manuscript. See Zumkeller, "Johannes von Retz" (pt. 1), 505ff.

The decisive argument against their identification is the fact that there is no common denominator between the hand of "D" and that of Johann of Retz. Retz's hand does appear in the Clm 27034, as the scribe of the fragment of Henry of Oyta's *Sermo de Nativitate BMV* (262ʳ–265ᵛ). Nor can "D" merely be a scribe for Johann; he is also a scholar in his own right. Trapp ("Clm 27034," 338–339) has advanced several plausible arguments for "D" 's authorship of a so-called *Lectura Oxoniensis*, which is partly in "D" 's hand and shows traces of revisions. Who then is "D"? Trapp's suggestion of Johann Berwart of Villingen cannot stand. In 1389, Berwart was not a doctor of theology but, rather, a master of arts. He held his *principia* on the *Sentences* with, among others, Peter of Pulkau, with whom he was authorized to lecture on the *Sentences* in the fall of 1403, more than a decade too late for consideration here; see Uiblein, "Zur Lebensgeschichte einiger Wiener Theologen des Mittelalters," 106, and *ATF*, I, 8. Another candidate might have been Wilhelmus Anglicus, a master active in Vienna during these years and possibly a student at Oxford (*AFA*, I, 569). But if Sommerfeldt was right to identify Wilhelmus as the scribe of Henry of Langenstein's *Epistola . . . de pace ecclesie universalis* in Heiligenkreuz, Stiftsbibliothek codex 290, 109ᵛ–113ʳ (fol. 110 wanting), then Wilhelmus Anglicus cannot be "D" either; see Sommerfeldt, "Zwei Schismatraktate Heinrichs von Langenstein," 438. I thank the Hill Monastic Manuscript Library, St. John's University, Collegeville, Minn., for providing handwriting samples from the

Fragment 5

Inc.: et generaliter omnes transe(?) secundum sensibiles qualitates in perpetuum . . . [63ᵛ].
Expl.: prima pars conclusionis est manifesta quia nulla earum aliquid indecens in Deo nec(?) impossibile ponitur [63ʳ].

The folio is bound recto for verso into the manuscript. It is an excerpt from a longer text, probably the last folio of a quire, as several catchwords at the bottom of 63ʳ suggest. The hand has no counterpart in the manuscript. The content is intriguing: the unidentified author discusses "quatuor opiniones vel ymaginationes de statu inferioris mundi quantum ad desinitionem vel permanentiam specierum in ipso" (63ʳ), ranging from (1) "nulla species elementarum manet preter humanam" to (4) "mundus inferior post universale iudicium statim vel post aliquod tempus reversus sit in cursum pristinum" (63ʳ). He concludes that all four are possible to God, "tamen solum primam esse de presenti ordinatione Dei consonat ex scripturis" (63ʳ).

Other natural-philosophical conclusions precede this discussion: e.g. "quod motus circularis non est celis a forma intrinseca substantiali(?) vel accidentalis(!) sicud motus rectus elemento . . ."

Fragment 6

Inc.: Quod autem conclusio sit falsa patet per argumentum suum quia sequitur tollit(?) maius malum [*illegible*] ponit minus, igitur plus proficit quam nocet [64ᵛ].
Expl.: sicut eius habitus est bonus [64ᵛ].

Folio 64ʳ is blank. The text begins at the very top of 64ᵛ and ends in the middle of a line, several blank lines before the bottom of the page. The fragment dis-

---

Heiligenkreuz codex.

It is possible, but by no means certain, that "D" is a student of Henry of Oyta, as Trapp suggests. Trapp's case rests on two arguments. The first is the statement "didici a vobis, Reverende Magister, quando legistis Evangelium Johannis" (82ᵛ), which Trapp interprets as a reference to Oyta's lost commentary on St. John ("Clm 27034," 332–333). But this remark in the first person is probably to be attributed to Johann of Retz rather than to "D." The second argument is based on a sketch for a bachelor's *vesperiae* (175ᵛ–177ʳ), which Trapp calls a "synopsis autographa" in Henry of Oyta's hand. But this fragment is (a) neither in Oyta's hand nor (b) an autograph. When one compares a microfilm of the so-called "synopsis autographa" with the autographs of Henry of Oyta's commentary on the Psalms (ÖNB 4235, 112ᵛ–113ʳ, and 3953, 100ᵛ–101ʳ, in particular, since these were the folios Trapp used for his identification), the hands are clearly distinguishable (compare especially the majuscules *A* and *I* and the minuscule *g*, among other striking examples). But even if this were Oyta's hand, the following mistakes were almost certainly made not by an author composing his text, but by a scribe misreading abbreviations: *propositionis*, crossed out and followed by *proportionis* (175ᵛb); later, *propositionem* crossed out and followed by *propositum* (177ʳa).

cusses degrees of evil in terms borrowed from the latitude of forms. There appear to be no quotations or references to other works; the author and the *suum* in the incipit remain unidentified. The hand has no counterpart in the manuscript; Bremis has left no traces of his activity on the folio, which water has badly damaged.

Fragment 7

Inc.: Queritur utrum sacerdos possit subditum suum ab excommunicatione absolvere. Et arguitur quod sic [66ʳ].
Expl.: quod tunc quodlibet sacerdos potest, si de maiore, tunc non potest; hoc est verum non actualiter sed potentialiter etc [66ᵛ].

Several corrections in a darker ink (and maybe in a different hand) indicate that the text is probably not an autograph. The author may be a lawyer: he prefers to quote canons rather than other authorities. One possible candidate is Henry of Odendorp, a doctor of laws from Orléans and one of the early leaders of the University of Vienna who transferred to Cologne in 1389.[28]

HENRY OF OYTA'S *Abbreviatio* OF WODEHAM'S COMMENTARY ON THE *Sentences* (18ʳ–21ᵛ) [FRAGMENT]

Inc.: Ihesus Christus totius scripture sacre principium atque finis esse dinoscitur ipsius igitur gratia dei rectrice ⟨†irectrice⟩ humiliter postulata, quero circa principium libri sententiarum, Utrum studium sacre theologie sit meritorium vite eterne [18ʳ].
Expl.: comparando autem eas ad invicem penes hoc quod una perfectius vel imperfectius excedit vel deficit ab adequata(?) [21ᵛ].

At the very bottom of 21ᵛ appear the words "correspondentia comprehensiva," very probably the catchwords of the next quire, which is missing. The fragment is listed in Stegmüller's *Repertorium*, which mistakenly extends the text to folio 54.[29] The copy is poor, with frequent misreadings of abbreviations and several large omissions, which the scribe later corrected in the margin. The main subdivisions of the argument are listed in the margins. Bremis has emphasized portions of the text in red ink and added a few corrections of his own (18ᵛ, 21ᵛ).

THE COMMENTARY ON THE *Sentences* BY JAMES OF ELTVILLE (JACOBUS DE ALTAVILLA), O. CIST. (89ʳ–192ᵛ) [FRAGMENT]

---

[28] One of the canons is "Omnis utriusque sexus," on which Henry of Odendorp wrote a commentary (ÖNB 5137, 1–76ʳ). For details about Odendorp, who was in Vienna in the late 1380s, see Fournier, "La Nation allemande," 386–431, passim.
[29] *RS*, nos. 40–41, I, 18.

Fragment A

Question 1:
Inc.: quia si angelus etc, nego consequentiam nam movens liberum potest absque resistentia successive movere [89^{r}a].
Expl.: ergo unus potest cognitionem alterius intuitive videre et tamen illa ratio fundatur super ista conclusio(!) igitur non concludit etc. Sic dicendum de ista questione [92^{v}b].

Question 2:
Inc.: Circa libertatem voluntatis quero istam questionem, Utrum voluntas creature rationalis libera cuiuslibet obiecti volitiva proprii sui actus vere sit activa et arguitur primo quod conclusio sit falsa [92^{v}b].
Expl.: Dico quod nullus potest se ipsum occidere propter se, sed si hoc vellet(?) aliquando hoc esset propter aliam causam ut patet ex dictis. Ad aliam quando [100^{v}b].

Fragment B

Inc.: Circa prologum primi sententiarum queritur primo utrum veritates theologice contrarientur seu repugnant veritatibus naturalis habitus et sensualis experientie. Arguitur primo quod non [101^{r}a].
Expl.: quia fides cum peccato mortali stare potest et tamen requiritur ad meritum, quia sine fide impossibile est placere deo etc [192^{v}a; rest of the folio is blank].

The text is written in two columns and consists of seven quires in at least five different hands. The first fragment (in HAND 2) is exceptionally clean. The other quires were copied by several scribes with whom Bremis was not always pleased, witness his numerous corrections and an occasional complaint.[30]

Stegmüller has identified Fragment B (101^r–192^v) as the first seventeen distinctions of Henry of Langenstein's commentary on the *Sentences*, bk. 1.[31] In this he was following a weighty scholarly tradition that went back at least to Konrad Heilig and Albert Lang.[32] This attribution was recently brought into question by Rudolf Damerau, who pointed to significant doctrinal differences between this commentary (also found in Munich, Bayerische Staatsbibliothek, Clm 11591) and the so-called *Lectura Parisiensis* (which survives in only two manuscripts, Alençon, Bibliothèque de la ville, codex 144; and Vienna, ÖNB

---

[30] "Hic deficit unum folium quasi propter maliciam scriptoris pro precio" (132^v). Bremis therefore must have paid his scribes proportionally to the length of the exemplar he gave them to copy (a known quantity), rather than according to the number of new manuscript folios completed. Although this strategy minimized excessively large handwriting, wide margins, and wasted paper, it did not eliminate cheating altogether.

[31] *RS*, no. 331, I, 155.

[32] See Heilig, "Kritische Studien zum Schrifttum," 105–176; and A. Lang, *Die Wege der Glaubensbegründung*, 213ff.

4319). Damerau attributed Clm 11591 to Henry of Altendorf (Henry of Hesse the Younger).[33] Justin Lang in turn tried to refute Damerau, but his arguments are not conclusive.[34]

The attribution to Langenstein can no longer hold. Already in Stegmüller's *Repertorium*, the incipits of the Langenstein and Jacobus de Altavilla commentaries are suspiciously similar, when not identical, for each of the four books.[35] More important, in an article that appeared well before the works of Damerau and Justin Lang, Damasus Trapp reported that Clm 11591, which Stegmüller had attributed to Langenstein, was in fact the work of James of Eltville, O. Cist.[36] The present fragment disproves the attribution to Langenstein on internal grounds. The crucial passage in Clm 11591 reads: "secundo arguit contra secundam conclusionem Gotscalis de Pomuk" (26^{r}a). The equivalent passage in ÖNB 4371 reads: "contra secundam conclusionem Gottschalk de Pornuli nostri ordinis p. ⟨= s.(?) = sacre(?)⟩ cisterciensis" (102^{r}b). Clearly Langenstein cannot have written these words, for he was a member of the secular clergy. Trapp's attribution of the text to the Cistercian Eltville is thus decisively confirmed. Langenstein may in fact have read his friend's commentary on the *Sentences* at Eberbach, but there is no longer any reason to believe that Langenstein composed an original *Lectura Eberbacensis* distinct from Eltville's work.[37]

As for Fragment A (89^r–100^v), it consists of portions of the fourth and fifth questions from book II of the same work.[38]

AEGIDIUS DE CAMPIS, QUESTIONS ON BOOK I OF THE
Sentences (193^r–246^v) [FRAGMENT]

Question 1:
Inc.: Utrum fides ewangelica sit summe auctoritatis obligativa cuiusli-

[33] Damerau, *Die Abendmalslehre des Nominalismus*, 32ff. More recently, Damerau has published a transcription and translation of ÖNB 4319, which he inexplicably considers to be the sole surviving copy of Langenstein's commentary; see *Der Sentenzenkommentar des Heinrich von Langenstein* (e.g. XV, xxxiii–xxxvii).

[34] J. Lang, *Christologie*, 60–61.

[35] *RS*, no. 384, I, 183f.

[36] Trapp, "Augustinian Theology in the Fourteenth Century," 146–274, esp. 252 n. 93.

[37] The tradition of a *Lectura Eberbacensis* composed by Langenstein derives from Schum's description of Erfurt, Ampl. fol. 118, which identifies the text with the Eltville incipit as the "questiones Hassonis super libris 4^{or} Sentenciarum, quas Hasso collegit et conscripsit pro lectura Eberbacensium"; see Schum, *Beschreibendes Verzeichniss*, 80. Heilig's classic article ("Kritische Studien zum Schrifttum," 105–176, 163ff) gave this inscription the currency it has today. Schum's remark (lvi) in the Erfurt catalogue is, however, apparently taken not from data in the manuscript, but from the Amplonian catalog of 1412. The information it provides is early, to be sure, but medieval cataloguers are no freer from mistakes than their modern counterparts. In this case, the information is only partially correct.

[38] They correspond to Munich, Bayerische Staatsbibliothek, Clm 11591, 245^{v}a–256^{v}b.

bet creature rationalis; et arguitur quod non: lex Christi non est summe auctoritatis [193ʳ].

Expl.: sed hoc arguit quandam familiaritatem ad eos dei et sic de Iudeis etc. [199ʳ].

Question 2:
Inc.: Utrum solum trinitati ineffabili beatifico sit fruendum; quod non [199ʳ].
Expl.: Ponitur etiam ut actus vitalis quia staret quod [213ᵛ; text breaks off here with 4–5 lines left blank].

Question 3:
Inc.: Consequenter circa materiam secunde et tertie distinctionis, utrum in lumine naturali sit communicabile Deum esse primum verum cognoscibile. Arguitur quod non quia tunc Deum per se notum et non fide credendum? [213ᵛ].
Expl.: istius articuli et per consequens totius questionis [221ʳ].

Question 4:
Inc.: Consequenter iuxta(?) tertiam distinctionem, Utrum misterium altissimum trinitatis [*illegible*] [221ʳ].
Expl.: [*illegible*] [228ʳ].

Question 5:
[A large red initial indicates the beginning of another question at 228ʳ, but it is impossible to decipher.]
Expl.: quod aliquis clare discernat inter supposita et tamen nullam videat habitudinem unius ad aliam etc. Nota hic defectum ratione exemplaris etc. Cum finis bonus est totum laudabile tunc et. A M E N [246ᵛ].

These folios are all written in the same hand. Only the first question appears to be both complete and legible. From 217ᵛ on, reading becomes very difficult even with ultraviolet light, for the badly faded ink prevents the paper from fluorescing. The last seven folios are severely damaged; large vertical cracks run down the center of each folio and compound the already dismal condition of the manuscript. Marked changes in legibility occur on the outer pages of several quires (216ᵛ–217ʳ, 239ᵛ-240ʳ), suggesting that some of the damage dates back to the fourteenth century, before the manuscript was even assembled into a single volume. Even if the physical condition of the manuscript were perfect, however, problems would remain: this copy was made from a defective exemplar, as the frequent gaps in the text, the incomplete second question, and the explicit of Question 5 indicate.

The attribution to Aegidius de Campis is based on a marginal note by the scribe: "responsio propria magistri Egidii de Campis et est conclusio sua ista" (209ᵛ). As the context indicates, the answer is indeed the author's own.[39]

---

[39] In his *Lectura super primum Sententiarum*, Aegidius included a set of rules governing

A brief survey of the authorities mentioned offers a glimpse of the interest of the commentary: the "doctor subtilis" (Duns Scotus) (194^r); William of Paris (194^r), Wilhlemus Antysodorensis (196^{r-v}, 198^r); Nicole Oresme (198^v, passim); Petrus Aureolus (199^v); Gregory of Rimini (200^v); John of Ripa (201^r, passim); Adam (Wodeham) (201^r); Baro (William of Ware) (202^v); Kilmiton (Richard Kilvington) (204^r); Holcot (197^r, passim), Bragwardyn (Thomas Bradwardine) (215^v); Ockham (227^r); Rodicen (presumably John of Rodington) (228^r), the "doctor solemnis" (Henry of Ghent) (209^r); and the "articuli Stephani episcopi Parisiensi," the articles condemned by Bishop Etienne Tempier of Paris in 1277 (210^r).

---

the logical doctrine of *suppositio* in Trinitarian theology; see Murdoch, "From Social into Intellectual Factors," 279, 315–316 n. 27. These rules, which also exist in another Viennese manuscript (Schottenstift 254 [230], 157^v–158^r), do not appear in the legible portions of the fragment. They probably occur in connection with distinction 7 or 33, which do not seem to have survived. Until further evidence is uncovered, the attribution must unfortunately rest on this single marginalium. For biographic data on Aegidius, see A. des Mazis, "Deschamps, Gilles," cols. 331–334.

BIBLIOGRAPHY

MANUSCRIPTS

For citations of these manuscripts in the text, see Index under the name of the city.

Alençon, Bibliothèque de la ville, codex 144.
Graz, Universitätsbibliothek, codices 443, 639, 1145.
Heiligenkreuz, Stiftsbibliothek, codex 290.
Klosterneuburg, Stiftsbibliothek, codices 41, 294, 820.
Melk, Stiftsbibliothek, codex 504.
Munich, Bayerische Staatsbibliothek, Clm 7456A, Clm 11591, Clm 17468, Clm 27034.
Paris, Bibliothèque de l'Arsenal, codex 522.
Paris, Bibliothèque nationale, Fonds latin 14580.
Tortosa, Archivo de la Catedral, codex 143.
Vatican City, Biblioteca Vaticana, Vat. lat. 3088.
Vienna, Österreichische Nationalbibliothek, codices lat. 4319, 4354, 4371, 4651, 4657, 4668, 4677, 4678, 4679, 4708, 4718, 4820, 4948, 4951, 4963, 5067, 5252, 13763.
Vienna, Schottenstift, codices 254, 269.
Vienna, Universitätsarchiv, Acta rectoratus, vol. 1; Acta Facultatis Artium, vol. 2.
Wilhering (Austria), Stiftsbibliothek, codex 43.

PRINTED WORKS

Abelard, Peter. *Dialectica*. Ed. L. M. de Rijk. Assen, 1970.
———. *Opera theologica*, vol. 2. Ed. E. M. Buytaert. Corpus Christianorum, continuatio mediaevalis, vol. 12. Turnhout, 1969.
Acta Facultatis Artium Universitatis Vindobonensis, 1385–1416. Ed. Paul Uiblein. Vienna, Graz, and Cologne, 1968.
Acta Facultatis Medicae Universitatis Vindobonensis. Vol. 1: *1399–1435*. Ed. Karl Schrauf. Vienna, 1894.
Adams, Marilyn McCord. "Ockham on Identity and Distinction." *Franciscan Studies* 36 (1976) 5–74.
———. "Universals in the Early Fourteenth Century." *CHLMP*, 411—439. Cambridge, Eng., 1982.

Akten der theologischen Fakultät der Universität Wien (1396–1508). Ed. Paul Uiblein. Vienna, 1978.

Altaner, Berthold. "Die Durchführung des Vienner Konzilsbeschlusses über die Errichtung von Lehrstühlen für orientalische Sprachen." *Zeitschrift für Kirchengeschichte* 52 (1933) 226–236.

———. "Zur Kenntnis des Hebräischen im Mittelalter." *Biblische Zeitschrift* 21 (1933) 288–308.

Altmann, Alexander. "*Ars rhetorica* as Reflected in Some Jewish Philosophers of the Italian Renaissance." In B. Cooperman, ed., *Jewish Thought in the Sixteenth Century*, 1–22. Cambridge, Mass., 1983.

Anselm of Canterbury. "De processione Spiritus Sancti." In *Opera omnia*, 6 vols., ed. F. S. Schmitt, II, 177–219. Rome, 1940.

Aquinas, St. Thomas, Siger of Brabant, and St. Bonaventure. *On the Eternity of the World*. Mediaeval Philosophical Texts in Translation, no. 16. Milwaukee, 1964.

Arendt, Paul. *Die Predigten des Konstanzer Konzils. Ein Beitrag zur Predigten- und Kirchengeschichte des ausgehenden Mittelalters*. Freiburg i. B., 1933.

Aristotle. *Prior Analytics*. Trans. A. J. Jenkinson. In W. D. Ross, ed., *The Works of Aristotle*, I. Oxford, 1928.

Aschbach, Joseph. *Geschichte der Wiener Universität im ersten Jahrhunderte ihres Bestehens*. Vienna, 1865.

Ashworth, Elizabeth J. "Mental Language and the Unity of Propositions: A Semantic Problem Discussed by Early Sixteenth-Century Logicians." *Franciscan Studies* 41 (1981) 61–96.

———. "Theories of the Proposition: Some Early Sixteenth-Century Discussions." *Franciscan Studies* 38 (1978) 81–121.

Auctarium Chartularii Universitatis Parisiensis. Vol. 1: *Liber procuratorum nationis Anglicanae (Alemanniae) in Universitati Parisiensi*. Ed. Heinrich Denifle and Emile Chatelain. Paris, 1894.

Auer, Johann. "Die aristotelische Logik in der Trinitätslehre der Spätscholastik. Bemerkungen zu einer Quaestio des Johannes Wuel de Pruck, Wien 1422." In Johann Auer and Hermann Volk, eds., *Theologie in Geschichte und Gegenwart* [Festschrift Michael Schmaus], 457–496. Munich, 1957.

Augustine. *The City of God*. Trans. G. G. Walsh and G. Monahan. Washington, D.C., 1952.

———. *De doctrina Christiana*. Corpus Christianorum, ser. lat., vol. 32. Turnhout/Tournai, 1962.

———. *De magistro*. Corpus Christianorum, ser. lat., vol. 29. Turnhout/Tournai, 1970.

———. *De Trinitate*. Corpus Christianorum, ser. lat., vol. 50–50A. Turnhout/Tournai, 1968.

———. *The Trinity*. Trans. Stephen McKenna. Washington, D.C., 1963.

Aventinus, Johannes Turmair. *Sämtliche Werke*. Munich, 1881–1908.

Baer, Yitzhak. *A History of the Jews in Christian Spain*, 2 vols. Trans. Louis Schoffman. Philadelphia, 1961, 1978.

Baldass, Peter von, Walther Buchowiecki, Rupert Feuchtmüller, and Wilhelm Mrazek, eds. *Gotik in Österreich*. Vienna, 1961.

Baron, Salo. *A Social and Religious History of the Jews*, 16 vols. New York, 1952–1976.

Bato, Ludwig. *Die Juden im alten Wien*. Vienna, 1928.

Baum, Elfriede. *Katalog des Museums Mittelalterlicher Österreichischer Kunst* [Österreichische Galerie, Wien, Kataloge, vol. 1]. Vienna and Munich, 1971.

Beatie, Bruce A. "Saint Katharine of Alexandria: Traditional Themes and the Development of a Medieval German Hagiographic Narrative." *Speculum* 52 (1977) 785–800.

Becker, Carl. *The Heavenly City of the Eighteenth-Century Philosophers*. New Haven, 1932.

Ben-Sasson, H. H., ed. *A History of the Jewish People*. Cambridge, Mass., 1976.

Berger, David. *The Jewish-Christian Debate in the High Middle Ages: A Critical Edition of the Niẓẓaḥon Vetus with an Introduction, Translation, and Commentary*. Philadelphia, 1979.

———. "Mission to the Jews and Jewish Christian Contacts in the Polemical Literature of the High Middle Ages." *American Historical Review* 91 (1986) 576–591.

Bernard, Paul. "Heresy in Fourteenth-Century Austria." *Medievalia et Humanistica* 10 (1956) 50–63.

———. "Jerome of Prague, Austria, and the Hussites." *Church History* 27 (1958) 3–22.

Bernstein, Alan E. *Pierre d'Ailly and the Blanchard Affair: University and Chancellor of Paris at the Beginning of the Great Schism* [SMRT, vol. 24]. Leiden, 1978.

Bettoni, Efrem. *Duns Scotus: The Basic Principles of His Philosophy*. Trans. Bernardine Bonansea. Washington, D.C., 1961.

Betts, R. R. "Jerome of Prague." *University of Birmingham Historical Journal* 1 (1947) 51–91.

Bezold, Fr. von. "Die ältesten deutschen Universitäten in ihrem Verhältnis zum Staat." *Historische Zeitschrift* 80 (1898) 436–467.

Binder, Karl. "Eine Anthologie aus Schriften mittelalterlicher Wiener Theologen." In *Dienst an der Lehre* [Wiener Beiträge zur Theologie, vol. 10], 201–261. Vienna, 1965.

———. *Die Lehre des Nikolaus von Dinkelsbühl über die unbefleckte Empfängnis im Lichte der Kontroverse* [Wiener Beiträge zur Theologie, vol. 31]. Vienna, 1970.

———. "Zum Einfluss des Duns Scotus auf Theologen der mittelalterlichen Universität Wien." In *Deus et homo ad mentem Ioannis Duns Scotus* [Acta Tertii

Congressus Scotistici Internationalis Vindobonae, 28 Sept. – 2 Oct., 1970; Studia Scholastico-Scotistica, vol. 5], 749–760. Rome, 1972.

Blumenkranz, Bernhard. *Die Judenpredigt Augustins. Ein Beitrag zur Geschichte der jüdisch-christlichen Beziehungen in den ersten Jahrhunderten.* Paris, 1973.

———. *Juden und Judentum in der mittelalterlichen Kunst.* Stuttgart, 1965.

———. *Le Juif médiéval au miroir de l'art chrétien.* Paris, 1966.

Bochenski, I. M. *A History of Formal Logic.* Trans. Ivo Thomas. Notre Dame, 1961.

Boehner, Philotheus. "The *Centiloquium* Attributed to William of Ockham." *Franciscan Studies* 22 [NS 1] (1941) 58–72 (pt. 1), 35–54 (pt. 2), 62–70 (pt. 3); 23 [NS 2] (1942) 49–60 (pt. 4), 146–157 (pt. 5), 251–301 (pt. 6).

———. *Collected Articles on Ockham.* Ed. E. M. Buytaert. St. Bonaventure, 1958.

———. "The Medieval Crisis of Logic and the Author of the *Centiloquium* Attributed to Ockham." *Franciscan Studies* 4 (1944) 151–170. Also in Boehner, *Collected Articles on Ockham.*

———. *Medieval Logic: An Outline of Its Development from 1250 to c. 1400.* Manchester, Eng., 1952; reprinted Westport, Conn., 1979.

Boeke, Enno. *Rondom het Paradijsverhaal.* Wassenaar, 1974.

Boh, Ivan. "Consequences." in *CHLMP*, 300–314. Cambridge, 1982.

Borchert, Ernst. *Der Einfluss des Nominalismus auf die Christologie der Spätscholastik nach dem Traktat De communicatione idiomatum des Nicolaus Oresme* [Beiträge . . . , vol. 35, 4–5]. Münster i. W., 1940.

Boyce, Gray Cowan. *The English-German Nation in the University of Paris during the Middle Ages.* Bruges, 1927.

Briquet, Charles Moïse. *Les Filigranes. Dictionnaire historique des marques du papier dès leur apparition vers 1282 jusqu'en 1600 . . . ,* 4 vols. Paris, 1907.

Browe, Peter. "Die Hostienschändungen der Juden im Mittelalter." *Römische Quartalschrift* 34 (1926) 167–197.

———. "Die Judenbekämpfung im Mittelalter." *Zeitschrift für katholische Theologie* 62 (1938) 197–231, 349–384.

———. *Die Judenmission im Mittelalter und die Päpste* [Miscellanea Historicae Pontificae, vol. 6]. Rome, 1942.

Brown, Jerome V. "Duns Scotus on the Possibility of Knowing Genuine Truth: The Reply to Henry of Ghent in the 'Lectura prima' and in the 'Ordinatio.' " *RTAM* 51 (1984) 136–182.

Brunner, Otto. *Die Finanzen der Stadt Wien, von den Anfängen bis ins 16. Jahrhundert.* In Otto Stowasser, ed., *Studien aus dem Archiv der Stadt Wien,* vol. 1/2. Vienna, 1929.

———. "Die Politik der Stadt Wien im späteren Mittelalter, 1396–1526." In *Historische Studien A. F. Přibram zum 70. Geburtstag dargebracht.* Vienna, 1929.

Büdinger, Max. "Über einige Reste der Vagantenpoesie in Österreich." *Sit-*

zungsberichte der Kaiserlichen Akademie der Wissenschaften (Vienna), Phil.-hist. Kl. 13 (1854) 314–339.

Buridan, John. *Sophisms on Meaning and Truth*. New York, 1966.

Burleigh, Walter. *De puritate artis logicae tractatus*. Ed. Philotheus Boehner. St. Bonaventure, 1955.

Campbell, Anna M. *The Black Death and Men of Learning*. New York, 1931.

Carpentier, Elisabeth. "Autour de la peste noire. Famines et épidémies dans l'histoire du xiv⁰ siècle." *Annales-Economies-Sociétés-Civilisations* 17 (1962) 1062–1092.

Chaloupecký, Vaclav. *L'Université Charles à Prague. Sa fondation, son évolution et son caractère au xiv⁰ siècle*. Prague, 1948.

Chartularium Universitatis Parisiensis. Vol. 3: *1350–1394*. Ed. Heinrich Denifle and Emile Chatelain. Paris, 1894.

Chazan, Robert. *Medieval Jewry in Northern France: A Political and Social History*. Baltimore and London, 1973.

"Chronicon Universitatis Pragensis, 1348–1413." In K. Höfler, ed., *Geschichtschreiber der Husitischen Bewegung in Böhmen* [Fontes Rerum Austriacarum, erste Abteilung, Scriptores, II] 13–47. Vienna, 1856; reprinted Graz, 1969.

Clagett, Marshall. *Nicole Oresme and the Medieval Geometry of Qualities and Motions*. Madison, 1968.

———. *The Science of Mechanics in the Middle Ages*. Madison, 1959, 1968.

Cobban, Alan B. *The Medieval Universities: Their Development and Organization*. London, 1975.

Cohen, Jeremy. *The Friars and the Jews: The Evolution of Medieval Anti-Judaism*. Ithaca and London, 1982.

———. "Scholarship and Intolerance in the Medieval Academy: The Study and Evaluation of Judaism in European Christendom." *American Historical Review* 91 (1986) 592–613.

Combes, André. "Facteurs dissolvants et principe unificateur au Concile de Constance." *Divinitas* 5 (1961) 299–310.

———. *Jean Gerson, commentateur dionysien. Les Notulae super quaedam verba Dionysii de Caelesti Hierarchia* [Études de Philosophie Médiévale, vol. 30]. Paris, 1940.

———. "Présentation de Jean de Ripa." *AHDLMA* 23 (1956) 145–242.

———. *La Théologie mystique de Gerson. Profil de son évolution*, 2 vols. Paris, 1963–1964.

Cooperman, Bernard, ed. *Jewish Thought in the Sixteenth Century*. Cambridge, Mass., 1983.

Copleston, Frederick. *A History of Philosophy*, 8 vols. Westminster, Md., 1941–1975.

Courtenay, William J. *Adam Wodeham: An Introduction to His Life and Writings* [*SMRT*, vol. 21]. Leiden, 1978.

———. *Covenant and Causality in Medieval Thought: Studies in Philosophy, Theology, and Economic Practice*. London, 1984.

Courtenay, William J.. "Late Medieval Nominalism Revisited: 1972–1982." *Journal of the History of Ideas* 44 (1983) 159–164. Also in Courtenay, *Covenant and Causality.*

———. "Nominalism and Late Medieval Religion." In C. Trinkaus and H. Oberman, eds., *The Pursuit of Holiness in Late Medieval and Renaissance Religion* [*SMRT*, vol. 10], 26–59. Leiden, 1974.

———. "Nominalism and Late Medieval Thought: A Bibliographical Essay." *Theological Studies* 33 (1972) 716–734. Also in Courtenay, *Covenant and Causality.*

Courtenay, William J., and Katherine Tachau. "Ockham, Ockhamists, and the English-German Nation at Paris, 1339–1341." *History of Universities* 2 (1982) 57–96.

Crowder, C.M.D. *Unity, Heresy, and Reform, 1378–1460: The Conciliar Response to the Great Schism.* New York, 1977.

Curtze, Maximilian. "Der Briefwechsel Regiomontans mit Giovanni Bianchini, Jacob von Speier und Christian Roder." In Maximilian Curtze, ed., *Urkunden zur Geschichte der Mathematik im Mittelalter und der Renaissance,* 187–336. Leipzig, 1902; reprinted New York, 1968.

Damerau, Rudolf. *Die Abendmalslehre des Nominalismus, ins besondere die des Gabriel Biel* [Studien zu den Grundlagen der Reformation, vol. 1]. Giessen, 1964.

———, ed. *Der Sentenzenkommentar des Heinrich von Langenstein* [Studien zu den Grundlagen der Reformation, vols. 15, 17]. Marburg, 1979, 1980.

David, Abraham. "Kara, Avigdor ben Isaac." *Encyclopaedia Judaica,* x, cols. 758–759. Jerusalem, 1972.

Davidson, Herbert. "Medieval Jewish Philosophy in the Sixteenth Century." In B. Cooperman, ed., *Jewish Thought in the Sixteenth Century,* 106–140. Cambridge, Mass., 1983.

Delumeau, Jean. *La Peur en Occident, XIVᵉ-XVIIIᵉ siècles.* Paris, 1978.

Denifle, Heinrich. *Die Entstehung der Universitäten des Mittelalters bis 1400.* Berlin, 1885.

Denis, Michael. *Wiens Buchdruckergeschicht[!] bis MDLX.* Vienna, 1782.

Denzinger, Heinrich, and Schönmetzer, Adolf, eds. *Enchiridion symbolorum, definitionum et declarationum de rebus fidei et morum,* 33rd ed. Freiburg, 1967.

De Rijk, L. M. *Logica Modernorum: A Contribution to the History of Early Terminist Logic,* 2 vols. Assen, 1962, 1967.

Documenta Mag. Joannis Hus vitam, doctrinam, causam in Constantiensi concilio actam et controversias de religione in Bohemia annis 1403–1418 motas illustrantia . . . Ed. Franz Palacký. Prague, 1869.

Douglas, Mary. *Purity and Danger: An Analysis of Concepts of Pollution and Taboo.* London, 1966.

Duhem, Pierre. *Le Système du monde,* 10 vols. Paris, 1913–1959.

Duns Scotus, John. *God and Creatures: The Quodlibetal Questions.* Trans. Felix Alluntis and Allan B. Wolter. Princeton, 1975.

————. *Opera omnia*, 25 vols. Ed. L. Wadding. Paris, 1891–1895.

————. *Opera omnia*. Ed. C. Balić. Vatican City, 1950–.

————. *Philosophical Writings*. Trans. Allan Wolter. Edinburgh, 1962; reprinted Indianapolis, 1962.

Durand, Dana B. *The Vienna-Klosterneuburg Map Corpus of the Fifteenth Century: A Study in the Transition from Medieval to Modern Science*. Leiden, 1952.

Ebendorfer von Haselbach, Thomas. *Chronicon Austriae*. Ed. Alphons Lhotsky. In *MGH, Scriptores*, NF 13. Stuttgart, 1957.

Ehrle, Franz, ed. *I più antichi statuti della Facoltà teologica dell'Università di Bologna*. Bologna, 1932.

————. *Der Sentenzenkommentar Peters von Candia, des Pisaner Papstes Alexanders V* [Franziskanische Studien, Beiheft 9]. Münster i. W., 1925.

Eidelberg, Schlomo. *Jewish Life in Austria in the Fifteenth Century, as Reflected in the Legal Writings of Rabbi Israel Isserlein and His Contemporaries*. Philadelphia, 1962.

Elie, Hubert. *Le Complexe significabile*. Paris, 1937.

Emmen, Aquilin. "Heinrich von Langenstein und die Diskussion über die Empfängnis Mariens. Seine Stellungnahme—Änderung seiner Ansicht—Einfluss." In Johann Auer and Hermann Volk, eds., *Theologie in Geschichte und Gegenwart* [Festschrift Michael Schmaus], 624–650. Munich, 1957.

Eubel, Konrad. "Zu dem Verhalten der Päpste gegen die Juden." *Römische Quartalschrift* 13 (1899) 29–42.

Eulenberg, Franz. *Die Frequenz der deutschen Universitäten von ihrer Gründung bis zur Gegenwart* [Abhandlungen der Sächsischen Gesellschaft der Wissenschaften, Phil.-hist. Kl., vol. 24, 2]. Leipzig, 1904.

Falk, F. "Der mittelrheinische Freundeskreis des Heinrich von Langenstein." *Historisches Jahrbuch* 15 (1894) 517–528.

Firnhaber, F. "Petrus de Pulka, Abgesandter der Wiener Universität am Konzil von Konstanz." *Archiv für Kunde österreichischer Geschichte* 15 (1856) 1–70.

Fletcher, J. M. "Wealth and Poverty in the Medieval German Universities, with Particular Reference to the University of Freiburg." In John Hale, Roger Highfield, and Beryl Smalley, eds., *Europe in the Late Middle Ages*, 410–436. London, 1965.

Fliche, Augustin, and Victor Martin, eds. *Histoire de l'Eglise des origines à nos jours*. Vol. 14: E. Delaruelle, E.-R. Labande, and Paul Ourliac, *L'Eglise au temps du Grand Schisme et de la crise conciliaire (1378–1449)*. Paris, 1962, 1964.

Fournier, Marcel. "La Nation allemande à l'université d'Orléans au XIVe siècle." *Nouvelle Revue de Droit Français et Étranger* 12 (1888) 386–431.

Frank, Isnard. *Hausstudium und Universitätsstudium der Wiener Dominikaner bis 1500* [Archiv für Österreichische Geschichte, vol. 127]. Vienna, 1968.

————. "Die Obödienzerklärung der österreichischen Herzöge für Papst Alexander V. (1409)." *Römische Historische Zeitschrift* 20 (1978) 49–76.

Frankl, Ludwig August. *Zur Geschichte der Juden in Wien*. Vienna, 1853.

Franzen, August, and Wolfgang Müller, eds. *Das Konzil von Konstanz. Beiträge zu seiner Geschichte und Theologie* [Festschrift Hermann Schäufele]. Freiburg, Basel, and Vienna, 1964.

Freddoso, Alfred, and Henry Schuurman. *Ockham's Theory of Propositions: Part II of the Summa Logicae.* Notre Dame, 1980.

Funkenstein, Amos. "Basic Types of Christian Anti-Jewish Polemics in the Later Middle Ages." *Viator* 2 (1971) 373–382.

Gabriel, Astrik. *The Mediaeval Universities of Pécs and Pozsony.* Notre Dame and Frankfurt, 1969.

Gál, Gedeon. "Adam Wodeham's Question on the 'Complexe Significabile' as the Immediate Object of Scientific Knowledge." *Franciscan Studies* 37 (1977) 66–102.

Gastfreund, Isaac. *Die Wiener Rabbinen seit den ältesten Zeiten bis auf die Gegenwart.* Vienna, 1879.

Gavigan, Johannes J. "De doctoribus theologiae O.S.A. in universitate Vindobonensi." *Augustinianum* 5 (1965) 271–364.

Gelber, Hester Goodenough. *Exploring the Boundaries of Reason: Three Questions on the Nature of God by Robert Holcot, O.P.* Toronto, 1983.

———. "The Fallacy of Accident and the *Dictum de Omni*: Late Medieval Controversy over a Reciprocal Pair." *Vivarium* (forthcoming).

———. "Logic and the Trinity: A Clash of Values in Scholastic Thought, 1300–1335." University of Wisconsin Ph.D. dissertation, 1974 [Ann Arbor: University Microfilms 74–24720].

———. "Ockham's Early Influence: A Question about Predestination and Foreknowledge by Arnold of Strelley, O.P." *AHDLMA* (forthcoming).

Gerson, Jean. *Œuvres complètes,* 10 vols. Ed. Palémon Glorieux. Paris, 1960–1973.

———. *Opera omnia,* 4 vols. Cologne, 1484.

Geschichte der Stadt Wien, 6 vols. (published by the Verein für Geschichte der Stadt Wien). Vienna, 1897–1918.

Geyer, Rudolf, and Sailer, Leopold. *Urkunden aus Wiener Grundbüchern zur Geschichte der Wiener Juden im Mittelalter.* Vienna, 1931.

Gilbert, Neal W. "Ockham, Wyclif, and the 'Via Moderna.' " In A. Zimmermann, ed., *Antiqui und Moderni,* 85–125. New York and Berlin, 1974.

Gilson, Etienne. *History of Christian Philosophy in the Middle Ages.* New York, 1955.

———. *Jean Duns Scot. Introduction à ses positions fondamentales.* Paris, 1952.

———. *La Philosophie au moyen âge,* 2 vols. Paris, [1922] 1976.

Gimpel, Jean. *The Medieval Machine: The Industrial Revolution of the Middle Ages.* New York, 1976.

Girgensohn, Dieter. *Peter von Pulkau und die Wiedereinführung des Laienkelches* [Veröffentlichungen des Max-Planck-Instituts für Geschichte, vol. 12]. Göttingen, 1964.

———. "Die Universität Wien und das Konstanzer Konzil." In A. Franzen and

W. Müller, eds., *Das Konzil von Konstanz*, 252–281. Freiburg, Basel, and Vienna, 1964.

Gladstein, Ruth. "Eschatological Trends in Bohemian Jewry during the Hussite Period." In A. Williams, ed., *Prophecy and Millenarianism*, 241–256. New York, 1980.

Glorieux, Palémon. "L'Année universitaire 1392–1393 à la Sorbonne à travers les notes d'un étudiant." *Revue des Sciences Religieuses* 19 (1939) 429–482.

Gold, Hugo. *Geschichte der Juden in Wien. Ein Gedenkbuch*. Tel Aviv, 1966.

Goldmann, Artur, ed. *Das Judenbuch der Scheffstrasse zu Wien (1389–1420)* [Quellen und Forschungen zur Geschichte der Juden in Deutsch-Österreich, vol. 1]. Vienna and Leipzig, 1908.

Gottlieb, Theodor. *Mittelalterliche Bibliothekskataloge Österreichs*. Vol. 1: *Niederösterreich*. Vienna, 1915.

Grabmann, Martin. *Die Geschichte der katholischen Theologie seit dem Ausgang der Väterzeit*. Freiburg i. B., 1933; reprinted Darmstadt, 1983.

Grajewski, Maurice J. *The Formal Distinction of Duns Scotus: A Study in Metaphysics* [The Catholic University of America Philosophy Series, vol. 90]. Washington, D.C., 1944.

Grant, Edward, ed. *A Sourcebook in Medieval Science*. Cambridge, Mass., 1974.

Graus, František. "The Crisis of the Middle Ages and the Hussites." In S. Ozment, ed., *The Reformation in Medieval Perspective*, 76–103. Chicago, 1971.

———. *Struktur und Geschichte. Drei Volksaufstände im mittelalterlichen Prag* [Konstanzer Arbeitskreis für mittelalterliche Geschichte, Vorträge und Forschungen, Sonderband 7]. Sigmaringen, 1971.

Greitemann, N. "Via antiqua en moderna op de universiteiten van Engeland, Frankrijk en Duitschland." *Studia Catholica* 6 (1929–1930) 149–163; 7 (1930–1931) 25–40.

Grössing, Helmuth. *Humanistische Naturwissenschaft. Zur Geschichte der Wiener mathematischen Schulen des 15. und 16. Jahrhunderts*. Baden-Baden, 1983.

Grossmann, Karl. "Die Frühzeit des Humanismus in Wien bis zu Celtis Berufung 1497." *Jahrbuch für Landeskunde von Niederösterreich*, NF 22 (1929) 150–325.

Grundmann, Herbert. "Sacerdotium—Regnum—Studium. Zur Wertung der Wissenschaft im 13. Jahrhundert." *Archiv für Kulturgeschichte* 34 (1951) 5–21.

———. "Vom Ursprung der Universität im Mittelalter." *Berichte über die Verhandlungen der Sächsischen Akademie der Wissenschaften zu Leipzig*, Phil.-hist. Kl., vol. 103, 2 (1957) [rev. ed. Darmstadt, 1960].

Grunwald, Kurt. "Lombards, Cahorsins and Jews." *Journal of European Economic History* 4 (1975) 393–398.

Grunwald, Max. *Geschichte der Wiener Juden bis 1914*. Vienna, 1926.

———. *Vienna*. Philadelphia, 1936.

Güdemann, Moritz. *Geschichte des Erziehungswesens und der Cultur der Juden in Deutschland während des Mittelalters und der Neuzeit*, 3 vols. Vienna, 1880–1888.

Guelluy, Robert. *Philosophie et théologie chez Guillaume d'Ockham*. Louvain and Paris, 1947.

Guerchberg, Séraphine. "La Controverse sur les prétendus semeurs de la 'Peste noire' d'après les traités de peste de l'époque." *Revue des Études Juives*, NS 8 (1948) 3–40.

Guttmann, Julius. *Philosophies of Judaism: The History of Jewish Philosophy from Biblical Times to Franz Rosenzweig*. Trans. David Silverman. New York, 1964.

Häfele, Gallus. *Franz von Retz. Ein Beitrag zur Gelehrtengeschichte des Dominikanerordens und der Wiener Universität am Ausgange des Mittelalters*. Innsbruck, 1918.

Hailperin, Herman. *Rashi and the Christian Scholars*. Pittsburgh, 1963.

Hansen, Bert. *Nicole Oresme and the Marvels of Nature: A Study of His De Causis Mirabilium, with Critical Edition, Translation, and Commentary* [PIMS, Studies and Texts 68]. Toronto, 1985.

Hantsch, Hugo. *Die Geschichte Österreichs*, 2 vols. Graz and Vienna, 1947.

Hardt, Hermann von der, ed. *Magnum Concilium Constantiense*, 6 vols. Frankfurt and Leipzig, 1697–1700.

Hartwig, Otto. *Henricus de Langenstein dictus de Hassia. Zwei Untersuchungen über das Leben und die Schriften Heinrichs von Langenstein*. Marburg, 1857.

Hauswirth, Ernest. *Abriss einer Geschichte der Benedictiner-Abtei U.L.F. zu den Schotten in Wien*. Vienna, 1858.

Heidingsfelder, Georg. *Albert von Sachsen. Sein Lebensgang und sein Kommentar zur Nikomachischen Ethik des Aristoteles* [Beiträge . . . , vol. 22, 3–4]. Münster i. W., 1921.

Heilig, Konrad J. "Kritische Studien zum Schrifttum der beiden Heinriche von Hessen." *Römische Quartalschrift* 40 (1932) 105–176.

———. "Leopold Stainreuter von Wien, der Verfasser der sogenannten Österreichischen Chronik der 95 Herrschaften. Ein Beitrag zur österreichischen Historiographie." *MIÖG* 47 (1933) 225–289.

———. "Mittelalterliche Bibliotheksgeschichte als Geistesgeschichte." *Zeitschrift für deutsche Kulturgeschichte* 1 (1935) 12–23.

Henle, R. J. *Saint Thomas and Platonism: A Study of the Plato and Platonici Texts in the Writings of Saint Thomas*. The Hague, 1956.

Henry, Desmond Paul. "Ockham and the Formal Distinction." *Franciscan Studies* 25 (1965) 285–292.

Henry of Ghent. *Summa questionum Ordinariarum*, 5 vols. Asti, 1520.

Henry of Langenstein. "Tractatus de contractibus." In J. Gerson, *Opera omnia*, IV, fols. 195–224. Cologne, 1484.

Herlihy, David. *Medieval and Renaissance Pistoia: The Social History of an Italian Town, 1200–1430*. New Haven and London, 1967.

Heytesbury, William. *On "Insoluble" Sentences*. Trans. Paul Vincent Spade. Toronto, 1979.

Hillenbrand, Eugen, ed. and trans. *Vita Caroli Quarti. Die Autobiographie Karls IV*. Stuttgart, 1979.

Hoffmann, Fritz. "Robert Holcot—Die Logik in der Theologie." In Paul Wilpert and W. P. Eckert, eds., *Die Metaphysik im Mittelalter. Ihr Ursprung und Ihre Bedenkung* [Miscellanea Mediaevalia, vol. 2], 624–639. Berlin, 1963.

———. *Die theologische Methode des Oxforder Dominikanerlehrers Robert Holcot* [*Beiträge . . .* , NF 5]. Münster i. W., 1972.

Hohmann, Thomas. *Heinrichs von Langenstein 'Unterscheidung der Geister' Lateinisch und Deutsch. Texte und Untersuchungen zu Ubersetzungsliteratur aus der Wiener Schule* [Münchener Texte und Untersuchungen zur deutschen Literatur des Mittelalters, vol. 63]. Zurich and Munich, 1977.

———. "Initienregister der Werke Heinrichs von Langenstein." *Traditio* 32 (1976) 399–426.

Hohmann, Thomas, and Georg Kreuzer. "Heinrich von Langenstein." In *Die deutsche Literatur des Mittelalters*, III, 763–773. Berlin, 1981.

[Holcot, Robert]. *Exploring the Boundaries of Reason: Three Questions on the Nature of God by Robert Holcot, O.P.* Ed. Hester Goodenough Gelber. Toronto, 1983.

———. *In quatuor libros Sententiarum quaestiones*. Lyon, 1518; reprinted Frankfurt, 1967.

Horowitz, Yeshua. "Kara, Menachem ben Jacob." *Encyclopaedia Judaica*, X, cols. 760–761. Jerusalem, 1972.

Hübl, Albert, ed. *Catalogus manu scriptorum qui in bibliotheca monasterii B.V.M. ad Scotos Vindobonae servantur*. Vienna and Leipzig, 1894.

———. "Die Schulen." In *GStW*, V. Vienna, 1918.

Huizinga, Johan. *The Waning of the Middle Ages*. Trans. F. Hopman. London, 1924.

Hummelberger, Walter, and Kurt Peball. *Die Befestigungen Wiens* [Wiener Geschichtsbücher, vol. 14]. Vienna, 1974.

Janik, Allan, and Stephen Toulmin. *Wittgenstein's Vienna*. New York, 1973.

Jenks, Stuart. "Judenverschuldung und Verfolgung von Juden im 14. Jahrhundert. Franken bis 1349." *Vierteljahrschrift für Sozial- und Wirtschaftsgeschichte* 65 (1978) 309–356.

John of Ripa. *Determinationes. Texte critique avec introduction notes et tables*. Ed. André Combes. Paris, 1957.

John of Salisbury. *The Metalogicon, a Twelfth-Century Defense of the Verbal and Logical Arts of the Trivium*. Trans. D. D. McGarry. Berkeley, 1955.

Jordan, Michael J. "Duns Scotus on the Formal Distinction." Rutgers Ph.D. dissertation, 1984 [Ann Arbor: University Microfilms, 84 24 118].

Jourdain, Charles. "De l'enseignement de l'hébreu dans l'université de Paris au XVᵉ siècle." In Jourdain, *Excursions historiques et philosophiques à travers le moyen âge*, 233–245. Paris, 1888.

Kahn, Léon. *Les Juifs à Paris depuis le VIᵉ siècle*. Paris, 1889.

Kałuża, Zenon. "Le chancelier Gerson et Jérome de Prague." *AHDLMA* 51 (1984) 81–126.

Kaminsky, Howard. *A History of the Hussite Revolution.* Berkeley and Los Angeles, 1967.

———. "Hussite Radicalism and the Origins of Tabor, 1415–1418." *Mediaevalia et Humanistica* 10 (1956) 102–130.

———. "The University of Prague in the Hussite Revolution: The Role of the Masters." In John Baldwin and Richard Goldthwaite, eds., *Universities in Politics: Case Studies from the Late Middle Ages and the Early Modern Period,* 79–106. Baltimore, 1972.

Kelter, Ernst. "Das deutsche Wirtschaftsleben des 14. und 15. Jahrhunderts im Schatten der Pestepidemien." *Jahrbücher für Nationalökonomie und Statistik* 165 (1953) 161–208.

Kerler, Dietrich. "Zur Geschichte der Besteuerung der Juden durch Kaiser Sigmund und König Albrecht II." *Zeitschrift für die Geschichte der Juden in Deutschland* 3 (1889) 1–13, 107–129.

Kern, Anton, ed. *Die Handschriften der Universitätsbibliothek Graz,* 3 vols. [Handschriftenverzeichnisse österreichischer Bibliotheken, Steiermark, vols. 1–3]. Leipzig, 1942; Vienna, 1956–1967.

Kestenberg, Ruth. "Hussitentum und Judentum." *Jahrbuch der Gesellschaft für Geschichte der Juden in der Čechoslovakischen Republik* 8 (1936) 1–25.

Kibre, Pearl. *The Nations in the Mediaeval Universities* [Mediaeval Academy of America, Publication 49]. Cambridge, Mass., 1948.

Kieckhefer, Richard. *Repression of Heresy in Medieval Germany.* Philadelphia, 1979.

Kink, Rudolf. *Geschichte der kaiserlichen Universität zu Wien,* 2 vols. Vienna, 1854.

Kisch, Guido. "The Jews in Medieval Germany: A Bibliography of Publications on Their Legal and Social Status, 1949–1969." *Revue des Études Juives* 130 (1971) 271–294.

———. *The Jews in Medieval Germany.* Chicago, 1949.

———. *Sachsenspiegel and Bible: Researches in the Source History of the Sachsenspiegel and the Influence of the Bible on Medieval German Law.* Notre Dame, 1941.

———. "The Yellow Badge in History." *Historia Judaica* 4 (1942) 95–144.

Kleine Klosterneuburger Chronik. Ed. H. J. Zeibig. In *Archiv für Kunde österreichischer Geschichtsquellen* 7 (1851) 227–252.

Kleineidam, Erich. *Universitas Studii Erffordensis. Überblick über die Geschichte der Universität Erfurt im Mittelalter, 1392–1521* [Erfurter Theologische Studien, vol. 14, 22]. Leipzig, 1964, 1969.

Klicman, Ladislav, ed. *Processus iudiciarius contra Jeronimum de Praga, habitus Viennae A. 1410–1412.* Historický Archiv, vol. 12. Prague, 1898.

———. "Der Wiener Process gegen Hieronymus von Prag, 1410–1412." *MIÖG* 21 (1900) 445–457.

Kneale, William, and Martha Kneale. *The Development of Logic.* Oxford, 1962.

Kniewasser, Manfred. "Die antijüdische Polemik des Petrus Alphonsi (getaugt 1106) and des Abtes Petrus Venerabilis von Cluny (✝ 1156)." *Kairos,* NS 22 (1980) 34–76.

Kohn, Roger. "Royal Power and Rabbinical Authority in 14th Century France." In David Blumenthal, ed., *Approaches to Judaism in Medieval Times,* II [Brown Judaic Studies, vol. 57], 133–148. Chico, Calif., 1985.

Koller, Gerda. *Princeps in ecclesia. Untersuchungen zur Kirchenpolitik Herzog Albrechts V. von Österreich* [Archiv für Österreichische Geschichte, vol. 124]. Vienna, 1964.

Kosegarten, Antje. "Zur Plastik der Fürstenportale am Wiener Stephansdom." *Wiener Jahrbuch für Kunstgeschichte* 20 (1965) 74–96.

Krauss, Samuel. *Die Wiener Geserah vom Jahre 1421.* Vienna and Leipzig, 1920.

Kren, Claudia. "Homocentric Astronomy in the Latin West: The *De reprobatione ecentricorum et epiciclorum* of Henry of Hesse." *Isis* 59 (1968) 269–281.

———. "A Medieval Objection to 'Ptolemy.' " *British Journal for the History of Science* 4 (1969) 378–393.

Kretzmann, Norman. "Syncategoremata, Sophismata, Exponibilia." In *CHLMP,* 211–245. Cambridge, Eng., 1982.

Kretzmann, Norman, Anthony Kenny, and Jan Pinborg, eds. *The Cambridge History of Later Medieval Philosophy, from the Rediscovery of Aristotle to the Disintegration of Scholasticism, 1100–1600.* Cambridge, Eng., 1982.

Kriegel, Maurice. *Les Juifs à la fin du moyen âge dans l'Europe méditerranéenne.* Paris, 1979.

Krieger, Gerhard. *Der Begriff der praktischen Vernunft nach Johannes Buridanus* [*Beiträge . . .* , NF vol. 28]. Münster i. W, 1986.

Krüger, Sabine. "Krise der Zeit als Ursache der Pest? Der Traktat *De mortalitate in Alamannia* des Konrad von Megenberg." *Festschrift Hermann Heimpel* [Veröffentlichungen des Max-Planck-Instituts für Geschichte, vol. 36], II, 839–883. Göttingen, 1972.

Kühnel, Harry. *Mittelalterliche Heilkunde in Wien* [Studien zur Geschichte der Universität Wien, vol. 5]. Vienna and Graz, 1965.

Kulisher, Josef. *Allgemeine Wirtschaftsgeschichte des Mittelalters und der Neuzeit,* 2 vols. Munich and Berlin, 1928.

Kurz, Franz. *Österreich unter Albrecht III.* Linz, 1827.

Kurze, Dietrich. "Häresie und Minderheit im Mittelalter." *Historische Zeitschrift* 229 (1979) 529–573.

Lang, Albert. *Die Entfaltung des apologetischen Problems in der Scholastik des Mittelalters.* Freiburg, Basel, and Vienna, 1962.

———. "Die ersten Ansätze zu systematischer Glaubensbegründung." *Divus Thomas* 26 (1948) 361–394.

———. *Heinrich Totting von Oyta. Ein Beitrag zur Entstehungsgeschichte der ersten deutschen Universitäten und zur Problemgeschichte der Spätscholastik* [*Beiträge . . .* , vol. 33, 4–5]. Münster i. W., 1937.

Lang, Albert. "Johann Müntzinger, ein Schwäbischer Theologe und Schul-
maister am Ende des 14. Jahrhunderts." In A. Lang, J. Lechner, and
M. Schmaus, eds., *Aus der Geisteswelt des Mittelalters* [*Beiträge* . . . , Suppl.
Band III, 2], 1200–1230.

———. "Die Katharinenpredigt Heinrichs von Langenstein. Eine program-
matische Rede des Gründers der Wiener Universität über den Aufbau der
Glaubensbegründung und die Organisation der Wissenschaften." *Divus
Thomas* 26 (1948) 123–159, 233–250.

———. *Die theologische Prinzipienlehre der mittelalterlichen Scholastik.* Freiburg
and Basel, 1964.

———. "Das Verhältnis von Schrift, Tradition und kirchlichem Lehramt nach
Heinrich Totting von Oyta." *Scholastik* 40 (1965) 214–234.

———. *Die Wege der Glaubensbegründung bei den Scholastikern des 14. Jahrhunderts* [*Beiträge* . . . , vol. 30, 1–2]. Münster i. W., 1930.

Lang, Justin. *Die Christologie bei Heinrich von Langenstein. Eine Dogmenhisto-
rische Untersuchung* [Freiburger Theologische Studien, vol. 85]. Freiburg,
Basel, and Vienna, 1966.

Lasker, Daniel. *Jewish Philosophical Polemics against Christianity in the Middle
Ages.* New York, 1977.

Lauer, Ch. "R. Meir Halevy aus Wien und der Streit um das Grossrabbinat in
Frankreich. Eine Studie über rabbinische Streitfragen im Mittelalter." *Jahrbuch der Jüdisch-literarischen Gesellschaft* 16 (1924) 1–42.

Launoy, Jean de. *Regii Navarrae Gymnasii Parisiensis Historia.* Paris, 1677.

Lauterer, Kassian. "Johannes von Retz OESA, Collatio in exequiis Mag. Con-
radi de Ebraco—Ein Nachruf für Konrad von Ebrach (✝ 1399)." *Cistercienser
Chronik* 68 (1961) 25–40.

———. "Konrad von Ebrach, S.O.Cist. (✝ 1399). Lebenslauf und Schrifttum." *Analecta Sacri Ordinis Cisterciensis* 17 (1961) 151–214; 18 (1962) 60–120;
19 (1963) 3–50.

Leff, Gordon. *The Dissolution of the Medieval Outlook: An Essay on Intellectual
and Spiritual Change in the Fourteenth Century.* New York, 1976.

———. *Gregory of Rimini: Tradition and Innovation in Fourteenth Century
Thought.* Manchester, 1961.

———. *Heresy in the Later Middle Ages: The Relation of Heterodoxy to Dissent
c. 1250 – c. 1450,* 2 vols. Manchester, 1967.

———. *Paris and Oxford Universities in the Thirteenth and Fourteenth Centuries.*
New York, 1968.

LeGoff, Jacques. *Time, Work, and Culture in the Middle Ages.* Trans. Arthur
Goldhammer. Chicago, 1980.

Lehmann, Paul. *Die Parodie im Mittelalter.* Munich, 1922.

———, ed. *Parodistische Texte. Beispiele zur lateinischen Parodie im Mittelalter.*
Munich, 1923.

Leinweber, Josef. "Ein neues Verzeichnis der Teilnehmer am Konzil von Pisa
1409. Ein Beitrag zur Frage seiner Ökumenizität." In Georg Schwaiger, ed.,

Konzil und Papst [Festgabe für Hermann Tüchle], 207–246. Munich, Paderborn, and Vienna, 1975.

Lerner, Robert. *The Heresy of the Free Spirit in the Later Middle Ages.* Berkeley and Los Angeles, 1972.

Lescún, Eliseo García. *La teología trinitaria de Gregorio de Rimini.* Burgos, 1970.

Lexicon Latinitatis Medii Aevi. Turnhout/Tournai, 1975.

Lhotsky, Alphons. *Aufsätze und Vorträge,* 5 vols. Ed. Hans Wagner and Heinrich Koller. Munich, 1976.

———. *Thomas Ebendorfer. Ein österreichischer Geschichtsschreiber, Theologe und Diplomat des 15. Jahrhunderts* [MGH, Schriften, vol. 15]. Stuttgart, 1957.

———. "Wien im Spätmittelalter." In Hans Wagner and Heinrich Koller, ed., *Alphons Lhotsky. Aufsätze und Vorträge,* IV, 19–144. Munich, 1976.

———. *Die Wiener Artistenfakultät, 1365–1497* [Österreichische Akademie der Wissenschaften, Sitzungsberichte, Phil.-hist. Kl., vol. 247, 2]. Vienna, 1965.

Lickteig, Franz-Bernard. *The German Carmelites at the Medieval Universities* [Textus et Studia Historica Carmelitana, vol. 13]. Rome, 1981.

Little, A. G. "The Franciscan School at Oxford in the Thirteenth Century." *Archivum Franciscanum Historicum* 19 (1926) 803–874.

Loeb, Isidore. "Les expulsions des juifs de France au XIVe siècle." In *Jubelschrift zum 70. Geburtstag des Prof. Dr. H. Graetz,* 31–56. Breslau, 1887.

Lohrmann, Klaus. "Die Juden im Wirtschaftsleben des mittelalterlichen Wien." In [Kurt Schubert], ed., *Judentum im Mittelalter,* 185–187. Eisenstadt, 1978.

Loomis, Louise Ropes, trans. *The Council of Constance: The Unification of the Church.* Ed. John Hine Mundy and Kennerly M. Woody. New York and London, 1961.

Loux, Michael J. *Ockham's Theory of Terms: Part I of the Summa Logicae.* Notre Dame, 1974.

Luschin von Ebengreuth, Arnold. "Die Handelspolitik der österreichischen Herrscher im Mittelalter." *Almanach der kaiserlichen Akademie der Wissenschaften* (Vienna) 43 (1893) 311–337.

Lütge, Friedrich. "The Fourteenth and Fifteenth Centuries in Social and Economic History." In Gerald Strauss, ed., *Pre-Reformation Germany,* 316–379. London, 1972.

Lytle, Guy Fitch. "Universities as Religious Authorities in the Later Middle Ages and Reformation." In Lytle, ed., *Reform and Authority in the Medieval and Reformation Church,* 69–97. Washington, D.C., 1981.

Maccoby, Hyam, ed. *Judaism on Trial: Jewish-Christian Disputations in the Middle Ages.* London and Toronto, 1982.

MacIntyre, Alasdair. "The Antecedents of Action." In Bernard Williams and Alan Montefiore, eds., *British Analytical Philosophy.* London, 1966. Reprinted in MacIntyre, *Against the Self-Images of the Age: Essays on Ideology and Philosophy,* 191–210. London, 1971; Notre Dame, 1978.

Madre, Alois. *Nikolaus von Dinkelsbühl. Leben und Schriften.* [*Beiträge* . . . , vol. 40, 4]. Münster i. W, 1965.

———. *Die theologische Polemik gegen Raimundus Lullus.* [*Beiträge* . . . , NF vol. 11]. Münster i. W, 1973.

Mahoney, Michael. "Mathematics." In David Lindberg, ed., *Science in the Middle Ages*, 145–175. Madison, 1978.

Maier, Anneliese. "Der literarische Nachlass des Petrus Rogerii (Clemens VI.) in der Borghesiana." *RTAM* 15 (1948) 332–356.

Maierù, Alfonso. "Logica aristotelica e teologia trinitaria. Enrico Totting da Oyta." In A. Maierù and A. Paravicini Bagliani, eds., *Studi sul XIV secolo in memoria di Anneliese Maier*, 481–512. Rome, 1981.

———. "Logique et théologie trinitaire dans le moyen âge tardif. Deux solutions en présence." In Monica Asztalos, ed., *The Editing of Theological and Philosophical Texts from the Middle Ages* [Acta Universitatis Stockholmiensis, Studia Latina Stockholmiensia, vol. 30], 185–212. Stockholm, 1986.

———. "Logique et théologie trinitaire. Pierre d'Ailly." In Zénon Kałuża and Paul Vignaux, eds., *Preuves et raisons à l'université de Paris. Logique, ontologie et théologie au XIVᵉ siècle*, 253–268. Paris, 1984.

———. "À Propos de la doctrine de la supposition en théologie trinitaire au XIVᵉ siècle." In E. P. Bos, ed., *Mediaeval Semantics and Metaphysics: Studies Dedicated to L. M. De Rijk* [Artistarum, Supplementa II], 221–238. Nijmegen, 1985.

———. *Terminologia logica della tarda scolastica.* Rome, 1972.

Maimonides, Moses. *The Guide of the Perplexed.* Trans. Schlomo Pines. Chicago, 1963.

The Manuale Scholarium: An Original Account of Life in the Mediaeval University. Trans. R. F. Seybolt. Cambridge, Mass., 1921.

Marcolino, Venício. "Der Augustinertheologe an der Universität Paris." In H. Oberman, ed., *Gregor von Rimini*, 127–194. Berlin and New York, 1981.

Marcus, Jacob. *The Jew in the Medieval World: A Source Book, 315–1791.* Philadelphia, 1938; New York, 1965.

Markowski, Mieczsysław. "Beziehungen zwischen der Wiener mathematischen Schule und der Krakauer astronomischen Schule im Licht der erhaltenen mathematisch-astronomischen Schriften in den Manuscripten der Österreichischen Nationalbibliothek in Wien und der Jagiellonischen Bibliothek in Krakow." *Mediaevalia Philosophica Polonorum* 18 (1973) 121–151.

Marrone, Steven P. *Truth and Scientific Knowledge in the Thought of Henry of Ghent.* Cambridge, Mass., 1985.

———. *William of Auvergne and Robert Grosseteste: New Ideas of Truth in the Early Thirteenth Century.* Princeton, 1983.

Martin, Dennis. "The Carthusian Nicholas Kempf: Monastic and Mystical Theology in the Fifteenth Century." University of Waterloo Ph.D. dissertation, 1981.

Die Matrikel der Universität Wien [Publikationen des Instituts für österreichische Geschichtsforschung, 6. Reihe]. Vol. 1: *1377–1450*, 2 parts. Graz and Cologne, 1954, 1956.

Mayer, Anton. *Die Bürgerschule zu St. Stephan in Wien. Eine historisch-pädagogische Studie*. Vienna, 1880.

Mazis, A. des. "Deschamps, Gilles." *Dictionnaire d'histoire et de géographie ecclésiastiques*, XIV, cols. 331–334. Paris, 1960.

Meier, Ludger. "Contribution à l'histoire de la théologie à l'université d'Erfurt." *RHE* 50 (1955) 454–479.

———. "Der Sentenzenkommentar des Johannes Bremer." *Franziskanische Studien* 15 (1928) 161–169.

Meigen. *See* Meyger.

Meissner, Alois. *Gotteserkenntnis und Gotteslehre nach dem englischen Dominikanertheologen Robert Holkot*. Limburg, 1953.

Mellinkoff, Ruth. "The Round, Cap-Shaped Hats Depicted on Jews in BM Cotton Claudius B. IV." In Peter Clemoes, ed., *Anglo-Saxon England*, II, 155–166. Cambridge, Eng., 1973.

Metzger, Thérèse, and Mendel Metzger. *Jewish Life in the Middle Ages: Illuminated Hebrew Manuscripts of the Thirteenth to the Sixteenth Centuries*. New York, 1982.

Meunier, Francis. *Essai sur la vie et les œuvres de Nicole Oresme*. Paris, 1857.

Meyger, Johann. *Tractatus distinctionum*. Vienna, 1482.

Michalksi, Konstanty. *La Philosophie au XIVᵉ siècle. Six études*. Ed. Kurt Flasch. Frankfurt, 1969.

Miskimin, Harry. *The Economy of Early Renaissance Europe, 1300–1460*. Cambridge, Eng., 1975.

Misset, E., and Pierre Aubry. *Les Proses d'Adam de Saint-Victor*. Paris, 1900.

Möhler, Wilhelm. *Die Trinitätslehre des Marsilius von Inghen*. Limburg, 1949.

Moody, Ernest A. "Buridan, Jean." *Dictionary of Scientific Biography*, II, 603. New York, 1970.

———. "Empiricism and Metaphysics in Medieval Philosophy." *The Philosophical Review* 57 (1958) 145–163.

———. *The Logic of William of Ockham*. New York, 1935; reprinted New York, 1965.

———. "The Medieval Contribution to Logic." In Moody, *Studies in Medieval Philosophy, Science, and Logic*, 371–392.

———. *Studies in Medieval Philosophy, Science, and Logic*. Berkeley and Los Angeles, 1975.

———. *Truth and Consequence in Mediaeval Logic*. Amsterdam, 1953; reprinted Westport, Conn., 1976.

Moore, George F. "Christian Writers on Judaism." *Harvard Theological Review* 14 (1921) 197–254.

Morrall, J. B. *Gerson and the Great Schism*. Manchester, 1960.

Mošin, Vladimir, and Seid M. Traljić. *Filigranes des XIIIe et XIVe siècles.* Zagreb, 1957.

Muldoon, James. *Popes, Lawyers, and Infidels: The Church and the Non-Christian World, 1250–1550.* Philadelphia, 1979.

Murdoch, John E. "The Development of a Critical Temper: New Approaches and Modes of Analysis in Fourteenth Century Philosophy, Science, and Theology." In Siegfried Wenzel, ed., *Medieval and Renaissance Studies*, No. 7, 51–79. Chapel Hill, 1978.

――――. "*Mathesis in philosophiam scholasticam introducta*: The Rise and Development of the Application of Mathematics in Fourteenth-Century Philosophy and Theology." In *Arts libéraux et philosophie au moyen âge* [Actes du Quatrième Congrès International de Philosophie Médiévale], 215–254. Paris and Montreal, 1969.

――――. "Philosophy and the Enterprise of Science in the Later Middle Ages." In Yehuda Elkana, ed., *The Interaction between Science and Philosophy*, 51–74. Atlantic Highlands, N.J., 1974.

――――. "From Social into Intellectual Factors: An Aspect of the Unitary Character of Late Medieval Learning." In John Murdoch and Edith Sylla, eds., *The Cultural Context of Medieval Learning* [Boston Studies in the Philosophy of Science, vol. 26], 271–339. Dordrecht and Boston, 1975.

――――. "*Subtilitates Anglicanae* in Fourteenth-Century Paris: John of Mirecourt and Peter Ceffons." In Madeleine Pelner Cosman, ed., *Machaut's World*, 51–86. New York, 1978.

Murdoch, John, and Edith Sylla. "The Science of Motion." In David Lindberg, ed., *Science in the Middle Ages*, 206–264. Madison, 1978.

Murdoch, John, and Edward Synan. "Two Questions on the Continuum: Walter Chatton (?), O.F.M. and Adam Wodeham O.F.M." *Franciscan Studies* 26 (1966) 212–288.

Murray, Alexander. *Reason and Society in the Middle Ages.* Oxford, 1978.

Newald, Richard. "Beiträge zur Geschichte des Humanismus in Oberösterreich." *Jahrbuch des Oberösterreichischen Musealvereines* 81 (1926) 156–223.

Newman, Louis Israel. *Jewish Influence on Christian Reform Movements* [Columbia University Oriental Studies, vol. 23]. New York, 1925.

Nicholas of Lyra. *Postilla super totam Bibliam.* Nürnberg, 1493.

Noonan, John T., Jr. *The Scholastic Analysis of Usury.* Cambridge, Mass., 1957.

Nuchelmans, Gabriel. *Theories of the Proposition: Ancient and Medieval Conceptions of the Bearers of Truth and Falsity* [North-Holland Linguistic Series, vol. 8]. Amsterdam and London, 1973.

Oberman, Heiko A. "Facientibus quod in se est Deus non denegat gratiam: Robert Holkot, O.P., and the Beginnings of Luther's Theology." *Harvard Theological Review* 55 (1962) 317–342. Reprinted in S. Ozment, ed., *The Reformation in Medieval Perspective*, 119–141. Chicago, 1971.

————. "Fourteenth-Century Religious Thought: A Premature Profile." *Speculum* 53 (1978) 80–93.

————, ed. *Gregor von Rimini. Werk und Wirkung bis zur Reformation.* Berlin and New York, 1981.

————. *The Harvest of Medieval Theology: Gabriel Biel and Late Medieval Nominalism.* Cambridge, Mass., 1963; rev. ed., Grand Rapids, Mich., 1967.

————. "The Shape of Late Medieval Thought: The Birthpangs of the Modern Era." In C. Trinkaus and H. Oberman, eds., *The Pursuit of Holiness.* Leiden, 1974.

————. "Some Notes on the Theology of Nominalism, with Attention to Its Relation to the Renaissance." *Harvard Theological Review* 53 (1960) 47–76.

Ockham, William of. "Dialogus de imperio et pontificia potestate." In *Opera omnia,* I.

[————]. *Ockham's Theory of Terms: Part I of the Summa Logicae.* Trans. Michael Loux. Notre Dame, 1974.

[————]. *Ockham's Theory of Propositions: Part II of the Summa Logicae.* Trans. Alfred Freddoso and Henry Schuurman. Notre Dame, 1980.

————. *Opera omnia.* Lyon, 1494–1496; reprinted London, 1962.

————. *Scriptum in librum primum Sententiarum: Ordinatio.* Eds. Stephen Brown and Gedeon Gál [*OT*, I–III]. St. Bonaventure, N.Y., 1967–1970.

————. *Summa logicae.* Eds. P. Boehner, G. Gál, and S. Brown [*OP*, I]. St. Bonaventure, N.Y., 1974.

O'Donnell, J. Reginald, ed. *Nine Mediaeval Thinkers: A Collection of Hitherto Unedited Texts* [PIMS, Studies and Texts, vol. 1]. Toronto, 1955.

Oedinger, Friedrich. *Über die Bildung der Geistlichen im späten Mittelalter* [Studien und Texte zur Geistesgeschichte des Mittelalters, vol. 2]. Leiden and Cologne, 1953.

O'Malley, John W. *Praise and Blame in Renaissance Rome: Rhetoric, Doctrine, and Reform in the Sacred Orators of the Papal Court, c. 1450–1521.* Durham, 1979.

Oresme, Nicole. *Le Livre du ciel et du monde.* Ed. Albert D. Menut and A. J. Denomy. Madison, 1968.

Overfield, James H. "Nobles and Paupers at German Universities to 1600." *Societas* 4 (1974) 175–210.

Oyta, Henry of. *Quaestio de Sacra Scriptura et de veritatibus Catholicis.* Ed. Albert Lang [*Opuscula et textus* . . . , fasc. 12]. Münster, 1953.

Ozment, Steven. *The Age of Reform, 1250–1550: An Intellectual and Religious History of Late Medieval and Renaissance Europe.* New Haven, 1980.

————. *Homo Spiritualis: A Comparative Study of the Anthropology of Johannes Tauler, Jean Gerson, and Martin Luther (1509–1516) in the Context of Their Theological Thought* [*SMRT*, vol. 6]. Leiden, 1969.

————, ed. *Jean Gerson: Selections from A Deo Exivit, Contra Curiositatem Studentium, and De Mystica Theologia Speculativa.* Leiden, 1969.

————, ed. *The Reformation in Medieval Perspective.* Chicago, 1971.

Ozment, Steven. "The University and the Church: Patterns of Reform in Jean Gerson." *Mediaevalia et Humanistica*, NS 1 (1970) 111–126.

Palacký, Franz, ed. *Urkundliche Beiträge zur Geschichte des Hussitenkrieges vom Jahre 1419 an*, 2 vols. Prague, 1873.

Panofsky, Erwin. *Renaissance and Renascences in Western Art*. Stockholm, 1960.

Paquet, Jacques, and Jozef IJsewijn, eds. *The Universities in the Late Middle Ages* [Mediaevalia Lovaniensia, ser. 1, studia 6; Publications de l'Institut d'Études Médiévales de l'Université Catholique de Louvain, 2ᵉ sér., vol. 2]. Louvain/ Leuven, 1978.

Pascoe, Louis. "Pierre d'Ailly: Histoire, Schisme, Antéchrist." In *Genèse et Débuts du Grand Schisme d'Occident (1362–1394)* [Colloques internationaux du CNRS, 586], 615–622. Paris, 1980.

Pelikan, Jaroslav. *The Christian Tradition: A History of the Development of Doctrine*, 5 vols. Vol. 4: *Reformation of Church and Dogma*. Chicago, 1984.

Pelzer, August, and Thomas Kaeppeli. "L'*Oeconomica* de Conrad de Megenberg retrouvée." *RHE* 45 (1950) 559–616.

Perger, Richard. "Beiträge zur Wiener Verfassungs- und Sozialgeschichte im Spätmittelalter." *Jahrbuch des Vereines für Geschichte der Stadt Wien* 32–33 (1976–1977) 11–41.

———. "Ein neues Geschichtswerk über den Wiener Stephansdom." *Unsere Heimat* 40 (1969) 70–88.

Perger, Richard, and Walter Brauneis. *Die mittelalterlichen Kirchen und Klöster Wiens* [Wiener Geschichtsbücher, vols. 19–20]. Vienna, 1977.

Perroy, Edouard. "A l'origine d'une économie contractée: Les crises du XIVᵉ siècle." *Annales-Economies-Sociétés-Civilisations* 4 (1949) 167–182.

Pez, Hieronymus. *Scriptores rerum Austriacarum veteres ac genuini . . .* , 2 vols. Leipzig, 1721–1725.

Pfeiffer, Franz, ed. *Das Buch der Natur von Konrad von Megenberg. Die erste Naturgeschichte in deutscher Sprache*. Stuttgart, 1861.

Piccard, Gerhard, ed. *Die Ochsenkopf-Wasserzeichen*, 3 vols. Stuttgart, 1966.

———, ed. *Die Turm-Wasserzeichen*. Stuttgart, 1971.

Pinborg, Jan. "Magister Abstractionum." *Cahiers de l'Institut du Moyen Âge Grec et Latin* 18 (1976) 1–4.

Pirenne, Henri. *Economic and Social History of Medieval Europe*. Trans. I. E. Clegg. London, 1936.

Powicke, F. M. *Ways of Medieval Life and Thought: Essays and Addresses*. New York, [1949] 1971.

Prantl, Carl. *Geschichte der Logik im Abendlande*, 4 vols. Berlin, 1855–1870; reprinted 1957.

Rankin, Oliver Shaw. *Jewish Religious Polemic of Early and Later Centuries: A Study of Documents Here Rendered in English*. Edinburgh, 1956.

Rapf, Cölestin. *Das Schottenstift* [Wiener Geschichtsbücher, vol. 13]. Vienna and Hamburg, 1974.

Rashdall, Hastings. *The Universities of Europe in the Middle Ages*, 3 vols. Rev. ed. F. M. Powicke and A. B. Emden. Oxford, 1936.

Redlich, Oswald, and Anton Schönbach. "Des Gutolf von Heiligenkreuz Translatio s. Delicianae." *Sitzungsberichte der kaiserlichen Akademie der Wissenschaften (Vienna)*, Phil.-hist. Kl., vol. 159, 2 (1908) 1–38.

Reeves, Marjorie. *The Influence of Prophecy in the Later Middle Ages: A Study in Joachimism*. Oxford, 1969.

Rennhofer, Friedrich. *Die Augustiner-Eremiten in Wien. Ein Beitrag zur Kulturgeschichte Wiens* [Cassiciacum, vol. 13]. Würzburg, 1956.

Repertorium Germanicum. Ed. Gerd Tellenbach. Vol. 2: *Urban VI., Bonifaz IX. und Gregor XII., 1378–1415*. Berlin, 1933.

[Richard of Campsall]. *The Works of Richard of Campsall*, 2 vols. Ed. Edward A. Synan. [PIMS, Studies and Texts, vols. 17, 58]. Toronto, 1968, 1982.

Rimini, Gregory of. *Lectura super primum et secundum Sententiarum*, 6 vols. Ed. D. Trapp and V. Marcolino. Berlin and New York, 1979–1981.

———. *Registrum generalatus, 1357–1358*. Ed. Albericks de Meijer. [Fontes Historiae Ordinis Sancti Augustini, ser. 1, vol. 1]. Rome, 1976.

Ritter, Gerhard. *Die Heidelberger Universität. Ein Stück deutscher Geschichte*. Vol. 1: *Das Mittelalter (1386–1508)*. Heidelberg, 1936.

———. "Romantic and Revolutionary Elements in German Theology on the Eve of the Reformation." In S. Ozment, ed., *The Reformation in Medieval Perspective*, 15–49. Chicago, 1971.

———. "Studien zur Spätscholastik I: Marsilius von Inghen und die okkamistische Schule in Deutschland." *Sitzungsberichte der Heidelberger Akademie der Wissenschaften*, Phil.-hist. Kl., vol. 12, 4 (1921) 1–209.

———. "Studien zur Spätscholastik II: Via antiqua und via moderna auf den deutschen Universitäten des XV. Jahrhunderts." *Sitzungsberichte der Heidelberger Akademie der Wissenschaften*, Phil.-hist. Kl., vol. 13, 7 (1922); reprinted Darmstadt, 1975.

Robson, J. A. *Wyclif and the Oxford Schools*. Cambridge, Eng., 1961.

Roover, Raymond de. "The Scholastic Attitude toward Trade and Entrepreneurship," *Explorations in European History*, 2nd ser., 1 (1963) 76–87. Reprinted in Julius Kirshner, ed., *Business, Banking, and Economic Thought in Late Medieval and Early Modern Europe*, 336–345. Chicago, 1974.

Ross, W. D., ed. *The Works of Aristotle Translated into English*, vol. 1. Oxford, 1928.

Roth, Bartholomäus. *Franz von Mayronis O.F.M. Sein Leben, seine Werke, seine Lehre vom Formalunterschied in Gott*. Werl i. W., 1936.

Roth, F.W.E. "Zur Bibliographie des Henricus von Hembuche de Hassia, dictus de Langenstein." *Beiheft zum Centralblatt für Bibliothekswesen* 1, 2 (1888–1889) 1–22.

Rubens, Alfred. *A History of Jewish Costume*. New York, 1967.

Rupprich, Hans. *Das Wiener Schrifttum des ausgehenden Mittelalters* [Sitzungsberichte der österreichischen Akademie der Wissenschaften, Phil.-hist. Kl., vol. 228, 5]. Vienna, 1954.

Sailer, Heinrich F. "Zur Geschichte der Preisbewegung in Niederösterreich in XIV. Jahrhundert." *Blätter des Vereines für Landeskunde von Niederösterreich*, NF 4 (1870) 104–122, 148–157, 178–184, 197–204, 268–277; NF 5 (1871) 6–17, 39–46, 92–94.

Salvadori, Giovanni. *Die Minoritenkirche in ihrer ältesten Umgebung. Ein Beitrag zur Geschichte Wiens*. Vienna, 1894.

Sarton, George. *Introduction to the History of Science*, 3 vols. Baltimore, 1927–1948.

Sauerland, H. von. "Rede der Gesandtschaft des Herzogs Albrecht III. von Österreich an Papst Urban VI. bei der Rückkehr der Länder des Herzogs Leopold III. unter die römische Obedienz, verfasst von Heinrich Hembuche, genannt von Langenstein oder de Hassia (c. 1387)." *MIÖG* 9 (1888) 448–458.

Schäffauer, Friedrich. "Nikolaus von Dinkelsbühl als Prediger. Ein Beitrag zur religiösen Kulturgeschichte des ausgehenden Mittelalters." *Theologische Quartalschrift* 115 (1934) 405–439, 516–547.

Schalk, Karl. "Zum Parteiwesen in Wien zu Ende des 14. Jahrhunderts." *MIÖG* 2 (1881) 458–459.

———. "Zur Finanzverwaltung Wiens am Ende des XIV. Jahrhunderts (1368–1385)." *Blätter des Vereines für Landeskunde von Niederösterreich*, NF 17 (1883) 3–55.

Scherer, J. E. *Die Rechtsverhältnisse der Juden in den deutsch-österreichischen Ländern*. Leipzig, 1901.

Schmeidler, Bernhard. *Das spätere Mittelalter von der Mitte des 13. Jahrhunderts bis zur Reformation*. Vienna, 1937; reprinted Darmstadt, 1980.

Schmeidler, Felix, ed. *Joannis Regiomontani Opera collectanea*. Osnabrück, 1972.

Scholem, Gershom G. *Major Trends in Jewish Mysticism*. New York, 1967.

Schorske, Carl E. *Fin-de-siècle Vienna: Politics and Culture*. New York, 1980.

Schrauf, Karl. "Die Universität." In *Geschichte der Stadt Wien*, II, pt. 2 (Vienna, 1905), 961–1017.

[Schubert, Kurt], ed. *Judentum im Mittelalter* [Katalog für die Ausstellung "Judentum im Mittelalter" im Schloss Halbturn, Burgenland, 1978]. Eisenstadt, 1978.

Schüler, Martin. *Prädestination, Sünde und Freiheit bei Gregor von Rimini* [Forschungen zur Kirchen- und Geistesgeschichte, vol. 3]. Stuttgart, 1934.

Schum, Wilhelm. *Beschreibendes Verzeichniss der Amplonianischen Handschriftensammlung zu Erfurt*. Berlin, 1887.

Schwarz, Arthur Zacharias, ed. *Die hebräischen Handschriften der k. k. Hofbibliothek zu Wien*. Vienna, 1914.

Schwarz, Ignaz. "Geschichte der Juden in Wien. Von ihrem ersten Auftreten bis zum Jahre 1625." In *GStW*, V, 1–64. Vienna, 1918.

———. *Das Wiener Ghetto. Seine Häuser und seine Bewohner*. Pt. 1: *Das Juden-*

viertel in der inneren Stadt bis zu seiner Aufhebung im Jahre 1421. Vienna and Leipzig, 1909.

Seibt, Ferdinand. *Karl IV. Ein Kaiser in Europa, 1346–1378.* Munich, 1978.

Seigel, Jerrold. *Rhetoric and Philosophy in Renaissance Humanism.* Princeton, 1968.

Seligsohn, Max. "Lipmann-Mühlhausen, Yom-Tob Ben Salomon." *The Jewish Encyclopedia*, VIII, 97–98. New York and London, 1904.

Shachar, Isaiah. *The Judensau: A Medieval Anti-Jewish Motif and Its History.* London, 1974.

Shank, Michael H. "Academic Benefices and German Universities during the Great Schism: Three Letters from Johannes of Stralen, Arnold of Emelisse, and Gerard of Kalkar, 1387–1388." *Codices Manuscripti* 7 (1981) 33–47.

———. "A Female University Student in Late Medieval Kraków." *Signs: A Journal of Women and Culture* 12 (1987) 373–380.

Siegris, Emmerich. "Die geplante Instandesetzung der Fassade des Hauses in Wien 1., Judenplatz Nr. 2, 'Zum grossen Jordan.'" *Unsere Heimat*, NF 15 (1942) 32.

Šmahel, František. "The Idea of the 'Nation' in Hussite Bohemia." *Historica* 16 (Prague, 1969) 143–247; 17 (Prague, 1969) 93–197.

———. "The Kuttenberg Decree and the Withdrawal of the German Students from Prague in 1409: A Discussion." *History of Universities* 4 (1984) 153–161.

———. "Leben und Werk des Magisters Hieronymus von Prag." *Historica* 13 (1966) 81–111.

Smalley, Beryl. *English Friars and Antiquity in the Early Fourteenth Century.* Oxford, 1960.

———. *The Study of the Bible in the Middle Ages.* Oxford, 1952.

Sommerfeld, Erich. "Ökonomisches Denken in Deutschland vor der frühbürgerliche Revolution. Der 'Tractatus de Contractibus' des Heinrich von Langenstein." Deutsche Akademie der Wissenschaften, Berlin-Ost, dissertation, 1969.

Sommerfeldt, Gustav. "Aus der Zeit der Begründung der Universität Wien." *MIÖG* 29 (1908) 291–322.

———. "Die Prophetien der hl. Hildegard von Bingen in einem Schreiben des Magisters Heinrich v. Langenstein (1383), und Langenstein's Trostbrief über den Tod eines Bruders des Wormser Bischofs Eckhard von Ders (um 1384)." *Historisches Jahrbuch* 30 (1909) 43–61, 297–307.

———. "Die Stellung Ruprechts III. von der Pfalz zur deutschen Publizistik bis zum Jahre 1400." *Zeitschrift für die Geschichte des Oberrheins*, NF 22 (1907) 291–319.

———. "Zu Heinrich von Oyta." *MIÖG* 25 (1904) 576–604.

———. "Zwei politische Sermone des Heinrich von Oyta und des Nikolaus von Dinkelsbühl (1388 und 1417)." *Historisches Jahrbuch* 26 (1905) 318–327.

———. "Zwei Schismatraktate Heinrichs von Langenstein. Sendschreiben an

König Wenzel von 1381 und Schreiben an Bischof Friedrich von Brixen, um 1384." *MIÖG*, Ergänzungsband 7 (1907) 436–469.

Spade, Paul. *The Mediaeval Liar: A Catalogue of the Insolubilia-Literature* [Subsidia Mediaevalia, vol. 5]. Toronto, 1975.

Spinka, Matthew, ed. *Advocates of Reform: From Wyclif to Erasmus* [Library of Christian Classics, vol. 14]. Philadelphia, 1953.

———. *John Hus at the Council of Constance*. New York, 1965.

Spitzer, Shlomoh. "Das Wiener Judentum bis zur Vertreibung im Jahre 1421." *Kairos* 19 (1977) 134–145.

[Stainreuter, Leopold]. "Die österreichische Chronik von den 95 Herrschaften," *MGH, Deutsche Chroniken*, vol. 6. Hanover and Leipzig, 1909.

Staudner, Gerda. "Die Wiener Juden als Geldgeber im Mittelalter." Philosophische Fakultät, Universität Wien, dissertation, 1966.

Stegmüller, Friedrich, ed. *Repertorium Commentatorium in Sententias Petri Lombardi*, 2 vols. Würzburg, 1947.

Steiman, Sidney. *Custom and Survival: A Study of the Life and Work of Rabbi Jacob Molin (Moelln) Known as the Maharil (c. 1360–1427) and His Influence in Establishing the Ashkenazic Minhag (Customs of German Jewry)*. New York, 1963.

Stein, S. *Jewish-Christian Disputations in Thirteenth-Century Narbonne* [Inaugural Lecture, University College, London, 22 October 1964]. London, 1969.

Steneck, Nicholas. *Science and Creation in the Middle Ages: Henry of Langenstein (d. 1397) on Genesis*. Notre Dame, 1976.

Stowasser, Otto H. "Zur Geschichte der Wiener Geserah." *Vierteljahrschrift für Sozial- und Wirtschaftsgeschichte* 16 (1922) 104–118.

———. "Zur inneren Politik Herzog Albrechts III. von Österreich." *MIÖG* 41 (1926) 141–149.

Strauss, Gerald, ed. and trans. *Manifestations of Discontent in Germany on the Eve of the Reformation*. Bloomington, Ind., 1971.

Stump, Eleonore. "Topics: Their Development and Absorption into Consequences." In *CHLMP*, 287–289. Cambridge, 1982.

Swanson, R. N. *Universities, Academics, and the Great Schism* [Cambridge Studies in Medieval Life and Thought, 3rd ser., vol. 12]. Cambridge, Eng., 1979.

Sylla, Edith Dudley. "Autonomous and Handmaiden Science: St. Thomas Aquinas and William of Ockham on the Physics of the Eucharist." In John Murdoch and Edith Sylla, eds., *The Cultural Context of Medieval Learning*, 349–391. Dordrecht and Boston, 1975.

———. "Medieval Concepts of the Latitude of Forms: The Oxford Calculators." *AHDLMA* 40 (1973) 223–283.

Synan, Edward A. "The Universal and Supposition in a *Logica* Attributed to Richard of Campsall." In J. R. O'Donnell, ed., *Nine Mediaeval Thinkers*, 183–232. Toronto, 1955.

————, ed. *The Works of Richard of Campsall*, 2 vols. [PIMS, Studies and Texts, vols. 17, 58]. Toronto, 1968, 1982.

Taber, Douglas. "The Theologian and the Schism: A Study of the Political Thought of Jean Gerson (1363–1429)." Stanford University Ph.D. dissertation, 1985.

Tabulae codicum manu scriptorum praeter Graecos et Orientales in Bibliotheca Palatina Vindobonensi asservatorum, 10 vols. Vienna, 1864–1868; reprinted Graz, 1965.

Tachau, Katherine. "French Theology in the Mid-Fourteenth Century." *AH-DLMA* 51 (1984) 41–80.

Ta-Shma, Israel Moses. "Mühlhausen, Yom Tov Lipmann." *Encyclopaedia Judaica*, XII, cols. 499–502. Jerusalem, 1972.

Thiel, Matthias. "Grundlagen und Gestalt der Hebräischkenntnisse des frühen Mittelalters." *Studi Medievali*, ser. 3, x, 3 (1969) 3–212.

Thorndike, Lynn. *The Sphere of Sacrobosco and Its Commentators*. Chicago, 1949.

————. *University Records and Life in the Middle Ages*. New York, 1944.

Thorndike, Lynn, and Pearl Kibre, eds. *A Catalogue of Incipits of Mediaeval Scientific Writings in Latin*, 2nd ed. rev. and aug. Cambridge, Mass., 1963.

Tomaschek, J. A., ed. *Die Rechte und Freiheiten der Stadt Wien*, 2 vols. Vienna, 1877.

Trachtenberg, Joshua. *The Devil and the Jews: The Medieval Conception of the Jew and Its Relation to the Modern Antisemitism*. New Haven, 1943.

Trapp, Damasus. "Augustinian Theology in the Fourteenth Century: Notes on Editions, Marginalia, Opinions, and Book-Lore." *Augustiniana* 6 (1956) 146–274.

————. "Clm 27034: Unchristened Nominalism and Wycliffite Realism at Prague in 1381." *RTAM* 24 (1957) 320–360.

————. "New Approaches to Gregory of Rimini." *Augustinianum* 2 (1962) 115–130.

————. "Peter Ceffons of Clairvaux." *RTAM* 24 (1957) 101–154.

————. "La tomba bisoma di Tommaso da Strasburgo e Gregorio da Rimini." *Augustinianum* 6 (1966) 5–17.

Trinkaus, Charles, and Heiko Oberman, eds. *The Pursuit of Holiness in Late Medieval and Renaissance Religion* [*SMRT*, vol. 10]. Leiden, 1974.

Trusen, Winfried. *Spätmittelalterliche Jurisprudenz und Wirtschaftsethik, dargestellt an Wiener Gutachten des 14. Jahrhunderts* [Vierteljahrschrift für Sozial- und Wirtschaftsgeschichte, Beiheft 43]. Wiesbaden, 1961.

Tuchman, Barbara. *A Distant Mirror: The Calamitous 14th Century*. New York, 1978.

Tweedale, Martin. "Abelard and the Culmination of the Old Logic." *CHLMP*, 143–157. Cambridge, Eng., 1982.

Uhlirz, Karl, ed. *Die Rechnungen des Kirchmeisteramtes von St. Stephan zu Wien*. Vienna, 1901–1902.

Uiblein, Paul. "Beiträge zur Frühgeschichte der Universität Wien." *MIÖG* 71 (1963) 284–310.

————. "Die ersten Österreicher als Professoren an der Wiener Theologischen Fakultät (1384–1389)." *Wiener Beiträge zur Theologie* 52 (1976) 85–101.

————. "Johann Stadel von Russbach. Ein Klosterneuburger Chorherr an der Wiener Universität." *Jahrbuch des Stiftes Klosterneuburg*, NF 4 (1964) 7–29.

————. *Ein Kopialbuch der Wiener Universität als Quelle zur österreichischen Kirchengeschichte unter Herzog Albrecht v.* [Fontes Rerum Austriacarum, zweite Abteilung, vol. 80]. Vienna, 1973.

————. "Die österreichischen Landesfürsten und die Wiener Universität im Mittelalter." *MIÖG* 72 (1964) 382–408.

[————], ed. *600 Jahre Universität Wien*. Vienna and Munich, 1965.

————. "Zu den Beziehungen der Wiener Universität zu anderen Universitäten im Mittelalter." In J. Paquet and J. IJsewijn, eds., *The Universities in the Late Middle Ages*, 168–189. Louvain/Leuven, 1978.

————. "Zur Lebensgeschichte einiger Wiener Theologen des Mittelalters." *MIÖG* 74 (1966) 95–107.

Ullmann, Walter. *The Origins of the Great Schism: A Study in Fourteenth Century Ecclesiastical History*. London, 1948.

Unterkircher, Franz, ed. *Katalog der datierten Handschriften in lateinischer Schrift in Österreich*. Vienna, 1969–.

Vancsa, Max. *Geschichte Nieder- und Oberösterreichs,*. 2 vols. Stuttgart and Gotha, 1927.

————. "Politische Geschichte von 1283 bis 1522." In *GStW*, ii, pt. 2, 499–591. Vienna, 1905.

Vanderjagt, Argo. "Henry of Langenstein." *Dictionary of the Middle Ages*, vi, 167. New York, 1985.

Van Steenbergen, Fernand. *Aristotle in the West: The Origins of Latin Aristotelianism*. Louvain/Leuven, 1970.

Verger, Jacques. "*Studia* et universités." In *Le scuole degli ordini mendicanti (secoli XIII-XIV)* [Convegni del Centro di Studi sulla Spiritualità Medievale, vol. 17], 175–203. Todi, 1978.

Vielmetti, Nikolaus. "Die Juden in Österreich während des Mittelalters. Historische Rahmen." In [K. Schubert], ed., *Judentum im Mittelalter*, 178–187. Eisenstadt, 1978.

Vignaux, Paul. *La Pensée au moyen âge*. Paris, 1938.

————. "Philosophie et théologie trinitaire chez Jean de Ripa." *Archives de Philosophie* 41 (1978) 221–236.

Voltelini, Hans von. "Die Wiener und Kremser Judeneid." *Mitteilungen des Vereines für Geschichte der Stadt Wien* 12 (1932) 64–70.

————. "Zur Wiener Stadtverfassung im 15. Jahrhundert." *Jahrbuch für Landeskunde von Niederösterreich*, NF 13–14 (1914–1915) 281–299.

Von der Hardt, Hermann. *Magnum oecumenicum Constantiense concilium de ecclesiae reformatione*, 6 vols. Frankfurt and Leipzig, 1697–1700.

Vooght, Paul de. *L'Hérésie de Jean Huss* [Bibliothèque de la Revue d'Histoire Ecclésiastique, fasc. 34]. Louvain, 1960.

———. "Jean Huss et ses juges." In A. Franzen and W. Müller, eds., *Das Konzil von Konstanz*, 152–173. Freiburg, Basel, and Vienna, 1964.

———. *Les Sources de la doctrine chrétienne d'après les théologiens du xive siècle et du début du xve siècle.* Paris, 1954.

Waissenberger, Robert, ed. *Vienna, 1890–1920.* New York, 1984.

Walde, Bernhard. *Christliche Hebraisten Deutschlands am Ausgang des Mittelalters.* Münster i. W., 1916.

Wappler, Anton. *Geschichte der theologischen Fakultät der k. k. Universität zu Wien.* Vienna, 1884.

Watkins, Renée Neu. "The Death of Jerome of Prague: Divergent Views." *Speculum* 42 (1967) 104–124.

Watt, D.E.R. "University Clerks and Rolls of Petitions for Benefices." *Speculum* 34 (1959) 213–229.

Wattenbach, W. "Die österreichischen Freiheitsbriefe. Prüfung ihrer Echtheit und Forschungen über ihre Entstehung." *Archiv für österreichischer Geschichtsquellen* 8 (1852) 77–119.

Wellesz, J. "Isaak b. Mose Or Sarua." *Monatschrift für Geschichte und Wissenschaft des Judentums* 48 (1904) 129–144, 209–213, 316–371, 440–456, 710–712.

Wieland, Georg. "The Reception and Interpretation of Aristotle's *Ethics.*" *CHLMP*, 657–672. Cambridge, Eng., 1982.

"Wiener Annalen (1349–1404)." In *MGH, Deutsche Chroniken*, vol. 6. Hanover and Leipzig, 1933.

Williams, Ann, ed. *Prophecy and Millenarianism: Essays in Honor of Marjorie Reeves.* New York, 1980.

Wilson, Curtis. *William Heytesbury and the Rise of Mathematical Physics* [Publications in Medieval Science, vol. 3]. Madison, 1960.

Winter, Ernst Karl. *Rudolph iv. von Österreich*, 2 vols. Vienna, 1934–1936.

Wodeham-Oyta, *Abbreviatio* = Goddam, Adam. *Super Quattuor libros Sententiarum . . .* [abbreviated by Henry of Oyta and edited by John Major]. Paris, 1512.

Wolf, Gerson. *Geschichte der Juden in Wien, 1156–1876.* Vienna, 1876.

———. *Die Juden* [Die Völker Österreich-Ungarns, vol. 70]. Vienna and Teschen, 1883.

Wolfson, Harry Austryn. "Notes on Proofs of the Existence of God in Jewish Philosophy." *Hebrew Union College Annual* 1 (1924) 575–596.

———. *Studies in the History of Philosophy and Religion*, vol. 1. Ed. I. Twersky and G. H. Williams. Cambridge, Mass., 1973.

———. *The Philosophy of the Church Fathers.* Vol. 1: *Faith, Trinity, Incarnation.* Cambridge, Mass., 1956.

Wulf, Maurice de. *Histoire de la philosophie médiévale*, vol. 3, 6th rev. ed. Paris, 1947.

Xiberta y Roqueta, B. M. *De scriptoribus scholasticis saeculi xiv ex ordine Car-

melitarum [Bibliothèque de la Revue d'Histoire Ecclésiastique, vol. 6]. Louvain, 1931.

Zeibig, H. J., ed. "Kleine Klosterneuburger Chronik." *Archiv für Kunde Österreichischer Geschichtsquellen* 7 (1851) 227–252.

Zeissberg, H. R. von. "Der österreichische Erbfolgestreit nach dem Tode des Königs Ladislaus Posthumus (1457–1458) im Lichte der habsburgischen Hausverträge." *Archiv für österreichische Geschichte* 58 (1879) 1–170.

Zimmermann, Albert, ed. *Antiqui und Moderni. Traditionsbewusstsein und Fortschrittsbewusstsein im späten Mittelalter* [Miscellanea Mediaevalia, vol. 9]. New York and Berlin, 1974.

Zumkeller, Adolar. "Ein Manuskript der Sentenzenlesung des Augustinertheologen Dionysius von Montina, fälschlich genannt Dionysius Cisterciensis." In *Miscellanea Martin Grabmann. Gedenkblatt zum 10. Todestag*, 73–87. Munich, 1959.

——. "Der Wiener Theologieprofessor Johannes von Retz, O.S.A. (✝ nach 1404) und seine Lehre von Urstand, Erbsünde, Gnade und Verdienst." *Augustiniana* 21 (1971) 505–540; 22 (1972) 118–184, 540–582.

Zykan, Marlene. *Der Stephansdom* [Wiener Geschichtsbücher, vols. 26–27]. Vienna, 1981.

INDEX

Abelard, Peter, xii, 60
Abraham of Temonaria, 147
absolute power of God, xii, 45, 47, 68n, 133
Adam of St. Victor, 57
Adams, Marilyn McCord, 68
Aegidius de Campis, 55, 217–18
Ailly, Pierre d', 87n, 103, 168n
Albert II of Habsburg, 147
Albert III of Habsburg, 11n, 13–14, 16, 19–22, 24, 26, 32, 37, 171, 173, 207; fiscal policies, 145–46; and revival of university, 147–48
Albert IV of Habsburg, 22, 171, 173
Albert V of Habsburg, 173, 178, 186, 191, 197–98
Albert of Saxony, 12, 13, 28, 29n, 32; *Sophismata*, 92n
Albertus Magnus, 11
Alençon, Bibliothèque de la ville, *codex 144*, 30n, 127n, 129n–133n, 216
Alexander V. *See* Peter of Candia
Alexander of Roes, 3–4
analytical languages, 27, 49
André de Neufchâteau, 129n
Anselm, 40, 50; rule of, 70, 75, 76, 90
apocalypticism, 167–68
apologetics, 43, 44, 75–76, 83, 84, 85n, 110, 131, 163–69, 172, 192, 194, 202; failure of, 167–69; historical approach, 166, 192; a moral matter, 156–61
Aquinas, Thomas, 5, 29, 42, 58n, 62, 63, 129
Arabic, 155
Arabs, 152, 189
Aristotle, 72
—and Christianity, 108–109, 124, 135–36
—commentary on: *Ethics*, 159n; *On the Heavens*, 32; the *Physics*, 32, 33; the *Prior Analytics*, 84
—excessive confidence in reason, 130ff

—and formal distinction, 125
—and Jews, 160–61
—logic: circumlocutions in, 126; compatibility with Plato, 81, 93, 109, 203; defects in, 73, 94, 122, 124; formality of, 72, 75, 79, 94, 120; and *insolubilia*, 124; modes of universalizing propositions, 108, 109; nonformality, 123; rejection of, 86, 133ff, 142, 170, 203; universal premises, 59n; universality of, 93, 94, 108–10, 121, 130–33, 169, 203
—and mysteries of faith, 96, 123–24
—*On the Heavens*, 50
—*Physics*, 50
—*Posterior Analytics*, 192–93
—predication, 69
—*Prior Analytics*, 69, 84, 124
—progress since, 50
—reception of, 134
—and *sophismata*, 125
—*Sophistical Refutations*, 95
—syllogizing, rules of, 58, 59, 60, 69, 72, 81, 94, 97, 119, 125, 202
and theology, 103, 112, 117, 119, 135–36, 142, 169–70, 194
—See also *dici de omni et nullo*; logic; syllogism
Arnold of Emelisse, 140n
Arnold of Seehausen, 49n, 55n, 117–20, 122, 125–26, 137–38, 165n; attacks on, 137, 173; commentary on the *Sentences*, 119
Arnold of Strelley, 71, 72, 123, 140; *Centiloquium theologicum*, 71–74, 140
Ashworth, Elizabeth J., 103
astronomy, ix, 139. *See also* comet of 1402; Jews; moon
Auer, Johann, 119, 122, 136–37
Augustine, 40, 50, 58n; citation of Isaiah, 124n, 194; *De Trinitate*, 59, 60; and Platonism, 134

Augustinerkirche, 10n, 17, 88
Augustinian Eremites, 10, 18, 87n, 88,
    173, 212; studium, 12n
Augustinianism, 29, 33n, 34, 83, 141, 182
Averroës, 5, 93, 161
Avicenna, 50
Avignon, 4, 5, 12, 14, 15, 89
Aygel, Johann, 198

Babenberg dukes, 7, 10
Bacon, Roger, 155
Baconthorp, John, 99n
Balardi, Jacob (Bishop of Lodi), 183–84
Bavaria, 10; duke of, 8n
Benedict IV, 11
Benedict XIII, 190
Benedictines, 10, 200. See also Melk
Berengar of Tours, 60
Berger, David, 164
Bernard of Clairvaux, 30, 124n
Berthold of Regensburg, 179n, 213n
Berthold of Wehingen, 14, 16
Binder, Karl, 30
Black Death. See plague of 1349
Boehner, Philotheus, 67, 83
Boethius, 11n, 69
Bologna (university and studia), 27, 35,
    87n, 155, 208–209
Bonaventure, 62–63, 118n
Boniface VIII, 4
Boniface IX, 22
Borchert, Ernst, 71n
Bradwardine, Thomas, 31, 181, 219
Bremer, Johannes, 36n
Bremis, Johannes, 36–56, 128n, 199; bi-
    ography, 36–38; daring theses, 54; li-
    brary, 54–55; notebook, 56, 138, 156,
    205–219; possible worlds, 44–45, 50n;
    principia debate, 34ff, 112ff; on the syl-
    logism, 43; on truth, 56
Brunner, Otto, 9
Bürgerschule, 10–11
Buridan, John, 23, 28, 32–33; attacked by
    Jerome of Prague, 176; commentary on
    the Ethics, 159n; questions on Physics,
    97n
Burleigh, Walter, 80, 104n, 125n, 129n

Campanus of Novara, 50

Campsall, Richard. See Richard of
    Campsall
Camus, Albert, 170, 204
Carmelites, 87, 130
Caspar the empiric, 198
Caspar Maiselstein, 178
Centiloquium. See Arnold of Strelley
Charles IV of Luxemburg, 12, 18, 144–45
Chatton, Walter, 90
Christian of Traunstein, 199
Clement VI, 12n
Clement VII, 15
Cohen, Jeremy, 169
coinage, 20, 148
collegium ducale, 19, 37–38, 148, 207; li-
    brary of, 88n, 207n
Cologne, 3; university of, 4n, 20, 21, 31,
    149n, 215
Combes, André, 53n, 141n
comet of 1402, 171n
complexe significabile, 100–102, 110, 129
conciliar movement, 152, 171
condemnations of 1277, 5, 219
Conrad of Ebrach, 35n, 85n, 212, 213n
Conrad of Megenberg, 11, 144
Conrad of Soltau, 17n
Constance, Council of, 31, 178–85, 190–
    91, 195, 203
contradiction, 114, 129, 170, 204; distin-
    guishing contradictory propositions
    from noncontradictory, 77; freedom
    from, 163; impossible to avoid, 135;
    principle of, 64, 67–68, 71, 80
Costesy, Henry, 100n
Councils: Lateran, 23–24, 61, 73, 79;
    Pisa, 173–74, 178. See also Constance
Courtenay, William J., xii, 54n
Cowton, Robert, 82–83, 95
Cracow, 178
Crescas, 165

Damerau, Rudolf, 30, 128, 216–17
Danube traffic, 7
demonstration, 43–44, 59, 68, 82; ge-
    nuses of, 184; refusal to give up, 159–
    62, 164; unsuitability of, 78, 193
descent, logical, 106–107
dici de omni et nullo, 84, 95ff, 115–16, 120–
    21, 126, 136; definition, 69; Ockham,

97; Oyta, 93ff; Wodeham, 95–97. *See also* fallacy of accident; Langenstein

difference. *See* distinctions

Dinkelsbühl, Nicholas of, 29n, 34n, 53n, 88n, 117ff, 173, 187, 200; accusations, 137, 173, 176; apologetic sermons, 191ff; autograph, 120n; commentary on Matthew, 194ff, 204; at Constance, 178–79, 183, 187, 195, 203; expediency, 196; and Hebrew books, 197; and Jerome of Prague, 176; and Jews, 192–96; logic and Trinity, 122–26, 136; monastic reform, 187; *Quaestiones communes*, 119–20; *Quaestiones magistrales*, 119, 122, 194; views on killing, 194

Dionysius of Montina, 87n

disputations, 32, 34–35, 42, 52, 58, 128, 140, 151–52, 181, 188, 211–12. *See also* Langenstein; principia; quodlibetal questions; Tortosa

distinctions: *a parte rei*, 62; Aquinas on, 62; Bonaventure on, 62; *ex natura rei*, 99; finite, 114n; formal, 63, 100n; formal nonreal, 99; infinitely small, 114; minimal, 48; rational, 62; real, 61, 114; real essential, 99; real nonessential, 99; Scotus on, 63ff. *See also* Langenstein; Ockham; Rimini; Wodeham

distribution, 98, 102, 103; *extra terminum*, 92, 130n; gender specific, 106–107; *infra terminum*, 92

Dominicans, 28n, 30, 42, 172

Douglas, Mary, 170

Duns Scotus, John, 30, 46, 47n, 52, 56, 63–65, 85, 219; and Augustine, 58n; confidence in reason, 78; on fallacy of accident, 69; on types of predication, 64, 73, 95. *See also* formal distinction

Duran, Profiat, 165

Dürer, Albrecht, 149n

Eberbach, 30, 55, 141, 168n

Eckehard of Ders, 168n

economy. *See* viticulture

Ehrle, Franz, 28, 37n

Erfurt, mss: *Ampl. F 118*, 217n; *Ampl. Q 125*, 156n; *Ampl. Q 150*, 96n

Erfurt, university of, 4n, 14n, 89, 114

eucharist, 59, 112

Euclid, 50

Eymeric, Nicholas, 142n

fallacy of accident, 69–71, 80, 82, 95; of equivocation, 70; figure of speech, 84

fideism, xii, 72, 78

formal distinction: Holcot and, 80; Langenstein and, 105–106; Ockham and, 65–71, 100; in philosophy, 64; Scotus and, 63–65. *See also* distinctions

formal identity, 105

formalizantes, 53n, 117n; Gerson attack on, 180

Francis of Mayronnes, 80n, 124n

Franciscans, 42, 53n

Frank, Isnard, 29

Franz von Retz, 42, 174, 208–209

Frederick of Gars, 22

Frederick of Nürnberg, 35n

Frederick II (Emperor), 10n, 142

Fünfkirchen, 38

Gelber, Hester G., 61, 65, 70, 81

Gerard of Kalkar, 17, 20, 27, 33

Gerson, Jean, 52, 179–80, 184, 203; attacks on *formalizantes*, 180; rhetoric and logic, 182; several logics, 180–81; travels to Austria, 187

Gilbert, Neal W., 31

Giles of Rome, 10, 129

Gilles des Champs. *See* Aegidius de Campis

Gilson, Etienne, 5n

God: attributes, 63, 66, 153–54, 156; degrees of perfection, 46; as master, 193; unity of, 163, 188–89. *See also* absolute power of God; Trinity

Gottschalk de Pomuk, 217

Göttweig, 188

Graz, Universitätsbibliothek: *codex 443*, 171n; *codex 639*, 89n, 112n; *codex 1145*, 96n

Gregory XI, 14

Greifswald, 12n

Guelluy, Robert, 67n

Gutolf of Heiligenkreuz, 3

Habsburg dukes: indebtedness, 147–48, 191; succession quarrels, 173; and Vienna, 8–9. *See also* Albert II; Albert III;

Habsburg dukes (*cont.*)
   Albert IV; Albert V; Leopold III; Leopold IV; Rudolph IV
Häfele, Gallus, 28n
Halevi, Meir ben Baruch, 160
Hebrew: fragments in Latin manuscripts, 199n; and Hussites, 188–89; instruction in, 150, 154–56
Heidelberg, university of, 4n, 6n, 12n, 17n, 21, 28n, 176–77
Heilig, Konrad, 128, 216
Heiligenkreuz: *codex 141*, 88n; *codex 290*, 213n
Henry of Altendorf, 217
Henry of Ghent, 40, 56, 90, 219
Henry of Hesse the elder. *See* Langenstein
Henry of Hesse the younger. *See* Henry of Altendorf
Henry of Kitzbühl, 178
Henry of Odendorp, 215
Henry of Oyta. *See* Oyta
heresy, 173, 176; accusations, 188ff. *See also* Hussites; Joachim of Fiore; Waldensians
Hermann of Treysa, 37n, 208n
Hermann Lurtz of Nürnberg, 113, 114n, 129; *Tractatus de paralogismis*, 128, 140
Heytesbury, William, 28, 32; *Rules for Solving Sophismata*, 125
Hildegard of Bingen, 168
Hofburg, 8
Hoffmann, Fritz, 78
Hohmann, Thomas, 97n
Holcot, Robert, 23, 31, 71n, 74–81, 90, 219; and Aristotle's syllogistic, 123, 140; Augustinian tendencies, 182; commentary on *Wisdom*, 78, 159; expository syllogism, 74, 76; justification of belief, 78, 166; logic of faith vs. natural logic, 75, 80, 85, 90; and Ockham, 97; plural verbs and singular subjects, 154; *Quaestiones*, 74–75, 77, 166; quodlibetal questions, 76–77, 97, 154; skepticism, 78; social determinants of belief, 75–76; syncategorematic terms, 77, 103; true propositions, 40
Hugolinus of Orvieto, 212
Huizinga, Johan, 4n

Hume, David, 139
Hundred Years' War, 3, 5
Hus, John, 175–76, 179–84, 186, 203; conformity to scripture, 196; as Jewish martyr, 189; and logic of scripture, 182
Hussites, xi, 171, 186–88, 191, 196–200, 204; and Jews, 188–89; weapon shipments, 189

immaculate conception, 41–42, 54, 124n, 139
incarnation, 59, 112
infidels, 86; and compulsion to believe, 75; conversion of, 158–61, 163–67
infinity, 40, 46–50, 63; infinitesimals, 46
instants, 48
intension and remission of forms, 49
Irblich, Eva, 205

James of Eltville (Jacobus de Altavilla), 29n, 141, 215–17
Jerome of Prague, 176–78, 186, 190, 203; as classical orator and philosopher, 185; confusion of logic and rhetoric, 184; trial in Constance, 179, 183; realism, 176–77; Viennese trial, 176–78, 183
Jewish-Christian relations, 143, 162
Jews: alleged host desecration, 191; and Aristotle, 161; astronomers, 150n; chronicles, 144n; conversion of, 168, 190; debates with, 155–56; destruction of synagogue, 198–99; early settlement in Austria, 142, 146–47; empirics, 198; of France, 151; and Great Plague, 143–44; greetings to, 155; Jewish hat, 148; *ketuba*, 140n; massacre in Vienna, 196–97; moneylending, 20, 144–45; obstacles to conversion, 158, 160, 166–67; polemics, 162, 169; in Prague, 161–63; privileges, 142–43, 191; rabbis, 157; raid on, 190; in Spain, 164; synagogue, 142, 146; and trinity, 164–65; usury, 144, 150, 157. *See also* Halevi; Kara; Klausner; Mühlhausen
Joachim of Fiore, 61, 168
Joannes de Montesono (Juan de Monzón), 41, 172
Johann Berwart of Villingen, 117ff, 125, 173, 213n

Johann Müntzinger, 155, 172
Johann of Randegg, 13n
Johann von Retz, 112n, 126n, 211–13
Johann Reuter, 22
Johann Sindrami, 179n
Johannes Brammart, 83n, 85n, 130n; influenced by Oyta, 87n, 117n
Johannes Bremis. *See* Bremis
Johannes of Haderdorff, 173
Johannes Langheim, 119n
Johannes of Stralen, 140
Johannes Wuel de Pruck, 119, 120n, 122
John Duns Scotus. *See* Duns Scotus
John of Hildesheim, 26
John of Holland, 32
John of Ripa, 45n, 52–53, 56, 100n, 117n, 180, 219
John of Rodington, 219
Jordan, Michael J., 63n
Judaei, Themo, 150n

Kabbalah, 162
Kalkar. *See* Gerard of Kalkar
Kara, Avigdor, 162–63, 188–89
Kara, Menahem ben Jacob, 162
Kelter, Ernst, 18n
Kern, Anton, 97n
Klausner, Abraham, 160
Klosterneuburg, 149n; chronicle, 196; Gerson in, 187
Klosterneuburg, Stiftsbibliothek: *codex 41*, 125n; *codex 294*, 112n, 212; *codex 296*, 54n; *codex 307*, 88n; *codex 820*, 96n
Krems, 160
Kutná Hora (Kuttenberg), 175–77

Lambert of Gelderen, 36–38, 173; disciple of Ripa, 52–53, 56, 117; *principia*, 112–13, 207–208; trial of Jerome of Prague, 176–77, 183, 186
Lanfranc of Bec, 60
Lang, Albert, 29, 89n, 216
Lang, Justin, 30, 128
Langenstein, Henry of, 193ff, 201ff
—apocalypticism, 167ff
—apologetics, 166, 202
—association with Oyta, 109–10
—astronomy, 139
—autographs, 34, 38, 155–56
—on disputation, 151–52, 193, 199–200
—at Eberbach, 55
—finances, 19, 148
—and generation of 1402, 120ff
—and Hermann Lurtz, 115, 128
—historiography, 29–30
—on immaculate conception, 42, 54, 139
—on intellectual progress, 58
—and Jews, 148ff
—letters, 20, 26, 140n, 168
—*Logic*: change of mind, 122ff, 128–29, 139, 142ff; *complexe significabile*, 129; distribution, 102–103; failure of *disamis*, 125–26, 136; formal distinction, 99, 103; nonformality of Aristotelian logic, 123, 132–36, 202; opposition to new syncategorematics, 103, 109; other distinctions, 99; and Plato, 124–25, 127, 132–35, 140, 203; real universals, 132, 134; supposition theory, 98ff, 103–104; and Trinity, 111ff, 131ff, 160; on universality of Aristotelian logic, 102, 130, 202
—move to Vienna, 6, 16–17, 30, 33, 142
—on new German universities, 21
—in Paris, 27, 32, 149–51
—relations with Albert III, 20–22
—sermons, 42n, 58n, 165
—study of Hebrew, 150, 154–56
—*translatio studii*, 6
—works: commentary on the *Sentences*: "Lectura Eberbacensis" (misattributed), 30, 55, 127, 216–17; "Lectura Parisiensis" (misplaced), 30n, 127–28; *Epistola concilii pacis*, 16, 150, 167; *Epistola pacis*, 152; "Informacio serenissimi principis," 26n; *Lectures on Genesis*, 33, 152–54, 172, 207; *Tractatus de dici de omni*, 96–109, 115, 121–23, 128, 169; *Treatise on contracts*, 20n, 22n, 149; *Treatise on the Hebrew Language*, 149–51, 193; "Von erchantnuss der sund," 22n
—See also *dici de omni et nullo*; distinctions; distribution; supposition
Langland, William, 5
latitude, 44; of creatable things, 45; of forms (*see* Oresme); of perfection, 48
Leff, Gordon, 85n

LeGoff, Jacques, 23n
Leonard of Carinthia, 35n
Leopold v of Babenberg, 7n
Leopold III of Habsburg, 20
Leopold IV of Habsburg, 173
Lhotsky, Alphons, 30
Liège, 9
Lipmann, Yom Tov. *See* Mülhausen
logic: circumlocutions in, 73, 86, 95, 126,
   165; of faith, 74–75; formality of, 72ff;
   natural vs. revealed, 76, 85; the neces-
   sary follows from anything, 113; and
   theology, 179. *See also* Aristotle, *dici de
   omni et nullo*, fallacy of accident; Hol-
   cot; Langenstein; Oyta; syllogism;
   Wodeham
Louis of Padua, 52, 100n
Lull, Ramón, 142n, 155

Madre, Alois, 119
magister abstractionum, 80n
Maierù, Alfonso, 105, 105n, 114
Maimonides, Moses, 161n, 162, 164
manuscripts. *See under name of city or li-
   brary*
Marsilius of Inghen, 17n, 28, 32; attacked
   by Jerome of Prague, 176; influenced
   by Oyta, 117n
Martin IV, 4
Martin V, 185
Mauleveld, 176
Mayer, Anton, 13n
Mayronnes, Francis of, 80n, 124n
medicine. *See* Avicenna; Aygel; Caspar
   the empiric; Vienna
Meier, Ludger, 36n
Meigen (Meyger), Johann, 36, 38, 53, 56,
   116–17; *principia* debates, 207–10; *Trac-
   tatus distinctionum*, 38, 116
Melk, 187
Melk, Stiftsbibliothek mss: *codex 40*, 89n;
   codex 178, 89n; *codex 504*, 194n–96n
Mestermann, Ludolf, 33, 175
millenarianism, 167–68
Möhler, Wilhelm, 117n
Moody, Ernest A., xiii, 72n
moon, 113
morenu, 161
Mülhausen, Yom Tov Lipmann, 161–62;

and Greek wisdom, 162; messianism,
   168, 189; *Sefer ha-Nizzahon*, 162
Munich, Bayerische Staatsbibliothek:
   Clm 3546, 49n, 161n; *Clm 7456A*,
   119n, 122n; *Clm 8867*, 34n, 89n, 112n;
   Clm 11591, 29n, 30n, 216–17; *Clm
   14687*, 11n; *Clm 17290*, 105n; *Clm
   17468*, 89n, 112n; *Clm 18146*, 172n;
   Clm 18147, 172n; *Clm 18364*, 112n;
   Clm 27034, 212–13
Munich, Universitätsbibliothek: *Incun.
   1166*, 124n
Murdoch, John E., 45, 49

nationalism, 17, 171
natural philosophy, 27, 32, 42, 44–48,
   113, 130, 133, 163, 207, 214. *See also*
   theology
Nicholas. *See also* Dinkelsbühl
Nicholas of Basel, 172
Nicholas of Höbersdorf, 179n
Nicholas of Lyra, 153–54, 167
nominalism, xii, xiii, 28–31, 33n

Oberman, Heiko A., 6n, 31, 78, 181
Ockham, William of, 5, 31, 58, 80–81,
   85, 96, 176, 219; attacked by Jerome of
   Prague, 176–77; commentary on, *Physics*, 32; on *dici de omni*, 97; and ecclesiastical tradition, 181; expository syllogism, 68–69; fallacy of accident, 70–71;
   formality of Aristotle's logic, 67, 71;
   and Gregory of Rimini, 83–85; and
   Holcot, 75, 77, 79, 97, 154; and Langenstein, 99–100; limits of formal distinction, 65ff, 100; *Ordinatio*, 65ff, 83;
   and Oyta, 90–91, 93–95; on principle
   of contradiction, 67–68; on rule of Anselm, 70; and Scotus, 65; and Strelley,
   72; *Summa logicae*, 66n, 67n, 68, 95, 97;
   on syncategorematics, 103; on truth,
   40; and Wodeham, 79–81
Ockhamism, 11, 28, 30
Oresme, Nicole, 42, 44, 50, 97n, 122,
   219
Oxford, 74n, 79, 86, 177, 213n; Bodl.,
   722 (2648), 23n; *Can. misc. 573*, 212n
Oyta, Henry of, 17n, 111, 122, 135–36,
   172; apologetics, 166; and *dici de omni*,

93; differences with Wodeham, 95; disciple of, 213; distribution, 92; eclecticism, 29; in Erfurt, 89; on fallacy of accident, 95; finances, 19; future contingent propositions, 30n; and Gregory of Rimini, 95–96; and Hermann Lurtz, 115; historiography, 29–30; immaculate conception, 42; and infidels, 123, 202; influence on Viennese students, 54n; influenced by Wodeham, 89ff, 109; and Johannes Bremis, 112; and Langenstein, 126–27, 136, 140; modes of universalizing propositions, 91ff, 121, 130; move to Vienna, 148; and orthodoxy, 171–72; in Paris, 27, 89; and Plato, 90ff, 125; in Prague, 17n, 34, 89; predication, 95n; relations with Albert III, 22; sermons, 42n; similarities with Langenstein, 97ff, 102, 106–109; students of, 117–22, 203; Trinitarian paralogisms, 89ff, 95; universality of logic, 90, 202; *via media*, 89–90; in Vienna, 17, 54, 89. *Works: Abbreviatio* of Wodeham's commentary on the *Sentences*, 54, 79, 80n, 94, 112n, 127n, 215; commentary on St. John (lost), 214n; commentary on Psalms, 214n; *Lectura textualis* of the *Sentences*, 89; *Quaestiones Sententiarum*, 34, 89ff, 98, 112, 122, 212; *Rapularium*, 128; treatise on contracts, 22, 149n

Padua, university of, 4n
Panofsky, Erwin, 149n
Paquet, Jacques, 14n
parable of tares, 157, 194
paralogisms. *See* Hermann Lurtz; Oyta; Trinity; Wodeham
Paris, 32, 34, 38, 52ff, 81, 128, 155; decline, 6; faculty of theology, 32, 100n; influence of Vienna, 30; manuscript, Bibliothèque de l'Arsenal, *codex 522*, 96n; manuscript, Bibliothèque nationale, *Fonds latin 14580*, 96n; university, 3, 15–17, 24, 26–27, 41, 87, 97, 177, 180. *See also* condemnations; Langenstein; Oyta
Passau, 18
Peter of Candia, 33n, 174

Peter Ceffons of Clairvaux, 150n, 210n
Peter Damian, 60
Peter Deckinger, 174, 179n
Peter Lombard, 61
Peter of Pulkau. *See* Pulkau
Peter Reicher of Pirchenwart, 55n
Peter of Spain, 28, 113n
Peter the Venerable, 165
Pierre d'Ailly. *See* Ailly, Pierre d'
Pigaz, Ralph, 125n
Pinborg, Jan, 80n, 105n
Pistoia, 9n
plague of 1349, 5, 18–19; later years, 19, 176
Plato: as alternative to Aristotle's logic, 123; heuristic ontology, 92–94, 109. *See also* Aristotle; Langenstein; Oyta; Wodeham
Poggio Bracciolini, 184–85
polemics. *See* Jews; Langenstein
Prague, 12, 17–18, 24, 36–38; clashes between Germans and Czechs, 17, 174ff; and Vienna, 163. *See also* Bremis; Hussites; Jews; Oyta
predication: adjectival, 126; formal, 82, 104n, 122; by identity, 82, 122; substantive, 126
principia to the *Sentences*, 111–12; Bremis, 39ff, 112ff; debates, 35ff, 205ff; definition, 35
prostitutes, 166
Pseudo-Scotus, 113n
Pulkau, Peter of, 55n, 117–22, 125–27, 137, 187–88; autograph, 120n; at Constance, 178–79, 183n, 186, 203; and Hebrew, 197; and heresy, 173, 176, 178; and Jews, 198

quodlibetal questions, 76–77, 199. *See also* Holcot

Rashdall, Hastings, 21, 28
realism, 28n, 30, 33n, 52. *See also* Lambert of Gelderen; John of Ripa; Langenstein; Plato; Wyclif
reason, 42, 67, 79, 83, 103; boundaries of, 63, 65, 74–75, 181; confidence in, 44; natural, 58, 72–73, 78, 90, 93; and revelation, 58ff; rules of reasoning, 43, 83

Regensburg, 10
Regiomontanus, 6n
Retz. *See* Johann von Retz; Franz von Retz
rhetoric, 161, 184–85. *See also* Gerson; Jerome of Prague
Richard of Bury, 74n
Richard of Campsall, 67n, 70, 90, 104n
Richard Kilvington, 219
Richard the Lionhearted, 7n
Richard Rufus of Cornwall, 80n
Rimini, Gregory of, 10, 68, 95, 122; commentary on the *Sentences*, 81–82; contra Ockham, 83–84; general of the order, 88–89
Rinkau, 114n
Ripa. *See* John of Ripa
Ritter, Gerhard, 28
Robert Holcot. *See* Holcot
Rome, 6, 14, 16, 37–38, 118, 134
rotulus, 37–38, 118, 200
Rudolph IV, 12–13, 144–45, 163
Rupert (Ruprecht) of the Palatinate, 21

Sacrosbosco, 11
Saint Catherine (of Alexandria), 158–59; iconography, 158n–59n; Langenstein sermon, 158ff
Saint Catherine of Siena, 5
Saint Jerome, 196
Saint Stephen's cathedral, 10; construction, 18; iconography, 149n; reckless preaching in, 186. *See also* Bürgerschule
Sarton, George, 29n
Scherer, Franz, 37n
Schism, ix, 4–5, 21, 24, 87, 152, 170ff; end, 185–86; as obstacle to conversion, 167; and Paris, 14–16, 32, 55; schismatics, 43. *See also* Constance
Schottenstift, 10, 17, 200
Schottenstift, mss: *codex 254 (230)*, 119n; *codex 269 (274)*, 119n
Schum, Wilhelm, 217n
Shem Tov, Joseph ben, 165
Sigismund (Emperor), 179
skepticism, xii, 78
Smalley, Beryl, 78
Sommerfeldt, Albert, 21n

Sommerfeldt, Gustav, 6n
sophismata, 74, 80, 125
"Sortes," 91n
Stainreuter, Leopold, 22, 146–47
Stegmüller, Friedrich, 215
Steneck, Nicholas, 34n
Stephen Marquart of Stockerau, 199
Suchenschatz, Michael, 128
supposition, 98, 103; formal, 105; formal-and-proper, 104; formal-essential, 104; formal-notional, 104; real-common, 104
syllogism: expository, 43, 68–69, 71–74, 76–77, 80–82, 84–86, 95, 184; *in barbara*, 43, 112, 125; *in bocardo*, 122n, 125; *in darii*, 125; *in disamis*, 125, 136; known naturally, 58n; petty, 181; singular vs. universal premises, 59n; topical, 68. *See also* Aristotle; logic
syncategorematic terms, 77, 108–109; new syncategorematics, 103, 127

theology, 58, 109; and apologetics, 44; and Aristotelian logic, 71, 74, 86, 98, 103, 112, 117, 119, 135–36, 142, 169–70, 194; and arts, 27, 34, 156ff; incomprehensibles of, 59; and metaphysics, 44–45; new knowledge in, 58; Paris faculty of, 15, 36, 52, 54–55, 89, 100n; relation to philosophy, 41–42, 44–45, 47–48, 51, 56, 83; and rules of reasoning, 43; undecidable propositions, 42; Vienna faculty of 12, 16–17, 26, 32–35, 39, 56, 88–89. *See also principia*; Trinity
Thomas of Strasbourg, 10, 88
Thomism, 29. *See also* Aquinas
Tortosa: disputation, 164–65, 190; manuscript, Archivo de la Catedral, *codex 143*, 96n
translatio studii, 5–6, 12
Trapp, Damasus, 29n, 55n, 212–13
trinitarian creature, 68n
Trinity: Augustine on, 59–60; Church Fathers on, 60; distinction between persons, 61; in Genesis, 152–53; incomprehensibility, 79; indemonstrability of, 131–32; and paralogisms, 59; personal attributes, 61; persons, 61ff, 156; vs. quaternity, 61; Talmud and

Midrash, 164. *See also* Holcot; Jews; Langenstein; Ockham; Oyta; Wodeham

trivium, 10

truth, theological, 40. *See also complexe significabile*

Uiblein, Paul, 11
Ulrich, Magister, 11n
universals, xii, 132, 134
Universities: foundations, 4n; student attrition rates, 14n; student poverty, 23–24. *See also under name of city*
Urban v, 12
Urban vi, 14–15
usury, 144, 150, 157, 169. *See also* Jews

Vancsa, Max, 8n
Vatican City, Biblioteca Vaticana, *Vat. Lat. 3088*, 96n–97n
via moderna, xiii, 28–29, 31
Vienna, *city*: finances, 19ff; and Habsburgs, 12ff, 18; history, 7ff; monasteries, 10–11; schools, 10ff; social structure, 8–9; taxation, 7–8; trade, 7–8. *See also* Albert iii; Jews; Rudolph iv
Vienna, Österreichische National-bibliothek, *codex Hebr. 218*, 149n
Vienna, Osterreichische Nationalbibliotek, *codices Lat: 213*, 11n; *1397*, 82n; *1515*, 88n; *3953*, 213n; *4017*, 168n; *4235*, 213n; *4319*, 127n, 128, 216–17; *4371*, 34–35, 39, 39n–41n, 43n–56n, 112n–114n, 205ff; *4354*, 192n–93n; *4384*, 168n; *4421*, 38n; *4423*, 38n; *4427*, 149n; *4575*, 38n; *4632*, 38n, 199n; *4635*, 38n; *4636*, 38n; *4651*, 152n–54n, 156n, 207; *4654*, 199n; *4657*, 199n; *4659*, 199n; *4668*, 120n, 126n, 199n; *4677*, 155n; *4678*, 160n; *4679*, 160n; *4708*, 112n; *4718*, 133, 134n–36n; *4795*, 199n; *4820*, 119n, 120n, 122n; *4842*, 88n; *4948*, 114n–16n; *4951*, 38n, 116n; *4963*, 38n, 116n; *5067*, 119n; *5113*, 174n; *5137*, 215n; *5252*, 33n, 125n; *5352*, 158n; *5424*, 33n; *13763*, 37n, 38n
Vienna, Universitätsarchiv, *Acta rectoratus*, vol. 1 [R 1]; *codex VII*, 37n. *See also* Schottenstift
Vienna, University of, 12; developmental approach to, 57; faculty of arts, acts, 37; faculty of law, 13n; faculty of theology, 16; statutes, 35n; and Habsburgs, 12; historiography, 27–34; matriculation records, 13–14; and Paris, 26–28; philosophical orientation, 27ff; poor students, 22ff; privileges, 11n, 26–27; procession, 23; viability, 20. *See also* Bremis; collegium ducale; Langenstein; Oyta; Paris; Prague; Saint Stephen's Cathedral
viticulture, 8–9, 19. *See also* wine
Vooght, Paul de, 183

Wagner, Richard, 87
Waldensians, 173, 188, 195
Walter of Bamberg, 87n, 130n; influenced by Oyta, 117n
Walter Disse, 130n
Wappler, Anton, 28n
Wiener Neustadt, 160
Wilhelmus Anglicus, 213n
Wilhering, Stiftsbibliothek, *codex 43*, 87n
William of Paris, 219
William of Ware, 219
wine, 19–20, 37
wisdom, 162. *See also* God
Wisdom of Solomon, 159; Holcot's commentary on, 159
Wittgenstein, Ludwig, 111
Wodeham, Adam, 54, 87n, 115, 123, 219; *Abbreviatio*, 215; appeal to Plato, 91, 125, 203; and Aristotle's syllogistic, 86; commentary on the *Sentences*, 79–80; *complexe significabile*, 110; and *dici de omni*, 95–97; and infidels, 202; influence in Vienna, 54, 56; moderate position, 89; and Oyta, 94–95, 109–10; on predication, 82; Trinitarian paralogisms, 79–81
Wolter, Allan, 41n
Wulf, Maurice de, 29n
Wyclif, John, 174–76

Zwettl, *codex 158*, 191n